A RECORD OF BUDDHIST MONASTERIES IN LO-YANG

Princeton Library of
Asian Translations

A RECORD OF BUDDHIST MONASTERIES IN LO-YANG

By Yang Hsüan-chih

Translated by Yi-t'ung Wang

Princeton University Press
Princeton, New Jersey

Published by Princeton University Press,
41 William Street, Princeton, New Jersey
In the United Kingdom: Princeton University Press,
Guildford, Surrey

Library of Congress Cataloging in Publication Data
will be found on the last printed page of this book

This book has been composed in Monophoto Bembo
by Asco Trade Typesetting Ltd. Hong Kong
ISBN 0-691-05403-7

Clothbound editions of Princeton University Press books
are printed on acid-free paper, and binding materials
are chosen for strength and durability.
Paperbacks, although suitable for personal collections,
are not usually suitable for library rebinding
Printed in the United States of America by
Princeton University Press, Princeton, New Jersey

Preparation of this volume was made possible in part
by a grant from the Translations Program
of the National Endowment for the Humanities,
an independent federal agency

Dedicated to my wife, An-chi Lou Wang
October 25, 1917 – February 23, 1981

One of the largest and earliest statues of Buddha, built ca. A.D. 460 during the Northern Wei dynasty in Yün-kang, P'ing-ch'eng (modern Ta-t'ung), its capital prior to A.D. 495. Height of head: 4.10m; statue, 13.37m. At the foot of the statue is An-chi Lou Wang.

Contents

List of Maps

List of Illustrations

Translator's Introduction

The *Lo-yang ch'ieh-lan chi* 洛陽伽藍記 (*A Record of Buddhist Monasteries in Lo-yang*)[1] by Yang Hsüan-chih 楊衒之,[2] is at once a masterpiece of literature and of history. Both descriptive and narrative in nature, it is accepted as a source of important materials by Buddhist and Confucian scholars alike. For this and other equally

[1] Abbreviated below as *Ch'ieh-lan chi*. This title is translated as *A Description of Buddhist Temples of Lo-yang* by Joseph Needham in his *Science and Civilisation in China* 3 (Cambridge, 1959), Bibliography A, p. 708. The major differences between his and my translation derive from "ch'ieh-lan," a Chinese transliteration for saṅghārāma, "temples" or "monasteries," or a park in which the Buddha and his followers could take pleasure. This term also appears in *WS* 114/24a 釋老志 which reads: 伽藍淨土, 理絕囂塵. "Ch'ieh-lan, being a land of purity, would naturally be isolated from the worldly dust." Throughout the following pages in the text, however, the author uses the Chinese character *ssu* 寺 as a substitute for *ch'ieh-lan*. In translating this character, I choose the word "monastery" for those that, on the basis of textual evidence, housed a large number of monks, but "temple" for those that housed only a few. "Nunnery" is of course applied to shrines that sheltered Buddhist nuns only.

Lo-yang ch'ieh-lan chi consists of five chapters, each dealing with one section of the city: the Inner City, East Lo-yang and Suburbs, South Lo-yang and Suburbs, West Lo-yang and Suburbs, and North Lo-yang and Suburbs. Each chapter constitutes an integral whole, with the name of the geographical division inserted between "Lo-yang" and "ch'ieh-lan chi." Hence, the chapter on the Inner City reads "Lo-yang ch'eng-nei ch'ieh-lan chi" 洛陽城內伽藍記. Such an arrangement suggests that *Lo-yang ch'ieh-lan chi* is only a collective title, with each chapter standing as a separate entity. It resembles in style the *San-kuo chih*, in which the *Wei-chih*, *Shu-chih*, and *Wu-chih* are component but independent units.

The *Lo-yang ch'ieh-lan chi* was known under different titles at different times. Three quotations from this work, one in *TPKC* (375/2a 再生類崔涵) and two in the *FYCL* (*SPTK so-pen* ed., 116/1386–1387 受生部感應緣, 43/511 變化部感應緣) refer, respectively, to the source as *T'a-ssu* 塔寺, *Lo-yang ssu-chi* 洛陽寺記, and *Lo-yang ssu chi-chuan* 洛陽寺記傳.

[2] For a discussion of the controversy over the author's name and his political career, see below.

convincing reasons, it has been held in high esteem by traditional Chinese scholars and contemporary Japanese sinologists.

Lo-yang, located on the north bank of the Lo River and to the south of the Yellow River, was the capital of the Eastern Chou (770–256 B.C.), the Later Han (A.D. 25–220), the Wei (A.D. 220–265) of the Three Kingdoms, and the Western Chin (A.D. 265–316) dynasties. In A.D. 495, under the reign of Emperor Hsiao-wen 孝文 (regnant A.D. 471–499; also known posthumously as Emperor Kao-tsu 高祖), it was again chosen as the capital of the nation by the ruling T'o-pa 拓跋 (also known as the Toba) aristocrats after nearly one hundred years of their intensive acculturation through contact with the Chinese. The move from the old capital in P'ing-ch'eng 平城 to Lo-yang, carried out in the face of stiff opposition, shifted the center of political, social, and economic activity from northern China to the central Yellow River Valley, and ushered in a period of spectacular growth in Buddhism in many areas: Buddhism as a form of religion,[3] Buddhist architecture, and Buddhist sculpture. At the height of this period, the capital city alone had more than one thousand temples and monasteries.[4] The rapid growth of Buddhism, particularly under the auspices of alien conquerors, was indeed unprecedented and unparalleled in Chinese history.

The unusual background of Yang Hsüan-chih, coupled with the rarity of extant works of this kind, makes the *Lo-yang ch'ieh-lan chi* extremely appealing to the Chinese mind. A classic completed in about A.D. 547—a date referred to in the author's preface—it sur-

[3] Wolfram Eberhard theorizes that the Toba patronage of Buddhism was "intended to break the power of the Chinese gentry" and that "the acceptance of Buddhism by rulers in the Far East always meant also an attempt to create a more aristocratic, absolutist regime" (*A History of China*, Berkeley and Los Angeles, 1971, p. 145). Such a sweeping statement can be accepted only with adequate textual evidence, which unfortunately is not provided by the author.

[4] Because Buddhism was so important in the Wei, the official compiler of the *History of Wei* (*Wei-shu*, I-wen facsimile ed.), in a departure from traditional historiography, devoted a treatise to Wei Buddhism and Taoism. For an English translation, see Leon Hurvitz, *Wei Shou on Buddhism and Taoism* (Kyoto, 1956). For a study of the treatise, see Tsukamoto Zenryū, *Gisho Shaku-Rō-shi no kenkyū* (Kyoto, 1961).

For a general study of Buddhist teaching in this period, see Ōchō Enichi, *Hokugi Bukkyō no kenkyū* (Kyoto, 1970), particularly the first section, dealing with Buddhist thought (*Shisō hen* 思想編). See also Hattori Katsuhiko, *Hokugi Rakuyō no shakai to bunka* (Kyoto, 1965), and his *Zoku* (Kyoto, 1968).

vives in its entirety. Few other works produced during the Northern Dynasties (A.D. 386–581) fared so well. Indeed, outside of the realm of pure literature and standard historical writings, only three other major works, the *Ch'i-min yao-shu*,[5] *Shui-ching chu*,[6] and *Yen-shih chia-hsün*,[7] are still extant.

The author's inclusion of important historical documents or literary masterpieces wherever appropriate is another outstanding feature of this work.[8] The work is divided into sections concerning the five geographical areas of the Lo-yang metropolis—the Inner City, and the Eastern, Southern, Western, and Northern Suburbs. These in turn are subdivided under such headings as temples, monasteries, nunneries, palace compounds, wards, and private residences. Accounts of past events, and the life histories of individuals participating in such events, are attached to records of the sites where the events occurred. These events and biographies are subsequently treated in detail by the author. Thus, in the entry on the Yung-ning Monastery (Monastery of Eternal Peace), where the tyrant Erh-chu Jung once stationed his armed forces, the author provides a minute account of the background of the nearly autonomous Erh-chu family, and the rise and fall of Erh-chu Jung. After the record of the successful entry of the Prince of Pei-hai into Lo-yang, a letter written by the renowned Tsu Ying and addressed to Emperor Chuang is recorded in full. In the same Yung-ning Monastery, Emperor Chuang, then a captive under Erh-chu Chao, was eventually strangled to death by the latter. A poem composed by the emperor shortly before his death is also included in its entirety.[9] Wang Su (A.D. 463–501), a deserter from the south, was first married to Lady Hsieh, but remarried a Wei

[5] Translated as *Important Arts for the People's Welfare* by Needham, *Science and Civilisation* 2, Bibliography A, p. 321.

[6] Translated as *Commentary on the Waterways Classic* by Needham, *Science and Civilisation* 3, Bibliography A, p. 714.

[7] For an English translation, see Teng Ssu-yü, *Family Instructions for the Yen Clan* (Leiden, 1968).

[8] From the *Ch'ieh-lan chi*, Yen K'o-chün 嚴可均 collected three prose writings into his *Ch'üan Hou-Wei wen* 全後魏文 (in *Ch'üan Shang-ku San-tai Ch'in-Han San-kuo Liu-ch'ao wen* 全上古三代秦漢三國六朝文, facsimile ed., Taipei, 1961), namely, the state paper investing Yüan Lüeh 元略 as the Prince of I-yang 義陽王 (11/12b–13a), Ch'ang Ching's 常景 epitaph for the Lo Bridge 洛橋銘 (32/7a–b), and Chiang Chih's 姜質 "T'ing-shan *fu*" 亭(庭)山賦 (54/9b–10a).

[9] See Chapter 1 at note 135.

princess after his arrival in the north. Soon afterwards, Lady Hsieh also came to the north, where she wrote a poem to her former husband recalling the intimate moments they had shared. To this the princess responded with a poem, urging her to erase whatever fond memories she might still have. Both poems are again included in their entirety, in the entry on the Cheng-chüeh Nunnery (Perfect Enlightenment Nunnery) in Ch'üan-hsüeh Ward (Ward of Exhortation to Study). The second poem is particularly noteworthy, since it reflects a new style of poetry, in which the same rhyming characters used in the first poem are repeated in the responding poem.[10]

The author of the *Lo-yang ch'ieh-lan chi* also paid attention to local folklore, such as ghost and fox stories, often blending sarcasm with wit in his report. The *Ch'ieh-lan chi* story about the ingratitude of K'ou Tsu-jen, who caused the death of his erstwhile benefactor, was almost immediately incorporated into Yen Chih-t'ui's (A.D. 531–591) *Yüan-hun chih*.[11] There are also stories about the God of the Lo River,[12] about a ghost who regained life after having been interred for twelve years,[13] about the spirit of Wei Ying, who appeared to accuse his wife of disloyalty to him,[14] and Sun Yen's wife, who allegedly was a fox.[15] In a similar fashion, he shows us a picture of hypocrisy and greed among contemporary Buddhist monks, by recording testimony supposedly delivered by three monks before Yama—the ruler over the dead and a judge in hell according to Indian mythology—and witnessed by Hui-i, a monk who regained life after having been dead for seven days.[16] As an example of those men of letters who made biased comments on the deeds of past monarchs,[17] and praised contemporaries with exaggeration, the

[10] Included in Ting Fu-pao's *Ch'üan Pei-Wei shih* (in *Ch'üan Han San-kuo Chin Liu-ch'ao shih*, I-wen facsimile ed.). See Chapter 3 at notes 81–91.

[11] See Chapter 4 at notes 27–55 under the Hsüan-chung Temple (Temple of Manifest Loyalty).

[12] See Chapter 3 at note 65 under the Ling-t'ai (Imperial Observatory).

[13] See Chapter 3 at notes 186–194 under the P'u-t'i Temple (Bodhi Temple).

[14] See Chapter 4 at notes 160–164 under the K'ai-shan Temple (Temple of Guidance to Goodness).

[15] See Chapter 4 at notes 147–152 under the Feng-chung Ward (Ward of Homage to the Deceased).

[16] See Chapter 2 at note 45 under the Ch'ung-chen Monastery (Monastery of Respect for Truth).

[17] Chao I's defense of Fu Sheng 苻生, a ruler traditionally denounced as a ruthless despot, is echoed by Liu Chih-chi (A.D. 661–721) in his highly regarded *Shih-t'ung*.

author quotes the words of Chao I, a hermit who claimed to be two hundred fifty years old at the time of writing.[18]

The author also demonstrates literary skill, particularly in his mastery of the literary style known as parallel prose (*p'ien-wen* 駢文). Distinct from rhymed prose, otherwise referred to as rhapsody, which had originated earlier, parallel prose was the dominant style of the period under discussion. In parallel prose, corresponding lines or sets of lines must be written with strict observance of regulations governing the distribution of tones and parts of speech. As an example, in Chapter 1 under the Yung-ning Monastery entry we have the following lines describing the pleasant atmosphere in a secluded area during the hot summer in congested Lo-yang:

lù-tùan fēi-ch'én,	pù yú yēn-yǔn chīh jùn;
路斷飛塵	不由渰雲之潤

Roads blocked off [from] flying dust, [but] not because of rain-carrying clouds' moisture;

ch'īng-fēng sùng-líang	ch'ǐ chìeh hó-hūan chīh fā
淸風送涼	豈藉合歡之發

The pure wind sends in the cold breeze, surely not because of the motion of round-fans.[19]

One can readily see the author's command of both sound and syntax, which seem to have come to the tip of his writing brush quite effortlessly. It is indeed largely because of this literary elegance that the work is often ranked with the *Shui-ching chu* as one of the most respected literary products of the period.[20]

For those particularly interested in China's relations with countries in the Western Regions and beyond, the author's inclusion of the travel account of the pilgrims Sung Yün and Hui-sheng (first quarter of the sixth century) is yet another monumental contribution. They passed through the land of T'u-yü-hun (in modern Tsing-hai), Shan-shan (Charklik), Tso-mo (Charchan), Mo-ch'eng (east of Uzun-tati),

[18] See Chapter 2 at note 78 under the Ch'ung-i Ward (Ward of Reverence for Righteousness).

[19] For *ho-huan*, see Chapter 1 at note 14.

[20] In the following pages great attention is paid to passages of special literary merit.

Khotan (Yü-tien), Udyāna (on the bank of modern Swat River), Ephthal (Russian Turkestan) and other countries, visiting various sacred Buddhist shrines and taking back to China a large number of Buddhist scriptures. The importance of their account is such that information on these areas preserved in the *Hsin T'ang-shu* treatise on geography may have been based on this work.[21] Obviously, a record of such importance deservedly received early scholarly attention; in 1903 the *Ch'ieh-lan chi* account was translated into French by the noted Sinologist Édouard Chavannes. Along with the *Fa-hsien chuan* 法顯傳 and the *Ta-T'ang Hsi-yü chi*, the record of Sung Yün and Hui-sheng has been extensively studied by Western and Oriental scholars,[22] and is treasured as one of the richest collections of source materials pertaining to China's relations with Central Asia in the sixth century.

On the other hand, the *Ch'ieh-lan chi* is perhaps as controversial as it is valuable. It remains uncertain whether the author's surname is 楊 (Yáng),[23] 陽 (Yáng),[24] or 羊 (Yáng),[25] or how long he had served in each of the following official positions: Warden of Ch'i-ch'eng (Ch'i-ch'eng *chün-shou* 期城郡守),[26] Grand Warden of Ch'i-ch'eng

[21] *Hsin T'ang-shu* (I-wen facsimile ed.) 40/13b ff.; also see Chapter 5.

[22] Among the leading scholars in this field, one may mention É. Chavannes, Alfred Foucher, Hsü Sung 徐松, Ting Ch'ien, Chang Hsing-lang, Shiratori Kurakichi, Matsuda Hisao, and Nagasawa Kazutoshi.

[23] Author's preface to the *Ch'ieh-lan chi* i, *Shih-t'ung* (*SPTK* ed.) 5/9b *Nei-p'ien* 內篇補注篇, and *Kuang Hung-ming chi* (*Taishō* ed.) 6/124 敍列代王臣滯惑解.

[24] *Kuang Hung-ming chi* 6/128: "a native of Pei-p'ing" 北平人.

[25] *Shih-t'ung t'ung-shih* (*SPPY* ed. with commentary by P'u Ch'i-lung, 1730 *chin-shih*) 5/12a; Chao Kung-wu, *Chao-te hsien-sheng Ch'ün-chai tu-shu chih* (*SPTK* ed.) 2B/9b 史部地理類.

[26] *Hsü Kao-seng chuan* (*Taishō* ed.) 1/427 "Biography of Bodhiruci" 菩提流支傳. Ch'i-ch'eng was established as a commandery during the Hsiao-ch'ang period 孝昌 (Filial and Prosperous) (A.D. 525–526). See *WS* 106C/21b 地形志.

Where applicable, translation of official titles are as given by Yü-ch'üan Wang, "An Outline of the Central Government of the Former Han Dynasty," *HJAS* 12, 1949; Rafe de Crespigny, *Official Titles of the Former Han Dynasty as translated and transcribed by H. H. Dubs* (Canberra, 1967); Hans Bielenstein, *Bureaucracies of Han Times* (Cambridge, 1980); Richard B. Mather, tr. *A New Account of Tales of the World* (Minneapolis, 1976); Robert des Rotours, *Le Traité des examens, traduit de la Nouvelle histoire des T'ang* (Paris, 1932); idem, *Traité des fonctionnaires et de l'armée*, 2 volumes (Leiden, 1948); Edward A. Kracke, Jr., *Civil Service in Early Sung China 960–1067* (Cambridge, 1953); and Charles O. Hucker, "Governmental Organization of the Ming Dynasty," *HJAS* 21, 1958, in their respective studies on the Han, Six

chün (Ch'i-ch'eng *chün t'ai-shou* 期城郡太守),[27] (the preceding title could have been an abbreviation of this), Court Guest (*Feng ch'ao-ch'ing*),[28] Supervisor of Archives (*Mi-shu chien*),[29] and Sergeant-at-Arms in the Office of the Commanding General of the Army (*Fu-chün-fu ssu-ma*).[30] We have too little textual evidence to make a final decision in this matter. In an attempt to reach a compromise, Chou Yen-nien suggests that 陽 is the surname, and that the author was perhaps the son of Yang Ku 陽固 and younger brother of Yang Hsiu-chih 陽休之. Native to the Wu-chung 無終 prefecture of the Pei-p'ing commandery 北平郡 (modern Chi-hsien 薊縣, Hopei), the Yang family was renowned for literary achievements. Chou Yen-nien's suggestion, however, is highly conjectural[31].

Other far more serious problems arise from the intermixing of the author's own notes with the main text. In the earlier editions, these were obviously separate, as asserted by Liu Chih-chi[32] and evidenced by some earlier quotations where certain notes were not included in the text. In later editions, however, there is no longer any demarcation between text and notes. Ku Kuang-ch'i (1776–1835), a noted bibliographer of the Ch'ing dynasty, believed that earlier editions

---

Dynasties, T'ang, Sung, and Ming institutions. Conflicts are many, and final decision of making the most appropriate choice is of course mine.

[27] *Li-tai san-pao chi* (*Taishō* ed.) 3/38; *Ta-T'ang nei-tien lu* (*Taishō* ed.) 4/270.

[28] *Ch'ieh-lan chi* 1/1a.

[29] *Kuang Hung-ming chi* 6/128.

[30] Author's preface to the *Ch'ieh-lan chi*.

[31] *Lo-yang ch'ieh-lan chi chu* (Shanghai, 1937) 5/9a–10a. His surmise is based upon *WS* 72/3a–12b 陽固傳, *Pei-shih* (I-wen facsimile ed.) 47/10b–13b 陽固傳 and 47/13b–18b 陽休之傳.

According to *WS*, Yang Ku had three sons but *PS* gives five, among whom four are identifiable (Hsiu-chih 休之, Ch'üan-chih 詮之, Ch'en-chih 綝之, and Chün-chih 俊之). The name for the remaining son, however, is still unknown. Cheng Ch'ien 鄭騫 agrees with Chou that the author was indeed Yang Ku's son ("Kuan-yü *Lo-yang ch'ieh-lan chi* ti chi-ko wen-t'i" 關於洛陽伽藍記的幾個問題 *Hsüeh-jen chou-k'an* 學人週刊, in the July 18, 1957 issue of the *Central Daily News* 中央日報, Taipei). Hsü Kao-juan (p. 48b) accepts the idea that Yang Hsüan-chih, as a man of letters, may have been influenced by Yang Ku, but feels that the two were not necessarily related.

Lo Ken-tse also touches on this subject in "*Lo-yang ch'ieh-lan chi* shih-lun" 洛陽伽藍記試論. See *Wen-hsüeh i-ch'an* 文學遺產 298 in the January 31, 1960 issue of the *Kuang-ming jih-pao* 光明日報, Peking. He offers no conclusion, however.

[32] *Shih-t'ung* 5/9b 補注篇.

used two sizes of characters, larger ones for the text and smaller ones for the notes.[33] Ch'en Yin-k'o (1890–1969) voiced his conviction that the addition of notes to the main text was a common practice among Buddhist monk-scribes of Yang Hsüan-chih's time, so the author may simply have followed what was being done by his contemporaries.[34]

In any event, Wu Jo-chun, in about 1834, pioneered the tedious but necessary task of separating the notes from the text. His work is entitled *Lo-yang ch'ieh-lan chi chi-cheng*. He was followed by T'ang Yen (*Lo-yang ch'ieh-lan chi kou-ch'en*, Shanghai, 1915); Chang Tsung-hsiang (*Lo-yang ch'ieh-lan chi ho-chiao*, Shanghai, 1930); the editors of the *Taishō shinshū daizōkyō* (Tokyo, 1922–1933), Chou Tsu-mo (*Lo-yang ch'ieh-lan chi chiao-shih*, Peking, 1963); Hsü Kao-juan (*Ch'ung-k'an Lo-yang ch'ieh-lan chi*, Taipei, 1960); and Iriya Yoshitaka (*Rakuyō garan ki*, in *Chūgoku koten bungaku taikei*, Tokyo, 1974). Fan Hsiang-yung's *Lo-yang ch'ieh-lan chi chiao-chu* (Shanghai, 1958) makes no attempt to separate the notes from the text. Although each work has its merits, my translation generally follows Hsü Kao-juan's relatively even-handed textual rearrangement.[35] Sections that comprise Yang Hsüan-chih's notes, as determined by Hsü Kao-juan, are indented in my translation.

Because the work has enjoyed such high respect, it has been printed in a great number of editions with substantial textual variants. There are perhaps two major editions: the Ju-yin-t'ang 如隱堂 edition (possibly edited by Lu Ts'ai 陸采 1497–1537), and Wu Kuan's 吳琯 (1571 *chin-shih* 進士) *Ku-chin i-shih* 古今逸史 edition. The latter was used as the basic text in the *Han-Wei ts'ung-shu* by Wang Mo (late eighteenth century). The Ju-yin-t'ang edition is the earliest and has therefore been the most respected. On the basis of the Ju-yin-t'ang text, the famous bibliophile Mao Chin (1599–1659) produced his *Chin-tai mi-shu* edition (also known as the Lü-chün-t'ing 綠君亭 ed.), which, in its turn, was incorporated into Wu Tzu-chung's *Chen-i-*

[33] *Ssu-shih-chai chi* (1849 ed.) 14/13a–b "*Lo-yang ch'ieh-lan chi* pa" 洛陽伽藍記跋.

[34] *Ch'en Yin-k'o hsien-sheng ch'üan-chi*, 3rd revised ed. (Taipei, 1977) A/600–605 "Tu *Lo-yang ch'ieh-lan chi* hou" 讀洛陽伽藍記後.

[35] Weng T'ung-wen also prefers Hsü's work over all others. See his "*Lo-yang ch'ieh-lan chi* pu-pien," an epilogue to the *Chin-tai mi-shu* 津逮祕書 (I-wen facsimile ed.).

t'ang ts'ung-shu in the early nineteenth century. The Ju-yin-t'ang edition was also used as the basic text by Chang Hai-p'eng (1755–1816) in his *Hsüeh-chin t'ao-yüan* (also known as the Chao-k'uang-ko 照曠閣 ed.) and again by Wu Jo-chun for his *Chi-cheng* edition.[36] The *Ssu-pu ts'ung-k'an* and *Ssu-pu pei-yao*, the two comprehensive collectanea published in modern times, reproduce the Ju-yin-t'ang and *Chi-cheng* editions, respectively.

Some editions of more recent years do not rely on one single earlier published edition. They consult different texts for the sake of collation. This is true of T'ang Yen, Chang Tsung-hsiang, the editors of the *Taishō shinshū daizōkyō*, Fan Hsiang-yung, Chou Tsu-mo, and Iriya Yoshitaka.

In the course of my translation, I have examined practically all the editions cited here, but I have relied on the Ju-yin-t'ang edition as the basic pilot text. Wherever applicable, I have also checked the text against collections of pre-Ming quotations, notably the *K'ai-yüan shih-chiao lu* (pertaining to the Yung-ning Monastery; *Taishō* ed.), the *Li-tai san-pao chi*, *Fa-yüan chu-lin*, *Yu-yang tsa-tsu* (*SPTK so-pen*), the *T'ai-p'ing yü-lan* (facsimile ed., Peking, 1959), and the *T'ai-p'ing kuang-chi* (1806 ed.). The source materials most valuable for the collation, however, are contained in the *Yüan Ho-nan chih* (*Ou-hsiang ling-shih* ed. by Miao Ch'üan-sun 1844–1919), in all probability an extract from the *Ho-nan chih* 河南志 of Sung Min-ch'iu 宋敏求 (1019–1079), who undoubtedly quoted extensively from the *Ch'ieh-lan chi*. Another rich repository of *Ch'ieh-lan chi* passages is preserved in the *Yung-lo ta-tien* (facsimile ed., Taipei, 1962) under the rhyming character *ssu* 寺 (temple or nunnery).

I have also availed myself of scholarly articles by contemporary authorities, notably those of Lao Kan,[37] Mori Shikazō,[38] Kuo Pao-

[36] For a study of different editions of the *Ch'ieh-lan chi*, see Hatanaka Jōen, "*Rakuyō garan ki* no sho hanpon to sono keitō," *Ōtani gakuhō* 30 (June 1951), 39–55; for other works on Buddhist temples of the same period, see Liu Ju-ling, "Liu-ch'ao ch'ieh-lan chi hsü-mu," *Shih-fan ta-hsüeh yüeh-k'an* 13 (1934), 40–58.

[37] "Pei-Wei Lo-yang ch'eng-t'u ti fu-yüan," *CYYCY* 20A (1948), 299–312.

[38] "Hokugi Rakuyōjō no kibo ni tsuite," *Tōyōshi kenkyū* 11:4 (1952), 36; 'Rō Kan shi no Hokugi Rakuyōjōzu-teki fukugen o hyōsu," *Tōyōgaku kenkyū* (Tokyo, 1970), pp. 229–243; "Itsu-shū-sho Sakurakukai to Hogugi Dai-Rakuyōjō," *Tōyōshi kenkyū* 11:4 (1952), 22–25.

chün,[39] Yen Wen-ju,[40] and Ho Ping-ti.[41] Annotations provided by Chou Tsu-mo and Fan Hsiang-yung, and to a lesser degree by Iriya Yoshitaka and T'ien Su-lan,[42] are often consulted. In addition, recent archaeological findings are also used.[43]

One may note that in this description of the splendor of numerous Buddhist monasteries and the military disturbances that took place there, the author takes little note of the reasons why Buddhism was so prosperous and influential at that time. He apparently considered such trends, however important, beyond the scope of his work. The translator has not attempted to add this information, since a number of scholarly works on this subject are readily available in many languages.

Between the inception and completion of my translation project, I was privileged to receive a Fulbright-Hays travel grant that funded my visit to Japan and Taiwan. While in Tōkyō and Kyōto, I consulted a great number of rare books housed in the Tōyō Bunko and Jimbun Kagaku Kenkyūjo. During my stay in Taiwan, I was most thankful to the Graduate School of History, National Taiwan University, and the National Science Council for their hospitality. I am also indebted to the Academia Sinica, which placed its collection of rare stele rubbings at my disposal. In February 1979, I was able to extend my research tour to the People's Republic of China, where, among other cities, I revisited the Yün-kang caves in Ta-t'ung, the Northern Wei capital prior to A.D. 495, and the Lung-men grottos in

[39] "Lo-yang ku-ch'eng k'an-ch'a chien-pao," in *K'ao-ku t'ung-hsün* 1 (1955), 9–21.

[40] "Lo-yang Han Wei Sui T'ang ch'eng-chih k'an-ch'a chi," in *K'ao-ku hsüeh-pao* 7 (1955), 117–136.

[41] "Pei-Wei Lo-yang ch'eng-kuo kuei-hua," *CYYCY, Symposium in Honor of Dr. Li Chi on His Seventieth Birthday* 1 (1965), 1–27; "Lo-yang, A.D. 495–534; A Study of Physical and Socio-Economic Planning of a Metropolitan Area," *HJAS* 26 (1966), 52–101.

[42] "*Lo-yang ch'ieh-lan chi* chiao-chu," in *Kuo-wen yen-chiu-so chi-k'an* 16 (Taipei, 1972), 1–164.

[43] Chung-kuo K'o-hsüeh-yüan K'ao-ku-yen-chiu-so Lo-yang kung-tso-tui (The Lo-yang Archaeological Team of the Institute of Archaeology, the Chinese Academy of Sciences), "Han-Wei Lo-yang-ch'eng ch'u-pu k'an-ch'a," *K'ao-ku* 4 (1973), 198–208; Lo-yang Po-wu-kuan (Lo-yang Museum), "Lo-yang Pei-Wei Yüan Shao mu," ibid., 218–224, 243.

Lo-yang, the capital after that date. There I had the opportunity to examine Buddhist statues and other sculptural objects both in the open and in grottos, sharpening my insight into the level of Buddhist arts achieved during the Northern Wei. I am particularly indebted to a National Endowment for the Humanities grant designated for the exclusive purpose of carrying out my translation project. I gratefully acknowledge the award of a sabbatical leave and research grants from the University of Pittsburgh that facilitated my efforts. I would like to express my sincere thanks to Professor Andrew H. Plaks and Ms. Michael Nylan of Princeton University, Ms. Margaret Case of Princeton University Press, Professors Richard B. Mather of the University of Minnesota, Yi-liang Zhou (Chou) 周一良 of Beijing University, Lien-sheng Yang 楊聯陞 of Harvard University, Whalen Lai of the University of California at Davis, and to my colleagues Professors David O. Mills, Edwin D. Floyd, and Katherine Carlitz for reading my manuscript and for making numerous suggestions. The translation is made more readable by the excellent editorial comments of Selina L. Wang 王華陵. I also want to thank Professor Keiko McDonald of the University of Pittsburgh, and Mr. Pao-liang Chu 朱寶樑 of the Harvard-Yenching Library for their bibliographical assistance. Patient and skillful typing of my manuscript was performed by Mrs. Kendall S. Stanley. To Mr. Vince Gutowski I am grateful for the two maps he prepared. Above all, I am deeply indebted to my wife, An-chi Lou 婁安吉, who always provides me with an environment most pleasant and conducive to the pursuit of my research activities.

Pittsburgh
February 1980

ADDITIONAL NOTE Five months after the completion of the first draft of this manuscript, my wife An-chi was found to be incurably ill. My daughter Selina and my son Theodore 王華歆 spent much time in assisting and comforting us both, at great inconvenience to themselves and their respective institutions. On February 23, 1981, An-chi peacefully and gracefully passed away, remarkably maintaining her composure to the end. Despite the hardship and depression we all experienced, my wife repeatedly encouraged us to get back to our work, and to put the finishing touches on this manuscript in which she had taken a keen interest from its inception. Although Anchi is no longer with us, she is an important part of this work, and so I dedicate it to her memory.

A RECORD OF BUDDHIST MONASTERIES IN LO-YANG

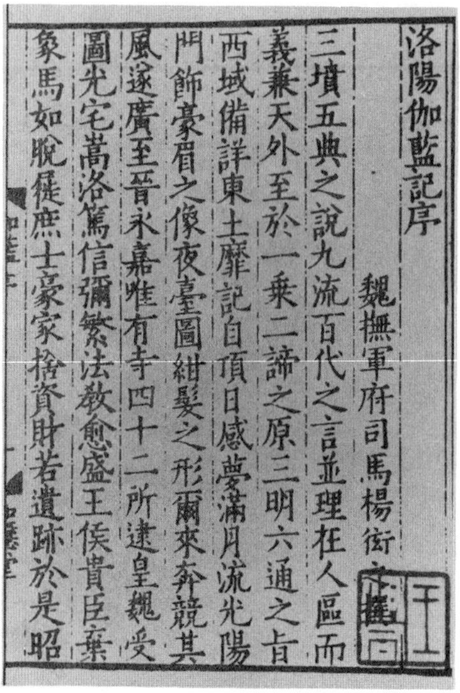

洛陽伽藍記序

魏撫軍府司馬楊衒之撰

三墳五典之說九流百代之言並理在人區而
義兼天外至於一乘二諦之原三明六通之旨
西域備詳東土靡記自頂日感夢滿月流光陽
門飾豪眉之像夜臺圖紺髮之形爾來奔競其
風遂廣至晉永嘉唯有寺四十二所逮皇魏受
圖光宅嵩洛篤信彌繁法教愈盛王侯貴臣棄
象馬如脫屣庶士豪家捨資財若遺跡於是昭

A. *Ju-yin-t'ang*

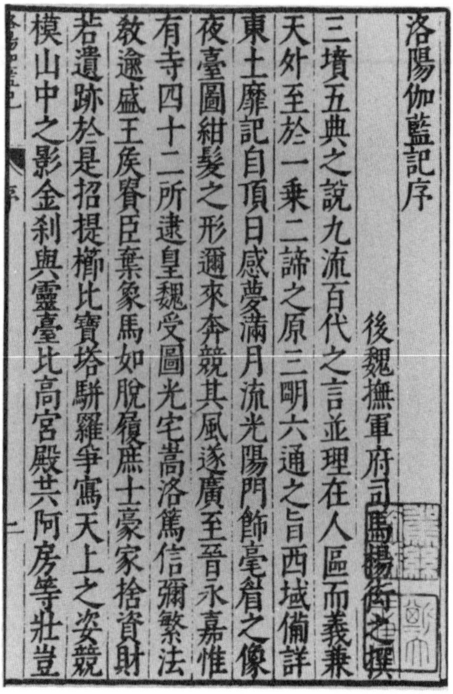

洛陽伽藍記序

後魏撫軍府司馬楊衒之撰

三墳五典之說九流百代之言並理在人區而義兼
天外至於一乘二諦之原三明六通之旨西域備詳
東土靡記自頂日感夢滿月流光陽門飾毫眉之像
夜臺圖紺髮之形邇來奔競其風遂廣至晉永嘉惟
有寺四十二所逮皇魏受圖光宅嵩洛篤信彌繁法
教逾盛王侯貴臣棄象馬如脫屣庶士豪家捨資財
若遺跡於是招提櫛比寶塔駢羅爭寫天上之姿競
模山中之影金剎與靈臺比高宮殿共阿房等壯豈

B. *Ku-chin i-shih*

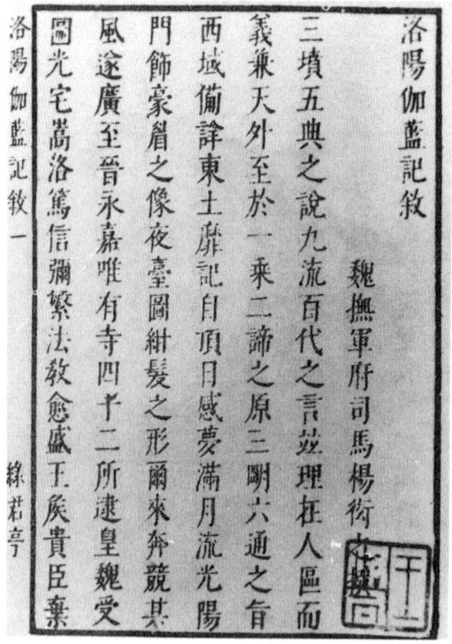

洛陽伽藍記敘

魏撫軍府司馬楊衒之撰

三墳五典之說九流百代之言竝理在人區而
義兼天外至於一乘二諦之原三明六通之旨
西域備詳東土靡記自頂日感夢滿月流光陽
門飾豪眉之像夜臺圖紺髮之形爾來奔競其
風遂廣至晉永嘉唯有寺四十二所逮皇魏受
圖光宅嵩洛篤信彌繁法教愈盛王侯貴臣棄

洛陽伽藍記敘一　　綠君亭

C. *Chin-tai mi-shu*

Fig. 1. Yang Hsüan-chih's Preface in three Ming editions

Preface to the *Lo-yang ch'ieh-lan chi*

by Yang Hsüan-chih

Sergeant-at-Arms in the Office of
the Commanding General of the Army of the Wei

The sayings [embodied in] the works of Three Emperors and Five Monarchs,[1] along with teachings [imparted by] the nine classes of literature and one hundred schools of philosophy,[2] have all prevailed in China and included ideas introduced from abroad. But such

[1] Literally, *san-fen wu-tien chih shou* 三墳五典之說 (*SPC* 6/37 gives *chi* 記 for *shou* 說), that is, books reputedly authored by two groups of exemplary emperors of Chinese antiquity. Fu-hsi 伏羲 (trad. 2852–2738 B.C.), Shen-nung 神農 (trad. 2737–2698 B.C.) and Huang-ti 黃帝 (the Yellow Emperor, trad. 2697–2598 B.C.) make up the first group of the mythical Three Emperors, and Shao-hao 少昊 (trad. 2597–2514 B.C.), Chuan-hsü 顓頊 (trad. 2513–2636 B.C.), Kao-hsin 高辛 (trad. 2435–2366 B.C.), Yao 堯 (trad. d. 2258 B.C.) and Shun 舜 (trad. 2317–2208 B.C.) are the Five Monarchs of the second group. This phrase is a direct quotation from the *Tso-chuan* 左傳 (I-wen facsimile *SSCCS* ed.) Chao 昭 12 45/36b–37a: 左史倚相趨過, 王曰:是良史也, 子善視之, 是能讀三墳五典八索九丘 . Legge 5, p. 641: "and E-sëang, the historiographer of the Left, passed by. 'There,' said the king, 'is an excellent historiographer. He can read the three Fun, the five Tëen, the eight Sih, and the nine K'ëw.'" Tu Yü's 杜預 (A.D. 222–284) comm.: 皆古書名. 孔安國尙書序云:伏羲, 神農, 黃帝之書, 謂之三墳, 言大道也. 少昊, 顓頊, 高辛, 唐, 虞之書, 謂之五典, 言常道也 . "All these are titles of ancient books. K'ung An-kuo's (pseudonyn) Preface to the *Shang-shu* reads: 'Books of Fu-hsi, Shen-nung, and the Yellow Emperor are known as the *San-fen*. They deal with the Great Way. Books of Shao-hao, Chuan-hsü, Kao-hsin, T'ang, and Yü are known as the *Wu-tien*. They deal with the Normal Way.'"

For a discussion of Yang's Preface, see Kanda Kiichirō, "Rakuyō garanki jo sakki," in *Tōyōshi kenkyū* 9 (July 1947), 71–94.

[2] Emending *chiu-liu pai-tai* 九流百代 to *chiu-liu pai-shih* 九流百氏 after *SPC* 9/89 and *Hsü Kao-seng chuan* 1/429. For the origin of 九流 (nine major schools of thought in pre-Han China), see *Han-shu pu-chu* (I-wen facsimile ed.) 30/51b.

The couplet reads 三墳五典之說, 九流百氏之言, 並理在人區 ,而利兼天下, which is actually modeled after the *Hou-Han shu* (I-wen facsimile *HHS* ed.) 118/27b 西域傳論:神迹詭怪, 則理絕人區; 威驗明顯, 則事出天外. "The magic perfor-

teachings as the law of the One Vehicle[3] and the Two Truths,[4] or the essence of the Three Insights[5] and Six Powers[6] acquired by the Buddha or an arhat—these were recorded in great detail in countries of the Western Regions, but scarcely touched upon in the Eastern Land.

When [Emperor Ming of the Han] saw in a dream the Buddha with a neck[7] shining as the sun and with a face as clear and as radiant as a full moon,[8] the emperor was so moved that an imperial order was given to have one statue of the Buddha[9] erected near the [K'ai-]yang Gate 開陽門 (Opening to the Morning Sun Gate) of the Southern Palace 南宮 and one near the [Ch'ang-]yeh Terrace [長]夜臺 (The

---

mances are simply too spectacular to be true in this world [of ours]; the proven efficacy of the [Buddhist] power can only occur outside of the universe." In Chapter 3 there is a couplet 商胡販客, 日奔塞下, which is yet another paraphrase of *HHS* (118/26b 西域傳論:馳命走驛, 不絕於時月; 商胡販客, 日款於塞下; q.v., Chapter 3, n. 165). "Companies of caravans rushed incessantly between the post stages in all seasons; barbarian tradesmen and peddlers daily came to pay tribute at our frontier lookouts." Both cases suggest that the author was an admirer of, and was much inspired by, the *HHS* style.

[3] That is, *i-ch'eng* 一乘, Mahāyāna (more strictly, Ekayāna), which, unlike Hīnayāna, purports to be the complete law of the Buddha.

[4] That is, *erh-ti* 二諦, reality 眞諦 (paramārtha) as opposed to the ordinary ideas of things 俗諦 (*saṁvṛti satya*). *Fa-men ming-i chi* (*Taishō* ed.) 199: 二諦, 一者世諦, 一名世諦, 亦名俗諦. 二者第一義諦, 亦名眞諦.

[5] That is, *san-ming* 三明 which includes: (1) insight into the normal conditions of self and others in previous lives (過去宿命明); (2) supernatural insight into future mortal conditions (未來天眼明); and (3) insight into the present mortal sufferings so as to overcome all passions or temptations (現在漏盡明). See *Chao-lun* (*Taishō* ed.) 158 涅槃無名論第四覈體第二:三明鏡於內, 神光照於外. 三明 is also given as 三達. See *Fa-men ming-i chi* 197: 三明一作三達, and *Fo-shuo p'u-sa pen-hsing ching* (*Taishō* ed.) A/108: 六通三達, 成一切智.

[6] That is, *liu-t'ung* 六通, the universal powers acquired by a Buddha or an Arhat through the degree of *dhyāna* (uninterrupted mental concentration). *Fa-men ming-i chi* 197: 一身通, 二天眼通, 三天耳通, 四他心通, 五宿命通, 六漏盡通.

[7] The text (la) gives *ting* 頂 and *SPC* (9/87) *ch'ing* 頃. Both characters are mistaken for *hsiang* 項, "neck." According to the *Han Hsien-tsung k'ai-fo-hua-fa pen nei-chuan* 漢顯宗開佛化法本內傳 (author unknown), as quoted in the *Kuang Hung-ming chi* 1/98 歸正篇, the emperor had a dream of the Buddha in A.D. 70, in which the latter appeared as a golden figure sixteen Chinese feet tall, with his neck emitting a stream of light. The text reads: 明帝永平[十]三年, 上夢神人. 金身丈六, 項有日光.

[8] That is, *man-yüeh* 滿月, a standard description of Buddha's face. See *Hsiu-hsing pen-ch'i ching* (*Taishō* ed.) 1/461.

[9] For the statue of Buddha above the K'ai-yang Gate, see *Li-huo-lun* 理惑論 as quoted in the *Hung-ming chi* (*Taishō* ed.) 1/5.

Eternal Night Terrace).[10] Special attention was given to depicting Buddha's eyebrows[11] and hair.[12] From this time[13] onward, Buddhism made rapid inroads in China and gained popularity throughout the nation.

During the Yung-chia period (A.D. 307–313) of the Chin dynasty, there were only forty-two Buddhist temples [in Lo-yang], but later when our imperial Wei accepted the heavenly mandate and chose the [same] Sung-Lo area as the site of our national capital, there was an increase in the number of Buddhist converts and those who lectured on Dharma.[14] Princes, dukes, and ranking officials donated such valuable things as elephants and horses,[15] as generously as if they were slipping shoes from off their feet. The people and wealthy families parted with their treasures as easily as with forgotten rubbish.[16] As a result, Buddhist temples[17] were built side by side, and stūpas rose up in row after row. People competed among themselves in making or copying the Buddha's portraits.[18] Golden stūpas matched the imperial observatory in height, and Buddhist lecture

[10] Ch'ang-yeh Terrace is the name of Emperor Ming's tomb, built while he was still alive.

[11] The Buddha is described as having dark hair and white eyebrows. See *Fo-shuo T'ai-tzu jui-ying pen-ch'i ching* (*Taishō* ed.) 1/474: 其髮紺青，眉間白毫，項出日光.

[12] The "white hair" is a standard mark in the statue of Buddha. It appears "between the eyes," hence is also known as "the third eye."

[13] Emending *erh* 爾 to *erh* 邇 after *IS* (1a).

[14] The text (1a) has a set of four sentences arranged in two comparable pairs, with two sentences for each pair. The first sentence in the first pair and the first sentence in the second pair each has four characters, whereas the second sentence of the first pair and the second sentence in the second pair each has six characters. The set of two pairs is therefore 4 × 6 and 4 × 6—the first example of such parallel prose in the text.

[15] The generous Prince Hsü-ta-na 須大拏 (Sudāna) was believed to have donated elephants, horses, and carriages. See Chapter 5 at note 117. The text indicates that Wei dignitaries were willing to donate whatever was needed in the cause of Buddhism.

[16] That is, *I-chi* 遺跡. *Wen-hsüan* (I-wen facsimile ed.) 29/3a 古詩十九首：不念攜手好，棄我如遺跡. "Forgetting the fondness [we shared] when holding our hands together/You are abandoning me without a single vestage [in your mind]."

[17] Literally *chao-t'i* 招提 (*catur-deśa*), meaning "four quarters"; that is, Buddhist temples to house monks coming from all directions.

[18] The text (1b) reads 爭寫天上之姿，競摹山中之影, of which 天上之姿 and 山中之影 both refer to Buddha's likeness. "The shadow of the mountain" may refer to an image of Buddha noted by Hui-yüan 慧遠 of Lu-shan 廬山. See his "Fo-ying ming" 佛影銘 as quoted in *Kuang Hung-ming chi*, pp. 197–198.

halls were as magnificent as the [ostentatiously wasteful] O-pang 阿房 [Palaces of the Ch'in dynasty (221–207 B.C.)]. Indeed, [Buddhist activity was so intense] that it was not merely a matter of clothing wooden [figures] in silk or painting earthen [idols] in rich colors.[19]

During the troubled years of Yung-hsi period 永熙 (Always Joyful) (A.D. 532–534),[20] the emperor moved to Yeh 鄴, accompanied by monks of various temples. It was not until the fifth year of the Wu-ting period 武定 (Conclusion of Military Operations) (A.D. 547)—also known as the Ting-mao 丁卯 year—that I revisited Lo-yang while on official duty. The outer and inner city walls lay in ruins, palaces were toppled, temples and monasteries were in ashes, and stūpas were no more than deserted graves. Walls were covered with wild vines, and streets were dotted with thorny bushes. Wild beasts lived under deserted stairways, and mountain birds bode in trees of abandoned courtyards. Wandering youngsters and cowherds walked back and forth through the nine intersections[21] of the city, while farmers and ploughers[22] grew crops on the grounds where palace towers once stood. Then I began to realize that it was not [Wei-tzu 微子 (12th cent. B.C.)] alone who lamented over the ruins of the Yin 殷 (trad. 1765–1123 B.C.),[23] and indeed any loyal Chou 周 (trad.

[19] The text (1b) 木衣綈繡, 土被朱紫 is a slightly modified quotation from Chang Heng's 張衡 "Hsi-ching fu" 西京賦 (*WH* 2/8a: 木衣綈錦, 土被朱紫) which E. R. Hughes (*Two Chinese Poets*, Princeton, 1960, p. 40) translates as "with the timbers adorned like the silk of robes, with the earth [walls] colored in red and purple." Originally, Chang Heng used this phrase to describe the luxurious residences in Ch'ang-an, but here Yang Hsüan-chih applied the similar wording to Buddhist temples in Lo-yang. "Figures" and "idols" are my addition. "Idols" may be symbolic of the grandeur of the formless Dharmakāya as visualized by Hui-yüan. See n. 18 above.

[20] In the seventh month (July to August) of the third year of the Yung-hsi period (A.D. 534), Emperor Hsiao-wu of the Wei was forced to move to Ch'ang-an. Three months later (October to November, A.D. 534), Emperor Hsiao-ching 孝靜 was enthroned in Yeh.

[21] *Shih-ching* (I-wen facsimile *SSCCS* ed.) 1.3/2a: (ode 7, verse 2) 兔罝: 施于中逵. Comm.: 逵, 九達之道. Here "nine" is used rather freely to mean "many."

[22] The text (1b) reads *keng-chia* 耕稼, which, in rhetorical terms, is not in agreement with *mu-shu* 牧豎 in the parallel sentence. The translation follows *SPC* (9/97) which gives *keng-lao* 耕老 instead.

[23] A reference to Wei-tzu, who lamented over the luxuriant wheat plants in the deserted ruins of the former Yin capital, prior to his trip to the Chou capital. *Shang-*

1122–256 B.C.) official would have been saddened at the sight of millet grown in deserted palace grounds![24]

Within and without the capital city there had been more than one thousand temples.[25] Today they are mostly demolished; one can not hear the tolling of bells at all. Out of fear that they might not be known to later generations, I have compiled this record. Nevertheless, it is rather difficult to give an account of every single temple, since there were simply too many[26] of them. I now keep a record of only the large temples, but I also select some small ones if there are auspicious or unusual stories pertaining to them. I have taken this opportunity to record actual events, including nonreligious affairs.[27] I started off with [temples] within the city, followed by those outside. I list the names of city gates in order to record the distance between the various temples. Altogether[28] there are five chapters.

Not a gifted narrator, I am afraid that I have overlooked [important points]. I only hope that gentlemen of later years will make additions to what I have missed.

In the seventeenth year of T'ai-ho 太和 (Grand Peace) (A.D. 493), [when] Emperor Kao-tsu [decided to] move the capital of the nation to Lo-yang, he ordered the Grand Minister of Public Works (*Ssu-t'u kung*), Mu Liang 穆亮, [to supervise] the construction of palaces which were completed two years later.[29] Names of city gates of Lo-yang followed those in use during the Wei and Chin periods.

---

shu ta-chuan (*SPTK so-pen*) 2/34 微子：微子將往朝周，過殷之故墟，見麥秀之蔪蔪，曰：此故父母之國，…志動心悲，…乃爲麥秀之歌.

[24] An allusion to the millet grown in the former palaces and ancestral shrines of the Chou court. *Shih-ching* 4.1/3b (preface to ode 65): 國風王城黍離序：黍離，閔宗周也. 周大夫行役，至於宗周，過故宗廟，宮室盡爲禾黍，閔周室之顚覆，彷徨不忍去，而作是詩也.

[25] T'ang Yung-t'ung estimates that at the end of the Wei period, there were 1,367 Buddhist temples in Lo-yang. See *Han-Wei Liang-Chin Nan-pei-ch'ao fo-chiao shih* (Shanghai, 1938), 2nd vol./70.

[26] Emending *tsui-to* 最多 to *chung-to* 衆多 after *SPC* 9/97.

[27] Adding the character *su* 俗 after *SPC* 9/97.

[28] Adding the character *fan* 凡 after *SPC* 9/97.

[29] The construction work was started in the tenth month (November–December) of the seventeenth year of T'ai-ho (A.D. 493) and completed two years later in the ninth month (October–November) of A.D. 495.

Both Li Ch'ung 李冲, Minister of State Affairs (*Shang-shu*), and Tung Chüeh 董爵, Court Architect (*Chiang-tso ta-chiang*), took part in the construction project. See *WS* 7B/13b; *YHNC* 3/1a.

There were three gates on the east side of the city wall. Starting from the north end, the first was known as Chien-ch'un Gate 建春門 (Gate of Establishing Spring).[30]

During the Han it was called Shang-tung Gate 上東門 (Upper East Gate), which was referred to in Juan Chi's 阮籍 (A.D. 210–263) poem "Walking out of the Upper East Gate."[31] During the Wei-Chin Period the name was changed to Chien-ch'un—a name kept in use by Emperor Kao-tsu.

Next to the south was the Tung-yang Gate 東陽門 (Gate of Eastern Sunlight).

During the Han it was known as Chung-tung Gate 中東門 (Central Gate on the East Side)[32] but it was changed to Tung-yang during the Wei-Chin period. Emperor Kao-tsu also kept this Wei-Chin name.

Still further to the south was the Ch'ing-yang Gate 青陽門 (Blue and Sunlit Gate).

Although during the Han it was known as the Wang-ching Gate 望京門 (Gate of Gazing at the Capital),[33] the name was changed to Ch'ing-ming Gate 清明門 (Gate of the Clear and Bright) during the Wei-Chin period. Emperor Kao-tsu later changed the name again to Ch'ing-yang.[34]

There were four gates[35] on the south side of the city wall.

The first gate[36] from the east end was known as the K'ai-yang Gate.

Long ago, after Emperor Kuang-wu of the Han 漢光武 (regnant A.D. 25–57) moved the capital to Lo-yang, and upon the

[30] The location of the Chien-ch'un Gate agrees with an entry in the *Ho-nan chün-[-hsien] ching-chieh pu* 河南郡[縣]境界簿 as quoted by Li Shan 李善 (d. A.D. 658) in his comm. for Hsieh Chuang's 謝莊 "Sung Hsiao-wu Hsüan Kuei-fei lei" 宋孝武宣貴妃誄 (*WH* 57/15b).

For differences in translating official titles and geographical names, see Hans Bielenstein, "Lo-yang in Later Han Times," *BMFEA* 48 (1976), 1–142.

[31] *WH* 23/4b 阮籍詠懷詩:步出上東門.

[32] The text (2a) reads *tung-chung* 東中, but both the *Shui-ching chu* (I-wen facsimile ed.) 16/25b 穀水注 and *YHNC* 2/4b 後漢城闕宮殿古蹟 give *chung-tung* 中東. Hence the translation.

[33] Also known as the *Hsüan-p'ing men* 宣平門 or *Mao-men* 旄門. See *YHNC* 24/6b.

[34] Also known as the *Shui-men* 稅門 and *Mang-men* 芒門. See *SCC* 16/25b.

[35] Emending *san* 三 to *ssu* 四 after *IS* (2a).

[36] Adding the character *men* 門 after *Chi-cheng* (2a)

completion of the gate, there had been no name for it. Suddenly one night a pillar appeared in the gate tower. Later, the K'ai-yang prefecture of the Lang-yeh 瑯琊 commandery (modern Yen-chou 兗州, Shantung) reported that a pillar attached to the south gate had flown away. A messenger was sent to inspect the lost pillar, and certified that this was the missing one. Consequently, the gate was named K'ai-yang. The name remained unchanged from Wei through Chin, and also under Emperor Kao-tsu.

Next to the west was the P'ing-ch'ang Gate 平昌門 (Gate of Peace and Prosperity).

During the Han it was called the P'ing Gate 平門 (Peace Gate),[37] but was renamed P'ing-ch'ang Gate during the Wei-Chin period. Emperor Kao-tsu kept the name unchanged.

Next to the west was the Hsüan-yang Gate 宣陽門 (Gate of Brilliant Sunlight).

During the Han it was called the Hsiao-yüan Gate 小苑門 (Gate of the Small Park), but was changed to Hsüan-yang during the Wei-Chin period. Emperor Kao-tsu kept the name in use.[38]

Still next to the west was the Chin-yang Gate 津陽門 (Gate of the Sunlit Ford).[39]

Known as the Chin-yang Gate in the Wei-Chin period, it was originally known as the Chin Gate 津門 (Ford Gate)[40] during the Han. Emperor Kao-tsu also retained the usage of the Wei-Chin name.

These were four gates on the west side of the city wall.

The first gate in the south was the Hsi-ming Gate 西明門 (Gate of Western Brilliance).

During the Han it was known as the Kuang-yang Gate 廣陽門 (Gate of Broad Sunlight), a name followed in the Wei-Chin period without change. Emperor Kao-tsu, however, changed it to Hsi-ming.

Next to the north was the Hsi-yang Gate 西陽門 (Gate of Western Sunlight).

[37] Also known as the *P'ing-men* 平門. The gate was built in A.D. 37 and reserved for royal processions. See *YHNC* 2/4a.

[38] A total of seventeen characters is added here after *CS* (11). Hence the translation.

[39] A total of six characters is added here after *Ho-chiao* (1a).

[40] The Lo River entered the city through this gate; hence the name.

During the Han it was called the Yung Gate 雍門 (Gate of Harmony)[41] but was changed to Hsi-ming[42] in the Wei-Chin period. Emperor Kao-tsu changed it again to Hsi-yang.

Next to the north was the Ch'ang-ho Gate 閶闔門 (The Heavenly Gate or the Gate of the Purple Palace in Heaven).[43]

During the Han it was known as the Shang-hsi Gate 上西門 (Upper West Gate). Above the gate were placed *chi* 璣 and *heng* 衡, astronomical instruments made, respectively, of bronze and jade. They were used to measure the movements of the sun, the moon, and the five constellations.[44] It was renamed Ch'ang-ho in the Wei-Chin period—a name kept in use by Emperor Kao-tsu.

Still farther to the north was the Ch'eng-ming Gate 承明門 (Receipt of Brilliance Gate).

The gate known as Ch'eng-ming was built on the orders of Emperor Kao-tsu. It faced the east-west main street and lay in front of the Chin-yung City 金墉城 (Golden-walled City).[45]

When the capital was moved to Lo-yang and the palaces were being built, Emperor Kao-tsu stayed in Chin-yung City. To the west of the city was the Wang-nan Temple 王南寺 (Temple to the South of His Majesty), frequented by the emperor when he discussed Buddhist doctrine with the monks. The gate was opened [to facilitate imperial visits]. Since the gate had no name, people referred to it as the New Gate, where princes and ranking officials gathered to greet the visiting emperor. The emperor spoke to Li Piao 李彪, the Chief Censor (*Yü-shih chung-wei*),[46] saying: "Ts'ao

[41] Also known as the Yung-ch'eng Gate 雍城門 ("a barrack-protected city"). See *YHNC* 2/2a.

[42] The gate corresponded to the Tung-yang Gate on the other side of the city wall. See *SCC* 16/20a.

[43] The Heavenly Gate is believed to be the south gate of the Purple Palace (Tz'u-wei-yüan 紫微垣) ("purple forbidden enclosure," name of the pole stars in ancient China; see Needham, *Science and Civilisation*, 3, 259).

[44] *Shu-ching* (I-wen facsimile *SSCCS* ed.) 3/4b 舜典：在璿璣玉衡，以齊七政. Legge 3, p. 33, "The Canon of Shun": "He examined the gem-adorned turning sphere, and the gem transverse *tube*, that he might regulate the seven Directions."

[45] It was built under Emperor Ming of the Wei in the northwestern section of Lo-yang. See *SCC* 16/9b. For recent archaeological discoveries of the Chin-yung City, see "Han-Wei Lo-yang ch'eng ch'u-pu k'an-ch'a," *K'ao-ku* 4 (1973), p. 207.

[46] Of humble origin, Li Piao had been a Court Secretary and Court Compiler under Emperors Kao-tsu and Shih-tsung. He died in A.D. 501. For more information about him, see *WS* 62/1a–20a.

Chih's 曹植 poem reads: 'I called on the emperor at the Ch'eng-ming Residence.'[47] So it is proper that the gate be named Ch'eng-ming." It was therefore so named.

There were two gates on the north side of the city wall. On the west end was the Ta-hsia Gate 大夏門 (Gate of Great China).

During the Han it was called the Hsia Gate 夏門 (Gate of China),[48] but was changed to Ta-hsia during the Wei-Chin period. Emperor Kao-tsu kept the name in use.[49] Emperor Hsüan-wu 宣武 (regnant A.D. 499–515)[50] had a three-storied tower built above it, reaching two hundred Chinese feet above the ground. All towers on the city gates of Lo-yang had only two stories, which were one hundred Chinese feet above the ground, except the one on the Ta-hsia Gate [which doubled the normal height]. Its beams thus appeared to pierce the clouds.

On the west side was the Kuang-mo Gate 廣莫門 (Gate of the Broad and Boundless).[51]

During the Han it was known as the Ku Gate 穀門 (Grain Gate),[52] but was changed to Kuang-mo in the Wei-Chin period. Emperor Kao-tsu retained the name. Westward from the Kuang-mo Gate, and stretching out as far as the Ta-hsia Gate, palaces and other buildings were linked to one another, obscuring the city walls.

Each gate was connected with [a thoroughfare] of three [lanes], wide enough to allow nine carriages to pass side by side.[53]

[47] Here the translation follows Hans Frankel's "Fifteen Poems by Ts'ao Chih, An Attempt at a New Approach," *JAOS* 84 (January–March 1964), 4. For Chinese text, see *WH* 24/3a 贈白馬王彪.

[48] Also known as the Hsia-ch'eng Gate 夏城門 ("Great China"; Hsia, name of the most ancient recorded dynasty is an analogy with China). See *YHNC* 2/5b.

[49] This sentence is added after *CS* (14).

[50] The text (3b) does not include these three characters Hsüan-wu-ti 宣武帝, "Emperor Hsüan-wu." *CS* (14) makes this addition after *YHNC* 3/2a.

[51] Kuang-mo is the name of one of the eight strong winds. It supposedly resides in the north. *Shih-chi hui-chu k'ao-cheng* (I-wen facsimile ed.) 25/12 律書:廣莫風居北方.廣莫者.言陽氣在下,陰莫陽廣大也;故曰廣莫.

[52] Also known as the Ku-ch'eng Gate (City of Grain) 穀城門. It faced the Mang Mountain further to the north. See *YHNC* 2/5b; *SCC* 16/14a.

[53] During the Chin, each thoroughfare consisted of three lanes. In the center was the imperial drive, which was flanked on either side by an earthen wall four Chinese feet high. The drive was open to ranking officials when performing ceremonial

duties, and the left and right lanes were for the use of the common people (the left was intended as an inbound lane, the right was outbound). Locust and willow trees were planted on both sides of the thoroughfare. The same thoroughfare arrangement was perhaps followed during the Wei. See *YHNC* 2/22a.

Side by side: that is, *chiu-kuei* 九軌. *Kuei* 軌 means the width between wheels of a carriage. See *Chou-li* (I-wen facsimile *SSCCS* ed.) 41/24b 考工記匠人:國中九經九緯, 經涂九軌. Cheng Hsüan's 鄭玄 (A.D. 132–200) comm.: 經緯之涂, 皆容方九軌, 軌謂軌廣.

Chapter 1

THE INNER CITY
(*Ch'eng-nei* 城內)

by Yang Hsüan-chih

Sergeant-at-Arms in the Office of
the Commanding General of the Army of the Wei

The Yung-ning Monastery[1] was constructed in the first year of the Hsi-p'ing period 熙平 (Prosperous and Peaceful) (A.D. 516), by decree of Empress Dowager Ling 靈太后, whose surname was Hu 胡. It was located one *li*[2] south of the Ch'ang-ho Gate on the west side of the Imperial Drive (*Yü-tao* 御道),[3] facing the palace grounds. To the east of the monastery was the Office of the Grand Commandant (*T'ai-wei fu*); to the west, the Ward of Eternal Health (Yung-k'ang *li* 永康里); to the south, the Office of Revealed Mysteries (*Chao-hsüan ts'ao*, that is, the Office of Religious Affairs).[4] On the north side, it bordered on the Tribunal of Censors (*Yü-shih t'ai*).

East of the Imperial Drive, and in front of the Ch'ang-ho Gate,

[1] For the construction of the Yung-ning Monastery, see also *TC* (I-wen facsimile ed.) 148/17b. There was another Yung-ning Monastery in the old capital of P'ing-ch'eng, which was the center of imperial activities. See WS 114/15b 釋老志. A description of this monastery, condensed from the same source, is available in Kenneth K. S. Ch'en's *Buddhism in China a Historical Survey* (Princeton, 1964, pp. 161–162). See also Laurence Sickman and Alexander Soper, *The Art and Architecture of China* (London, 1956), p. 229; Mizuno Seiichi, "Rakuyō Eineiji kai," in *Kōkogaku ronsō* 10 (January 1939), 111–128. For recent archaeological discoveries of the remains of this monastery, see "Han-Wei Lo-yang-ch'eng ch'u-pu k'an-ch'a," *K'ao-ku*, pp. 204–205. See also William C. White, *Tombs of Old Loyang* (Shanghai, 1934); *Tomb Tile Pictures of Ancient China* (Toronto, 1939).

[2] A measure of distance, one *li* is roughly the equivalent of one-third of an English mile. It also means a ward.

[3] Also known as T'ung-t'o *chieh* 銅駝街, "Bronze Camel Street."

[4] Also known as the Office to Oversee Merits (*Chien-fu ts'ao*) when the Northern Wei capital was still in P'ing-ch'eng. "Hsüan" here refers to Buddhist affairs instead

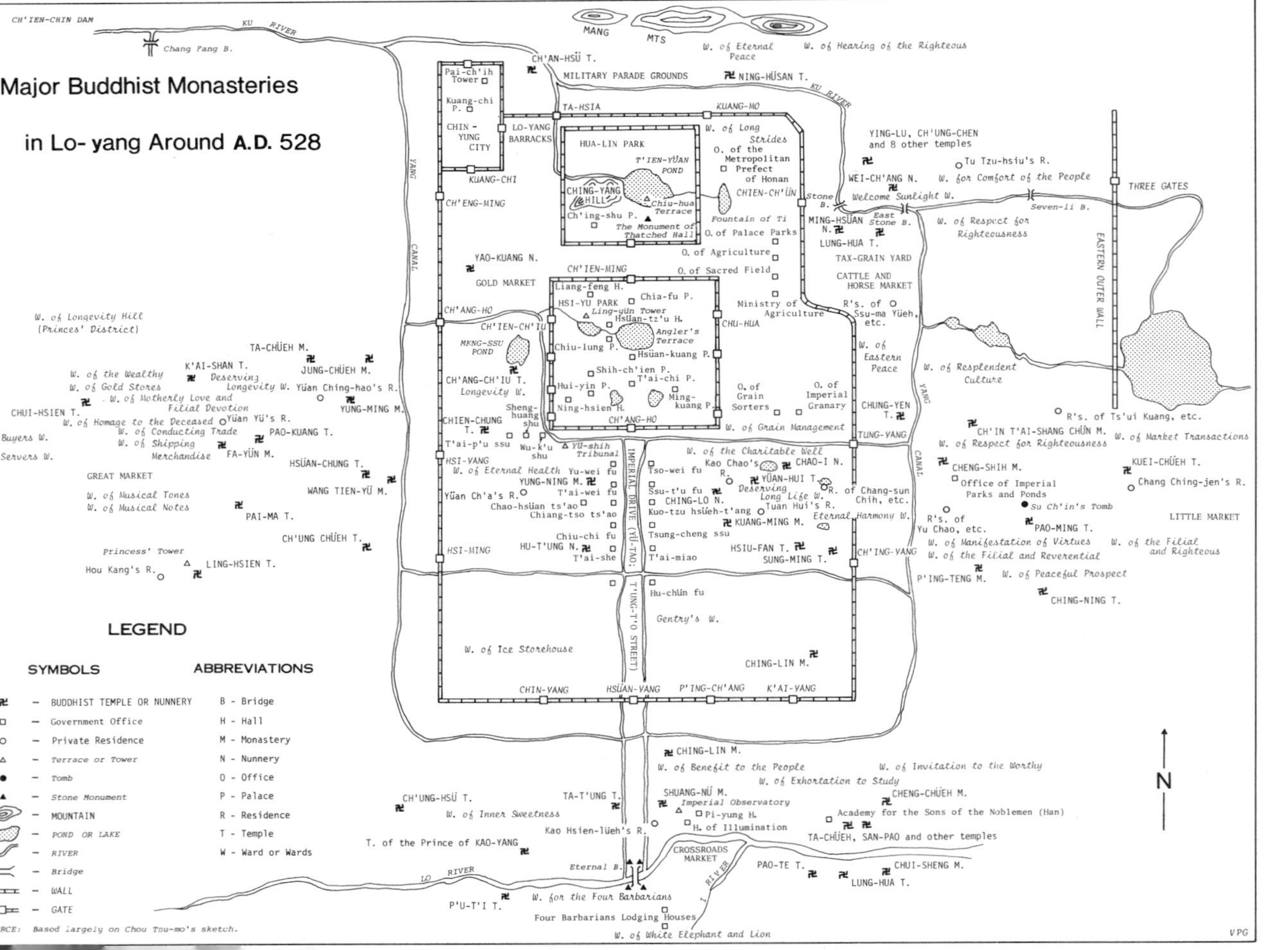

Major Buddhist Monasteries
in Lo-yang Around A.D. 528
CH'IEN-CHIN DAM
KU RIVER
Chang Fang B.
MANG MTS
W. of Eternal Peace
W. of Hearing of the Righteous
CH'AN-HSÜ T.
MILITARY PARADE GROUNDS
NING-HÜSAN T.
Pai-ch'ih Tower
Kuang-chi P.
CHIN-YUNG CITY
LO-YANG BARRACKS
KUANG-CHI
CH'ENG-MING
TA-HSIA
KUANG-MO
HUA-LIN PARK
T'IEN-YÜAN POND
CHING-YANG HILL
Chiu-hua Terrace
Ch'ing-shu P.
The Monument of Thatched Hall
W. of Long Strides
O. of the Metropolitan Prefect of Honan
CHIEN-CH'UN
Fountain of Ti
O. of Palace Parks
O. of Agriculture
O. of Sacred Field
Ministry of Agriculture
CHU-HUA
YING-LU, CH'UNG-CHEN and 8 other temples
Tu Tzu-hsiu's R.
WEI-CH'ANG N.
W. for Comfort of the People
Welcome Sunlight W.
Stone B.
East Stone B.
Seven-li B.
THREE GATES
MING-HSÜAN N.
LUNG-HUA T.
W. of Respect for Righteousness
TAX-GRAIN YARD
CATTLE AND HORSE MARKET
R's. of Ssu-ma Yüeh, etc.
EASTERN OUTER WALL
W. of Eastern Peace
W. of Resplendent Culture
YANG CANAL
YAO-KUANG N.
GOLD MARKET
CH'IEN-MING
Liang-feng H.
HSI-YU PARK
Chia-fu P.
Ling-yün Tower
Hsüan-tz'u H.
Angler's Terrace
CH'ANG-HO
CH'IEN-CH'IU
MENG-SSU POND
Chiu-lung P.
Hsüan-kuang P.
Shih-ch'ien P.
T'ai-chi P.
Hui-yin P.
Ming-kuang P.
Ning-hsien H.
O. of Grain Sorters
O. of Imperial Granary
CHUNG-YEN T.
W. of Grain Management
TUNG-YANG
CH'ANG-CH'IU T.
Longevity W.
CHIEN-CHUNG T.
Sheng-huang shu
T'ai-p'u ssu
Wu-k'u shu
YÜ-shih Tribunal
IMPERIAL DRIVE (YÜ-TAO; T'UNG-T'O STREET)
HSI-YANG
W. of Eternal Health
Yu-wei fu
YUNG-NING M.
Yüan Ch'a's R.
T'ai-wei fu
Chao-hsüan ts'ao
Chiang-tso ts'ao
Chiu-chi fu
HU-T'UNG N.
T'ai-she
HSI-MING
W. of the Charitable Well
Kao Chao's R.
CHAO-I N.
Tso-wei fu
YÜAN-HUI T.
Ssu-t'u fu
Deserving Long Life W.
R. of Chang-sun Chih, etc.
CHING-LO N.
Tuan Hui's R.
Kuo-tzu hsüeh-t'ang
KUANG-MING M.
Eternal Harmony W.
Tsung-cheng ssu
HSIU-FAN T.
SUNG-MING T.
T'ai-miao
CH'ING-YANG
Hu-chün fu
Gentry's W.
W. of Ice Storehouse
CHING-LIN M.
CHIN-YANG
HSÜAN-YANG
P'ING-CH'ANG
K'AI-YANG
W. of Longevity Hill (Princes' District)
TA-CHÜEH M.
K'AI-SHAN T.
JUNG-CHÜEH M.
W. of the Wealthy
Deserving Longevity W.
W. of Gold Stores
Yüan Ching-hao's R.
W. of Motherly Love and Filial Devotion
YUNG-MING M.
CHUI-HSIEN T.
W. of Homage to the Deceased
Yüan Yü's R.
W. of Conducting Trade
PAO-KUANG T.
Wine Buyers W.
W. of Shipping Merchandise
Wine Servers W.
FA-YÜN M.
HSÜAN-CHUNG T.
GREAT MARKET
WANG TIEN-YÜ M.
W. of Musical Tones
W. of Musical Notes
PAI-MA T.
CH'UNG CHÜEH T.
Princess' Tower
LING-HSIEN T.
Hou Kang's R.
R's. of Ts'ui Kuang, etc.
CH'IN T'AI-SHANG CHÜN M.
W. of Market Transactions
W. of Respect for Righteousness
CHENG-SHIH M.
KUEI-CHÜEH T.
Office of Imperial Parks and Ponds
Chang Ching-jen's R.
Su Ch'in's Tomb
LITTLE MARKET
R's. of Yu Chao, etc.
PAO-MING T.
W. of Manifestation of Virtues
W. of the Filial and Righteous
W. of the Filial and Reverential
P'ING-TENG M.
W. of Peaceful Prospect
CHING-NING T.
CHING-LIN M.
W. of Benefit to the People
W. of Invitation to the Worthy
W. of Exhortation to Study
CH'UNG-HSÜ T.
TA-T'UNG T.
SHUANG-NÜ M.
Imperial Observatory
CHENG-CHÜEH M.
W. of Inner Sweetness
Pi-yung H.
Academy for the Sons of the Noblemen (Han)
Kao Hsien-lüeh's R.
H. of Illumination
TA-CHÜEH, SAN-PAO and other temples
T. of the Prince of KAO-YANG
CROSSROADS MARKET
LO RIVER
Eternal B.
I RIVER
PAO-TE T.
CHUI-SHENG M.
LUNG-HUA T.
P'U-T'I T.
W. for the Four Barbarians
Four Barbarians Lodging Houses
W. of White Elephant and Lion
N
LEGEND
SYMBOLS
BUDDHIST TEMPLE OR NUNNERY
Government Office
Private Residence
Terrace or Tower
Tomb
Stone Monument
MOUNTAIN
POND OR LAKE
RIVER
Bridge
WALL
GATE
ABBREVIATIONS
B - Bridge
H - Hall
M - Monastery
N - Nunnery
O - Office
P - Palace
R - Residence
T - Temple
W - Ward or Wards
SOURCE: Based largely on Chou Tsu-mo's sketch.
VPG

Map I

was the Office of the Imperial Guards of the Left (*Tso-wei fu*), and south of that was the Office of the Minister of Public Instruction (*Ssu-t'u fu*). South of the *Ssu-t'u fu* was the Academy for the Sons of the Noblemen (*Kuo-tzu hsüeh-t'ang*), which contained [three] statues—Confucius in the center, flanked on one side by Yen Yüan 顏淵 [514–483 B.C., a favorite disciple of Confucius, 551–479 B.C.], inquiring about the meaning of good-heartedness, and on the other side by Tzu-lu 子路 [543–480 B.C., another favorite disciple of Confucius], asking about government. South of the academy was the Office of the Imperial Clan (*Tsung-cheng ssu*), and beyond that the Shrine of Imperial Ancestors (*T'ai-miao* 太廟). Further to the south was the Office of the Protector of the Army (*Hu-chün fu*), and finally the Gentry's Ward (I-kuan *li* 衣冠里).

On the west of the Imperial Drive was the Office of the Imperial Guards on the Right (*Yu-wei fu*), and south of that was the Office of the Grand Commandant.

Extending southward, in order, were the Office of the Court Architect (*Chiang-tso ts'ao*), the Office of *Chiu-chi fu*, "Nine-story" Office,[5] and the Temple of the Earth (*T'ai-she* 太社). At the southernmost edge was the Ward of Ice Storehouse (Ling-yin *li* 凌陰里)[6] where ice had been stored for the use of the previous four reigns.[7]

Within the precincts [of the monastery] was a nine-storied wooden stūpa. Rising nine hundred Chinese feet above the ground, it formed the base for a mast that extended for another one hundred Chinese feet; thus together they soared one thousand Chinese feet

of Taoist teachings, which is the traditional meaning of this word. For *Chien-fu ts'ao*, see *WS* 114/17a 釋老志.

[5] The function of this office is not clear. The text may be in error.

[6] Ling-yin, meaning "Ice Storehouse," appeared for the first time in the *Shih-ching* 8.1/21b (ode 154, verse 8, line 2) and is the same term that Arthur Waley translated as "Cold Shed" in the *Book of Songs* (New York, 1960), p. 167.

[7] The text reads *ssu-ch'ao shih* 四朝時, in which *ssu* 四 is probably a corruption for *chung* 中. *Chung-ch'ao* 中朝, a term frequently used in this work, referring to the four reigns of the Western Chin (A.D. 265–316), when the national capital was in Lo-yang. It is also a term used in *SCC* (15/13a under Lo-shui). The author never used this term *ssu-ch'ao* elsewhere.

PC (111–112) suggests that *ssu-ch'ao* 四朝 might be an error for *hsi-ch'ao* 西朝 (Western Dynasties), a term often used by intellectuals of the Southern Dynasties to refer to Lo-yang, or to dynasties with Lo-yang as their national capital. Since Yang Hsüan-chih was a subject of the Northern Dynasties, however, it does not seem likely that he would use the same term for Lo-yang that his southern counterparts did.

above the ground, and could be seen as far away from the capital as one hundred *li*. In the course of excavating for the construction of the monastery, thirty golden statues were found deep underground; this was interpreted as an auspicious reward for the empress dowager's conversion to Buddhism. As a result, she spent all the more lavishly on its construction.

On the top of the mast was a golden jar inlaid with precious stones. It had the capacity of twenty-five piculs.[8] Underneath the bejeweled jar were thirty tiers of golden plates to receive the dew. Golden bells hung from each of the plates. In addition, chains linked the mast with each of the four corners of the stūpa. Golden bells, each about the size of a stone jar, were also suspended from the linkworks.

There were nine roofs, one for each story, with golden bells suspended from the corner of each one, totaling 120 in all. The stūpa had four sides, each having three doors and six windows. Painted in vermillion, each door had five rows of gold nails. Altogether there were 5,400 nails on twenty-four panels of twelve double doors. In addition, the doors were adorned with knockers made of golden rings. The construction embodied the best of masonry and carpentry. The elegance of its design and its excellence as an example of Buddhist architecture was almost unimaginable. Its carved beams and gold door-knockers fascinated the eye. On long nights when there was a strong wind, the harmonious jingling of the bejeweled bells could be heard more than ten *li* away.

North of the stūpa was a Buddhist hall, which was shaped like the Palace of the Great Ultimate (T'ai-chi *tien* 太極殿). In the hall was a golden statue of the Buddha eighteen Chinese feet high, along with ten medium-sized images—three of sewn pearls, five of woven golden threads, and two of jade. The superb artistry was matchless, unparalleled in its day.

The monastery had over one thousand cloisters for the monks, both single cloisters and multilevel ones, decorated with carved beams and painted walls. The doors, painted in blue designs, had carved windows.[9] The beauty of the cloisters was beyond description. Luxuriant cypress, juniper, and pine trees brushed the eaves of the building, while bamboo groves and aromatic plants lined the

[8] A picul is the equivalent of 100 catties or 10 *tou*.

[9] The text (1/2b) reads *ch'ing-so i-shu* 靑瑣綺疏. For the origin of *ch'ing-so* 靑瑣, see *WH* 2/4a 張衡西京賦. Blue was the ornamental color reserved for imperial use during the Han.

courtyards and stairways. [For this monastery] Ch'ang Ching wrote a stone inscription that reads [in part]: "Even the Grand Hall on Mt. Sumeru[10] and the Palace of Purity in Tuṣita Heaven[11] are no match for this."

Here were kept all the sūtras and Buddhist images presented by foreign countries. The walls of the monastery were all covered with short rafters beneath the tiles in the same style as our contemporary palace walls. There were gates in each of the four directions. The tower on the South Gate rose two hundred Chinese feet above the ground, had three stories, each with an archway, and was shaped like the present-day Tuan-men 端門 (meaning South Gate) of the palace grounds. On the gate and latticed windows were paintings of patterned clouds and colored fairies—all magnificent and beautiful.

Under the archway were images of four guardians and four lions, adorned with gold, silver, pearls, and rare stones. Such an imposing and splendid scene could not be found elsewhere.

The East and West Gates resembled the South Gate, except that the towers had only two stories. The North Gate had no tower; in this it resembled the Wu-t'ou Gate 烏頭門 (Black-head Gate).[12]

Outside the four gates were planted green locust trees on the bank of clean streams.[13] Travelers in the capital city often took shelter there. On the street, the freedom from dust in the air was not the result of moisture from the rain clouds; the cooling effect accompanying the pleasing breeze did not originate from round-shaped fans.[14] [Instead, they were blessings of this physical environment.][15]

[10] The text reads *Hsü-mi pao-tien* 須彌寶殿, the Grand Hall of Sumeru. According to Hsüan-tsang (*Ta-T'ang Hsi-yü chi*, *SPTK so-pen* 1/3), Sumeru is the name of a holy mountain that, in Hindu mythology, holds up the heavens.

[11] The text reads *Tou-shuai ching-kung* 兜率淨宮, meaning the Palace of Purity in Tusita where Maitreya dwells.

[12] It is also known as Ling-hsing Gate 櫺星門, with towers on each side. Its height varied from eight to twenty-two Chinese feet. See Li Chieh's *Ying-tsao fa-shih* (facsimile ed., Shanghai, 1954), 6/122–125, 32/62–63.

[13] Literally, *lü-shui* 綠水, azure waters.

[14] The Chinese name for this type of fan is *ho-huan* 合歡. For its origin, see *WH* 27/11b 班婕妤怨歌行. *Ho-huan* (*acacia*) is also the name of a tree. Its exuberant leaves grow in thick profusion, but each one yields to the wind separately, producing a pleasant breeze for those enjoying shade underneath. See Ts'ui Pao, *Ku-chin chu* (*IS* ed.) B/1b. The author uses this term as a pun.

[15] The text (1/3a), which consists of two pairs of parallel sentences in alternating

Ch'ang Ching, Drafter of the Central Secretariat (*Chung-shu she-jen*), was ordered by the court to prepare a stone inscription for the monastery.[16]

[Ch'ang] Ching, styled Yung-ch'ang 永昌, was a native of Ho-nei 河內.[17] He was known nationally for his sagacity and learning. In the nineteenth year of the T'ai-ho period (A.D. 495), Emperor Hsiao-wen, impressed by his talents, promoted him to the post of Erudite of the Law (*Lü-hsüeh po-shih*). Thus he was often consulted on difficult legal cases. In the early Cheng-shih period 正始 (The Beginning of Justice) (*ca.* A.D. 504),[18] he was ordered to codify a permanent legal system with Kao Seng-yu 高僧祐, Associate Censor in charge of Drafting (*Chih-shu shih-yü-shih*); Wang Yüan-kuei 王元龜, Commander of the Plumed Forest Guards [so named because the many feathers around the arrows

---

four- and six-character form, is an excellent example of the author's mastery of the parallel prose style. As an example of free translation, the whole paragraph, including this passage, can be rephrased and translated as follows: "Deep blue-green locust trees were planted outside the four gates along the banks of a sparkling stream, offering a welcome retreat for the travelers in the capital who often took shelter there. People on the street delighted in its freedom from both the gusts of dust-laden wind [and the suffocating heat]. The enticing beauty of this spot no more derived from the presence of billowing cumulus clouds hanging heavy with moisture, than from the gentle breeze of the round-shaped fans. [Rather, it was a fortuitous confluence of all nature's friendliest elements.]" Also see the Introduction.

[16] Ch'ang Ching was a leading essayist, jurist, and government official near the end of the Northern Wei dynasty (A.D. 386–534). Two rubbings of his stele inscriptions are still available today: one for Yüan Hsing 元興 (dated A.D. 542) and the other for the Chief of Buddhist Nuns Tz'u-ch'ing 慈慶 (dated A.D. 524). See Chao Wan-li, *Han-Wei Nan-pei-ch'ao mu-chih chi-shih* (Peking, 1956), plates 42 and 239.

For the biography of Ch'ang Ching, see *WS* 82/5a–13a. This is an important source of information about the legal history of the Northern Wei, because no other work provides nearly as complete a list of participants and their respective official titles.

[17] During the Northern Wei, Ho-nei commandery belonged to Huai province 懷州. See *WS* 106A/23b 地形志. Yeh-wang 野王 was the capital city of Ho-nei commandery.

[18] According to *Ts'e-fu yüan-kuei* and other sources quoted by Ch'eng Shu-te (*Chiu-ch'ao lü k'ao*, facsimile ed., Taipei, 1965, 5/409), the codification took place in A.D. 504.

and the butts gave the appearance of a forest] (*Yü-lin chien*); Tsu Ying,[19] Secretary in the Department of State Affairs (*Shang-shu lang*); and Li Yen-chih 李琰之,[20] Cavalier Attendant (*Yüan-wai san-ch'i shih-lang*). The Prince of P'eng-ch'eng 彭城王 [Yüan] Hsieh 元勰,[21] the Grand Preceptor (*T'ai-shih*), and Liu Fang 劉芳,[22] Governor (*Tz'u-shih*) of Ch'ing-chou 青州, were also ordered to take part in these deliberations. In examining the existing regulations and checking ancient clauses against the current ones, [Ch'ang] Ching exhibited his organizational ability. The law, in twenty chapters, was adopted and at this writing is still in use. In cooperation with [Liu] Fang, he suggested names for the palaces, halls, roads, wards, and suburbs of Lo-yang. Later, he was transferred from the capital post to be the Prefect (*Ling*) of Ch'ang-an. His contemporaries compared him to P'an Yüeh 潘岳.[23] After this he served as the Drafter of the Central Secretariat, Attending Secretary within the Imperial Yellow Gate (*Huang-men shih-lang*), Supervisor of Archives, Governor of Yu-chou, and Palatine Ceremonially Equal to the Three Authorities (*Yu-chou tz'u-shih i-t'ung san-ssu* 幽州刺史儀同三司).[24] Because of [his successful official career], his disciples felt much honored.

Even though Ch'ang Ching had at times served as a close attendant to the emperor in the capital and at other times served as governor outside of it, he led an ascetic and simple life, working the same as an ordinary farmer. His only possessions consisted of classical and historical books, which filled his carriages when travel-

[19] For his biography, see *WS* 82/20–4b.

[20] For his biography, see *WS* 82/1a–2a.

[21] For his biography, see *WS* 19B/2b–22b.

[22] For his biography, see *WS* 55/7a–16a.

[23] P'an Yüeh (A.D. ?–300) was a noted man of letters of the early Chin Dynasty. For his biography, see *Chin-shu chiao-chu* (I-wen facsimile ed.) 55/11a–21b. He had been the prefect of Ch'ang-an; hence the allusion.

[24] For 黃門侍郎, my translation follows Teng Ssu-yü, *Family Instructions for the Yen Clan* (Leiden, 1968), xxii. *I-t'ung san-ssu* (Palatine Ceremonially Equal to the Three Authorities) is an honorific title reserved for veteran high-ranking officials. It carried little real power, and its function varied from time to time. Teng Chih 鄧騭 of the Later Han Dynasty was the first official to hold this title. In A.D. 106 he was given this title in addition to his post of General of Chariots and Horsemen (*Chü chiang-chün*). See *HHS* 16/11a.

ing and his shelves when at home. Several hundred essays written by him and prefaced by Feng Wei-po 封暐伯,[25] the Supervising Secretary (*Chi-shih*), are still available today.

After the ornamentation was finished, Emperor Ming 明帝 (regnant A.D. 515–528) and Empress Dowager [Hu] both ascended [the tower]. They viewed the palaces [as if] in their own palms, and gazed down upon the national capital [as if] in their own courtyard. To keep the interior of the palaces from public view, people were denied access to the tower.

Hu Hsiao-shih 胡孝世, Metropolitan Prefect of Ho-nan (Honan *yin* 河南尹) and I once ascended the tower. In truth, it seemed as if the clouds and rain were below us!

The monk Bodhidharma 菩提達摩 of the Western Regions (Hsi-yü 西域) was a native of Persia.[26] He came from the desolate frontier to visit China. Having seen the golden plates making dazzling reflections of the sunlight and shining into the clouds, and having heard the ringing of bejeweled bells lofted into the sky by the wind, he sang praises of this extraordinary artistic achievement.

Bodhidharma claimed at that time to be one hundred fifty years old. But during his extensive travels, which had taken him to every corner of many countries, nowhere in the sullied world[27] had he seen a monastery as elegant and beautiful as this one. Not even in

[25] Feng Wei-po, the eldest son of Feng Kuei 封軌, was a native of Po-hai commandery 渤海郡 (in modern Hopei). He was chosen as Erudite of the Imperial Academy (*T'ai-hsüeh po-shih*) in recognition of his learning. For his biography, see *WS* 32/14b–16b.

[26] The dates and life of Bodhidharma (ca. A.D. 461–534) remain controversial. Some maintain that he was an Indian prince who came to Canton by sea in A.D. 520 or 527. Others assert that he was a native of Persia and lived more than 150 years before he suddenly disappeared. At first invited by Emperor Wu of the Liang 梁武帝 (regnant A.D. 502–549) to stay in Nanking, he eventually went to live in Sung Mountain (north of modern Teng-feng prefecture 登封, Honan) under the Northern Wei. He was generally accepted as the first patriarch of the Ch'an School 禪宗 in China. See Tao-yüan, *Ching-te ch'uan-teng lu* (*SPTK* ed.) 3/1b–9b, and Ch'en, *Buddhism in China*, pp. 352–353.

For a study of the Western Regions, see Hori Kentoku, *Kaisetsu Seiiki ki* (Tokyo, 1912); and for a description of Buddhism in that area, see Hatani Ryōtai, *Seiiki no Bukkyō* (Kyoto, 1914). See also Funaki Katsuma, "Hokugi no Seiiki kōtsū ni kansuru shomondai" I in *Fukuoka Nishi Nihon shigaku* 4 (1950) 46–69; II in *Hakusan shigaku* (Tōyō Daigaku Hakusan Shigakkai), 2 (1956), 1–10.

[27] Literally, Yen-fou[-chou] 閻浮[州], Jambu-dvīpa.

Buddha's realm of ultimate things[28] was there anything like this. He chanted namah—an expression of complete submission to the Buddha—and held his palms together for several days after having seen it.

In the second year of the Hsiao-ch'ang period (A.D. 526), a hurricane upturned many houses and uprooted many trees [in Lo-yang]. The golden vase on top of the mast was also blown off by the wind and fell more than ten Chinese feet into the ground. [The court] once again ordered workers to recast a new vase.

In the first year of the Chien-i period 建義 (To Establish Justice) (A.D. 528), Erh-chu Jung 爾朱榮, Prince of T'ai-yüan 太原王, stationed his army and cavalry in this monastery.[29]

> [Erh-chu] Jung, styled T'ien-pao 天寶, was a native of Northern Hsiu-jung commandery 北(地)秀容.[30] For [two] generations his father and he had held the title Chieftain of the First Rank in Charge of the People (*Ti-i ling-min ch'iu-chang*),[31] Duke

[28] The text (1/4a) reads *chi-wu-ching-chieh* 極物境界.

[29] For a comparable account of Erh-chu Jung's rise to power and his eventual downfall, see *WS* 74/1a–15a.

[30] The text (1/46) gives Pei-ti Hsiu-jung 北地秀容. Pei-ti (in modern Kansu) was the name of a commandery geographically removed from Hsiu-jung, thus indicating the character *Pei* 北 as an interpolation. On the other hand, in the "Treatise on Geography" (*Ti-hsing chih* 地形志) in *WS* (106A/17b–18a), a Hsiu-jung commandery (established in A.D. 410) in Ssu-chou 肆州 (created as a *chen* 鎮—military post—in A.D. 405 but changed to a province in A.D. 445), and a Hsiu-jung prefecture (modern Hsin-hsien 忻縣, Shansi) are mentioned. No mention is made of Pei (Northern) Hsiu-jung. The biography of Erh-chu Jung (*WS* 74/1a–b), however, records that at one time Emperor T'ai-tsu (regnant A.D. 386–409) considered transferring Erh-chu Yü-chien 爾朱羽健 (Erh-chu Jung's great-grandfather) from Pei Hsiu-jung to Nan 南 (Southern) Hsiu-jung, the latter covering an area of 300 square *li*—almost three times the normal size of a prefecture. The size itself seems to indicate that both Pei Hsiu-jung and Nan Hsiu-jung were commanderies instead of prefectures. Furthermore, citing a prefecture instead of a commandery in a biography to identify an individual geographically would be a departure from the traditional style of historical writing.

For general background of the tribal structure Erh-chu Jung headed, see Zhou Yi-liang, "Pei-ch'ao ti min-tsu wen-ti yü min-tsu cheng-ts'e," *Wei-Chin Nan-pei-ch'ao shih lun-ts'ung* (Peking, 1963), p. 159.

[31] According to *WS* (74/1a), since the time of Erh-chu Jung's great-grandfather, Erh-chu Yü-chien, the head of the Erh-chu family had also been the chieftain with jurisdiction over all tribesmen. The chieftains ranged from the first to third rank. See also Zhou Yi-liang, "Ling-min ch'iu-chang yü liu-chou tu-tu," in *Wei-Chin Nan-pei-ch'ao shih lun-ts'ung*, p. 188.

of Po-ling Commandery 博陵郡公,[32] exercising jurisdiction over more than eight thousand groups[33] of tribesmen. He was in possession of scores of thousands of horses,[34] and his wealth equaled that of [the vassal of] a rich kingdom.[35]

In the second month of the first year of the Wu-t'ai period 武泰 (Mighty and Peaceful) (March 31, A.D. 528),[36] Emperor [Su-tsung 肅宗] died without an heir. [Yüan] Chao 元釗, heir to the Prince of Lin-t'ao 臨洮王, was chosen as successor. At the time of his ascension, the [young] emperor was only three years old. The Empress Dowager [Hu 胡], obsessed by her greedy desire for control of the government, [chose] and enthroned [this infant emperor].[37]

[Erh-chu] Jung spoke to Yüan T'ien-mu 元天穆, Governor of Ping-chou 并州:[38] "When the [late] emperor died[39] at nineteen years of age, people still considered him an immature ruler. How

[32] The text implies that the family had the hereditary title Duke of Po-ling. According to *WS* (74/3a), however, Erh-chu Jung was the first to receive this title.

[33] Literally *pu-lo* 部落, a tribe.

[34] *WS* 74/2a reads: "Cattle, sheep, camels, and horses are divided into herds by color and measured by the number of valleys they grazed."

[35] Literally *fu-teng t'ien-fu* 富等天府, "as rich as the heavenly treasury." For the origin of *t'ien-fu*, see *Chan-kuo-ts'e* (*SPTK so-pen*) 3/30: 此所謂天府, 天下之雄國也. James I. Crump, Jr., tr., *Intrigues: Studies of the Chan Kuo Ts'e* (Ann Arbor, 1964), p. 32: "truly an arsenal of nature, the most awesome state in the land!"

[36] The exact date of the imperial demise is as given in *WS* 9/29a–b. According to *WS* 74/4b, however, it should be April 1.

[37] That is, Yüan Yü 元愉, son of Emperor Hsiao-wen and originally known as Prince of Ching-chao 京兆王. Lin-t'ao was his posthumous title. See *WS* 22/4b; 9/29b.

Upon the death of Emperor Su-tsung, Empress Dowager Hu proclaimed the enthronement of the child of Lady P'an (literally, P'an *Ch'ung-hua* 潘充華, *Ch'ung-hua* being one of many titles for palace women), said to be a baby boy. A few days later, when the nation recovered somewhat from the initial shock of the imperial demise, she announced that Lady P'an's baby was really a girl, but, since a male successor was urgently needed, she had selected the son of Yüan Pao-hui 元寶暉 as the new emperor. He was then only three years old. See *PS* 13/21a.

[38] Yüan T'ien-mu was a member of the imperial household. He and Erh-chu Jung, as noted elsewhere, were sworn brothers. See *PS* 15/8b Ping-chou had its capital in Chin-yang 晉陽 (modern T'ai-yüan prefecture 太原, Shansi).

[39] Literally, *yen-chia* 晏駕, "late to the carriage." It was customary for the emperor to hold court audience early in the morning. *SC* 79/28 范雎傳:宮車一日晏駕, "If

much less likely that an infant, as yet unable to speak, can rule the nation so that we may expect peace and prosperity? For generations we [of my family] have received court favor. I can not sit idly by, watching success turn to failure. Now I would like to lead a five thousand iron-armored[40] cavalry to hurry to express their grief at the imperial grave and at the same time inquire from attending ministers the causes leading to the imperial death.[41] How would you respond, in all honesty, [to my proposal]?"[42]

[Yüan T'ien-]mu replied: "For generations your Lordship has ruled the Provinces Ping-chou and Ssu-chou 肆州 with outstanding courage and ability.[43] Among your tribesmen, you have ten thousand archers. I[-yin] 伊[尹] (18th cent. B.C.) or Huo [Kuang] 霍光 (d. 68 B.C.)[44] would be seen again if you could carry out the deposal of [the unworthy] and enthronement [of the worthy]."[45]

That day [Erh-chu] Jung and [Yüan T'ien-]mu exchanged vows to become sworn brothers. [Yüan T'ien-]mu was senior in

---

one day the palace carriage should come out late...." Ying Shao's 應劭 (ca. A.D. 140–ca. 206) commentary: 天子當晨起早作, 如方崩殞, 故稱晏駕, "The emperor should rise up in the morning and start working early. If he has just passed away, he is known 'to be late to his carriage.'"

[40] *IS* (1/4a) gives *t'ieh-ma san-ch'ien* 鐵馬三千. For *t'ieh-ma*, see *WH* 56/6b 陸倕石闕銘: 鐵馬千羣. Li Shan's commentary: 鐵馬, 鐵甲之馬, "By iron-horses, we mean those that are iron-armored."

[41] It was believed that the emperor died unnaturally; hence Erh-chu Jung's provocative inquiry.

[42] According to *TC* 152/6b and *WS* 74/5b, the deceased emperor had secret plans authorizing Erh-chu Jung to stage an armed coup d'état in the capital, thus ridding himself of Cheng Yen 鄭儼 and Hsü Ho 徐紇, two powerful officials faithful to the empress dowager but disloyal to the emperor. Knowing what might happen, and with the empress dowager's concurrence, Cheng Yen and Hsü Ho allegedly poisoned the emperor.

[43] Here the translation follows *CT* (1/5b), which has an additional phrase *ying-wu chih lüeh* 英武志略.

[44] I-yin, a prime minister of the Yin 殷 dynasty, dethroned Emperor T'ai-chia 太甲 (regnant 1753–1721 B.C.) See *Shu-ching* 8/17a–24a. Huo Kuang of the Western Han enthroned Liu Ho 劉賀, King of Ch'ang-i 昌邑王, after the death of Emperor Chao 昭帝 (regnant 86–74 B.C.), but later elevated Emperor Hsüan 宣帝 (regnant 73–49 B.C.) as a replacement for the King of Ch'ang-i when the latter was found to be incompetent. See *HS* 68/4b ff.

[45] *Hsing fei-li chih shih* 行廢立之事, "to handle such matters as dethronement and enthronement."

age, so [by convention] he was treated as the elder brother [with the accompanying respect]. [Erh-chu] Jung, however, was recognized as the sworn leader, so that [Yüan T'ien-]mu bowed to the other for courtesy's sake.

They then secretly discussed the senior members of the royal household, unsure as to who deserved the imperial mandate.[46] Subsequently, Chin-yang men cast gold figures for the prospective rulers;[47] none but [the statue of] the Prince of Ch'ang-lo 長樂王, [Yüan] Tzu-yu 元子攸, was dignified or an especially good likeness. As a result, [Erh-chu] Jung was in favor of the Prince of Ch'ang-lo. An old and skilled slave, Wang Feng 王豐,[48] was sent to enter Lo-yang, requesting that he be the next ruler. [The Prince of] Ch'ang-lo immediately accepted the offer and set a date for concerted action. [Erh-chu] Jung dressed his three armies in white,[49] and marched southward under unfurled flags.

When she heard of [Erh-chu] Jung's uprising, the empress dowager called the various dignitaries for a meeting. None of the royal clan was willing to offer advice, as each had ill feelings against her, for she had alienated them by garnering all [imperial] favors. Only Hsü Ho,[50] Attending Secretary within the Imperial Yellow Gate, said: "Erh-chu Jung is a petty barbarian of Ma-i 馬邑[51] of mediocre abilities. Notwithstanding his own [limited] virtue and strength, he is now thrusting his sword against the court. This we may compare to the praying mantis's attempt to halt the wheels of

[46] Literally, *tang-pi* 當璧, "he who worships right over the jade"; that is, the one ruler approved by the god. The expression originates from the *Tso-chuan* Chao 13 46/9a: 當璧而拜者, 神所立也. Legge 5, p. 650: "He who worships right over his *pieh* shall be he whom your Spirits have appointed."

[47] It was customary during the Wei to cast a statue in the likeness of candidates for the titles of Empress and Monarch. Only those whose statues came out of the mold with perfect features would be chosen. See Chao I, *Nien-erh-shih ta-chi* (*SPPY* ed.) 14/14a under 後魏以鑄像卜休咎.

[48] *WS* 76/6a reads Wang Hsiang 王相. He was a *ts'ang-t'ou* 蒼頭. For more information about this term, see Martin C. Wilbur, *Slavery in China during the Former Han Dynasty, 206 B.C.–A.D. 25* (revised ed., New York, 1967), p. 69.

[49] A symbol of mourning for the death of the emperor.

[50] The text (1/5b) reads Hsü T'ung 徐統, *T'ung* being a scribal mistake for *Ho* 紇.

[51] The name of a Han prefecture used loosely to refer to Shuo-chou 朔州 (modern Shuo-hsien 朔縣, Shansi) during the Northern Wei. It was first established during the Ch'in to guard against the Hsiung-nu raids. See *HS* 28b/38a Yen Shih-ku's 顏師古 commentary quoting the 晉太康地記.

a chariot with its front legs,[52] or to one who lies atop piled firewood until he is burnt to death.[53]

"We have enough guardsmen and civilian officers for a fight. We have only to defend Ho-ch'iao 河橋 (the Yellow River Bridge)[54] and watch [the enemy's] possible intentions. Since Erh-chu Jung's army has come from over one thousand *li* away, it will be tired. We will certainly break them, since our army is rested while his has been overworked."

The empress dowager accepted [Hsü] Ho's advice. She then ordered Inspectors General Li Shen-kuei 李神軌[55] Cheng Chi-ming 鄭季明,[56] and others to guard Ho-ch'iao with five thousand soldiers under their command. On the eleventh of the fourth month (May 15, A.D. 528), Erh-chu Jung passed through Ho-nei[57] and arrived at Kao-t'ou Post 高頭驛,[58] where the Prince of Ch'ang-lo had gone north to the Yellow River from Lei-p'i 雷陂. Seeing that Ch'ang-lo had fled, [Li] Shen-kuei and [Cheng] Chi-ming opened the gates [at Ho-ch'iao] and surrendered. On the twelvth (May 16), [Erh-chu] Jung's army was north of the Mang Mountains 芒山, and in the open fields of Ho-yin 河陰. On the thirteenth (May 17), an edict was issued that all officials were to have an imperial audience immediately; all those who complied were massacred. Altogether three thousand[59] princes and high-ranking government officials were killed. On the fourteenth (May

[52] This is a reference to *Chuang-tzu* (*SPTK so-pen*) 3/37, which points out the folly of the mantis's overconfidence.

[53] This is the philosopher Chia I's 賈誼 (201–169 B.C.) analysis of the political situation the Western Han Court then faced: to sleep atop piled firewood and consider oneself safe until the flame reaches him from below.

[54] A strategic outpost of Lo-yang; south of Meng-hsien 孟縣 and north of Lo-yang. it was originally built at Tu Yü's order in A.D. 274 at Fu-p'ing Ford 富平津 (south of modern Meng-hsien, Honan). See *Chin-shu* 3/22b; 34/21b.

[55] Son of Li Ch'ung 李崇. For more information, see Li Ch'ung's biography in *WS* 66/12a–b.

[56] Grandson of Cheng Te-hsüan 鄭德玄. For more details, see *WS* 56/14b–15a.

[57] In modern Ch'in-yang 沁陽, Honan.

[58] *WS* 74/6a reads Kao-chu 高渚. This meeting took place on May 13, A.D. 528. Ch'ang-lo's elder brother Yüan Shao 元劭, Prince of P'eng-ch'eng 彭城王, and younger brother Yüan Tzu-cheng 元子正, Prince of Shih-p'ing 始平王, also accompanied him.

[59] The exact number killed is unknown. Estimates vary from more than thirteen hundred (*WS* 74/6b) to more than two thousand (*WS* 10/2a; *TC* 152/10b).

18), the emperor entered the capital city, granted an amnesty, and changed the regnal period to the first year of Chien-i. This was, then, Emperor Chuang.

This was a period when the nation had just undergone severe military disturbances, resulting in the liquidation of many dignitaries. Those who had fled were too frightened to appear. Emperor Chuang ascended the T'ai-chi [Palace][60] and granted a general amnesty,[61] but Shan Wei 山偉, the Cavalier Attendant-in-Ordinary (*San-ch'i ch'ang-shih*), was the only official who came out to the southern watchtower to express thanks for the imperial blessing.[62] More honorific titles were given to [Erh-chu] Jung and [Yüan T'ien-]mu: for [Erh-chu] Jung, Commissioner Holding Imperial Credentials (*Shih ch'ih-chieh*), Generalissimo in Charge of Internal and External Military Affairs (*Chung-wai chu chün-shih ta-chiang-chün*). Palatine [Ceremonially Equal to the Three Authorities] (*K'ai-fu* 開府), Great General in the North (*Pei-tao ta-hsing-t'ai* 北道大行臺), Generalissimo, Inspector General of Military Operations in Ten Provinces (*Tu-tu shih-chou chu chün-shih ta-chiang-chün*), Commander of Left and Right [Palace Guards] (*Ling tso-yu* 領左右),[63] and Prince of T'ai-yüan 太原王; for [Yüan T'ien-]mu, Chief Palace Attendant (*Shih-chung*), Grand Commandant (*T'ai-wei kung*), Hereditary Governorship of Ping-chou (*Shih-hsi* Ping-chou *tz'u-shih* 世襲并州刺史), and Prince of Shang-tang 上黨王. Members of his family having never before held government posts were appointed as ranking ministers, governors, and prefects. They were too numerous to be counted.

[60] T'ai-chi was the main hall in the palace complex. It was first built in A.D. 235 to hold important ceremonies. See *Wei-chih* (in *San-kuo chih chi-chieh*, Peking, 1957), 3/32a.

[61] Literally, *Chieh-wang ch'ui-jen* 解網垂仁, "loosene the net [of the law] and bestow benevolence," a reference to King T'ang 湯, founder of the Shang dynasty (trad. 1765–1123 B.C.), who advocated that three of the four corners of a hunter's net be opened up to give captives a chance to flee. See *SC* 3/8–9.

[62] Shan Wei, a native of Lo-yang, was on duty in the palace as the Grandee Remonstrant (*Chien-i ta-fu*) when the purge took place in Ho-yin (east of modern Meng-chin 孟津, Honan) He was therefore saved from the massacre. For his biography, see *PS* 50/18a–19b.

[63] *Ling tso-yu* 領左右 is perhaps an abbreviation for *Ling-chün tso-yu* 領軍左右, who had authority over imperial guards. Yüan Ch'a (executed in A.D. 526) also held this title in previous years. See *WS* 16/18b.

By the twentieth [May 24], [people] in Lo-yang were still fearful of their fate[64] and ill at ease. Both the living and the dead [had cause to] resent the current state of affairs; everyone entertained conflicting ideas [as to how to cope with the situation]. The wealthy houses and powerful families gave up their residences and competed in fleeing [so as not to be caught], while the poor man and lowly fellow raced away with their children strapped on their backs. Thereupon an edict was issued [saying that] all those who were unjustly killed would be awarded posthumous honors. Those of Rank III and above were to receive the title of Three Lords; Rank V and above, President or Vice President of the Imperial Secretariat,[65] and Rank VII and above, Governor. Commoners were appointed as grand wardens and governors in charge of military zones. As a result, people seemed somewhat pacified.

The emperor took [Erh-chu] Jung's daughter as the empress,[66] and advanced [Erh-chu] Jung to the post of Pillar of the State (*Chu-kuo*), Generalissimo (*Ta-chiang-chün*), Chief of Ministers (*Lu Shang-shu shih*), with other posts unchanged. [Yüan T'ien-]mu was promoted to Generalissimo, with other posts all unchanged. In the fifth month (May–June A.D. 529), Yüan Hao 元顥, Prince of Pei-hai, again entered Lo-yang and assembled his army in this monastery.

[Yüan] Hao was Emperor Chuang's cousin.[67] Toward the end of the Hsiao-ch'ang period (A.D. 525–527), he stationed his army in Chi commandery 汲郡. He fled to the south and surrendered to

[64] A reference to *Shih-ching* 12.3/22a (ode 200, verse 5, line 2) 巷伯：勞人草草, to which the subcommentary reads: 草草者, 憂將妄得罪也. Arthur Waley translated the *Shih-ching* text as "the toiler lives in woe" (*Book of Songs*, p. 315).

[65] The text reads *Ling-p'u* 令僕, which is an abbreviation for *Shang-shu-ling* 尙書令 and *Shang-shu p'u-yeh* 尙書僕射. Compare with Richard Mather's translation in his *A New Account of Tales of the World* (Minneapolis, 1976), p. 188.

[66] This lady was formerly a consort of Emperor Hsiao-chuang's nephew, known in history as Emperor Ming. For this reason Emperor Hsiao-chuang was reluctant to take her as his wife. Finally he acceded on the advice of Tsu Ying, a man of great literary fame. See *PS* 48/4b.

[67] Emperor Hsiao-chuang's father and Yüan Hao's father were brothers. In A.D. 528, Yüan Hao held the titles of Chief Palace Attendant, Generalissimo of the Whirling Cavalry, Palatine Ceremonially Equal to Those of the Three Authorities and Governor of Hsiang-chou 相州刺史. See *WS* 21A/33a.

Hsiao Yen 蕭衍 [Emperor of Liang 梁, regnant A.D. 502–549], after hearing of Erh-chu Jung's capture of Lo-yang. In A.D. 529, [Yüan] Hao took Lo-yang; Emperor Chuang withdrew to the north.[68] Consequently, [Yüan] Hao ascended the throne, changing the name of the year to that of Chien-wu 建武 (To Establish Military Strength) (A.D. 529).

[Yüan] Hao wrote a letter to Emperor Chuang, which reads: "Since the Great Way is hidden, the government[69] has not striven for the common good.[70] Misfortunes and good fortune do not come in the right order,[71] and the idea that only worthies should hold office is no longer observed. We hope to realize [the exemplary virtues] of the Five Emperors,[72] without relying on [imperial] armies.[73] As a result,[74] We consider [the honor] of a monarch as nothing more than dregs, and the throne as a mere trifle.[75] It is not that We desire the honor of being emperor. How

[68] Emperor Hsiao-chuang fled the capital on June 15, arriving at Ho-nei the following day. Yüan Hao entered Lo-yang on June 17, A.D. 529. See *WS* 10/8b.

[69] Literally, *t'ien-hsia* 天下, "the nation."

[70] A reference to *Li-chi* (I-wen facsimile *SSCCS* ed.) 21/3a: 大道之行也, 天下爲公, "If the Great Way is observed, the whole nation will strive for the common good." Here the meaning is used in reverse.

[71] The text reads *huo-fu-pu-chui* 禍福不追. *CS* (1/36) suggests *chui* 追 as an error for *shu* 述; hence the translation.

[72] The Five Emperors commonly include Huang-ti (trad. 2697–2598 B.C.) Chuan-hsü, Ti-K'u 帝嚳 (also known as Kao-hsin), Ti-Yao, and Ti-Shun. They were supposedly more interested in national welfare than personal glory.

[73] In olden days, the emperor had the right to maintain six armies, whereas feudal lords could keep only three. *Tso-chuan* Ch'eng 成 3 26/5a: 晉作六軍. Legge 5, p. 353: "Tsin constituted six armies." Comm.: 六軍, 僭王也; 萬二千五百人爲軍, "[To have] six armies [by a feudal lord] is usurping the imperial authority. Each army consists of 12,500 men."

[74] I follow *CS* (1.36) which suggests *cheng* 正 as an error for *shih* 是.

[75] The text reads *k'ang-p'i wan-ch'eng, tzu-chu ta-pao* 糠粃萬乘, 錙銖大寶. *K'ang-pi* 糠粃 means husks of rice, that is, valueless; *wen-ch'eng* 萬乘, ten thousand combat chariots (each drawn by a team of four horses) in the possession of a powerful monarch; *tzu-chu* 錙銖, small measure of weight. For the origin of *wan-ch'eng* 萬乘, see *Meng-tzu* 孟子 (I-wen facsimile *SSCCS* ed.) 1A/2a 萬乘之國, "a state of 10,000 carriages." Chao Ch'i's 趙岐 (d. A.D. 201) commentary: 萬乘, 兵車萬乘, 謂天子也, "By 10,000 chariots it means 10,000 combat chariots, the owner of which is the Son of Heaven." For *tzu-chu* 錙銖, see *Li-chi* 59/11a–b 儒有上不臣天子, 下不事諸侯, "Some Confucians were unwilling to serve as ministers of the Son of Heaven, above; or of the feudal lords, below." Sub-comm: 雖分國以祿之,

little appetite We would have for the riches of a nation![76] However, [We were forced to act] after Erh-chu Jung's entry into Lo[-yang] last year; though he desired at first to raise troops in the king's service he ended by usurping the Wei. He applied his treasonous sword to the ruler [who should be held in respect as one's own] parents, and struck the ranking officials with knife blades and arrowheads. He intended to kill all members of the [imperial] Yüan household, young and old alike. He was as ambitious as Ch'en Heng 陳恒, who [eventually] usurped the Ch'i,[77] and he was not without a scheme identical to those of the Six Ministers who dismembered the Chin Kingdom.[78] Only because of the turmoil prevailing in the nation does Erh-chu Jung hesitate to commit an outright usurpation. For the time being he observes the [existing] relations between ruler and subject, and makes a pretense of abiding by ceremonial etiquette. He murdered two [of my ministers'] brothers,[79] and stood by as a dictator[80] to wait for the right moment for action. How much longer will he remain a loyal subject? We, downcast at seeing this, traveled a long distance to the south of the Yangtze. With tears [We] besought the Liang to swear revenge of the insult. Like wind We flew to Chien-yeh 建業 (that is, Nanking, the capital of the Liang); like lightning [We] rushed to the Three Rivers,[81] hoping to hold [Erh-chu] account-

---

視之如錙銖, 不貴重也, "Even if they were given a fief as their salary, they would look at the fief as husks of rice: they attach no value to it." For *ta-pao* 大寶, see *I-ching* (I-wen facsimile *SSCCS* ed.) 8/4a: 聖人之大寶曰位. Richard Wilhelm, tr., *The I Ching or Book of Changes* (New York, 1950), 1, 352: "It is the great treasure of the holy sage to stand in the right place."

[76] Literally, *liu-ho chih fu* 六合之富, "the riches from all six directions" (that is, the four corners of the globe, plus heaven above and earth below).

[77] Ch'en Heng, otherwise known as T'ien Ch'ang 田常, killed Duke Chien 簡 in 479 B.C. and enthroned Duke P'ing 平 of the Ch'i. His family later became the real ruling house of the same state. See *SC* 46/9ff.

[78] During the period of Warring States (450?–221 B.C.) Han 韓, Chao 趙, Wei 魏, Fan 范, Chung-hang 中行, and Chih 智 were the six most powerful ministerial clans, which usurped and thus weakened the Chin 晉 authority. In the end, the first three clans divided the Chin into separate kingdoms. See *SC* 39/88–94.

[79] Both the emperor's elder brother Shao, King Superior-to-all (Wu-shang-wang 無上王), and his younger brother Yüan Tzu-cheng were killed in the Ho-yin massacre.

[80] Literally, *tu-fu chieh-li* 獨夫介立, "the solitary man nobly stands out."

[81] That is, the Yellow River, the Lo, and the I Rivers.

able for his crimes, to release you [my minister] from shackles and handcuffs,[82] to show sympathy for my close relatives who are also deeply offended, and to undo the noose from which the masses are hung upside down.[83] We thought that you, with clear vision, would act in unison with Us, come to see Us in person, recount the sorrowful experience [We both have undergone,] and take concerted action against the vicious Chieh 羯 [barbarian].[84] I had no idea that the moment We marched through the Ch'eng-kao Pass 成皋, you would cross the river for the north. Although [We realize] that the villain's pressure on you and your subsequent loss of freedom [might have caused you to flee], it is also possible that you suspect Our intentions and may even consider Us greedy.[85]

"We heaved long sighs when We heard of your movement, and felt distressed as We [thoughtfully] fingered Our lapel. Why? The relationship between you and us is not one of remote kin;[86] we are separate leaves on forked branches. Our fates are interwined.

[82] *Chou-li* (I-wen facsimile *SSCCS* ed.) 36/11b: *chung-tsui chih-ku* 中罪桎梏. Cheng Hsüan's 鄭玄 (A.D. 132–200) commentary: 在手曰桎, 在足曰梏.

[83] *Meng-tzu* 3A/3b: 當今之時，萬乘之國行仁政，民之悅之，猶解倒懸也. D. C. Lau, tr., *Mencius* (Baltimore, 1970), p. 76: "At the present time, if a state of ten thousand chariots were to practice benevolent government, the people would rejoice as if they have been released from hanging by the heels." Chao Ch'i's commentary: 倒懸, 喻困苦也, "*Tao-hsüan* means distress."

[84] Literally *hsiung* Chieh 兇羯, "the vicious Chieh." Chieh is the name of a tribe that since Shih Lo's 石勒 time had inhabited northern Shansi—a region from which Erh-chu Jung came.

[85] The text reads *ch'i-chien ts'ai wo* 棄劍猜我. *CC* 1/29 n. 111 suggests that *ch'i* 棄 may be an error for *so* 索, which refers to a story about the brothers Yü-kung 虞公 and Yü-shu 虞叔 of the state of Yü 虞 of the Ch'un-ch'iu 春秋 (722–481 B.C.) period. On one occasion, Yü-shu gave his brother a jade upon request, but declined to give him a sword when approached the second time. See *Tso-chuan* Huan 桓 10 7/7a–b. Legge 5, p. 55: "The 3d brother of the duke of Yu had a *valuable* piece of jade, which the duke asked of him. He refused it, but afterwards repented, saying, 'There is a proverb in Chow, "A man may have no crime; that he keeps his *pieh* is his crime." This jade is no use to me;—shall I buy my hurt with it?' He then presented it to the duke, who went on to ask a precious sword which he had. The young brother then asked *to himself*, 'This man is unsatiable; his greed will reach to my person.' He therefore attacked the duke, who was obliged to flee to Kung-ch'e."

[86] Literally, *chen chih yü ch'ing, hsiung ti fei yüan* 朕之與卿, 兄弟非遠, "Our relationship is not one of the remote brothers." Actually, both were grandsons of Emperor Hsien-wen 顯文 (regnant A.D. 466–471) and therefore by Chinese standards were still brothers of the same household.

Even at a time of domestic squabbles, [quarreling brothers] should unite with each other to resist foreign incursions.[87] How much more true is it between the two of us, who have been extremely intimate. Nothing is more urgent than rendering a helping hand to one's own brothers in the current crisis.[88] What cause is there to abandon close relatives while approaching their enemies?

"Furthermore, signs of Erh-chu Jung's insubordination are visible in all parts of the nation.[89] [Men], whether wise or foolish, are aware of his conspiracy against the state of Wei. However clear-minded, you are questioning the unquestionable,[90] entrusting your fate to wolves, handing over your body to a tiger's mouth, abandoning your close relatives, assisting the outlaw, and fighting your own brothers. If you capture even an inch of land, the land belongs to [Erh-chu] Jung in the first place; if you seize cities, you can under no circumstances possess them. You are only endangering your own country while widening the interests of the enemy invaders. All literati are ashamed of it: you are gladdening the heart of the usurper [Wang] Mang [王]莽,[91] and giving strength to assist [the tiger-killer] Pien Chuang 卞莊![92]

"Now, the rise or fall of our nation depends on the two of us. If

[87] *Shih-ching* 9.2/14b (ode 164, verse 4, lines 1 and 2): 小雅常棣：兄弟鬩於牆，外禦其務. Comm.: 務, 侮也. Waley, *Book of Songs*, p. 203: "Brothers may quarrel within the walls/But outside they defend one another from insult."

[88] *Shih-ching* 9.2/13a–14b (ode 164, verse 1, lines 3 and 4): 凡今之人，莫如兄弟; (verse 3, lines 1 and 2): 脊令在原，兄弟急難. Waley, *Book of Songs*, p. 203: "Of men that now are/None equals a brother;" "There were wagtails on the plain/When brothers are hard pressed, . . ."

[89] The text (1/8a) reads *pao yü p'ang-wu* 暴於旁午, "exposed [to the nation] in length and width." *P'ang-wu* 旁午 is a phrase used in *HS* 68/9a *shih-che p'ang-wu* 使者旁午, which, according to Yen Shih-ku's commentary, means *tsung-heng* 縱橫, "vertical and horizontal," that is, everywhere.

[90] The text (1/8a) *ch'ing nai ming-pai, i-yü pi-jan* 卿乃明白，疑於必然 may contain some errors. The meaning is not at all clear.

[91] A reference to Wang Mang (33 B.C.–A.D. 23), who usurped the Han and established a new dynasty for himself in 9 A.D.

[92] An allusion to the parable recorded in *Chan-kuo-ts'e* (3/37–38) about the tiger-killer Pien Chuang, who was advised by Kuan Yü 管與 to wait for the right moment to act: "The two tigers are feeding on a bull. They will struggle for larger share if the meat tastes good, and struggle will necessarily lead to a fight. If they fight, the big tiger will be wounded and the small one killed. If you stab the wounded one, you will then enjoy the fame of killing two tigers with one stroke."

Heaven helps the lawful and supports our righteous venture, the imperial Wei will then enjoy boundless prosperity. If, on the other hand, Heaven is not yet satiated with disturbances, the Chieh barbarians 胡羯 will then survive, hooting like owls and snapping like wolves, and devouring provisions north of the river. This will be good fortune for [Erh-chu] Jung and a calamity for you.

"You are no stranger to me; indeed, you are my own brother.[93] For this reason We are sending you this foot[-long] letter to express Our feelings; you should think it over carefully. Considering [this matter] only in terms of justice and righteousness,[94] your riches and high position will then be guaranteed. It is unwise to be a follower [of Erh-chu Jung]. We shall never eat our words lest we treat each other as 'fish and meat' (that is, kill each other). Be careful to make the most auspicious choice. Do nothing which you would regret later."

This is the writing of Tsu Ying, the Attending Secretary within the Imperial Yellow Gate.[95]

At this time the emperor was in the city of Ch'ang-tzu 長子,[96] to which place the Prince of T'ai-yüan and the Prince of Shang-tang rushed to cope with the emergency. In the sixth month (July), the imperial army beseiged Ho-nei, which was being defended for [Yüan] Hao by Yüan T'ao-t'ang 元桃湯,[97] the Grand Warden (*Tai-shou*), and [Yüan] Chen-sun 元珍孫,[98] the Superintendent of

[93] Literally, *ch'i-i i-jen* 豈伊異人, which is a reference to the *Shih-ching* 14.3/12 (ode 217, verse 2, lines 5 and 6) 小雅頍弁. The quotation is followed by another line, *hsiung-ti chu lai* 兄弟俱來. Waley, *Book of Songs*, p. 206: "Why give them to other men?/Your brothers must all come."

[94] The text (1/8b) reads *chien-li shih-t'u* 兼利是圖. I follow the *CT* (1/9b), which offers the alternate *i* 義 for *chien* 兼.

[95] The text incorrectly gives *Jung* 榮 for *Ying* 瑩. Tsu Ying's biography (*PS* 47/25a) does not include this document. The text (1/8b) gives his official title as *Huang-men lang* 黃門郎, but my translation follows the *PS* biography, which gives *Huang-men shih-lang* 黃門侍郎.

[96] It was part of Shang-tang commandery (modern Ch'ang-tzu 長子, Shansi) during the Northern Wei.

[97] *WS* 10/9a and 74/11a refer to this man as Yüan Hsi 元襲. According to his stele inscription (*MCCS* 4/25a–b, plate 112), he was the son of Yüan Wu-kung 元武公, Governor of Lo-chou 洛州刺史, and grandson of the Prince of Ching-chao 京兆王. He died on July 12, A.D. 529.

[98] He was a renowned general of his time, but not much information about him is available. Se *WS* 73/12a.

the Imperial Clan (*Tsung-cheng*) and concurrently the General of Chariots and Horsemen, and others. They managed to withstand the attacks. At that time, the generals, as well as soldiers, were worn out from the summer heat. The Prince of T'ai-yüan wanted to have the emperor visit Chin-yang, waiting until the following autumn before launching a major campaign. Before a decision was reached, he summoned Liu Chu 劉助 for divination.[99] [Liu] Chu replied, "We will certainly win." Thereupon, when it was daylight, they made a concentrated assault which, as [Liu Chu] predicted, was successful. Both Yüan T'ao-t'ang and Yüan Chen-sun were beheaded, in order to overawe the three armies.

After learning that Ho-nei had fallen, [Yüan] Hao personally led his court officials to encamp at Ho-ch'iao, and specially assigned [Yüan] Yen-ming 元延明,[100] Prince of An-feng 安豐王 and the Chief Palace Attendant to guard Hsia-shih 硤石.[101] In the seventh month (August), the emperor arrived at Ho-yang 河陽, keeping [Yüan] Hao across the river in sight. The Prince of T'ai-yüan ordered Erh-chu Chao 爾朱兆 (nephew of Erh-chu Jung), the General of Chariots and Horsemen, secretly to lead his army across the river. He defeated [Yüan] Yen-ming at Hsia-shih. Learning of [Yüan] Yen-ming's ill fate, [Yüan] Hao also fled. All Chiang 江 (the Yangtze River) and Huai 淮 (the Huai River) soldiers under his command, some five thousand strong, were disarmed,[102] sobbing to each other while shaking hands and bidding farewell.[103] Accompanied by several scores[104] of cavalry, [Yüan] Hao sought to flee to Hsiao Yen. Upon arrival at Ch'ang-she 長社, however, he was beheaded by the local people,[105] who

[99] *WS* 91/1b reads Liu Ling-chu 劉靈助.

[100] Before this assignment, he was Acting Chief of Ministers (*Ling shang-shu ling*) and Grand Marshal (*Ta ssu-ma*). After the defeat, he went to the rival south and eventually died in service under Liang dynasty. See *WS* 20/5b–6a.

[101] West of Ma-chu 馬渚 in Meng-chin of Honan, where a ford was located.

[102] The text (1/9a) reads *chieh-chia hsiang-ch'i* 解甲相泣, which gives no indication whether they were disarmed or removed their armor voluntarily. Another entry in the same work (2/13b–14a under the P'ing-teng Monastery 平等寺), however, states that "all the five thousand Chiang-Huai soldiers under his command were captured, without a single one able to return home." The translation follows this account.

[103] Based on *IS* 1/7a, Chou Tsu-mo (*CS* 1/40) suggests *lieh* 列 as an error for *pieh* 別; hence the translation.

[104] Emending *shu-ch'ien* 數千 to *shu-shih* 數十 after *IS* 1/7a.

[105] According to *WS* 10/9b, Chiang Feng 江豐, a soldier stationed in Lin-ying

subsequently sent his head to the capital of the nation. On the 20th (September 8), the emperor returned to Lo-yang. The Prince of Tai-yüan, while keeping his old titles, was given the additional title Pillar of Heaven and Generalissimo (*T'ien-chu ta-chiang-chün* 天柱大將軍). The Prince of Shang-tang was promoted to the post of Grand Steward (*T'ai-tsai*), while keeping his other titles.

In the third year of the Yung-an period 永安 (Permanent Peace) (A.D. 530), the rebel Erh-chu Chao imprisoned Emperor Chuang in the monastery.

Presently, the Prince of T'ai-yüan, because of his high position and unusual achievements, had become arrogant and overbearing. He arbitrarily passed out favors to the undeserving, and denied recognition to the worthy. Angrily,[106] the emperor said to his attendants, "We would rather die [with honor] like the Duke of Kao-kuei-hsiang 高貴鄉公[107] than live [in disgrace] like Emperor Hsien of the Han 漢獻帝 [the last Han emperor, who abdicated in A.D. 220]!" On the 25th of the ninth month (November 1, A.D. 530), pretending that a crown prince had been born,[108] the emperor invited [Erh-chu] Jung and [Yüan T'ien-]mu to the court, where he personally killed [Erh-chu] Jung in the Ming-kuang Palace 明光殿 (Sacred Light Palace).[109] Lu Hsien 魯暹,[110] a soldier in hiding, killed [Yüan T'ien-]mu. [Erh-chu] Jung's heir apparent and the chieftain of his tribesmen (*pu-lo ta-jen* 部落大人), [P'u-t'i

---

臨穎, was the real murderer. *MCCS* (plate 182) gives the twenty-first of the seventh month in the third year of Yung-an 永安 (Permanent Peace) (August 29, A.D. 530) as the date of his death (at the age of thirty-six), but the "third year" is an obvious error for the second year. Hence, the correct date should be September 9, A.D. 529, just a few days after his defeat. The date given by *WS* 10/9b is September 11, A.D. 529, a discrepancy resulting from the date of his actual death and the date when the court received the report.

[106] I follow *CS* (1/41) to emend *k'ung* 恐 to *nu* 怒.

[107] The text (1/4b) incorrectly reads *ch'ing* 卿 for *hsiang* 鄉. The duke rose against the dictator Ssu-ma Chao 司馬昭 (A.D. 211–265), but was killed by the latter's subordinates in A.D. 258. See *Wei-chih* 4/55b–56b; P'ei Sung-chih's 裴松之 (A.D. 372–451) commentary quoting *Han-Chin ch'un-ch'iu* 漢晉春秋.

[108] The prince was actually born ten days later, on November 11, A.D. 530. See *TC* 154/16a.

[109] The text reads Kuang-ming Hall 光明殿, but both *YHNC* 3/2b and *MCCS* (plate 46.2) give Ming-kuang 明光. Hence, the translation.

[110] *WS* 74/14a gives Lu An 魯安 as the man's name. Erh-chu Jung died at the age of thirty-eight (*WS* 74/14b); Yüan T'ien-mu, at forty-two (*MCCS* plate 46.2).

菩提], were also slain. [Erh-chu] Jung's subordinate, Erh-chu Yang-tu 爾朱陽都, General of Chariots and Horsemen, and others, twenty in all,[111] who had entered the Chu-hua Gate 朱華門 (Vermillion-Radiant Gate)[112] in the company of their leaders, were cut down by an ambush. Only Erh-chu Shih-lung 爾朱世隆 [cousin of Erh-chu Jung], the Vice President on the Right, Department of State Affairs (*Yu p'u-yeh*) had been at home all the time. After hearing of [Erh-chu] Jung's death, he assembled [Erh-chu] Jung's troops, setting the Hsi-yang Gate[113] afire and rushing to Ho-ch'iao. On the first of the tenth month (November 6), [Erh-chu] Shih-lung and the Princess of Pei[114]-hsiang commandery 鄉公主 [Erh-chu Jung's wife], offered sacrifices to the deceased at Prince Feng's Monastery 馮王寺[115] on the Mang Mountains, and donated bolts of silk to the abbot in return for the happiness of the departed. Erh-chu Hou T'ao-fa 爾朱侯討伐 [member of the Hou 侯 clan who had surrendered to Erh-chu Jung] and Erh-chu Na-lü Kuei 爾朱那律歸[116] [member of the Na-lü 那律 clan who had surrendered to Erh-chu Jung], were then ordered to lead one thousand cavalry all clad in white [as an expression of sadness] to come to the outer city walls to ask for the body of the Prince of T'ai-yüan and mourn. Ascending the Ta-hsia Gate and looking at them, the emperor dispatched the clerk (*chu-shu*)[117] Niu Fa-shang 牛法尚 to announce to [Erh-chu Na-lü] Kuei and others: "The Prince of T'ai-yüan, unable to crown his achievements with a successful conclusion, secretly plotted usur-

[111] *TC* 154/13b gives Erh-chu Yang-tu's name as 爾朱陽覩, and the number killed as thirty.

[112] The text (1/9b) reads Tung-hua Gate 東華門, but the *IS* (1/7b) gives Chu-hua Gate 朱華門, which agrees with the location given in the map of *YHNC* (not marked with chapter or page numbers).

[113] Also known as Hsi-ming Gate 西明門. See *TC* 154/14a Hu San-hsing's 胡三省 (A.D. 1230–1302) commentary.

[114] I follow *CS* (1/42) to add the character *pei* 北.

[115] The monastery was donated by Feng Hsi 馮熙, Emperor Kao-tsu's maternal uncle. Feng Hsi financed the construction of seventy-two temples, mostly in hilly areas. See *WS* 83A/7b–9a.

[116] On the basis of the text following, this man's given name should be Kuei. He may have been a member of a Na-lü clan, which adopted the Erh-chu surname after its adherence to the latter.

[117] Translated as clerk by Teng Ssu-yü, *Family Instructions* (p. 115, n. 1).

pation. The imperial law [treats everyone equally], does not [favor or recognize] special relatives, and therefore punishes [the prince] in the spirit of justice. Only [Erh-chu] Jung himself was guilty; no others will be implicated. Why do you not surrender? All your posts and titles will remain just as before."

[Erh-chu Na-lü] Kuei replied: "Your subject accompanied the Prince of T'ai-yüan to come to court to pay tribute to Your Majesty. But now he has been abruptly killed. Your subject wants to return to Chin-yang, but he cannot return empty-handed. I beg to have the Prince of T'ai-yüan's body to bury; then neither the living nor the dead will have cause for complaint."

As he uttered these words, his tears fell as rain, for he could not control his grief. The assembled barbarians cried out bitterly, their voices shaking the capital. The emperor upon hearing them was also saddened. Chu Yüan-lung 朱元龍,[118] the Chief Palace Attendant, was ordered to bestow on [Erh-chu] Shih-lung an iron tablet,[119] promising permanently to exempt him from the death penalty, and letting him keep all his government posts as before.

In reply [Erh-chu] Shih-lung spoke to [Chu] Yüan-lung: "The accomplishments of the Prince of T'ai-yüan fill [the space between] heaven [above] and earth [below], and he exerted his best efforts to save the masses from hardship. With utmost sincerity he served his nation, a fact to which the gods bear witness. As the Prince of Ch'ang-lo broke his promise, he slew the loyal and virtuous. Now how can I have confidence in the two lines inscribed on this iron [tablet]? I shall avenge the Prince of T'ai-yüan, and shall never surrender and return to him."

Noting that [Erh-chu] Shih-lung referred to the emperor as Prince of Ch'ang-lo, [Chu] Yüan-lung sensed his disloyalty, and reported his words to the emperor. The emperor then took some valuable holdings from the treasury, and had them placed outside the western gate. He solicited volunteers who were willing to die

[118] Chu Jui 朱瑞, styled Yüan-lung, had been a confidant of Erh-chu Jung but later served the emperor as a trsuted official. He was executed in A.D. 531 upon Erh-chu Chao's entry into Lo-yang. See *WS* 80/1a–2b.

[119] The tablet was shaped like a folded tile, on which the receiver's name, official title, and merits were fully engraved. It was in two halves, to be retained respectively by the receiver and the court. It was given only to the most outstanding officials. For a historical survey and the system of bestowal of such tablets during the Ming period, see Ling Yang-tsao, *Li-shuo-pien* (*Ling-nan i-shu* ed.), 40/7 a–b.

for the nation, and within a day he had enlisted ten thousand men, who fought [Erh-chu Na-lü] Kuei and others in the suburbs. The fighting spirit of the rebels was undiminished, however. [Erh-chu Na-lü] Kuei and his associates had often fought on the field of battle, and were skillful at sword fighting.[120] The capital recruits, on the other hand, had no combat experience. Although they were principled and brave, their strength was no match for their hearts. After three days of continuous fighting, the bandits [the ones who should not have had long to live] did not tire. The emperor then posted a reward for those who could destroy the bridge. Li Miao 李苗,[121] a diver from Han-chung 漢中, set the bridge afire from upstream. [Erh-chu] Shih-lung, seeing that the bridge had caught fire, plundered the populace and marched northward to the T'ai-hang Range 太行山. The emperor ordered Yüan Tzu-kung 源子恭, the Chief Palace Attendant, and Yang K'uan 楊寬, Attending Secretary within the Imperial Yellow Gate, to take command of thirty thousand foot and mounted soldiers, and encamp at Ho-nei.[122] Upon arrival at Kao-tu 高都 (in Chien-chou 建州), [Erh-chu] Shih-lung installed [Yüan] Yeh 元曄, Prince of Ch'ang-kuang 長廣王[123] and Grand Warden of T'ai-yüan 太原太守 as ruler, who changed the regnal name to Chien-ming 建明[124] (To Establish Enlightenment). Eight members of the Erh-chu family were themselves honored as princes.[125]

The Prince of Ch'ang-kuang [chose] Chin-yang as his capital, and dispatched Erh-chu Chao, the Prince of Ying-ch'uan 潁川王, to

[120] For the origin of fencing as an art, see *SC* 127/13: 齊張仲曲成侯以善擊刺,學用劍,立名天下.

[121] The text gives the man's name as Li Hsün 李荀. I follow *CS* (1/44), which changes Hsün 荀 to Miao 苗 in accordance with *WS* (10/13b and 71/32b–33a) texts.

[122] For Yüan Tzu-kung's and Yang K'uan's role in other military operations in later years, see *WS* 41/19a–b and *PS* 41/44b.

[123] Ch'ang-kuang was the grandson of the Prince of Nan-an 南安王. At this time he was Acting Governor of Ping-chou and Grand Warden of T'ai-yüan. Later, he was dethroned by Erh-chu Shih-lung. See *WS* 19C/17b–18a.

[124] The character after *chien* 建 is missing in the text (1/11a). It should be *ming* 明.

[125] According to *WS* (75/1a–17b), only seven members of the Erh-chu family were made princes, namely: Chao 兆 (Prince of Ying-ch'uan 潁川王), Chih-hu 智虎 (Prince of An-ting 安定王), Yen-po 彥伯 (Prince of Po-ling), Chung-yüan 仲遠 (Prince of P'eng-ch'eng), Shih-lung (Prince of Lo-p'ing 樂平王), Tu-lü 度律 (Prince of Ch'ang-shan 常山王), and T'ien-kuang 天光 (Prince of Kuang-tsung 廣宗王). *TC* (154/18a–19a) lists all but Erh-chu Chih-hu.

lead an army toward the capital, [Lo-yang].[126] After a victory over [Yüan] Tzu-kung, [Erh-chu Chao] crossed the Yellow River at Lei-p'i, and subsequently captured the emperor at the Shih-ch'ien Palace 式乾殿 (Respecting the Heavenly Way). At first the emperor thought it impossible that Erh-chu [Chao] would soon sail across the turbulent Yellow River rapids, but, unexpectedly, on the day of crossing, the water was so shallow that it did not even come up to the belly of a horse. [Erh-chu] Chao's army therefore did not use boats, but waded across the current. The emperor thus met with disaster. Since the beginning of written history, nothing like this had ever happened.

[Yang] Hsüan-chih commented: In olden times, when Emperor Kuang-wu (regnant A.D. 25–57) received the heavenly mandate, the frozen Hu[-t'o] 滹沱 River served as a bridge for him to cross.[127] When [Emperor] Chao-lieh's 昭烈 (regnant A.D. 221–223) career changed for the better, the horse Ti-lu 的盧 (White Forehead) jumped up out of a muddy creek[128] to carry him through his trouble. All these were in agreement with heaven and blessed by the gods in heaven. As a result, [both men] were able to save the world and give great protection to the masses. Now, with regard to such a man as [Erh-chu] Chao: his eyes are

[126] The text (1/11a) reads *ching-shih* 京師, meaning Lo-yang.

[127] At the early stage of Emperor Kuang-wu's 光武 career, he was chased by the army of Wang Lang 王郎, a serious contender for the empire in Ho-pei. After reaching the approaches of the Hu-t'o River, with Wang Lang's troops closing in, Kuang-wu and his associates were frightened at the prospect of having no boats to take them across the river. Suddenly there was a quick freeze, so they managed to escape from their pursuers. See HHS 50/3b, 王霸傳 and Hans Bielenstein, "The Restoration of the Han Dynasty, with Prolegomena on the Historiography of the *Hou Han Shu*," 1–3 *BMFEA* 26 (1954), 1–209; 31 (1959), 1–287; 39 (1967) 1–198.

[128] After the defeat of Yüan Shao 袁紹 (d. A.D. 202), with whom Liu Pei 劉備 (A.D. 162–223) was associated, Liu Pei went to attach himself to Liu Piao 劉表 (d. A.D. 208), then Governor of Ching-chou 荊州刺史. Liu Piao was afraid of being overshadowed by Liu Pei, so he treated Liu Pei with little warmth. On one occasion Ts'ai Mao 蔡瑁, Liu Piao's subordinate, planned to seize Liu Pei during a meeting. Noticing the immediate danger, Liu Pei secretly left the meeting, but during the flight his horse became stuck in a stream outside the city of Hsiang-yang 襄陽. In desperation, Liu Pei said to the horse: "Ti-lu, now we are in trouble. Do your best [to get out]." As a result, the horse jumped forward for a distance of thirty Chinese feet, bringing Liu Pei to safety. See *Shu-chih* 蜀志 (in *San-kuo-chih chi-chieh*) 32/11a–b; P'ei Sung-chih's commentary quoting *Shih-yü* 世語.

like hornets'; his voice, like that of a jackal; and his behavior, like the worst kind of an owl or *ching* 獍[129] [animal]. Relying on military power and accustomed to committing atrocities,[130] he murdered his own monarch. If only the holy spirits (*huang-ling* 皇靈) had a conscience, they should bear witness to this evil character [and do everything possible to punish him]! Quite to the contrary, they caused the Meng Ford 孟津 to have water only up to the [horses'] knees, and thus encouraged [Erh-chu Chao] to carry out his wicked designs. The *Book of Changes* says, "The Way of Heaven is to bring calamity [to those who act] beyond reasonable limitations, and ghosts and spirits benefit [those who act with] restraint."[131] This is proof that the saying is groundless.

At that time [Erh-chu] Chao encamped his army in the office of the Department of State Affairs (*Shang-shu-sheng* 尙書省), where he set up bells and drums as would the Son of Heaven, and put up a timepiece known as *lou-k'e* 漏刻 (clepsydra)[132] in the courtyard. Imperial consorts and princesses were all detained in his tent. He locked the emperor in the tower of the monastery. At that time, in the twelfth month (January–February), the emperor, troubled by the cold, asked [Erh-chu] Chao for a headscarf, but [Erh-chu] Chao declined.[133] Subsequently, he sent[134] the imprisoned em-

[129] In Chinese mythology, the owl is believed to be a bird of prey that feeds on its mother, whereas the *ching* (same as *p'o-ching* 破鏡) is an animal that eats its father. See *HS* 25A/23b Meng K'ang's 孟康 commentary. According to another source, the *ching* eats its mother, not father. See Jen Fang, *Shu-i chi* (*Han-Wei ts'ung-shu* ed.) A/7a.

[130] For the origin of *tsu-ping an-jen* 阻兵安忍, see *Tso-chuan* Yin 隱 43/16b: 阻兵而安忍. Legge 5, p. 16: "Chow-yu relies on his military force, and can do cruel things." Tu Yü's commentary: 阻, 恃兵也.

[131] *I-ching* 2/31b–32a: 天道虧盈而益謙, 地道變盈而流謙, 鬼神害盈而福謙. Wilhelm, *I Ching*, 1, 67–68, Hexagram no. 15 Ch'ien–Modesty: "It is the law of heaven to make fullness empty and to make full what is modest.... It is the law of earth to alter the full and to contribute to the modest.... It is the law of fate to undermine what is full and to prosper the modest."

[132] A pot that contained water and that had a hole in the bottom. An arrow was placed in the pot to mark the amount of water it had leaked as a measure of the time. The pot was an emblem of imperial authority. *Shih-ching* 5.1/12b (ode 100, verse 1, line 1): 國風東方未明. Sub-comm. (5.1/14b): 蓋天子備官, 挈壺掌漏, 鷄人告寺.

[133] *TC* 154/20b Hu San-hsing's commentary: *t'ou-chin so-wei p'a-t'ou* 頭巾所謂袹頭.

[134] The text (1/12a) reads *huan* 還, which, as *CS* (1/4b) suggests, is an error for *sung* 送. Hence the translation.

peror to Chin-yang, where the latter was hanged at the San-chi Temple 三級寺 (Three-storied Temple).[135] On the point of death, the emperor prayed to Buddha, asking that he never be reborn as an emperor. Further, he composed a poem, with five characters per line, which reads:

Power has left me, and the path of life is hastening [to the end].
Haunted by worries, my road of death is long.
Regretfully, I have left my palace gate,[136]
Sorrowfully, I now enter the nether world.
Once the underground tunnel is closed,
How could there be further light in the dark hall?
Meditative birds cry in the green pines,
The mournful wind blows through the white willows.
I have ever heard that death is suffering,
But never thought I myself would meet it!

It was not until the winter of the first year of T'ai-ch'ang 太昌 (Great Prosperity) (A.D. 532) that the imperial coffin was escorted back to Lo-yang, and interred in [the imperial tomb known as] Ching-ling 靖陵.[137] The emperor's five-character poem was then used as the pallbearers' song [to which rhythms the men pulled in unison]. Men, both in and out of the court, were all deeply saddened when they heard it. The witnesses among the populace all covered their faces with their hands and cried.

In the second month of the third year of Yung-hsi (March A.D. 534), the stūpa caught fire. The emperor ascended the Ling-yün Tower 淩雲臺 (The Cloud-breaching Tower)[138] to watch the fire, dispatching [Yüan] Pao-chü 元寶矩,[139] the Prince of Nan-yang 南陽王, and Chang-sun Chih 長孫稚, Chief of Ministers[140] to lead a

[135] The meaning of this temple's name is unclear.

[136] Literally, *kuo-men* 國門, "gate of the nation."

[137] *WS* 10/15b reads Ching-ling 靜陵, *ching* 靜 being a phonetic variant of 靖.

[138] According to *YHNC* (2/19b), the Ling-yün Tower was built in A.D. 221 on the order of Emperor Wen 文帝 (regnant A.D. 220–226). It was two hundred Chinese feet high; from the top of it one could see as far as Meng Ford.

[139] For the date of the fire, see also O. Siren, "Chinese Architecture," in *Encyclopaedia Britannica* (1971), 5, 556.

Pao-chü was the son of Yü 愉, Prince of Ching-chao. In A.D. 535, he succeeded Emperor Ch'u 出帝 as the ruler of the Western Wei. See *WS* 12/2a–b.

[140] For his biography, see *WS* 25/4b–7a.

contingent of one thousand *yü-lin* ("plumed forest")[141] palace guards to fight the fire. Not one but left with sorrow and pity, tears streaming down. The fire, which had started on the eighth floor, was worse by the early morning. At that time there was thunder, rain, and darkness, and hail mixed with snow. The common people and Buddhist devotees all came to watch the fire. The sound of wailing shook the capital. Three[142] fully ordained monks[143] hurled themselves into the fire and died. The blaze lasted for three months before it was extinguished. There were flames that went underground around pillars, leaving a smoky smell even one year[144] later.

In the fifth month of that year (May–June A.D. 534), someone came from Tung-lai commandery 東萊郡,[145] saying: "We saw a stūpa in the seas, which was bright and luminous and looked like new. People on the seas all saw it. But suddenly a mist came up and obscured the stūpa." In the seventh month (August 21, A.D. 534), the Prince of P'ing-yang 平陽王,[146] seized upon[147] by Hu-ssu Ch'un 斛斯椿,[148]

[141] A term for horsemen who normally guarded the palaces and the national capital. The office was first institutionalized under Emperor Wu (regnant 140–87 B.C.) of the Western Han.

[142] *K'ai-yüan shih-chiao lu* (6/541) gives "two" rather than "three" monks.

[143] Literally *pi-ch'iu* 比丘, a transliteration of bhikṣu, meaning a fully ordained monk as opposed to a novice śramaṇa.

[144] The text (1/12b) has *yu huo ju ti hsün chu* 有火入地尋柱, which is different from the *IS* (1/10a): *yu ju ti chu huo hsün chu* 有入地柱火尋柱. Neither version makes good sense, however.

[145] The text reads Hsiang-chün 象郡, a commandery that did not exist during the Wei. *CS* (1/48) suggests Tung-lai instead. Tung-lai belonged to Kuang-chou 光州 (modern Yeh-hsien 掖縣, Shantung). The story was fabricated by followers of Kao Huan 高歡 (A.D. 496–547), founder of the Northern Ch'i dynasty (A.D. 550–557), who started his career in the same Tung-lai area. See *Pei-Ch'i shu* (I-wen facsimile ed.) 2/1a. It may be noted that the *PCS* wording of this event is almost identical with Yang Hsüan-chih's account.

[146] Known in history as Emperor Ch'u or Emperor Hsiao-wu 孝武. See *WS* 11/9b–20b.

[147] The text reads *shih* 使, but *K'ai-yüan shih-chiao lu* gives *hsia* 挾.

[148] Hu-ssu Ch'un was a shrewd general and politician, who first served the interest of the Erh-chu clan and then turned against it. He repeated the same performance to Kao Huan, who was not trusted by Emperor Hsiao-wu (regnant A.D. 532–534), known as the Prince of P'ing-yang before his enthronement. Hu-ssu Ch'un therefore escorted the emperor to Ch'ang-an, the stronghold of Yü-wen T'ai 宇文泰 (A.D. 506–557), Kao Huan's deadly rival. For his biography, see *WS* 80/4a–6b.

fled to Ch'ang-an.[149] In the tenth month (November–December, A.D. 534), the capital was moved to Yeh.[150]

The Chien-chung Temple 建中寺 (Temple of Establishing the Mean)[151] was built [on the order of] Erh-chu Shih-lung, Prince of Lo-p'ing, in the first year of P'u-t'ai 普泰 (Universal Prosperity) (A.D. 531) when he was President of the Department of State Affairs (*Shang-shu ling*). Originally, it was the residence of the eunuch Liu T'eng 劉騰, Minister of Public Works.[152] The rooms were extremely luxurious, using [larger] beams and pillars than were permitted by law. Verandas and corridors of the house were a full *li* long. The hall was comparable to the Hsüan-kuang Palace 宣光殿 (Light-radiating Palace), and the gate was a match for the Ch'ien-ming Gate 乾明門 (Gate of Heavenly Brightness). In size and magnificence, no prince's house could match this one.

It was located in the so-called Yen-nien Ward 延年里 (Longevity Ward), north of the Imperial Drive and inside the Hsi-yang Gate. To the east of Liu T'eng's residence was the Court of the Imperial Stud (*T'ai-p'u ssu*), to the east of the court was the Bureau of Imperial Carriages (*Sheng-huang shu*).[153] To the east of the stable was the Office of the Prefect in Charge of Military Provisions (*Wu-k'u shu*),[154] which was also the arsenal of Prince Wen of the Ssu-ma

[149] Kao Huan also encamped his army in this monastery following Emperor Ch'u's flight to Ch'ang-an. See *PCS* 2/5b.

[150] The exact date is not given in *PCS*. According to *TC* (156/28b–29a), the Emperor of Eastern Wei left Lo-yang on November 17 and arrived in Yeh on December 2, A.D. 534.

[151] For the origin of 建中, see the *Shu-ching* 8/9a 仲虺之誥:王懋昭大德,建中於民. Legge 3, p. 182, "The Announcement of Chung-hwuy": "Exert yourself, O king, to make your great virtue illustrious, and set up the *pattern of the* Mean before the people."

[152] Liu T'eng gained influence in palace quarters under Emperor Kao-tsu, but had become extremely powerful under Empress Dowager Hu. In cooperation with Yüan Ch'a, he murdered the Prince of Ch'ing-ho and put the empress dowager under house arrest. See *WS* 94/16a–18a.

[153] *Sheng-huang*, otherwise known as *fei-ma* 飛馬, was the name of a legendary horse that looked like a fox with a horn on its back. It was said to have a life span of one thousand years. See *Huai-nan-tzu* 淮南子 (*SPTK so-pen*) 6/42 Kao Yu's 高誘 (fl. A.D. 205–212) commentary.

[154] For *wu-k'u* 武庫, see *WH* 2/8a 張衡西京賦:武庫禁兵. (According to Hsüeh Tsung's 薛綜 commentary, it refers to the official in charge of weapons for the

family 司馬文王 (A.D. 211–265) when he was the prime minister (*Hsiang-kuo*)[155] of the Wei.[156] On the east it reached the Palace Gate of Ch'ang-ho.

To the south[157] and inside the Hsi-yang Gate was Yung-k'ang Ward 永康里 (Ward of Eternal Health), in which was located the residence of Yüan Ch'a 元叉,[158] the General Directing the Army (*Ling-chün chiang-chün*). A stone tablet unearthed from a deserted well indicated that this had been the site of the former residence of Hsün Yü 荀彧 (A.D. 163–212), Grand Commandant of the Han.[159]

During the Cheng-kuang period 正光 (Impartial Light) (A.D. 520–524), Yüan Ch'a assumed dictatorial powers, and, with [Liu] T'eng as his chief [fellow] conspirator, placed the empress dowager under house arrest at Yung-hsiang 永巷 (Eternity Lane).[160]

---

emperor.) During the Chin, *wu-k'u* was under the supervision of the Commandant of the Palace Guards (*Wei-wei* or *Wei-wei ch'ing*).

155 That is, Ssu-mu Chao. He was a usurper of the Wei and had been its prime minister (A.D. 263–265).

156 The following two paragraphs were not quoted in the *YLTT* (13822/8b–9a), and may therefore have been interpolations.

157 The character *nan* 南 is added after *CT* (1/15a) and *YHNC* (3/5a).

158 In many editions *I* 乂 is written as *Ch'a* 叉. *Ch'a* 叉 agrees with his secondary courtesy name, Yeh-ch'a 夜叉, which includes the same character *ch'a* 叉. On the other hand, *I* 乂 also makes sense, for he had the courtesy name Po-chün 伯儁—*I* 乂 and *Chün* 儁 both mean "outstanding." (*Shu-ching* 40/20b: 俊乂在官. Ma Jung's 馬融 (A.D. 79–166) commentary: 才德過千人爲俊, 百人爲乂. Yüan Ch'a's stele (*MCCS* plate 78) also gives 乂, but I follow his biography in *WS* 16/15a.

159 Grand Commandant was the posthumous title awarded in A.D. 265. In A.D. 189, Hsün Yü joined the headquarters of Ts'ao Ts'ao 曹操 (A.D. 155–220; founder of the Wei dynasty of the Three Kingdoms) and became the latter's trusted advisor, but lost his favor when Hsün Yü objected Ts'ao Ts'ao's ennoblement as duke in A.D. 212. Hsün Yü subsequently committed suicide. See *Wei-chih* (10/21a) comm. quoting the *Wei-shih ch'un-ch'iu* 魏氏春秋 and Ch'en Ch'i-yün (Chen Chi-yun), *Hsün Yüeh (A.D. 148–209), The Life and Reflections of an Early Medieval Confucian* (Cambridge, 1975), pp. 165–166.

Empress Dowager Hu and the Prince of Ch'ing-ho formed a powerful clique and controlled the government between A.D. 515 and 520, but in the latter year they were overthrown by Yüan Ch'a and Liu T'eng, who were at first protégés of the empress.

160 After the assassination of Prince of Ch'ing-ho, Yüan Ch'a and Liu T'eng kept Empress Dowager Hu under house arrest in the Hsüan-kuang Palace, locked within the Yung-hsiang Gate, and shut off from the outside. Liu T'eng himself took possession of the key of the lock. Even Emperor Shih-tsung was not permitted to visit the empress. Yüan Ch'a, on his part, took command of the palace guards, and

[Yüan] Ch'a was the son of [Yüan] Chi 繼, Prince of Chiang-yang 江陽王, and brother-in-law to the empress dowager. In the early Hsi-p'ing period (A.D. 516–518), Emperor Ming (that is, Su-tsung), then still very young,[161] was at the mercy of powerful members of the royal household.[162] The empress dowager appointed Yüan Ch'a as Chief Palace Attendant, Commander of Left and Right [Palace Guards], over whom he had absolute authority. She treated him as a confidant, but, unexpectedly, she was imprisoned at Yung-hsiang [by the same person she had trusted] for six years. The empress dowager cried and said: "I brought up the tiger which bites me; I nurtured the small serpent which has now grown into a large snake."[163]

After returning to power in the second year of the Hsiao-ch'ang period (A.D. 526), the empress dowager executed Yüan Ch'a and others, and confiscated [Liu] T'eng's land holdings and his residence. By the time of Yüan Ch'a's execution, [Liu] T'eng had already died.[164] Mulling over Liu T'eng's crime, the empress dowager ordered that his tomb be opened up and his remains be dismembered, so that his soul would have no place to return to. The residence was given to [Yüan] Yung 元雍, the Prince of Kao-yang 高陽王. [After the prince's death] in the first year of the Chien-i ["i" is an error for "ming" 明] period (A.D. 530), Erh-chu Shih-lung, the Prince of Lo-p'ing and the President of State Affairs, converted this residence into a

made decisions about national affairs. In A.D. 525, however, the empress regained her lost power and took revenge on Yüan Ch'a and even the remains of Lui T'eng. See *WS* 16/15a–20a; 94/16a–18a.

The Yung-hsiang was traditionally used as a prison for guilty women in the palace. See Chang Tsung-hsiang, ed., *Chiao-cheng San-fu huang-t'u* (Shanghai, 1958) 6/53.

[161] Emperor Ming was born on April 8, A.D. 510 and enthroned on February 12, A.D. 515. See *WS* 9/1a.

[162] That is, Prince of Kao-yang 高陽王 (Emperor Ming's granduncle; *WS* 21A/20a–26a), Prince of Jen-ch'eng 任城王 (Emperor Ming's great-granduncle; *WS* 19B/2b–22b), Prince of Kuang-p'ing 廣平王 (*WS* 22/5a–6b; *PS* 19/35a), and Prince of Ch'ing-ho (Emperor Ming's uncle; *WS* 22/5a–6b) had been ranking officials at the court.

[163] Hui 虺 is a small snake growing big. *Kuo-yü* (*SPTK so-pen*) 19/137: 如虺弗摧, 爲蛇將若何, "If you do not kill a snake when it is small, what can you do when it grows big?" Wei Chao's 韋昭 (A.D. 204–274) comm.: 虺, 小蛇大也, "*Hui* is a small snake growing big."

[164] Liu T'eng died in the third month (April) of A.D. 523, but Yüan Ch'a was killed three years later (April 17, A.D. 526). See *MCCS* plate 78.

temple where rites were performed to insure [Erh-chu] Jung's posthumous happiness. The temple was the so-called abode of immortals, with its red gates and yellow pavilions. The front hall was converted into a shrine called the Buddha Hall and the rear section was made into a lecture hall. Gold and silver lotus flowers and silk canopies covered every inch of space. There was a Liang-feng Hall 涼風堂 (Hall of Cooling Breezes) where [Liu] T'eng used to avoid the heat. It was always chilly and cold, free from flies all the summer. There were trees one thousand or ten thousand years old.[165]

The Ch'ang-ch'iu Temple 長秋寺 (Temple of the Prolonger of Autumn) was established by Liu T'eng, and so named because [Liu] T'eng had once been the Grand Prolonger of Autumn (*Ch'ang-ch'iu [ling] ch'ing*).[166] It was located one *li* to the north of the Imperial Drive, inside the Hsi-yang Gate, also within the Yen-nien Ward.

The site was the same as the Gold Market 金市 of the Western Chin.[167]

To the north of the temple was the Meng-ssu Pond 濛汜池 (Sunset Pond)[168] which contained water during the summer but dried up in the winter.

The temple has a three-storied stūpa, [topped with] a golden plate (*chin-p'an* 金盤) [to collect dew] and an auspicious flagstaff that could be seen in the city. There was a statue of a six-tusked white elephant carrying on its back Śākyamuni in the void.[169] The sumptuous Bud-

[165] Liu Hsin, *Hsi-ching tsa-chi* (*SPTK so-pen*) 1/4: 漢[上林苑有]千年長生樹十株,萬年長生樹十株, "In the [Shang-lin Park] of the Han, there were ten ever-growing trees [each] one thousand years old, and ten ever-growing trees [each] ten thousand years old." For the authenticity of this work, see Lao Kan, "Lun *Hsi-ching tsa-chi* chih tso-che chi ch'i ch'eng-shu shih-tai," *CYYCY* 33 (1962), 19–34.

[166] The text is *Ch'ang-ch'iu ling-ch'ing* 長秋令卿 (Grand Prolonger of Autumn), but *WS* 94/16b gives *Ch'ang-ch'iu ch'ing* 長秋卿. *Ling* 令 (minister) is an obvious interpolation.

[167] One of the three markets in Lo-yang during the Chin: Gold Market, Horse Market, and the Lo-yang City Market. See *WH* 16/3a 潘岳閑居賦; Li Shan's comm. quoting Lu Chi's 陸機 (A.D. 261–303) *Lo-yang chi* 洛陽記. *YHNC* 2/27b lists the P'ing-lo Market 平樂市, Gold Market, and Horse Market as the three markets.

[168] This pond was named after Meng-ssu, believed to be the place where the sun sets. See *Ch'u-tz'u* (*SPTK so-pen*) 3/48: 出自暘谷,入于濛汜. "The sun rises from the Yang-ku, and sets in Meng-ssu." David Hawkes translates Meng-ssu as "the Vale of Darkness." See his *Ch'u Tz'u, the Songs of the South* (London, 1959), p. 47.

[169] Believed to be an actual scene when Buddha was born. See *FYCL* 14/154.

dhist decorations were all made of gold or jade, with a distinctive workmanship difficult to describe. As a rule, this statue would be carried out [of the temple] and put on parade on the fourth day of the fourth month,[170] behind such [man-made] animals as *pi-hsieh* 辟邪[171] and lions. [Variety shows would be held, featuring] sword-eaters, fire-spitters,[172] galloping horses, flagstaff climbers,[173] and rope-walkers—all being [demonstrations] of unusual skills. Their spectacular techniques and bizarre costumes were unmatched in the capital. Wherever the statue stopped, spectators would encircle it like a wall. Stumbling and trampling on each other, people in the crowd often suffered casualties.

The Yao-kuang Nunnery 瑤光寺 (Jade-sparkle Nunnery) was constructed [on the order of Emperor] Hsüan-wu, (regnant A.D. 499–515) whose posthumous title was Shih-tsung.[174] It was located on the north side of the Imperial Drive, inside the Ch'ang-ho city

[170] *CS* (1/52) suggests the character *ssu* 四 as an error for *ch'i* 七, the seventh day of the fourth month being the eve of Buddha's birthday, so all Buddhist statues from leading temples in Lo-yang would be assembled prior to next day's parade. But Iriya Yoshitaka (1/29, note 205) believes that the parade could be held any day between the first and fourteenth day of the fourth month, so the original text is not necessarily in error.

[171] A fabulous animal with two horns believed to have the ability to ward off evil influences. See *HS* 96A/29a 西域傳上：[烏弋山離國王]而有桃拔，師子，犀牛，"[The king of the state of Wu-i-shan-li] has *t'ao-pa*, lions, and *hsi-niu*." 孟康曰：桃拔一名符拔，似鹿長尾，一角者或爲天鹿者，兩角或爲辟邪，師子似虎，正黄有髯耏，尾端茸毛大如斗 Meng K'ang's commentary: "*T'ao-pa* is also known as *fu-pa*. It resembles a long-tailed deer. If it has one horn, it may be a 'heavenly deer,' if it has two horns, it may be a *pi-hsieh*. The lion looks like a tiger, with a pure yellow [skin] and whiskers as those of a tiger. The tail has hair as bulky as a bushel."

[172] This entertainment may have its origin the Western Region countries. *FYCL* 76/916 quoting Ts'ui Hung's 崔鴻 *Pei-Liang lu* 北涼錄：玄始十四年七月，西域貢吐刀嚼火，祕幻奇伎. "In the seventh month of the fourteenth year of Hsüan-shih (August–September, A.D. 425), Western Region countries presented [to the court] magicians capable of swallowing knives, biting fires, and such other mysterious and wonderous skills."

[173] Emending *yüan* 緣 to *ts'ai* 綵 after *CS* 1/53.

[174] Emperor Hsüan-wu (regnant A.D. 499–515), son of Emperor Kao-tsu (regnant A.D. 471–499), was an enthusiastic supporter of Buddhism both in and out of the court. Toward the end of his reign (A.D. 515), there were 13,727 temples in the nation. He was responsible for the construction of cave statues at Lung-men near Lo-yang. See *WS* 8/25a and 114/19a–20b.

gate,[175] and two *li* east of the Ch'ien-ch'iu Gate 千秋門 (Gate of Long Life).[176]

Inside the Ch'ien-ch'iu Gate and to the north of the drive was the Hsi-yu Park 西遊園 (Western Journey Park) in which was the Ling[177]-yün Tower, built [on order of] Emperor Wen of the Wei (regnant A.D. 220–226). On the tower was an Octagonal Well (*Pa-chiao ching* 八角井), to the north of which Emperor Kao-tsu (that is, Hsiao-wen, regnant A.D. 471–499) had Liang-feng Hall 涼風觀 (Hall of Cooling Breezes) constructed. Having ascended the tower, one could gaze into the distance and see the whole valley of the Lo River. Underneath the tower were a blue lake and a curved pond. To the east of the tower was the Hsüan-tz'u Hall 宣慈觀 (Hall in Praise of Maternal Love) which rose one hundred Chinese feet from the ground. To the east of the Hall was an Angler's Terrace (*Tiao-t'ai* 釣臺),[178] shaped like a magic fungus, made up by placing one piece of wood on top of another. It stood above the lake and rose two hundred Chinese feet from the ground. [So tall was it that] breezes were generated near the windows, and clouds gathered around the beams. [In the hall] with red pillars and carved rafters, one can see pictures of the various immortals. A whale, cut from stone, was placed against the Angler's Terrace so that it appeared at one and the same time to be jumping up from the ground and descending from the air. To the south of the Angler's Terrace was the Hsüan-kuang Palace; to the north, the Chia-fu Palace 嘉福殿 (Palace of Exalted Happiness); to the west, the Chiu-lung Palace 九龍殿 (Palace of Nine Dragons). In front of [the latter] palace a lake was created by the water spewed forth by the nine dragons.[179] Altogether there were four palaces, all connected by corridors leading to the magic fungus [terrace]. During the

[175] Both the palace and the city of Lo-yang had a gate known as Ch'ang-ho. The character *ch'eng* 城 is added in accordance with Wu Jo-chun's ed. (*Chi-cheng* 2b).

[176] The Ch'ien-ch'iu Gate was the west gate of the palace that faced the Ch'ang-ho.

[177] The text (1/15b) reads *ling* 淩, but both *Wei-chih* (2/48b) and *YHNC* 2/19b give the variant *ling* 陵.

[178] "Angler's Terrace" has a special meaning in the mind of the Chinese. Lü Wang 呂望 (11th and 12th cent. B.C.), a great statesman of the Chou, lived an angler's life before attaining political prominence, and Yen Kuang 嚴光 (styled Tzu-ling 子陵), a good friend of the founder of the Later Han, preferred to spend his days as an angler even after he was offered a high position in the government.

[179] The construction of the Palace of Nine Dragons and the accompanying waterworks was completed in A.D. 235, but they later fell into ruin. Some of them

thirty hottest days[180] of summer, the emperor stayed in the fungus-shaped terrace to avoid the heat.

[In the nunnery] there was a five-storied stūpa that rose five hundred Chinese feet from the ground. Its "immortals' palms"[181] soared into the sky; its bells hung from the clouds. The dexterity of workmanship matched that of the Yung-ning Monastery. The five hundred or more rooms in the nuns' quarters and lecture halls presented a spectacular view of an unbroken line of carved window-panes. One could go straight from the door of one room to any one of the others. There were rare trees and aromatic plants too numerous to be listed. Such trees and plants as *niu-chin* 牛筋 (that is, *ch'ou-* 杻 or *i-*檍) evergreens,[182] hollies (*kou-ku* 狗骨 or *kuo* 枸),[183] water lilies (*chi-t'ou* 雞頭),[184] and mallows (*ya-chiao* 鴨脚)[185] were all here.

were restored by the Northern Wei on the same site. See *SCC* 16/16a–b; *Wei-chih* 3/32b–34b.

[180] Literally *san-fu* 三伏, *fu* 伏 meaning to hide. The term is derived from an astrologer's assertion that the element "metal" was afraid of the element "fire," so during a period of three consecutive ten-day cycles (approximately between June 21 and August 7), when the weather was the hottest, "metal" would try to hide from "fire"; hence the term. See *Kuang-yün* (*SPPY* ed.) 5/4a and Derk Bodde, *Festivals*, "Day of Concealment," pp. 317–325.

[181] The immortal's palm was an ornament designed to collect dew as a gift of heaven, the consumption of which would promote longevity. See *SC* 12/12: 其後則又作栢梁, 銅柱, 承露僊人掌之屬矣, Later, such things as cypress beams, copper pillars, immortal's palms to collect dew, and others were made." According to *CC* (1/49, n. 12), which quotes a *HS* entry (25A/25a: 其後又作柏梁, 銅柱, 承露僊掌之屬矣, "Later, cypress beams, copper pillars, immortal's palms to collect dew, and other such things, were made." Su Lin's commentary: 蘇林曰:僊人手掌擎盤承甘露, "Plates held in the palm of immortal's hand are used to collect dew."). It was not a palm but rather a plate held in the hand of the immortal that was used as a dew collector.

[182] Lu Chi, *Mao-shih ts'ao-mu niao-shou ch'ung-yü shu* (*Ts'ung-shu chi-ch'eng* ed.) A/26–27: 杻, 檍也, 葉似杏而尖, 白色, 皮正赤, 爲木多曲少直…, 人或謂之牛筋, "*Ch'ou* is the same as *i*. Its leaves are like those of apricot trees, but more pointed. The color is white. The bark is solid red. Trunks are mostly crooked; few of them are straight.... Others also call them *niu-chin*."

[183] Lu Chi, *Mao-shih ts'ao-mu niao-shou ch'ung-yü shu*. A/36: 枸樹, 山林, 其狀如櫨, 一名枸骨, "*Kou* are mountain bushes. They look like *lu* and are also known as *kou-ku*."

[184] *CMYS* 6/26b: [芡]一名雞頭, 一名雁喙…. 由子形上花似雞冠, 故名曰雞頭, "[*Ch'ien*] is also known as *chi-t'ou* and *yen-hui*.... Since its flowers look like a cock's comb, it is also known as *chi-t'ou*."

[185] *CMYS* 3/1b: 按今世葵有紫莖白莖二種, 種別復有大小之殊, 又有鴨脚

Imperial consorts,[186] as well as ladies of the harem,[187] studied Buddhism here. Women of nobility interested in Buddhist studies also shaved their head and bade farewell to their parents, to come to lodge at this nunnery. Putting aside their precious and beautiful ornaments, they dressed instead in Buddhist robes and devoted themselves to the Eight Correct Ways,[188] and adhered to the one Buddha-vehicle.[189] In the third year of the Yung-an period (A.D. 530), when Erh-chu Chao entered Lo-yang, he let his soldiers loose to plunder. Several scores of barbarian horsemen went into the Yao-kuang Nunnery where they ravished the nuns. As a result, the nunnery became the subject of ridicule. People of the capital would say: "Hurry up, you males of Lo-yang! Plait your hair in the barbarian fashion, so the nuns of the Yao-kuang Nunnery will take you as their husbands."[190]

To the north of the Yao-kuang Nunnery was the Ch'eng-ming

葵也, "It may be noted that there are two kinds of mallows: one with purple stalks and the other with white stalks. There are also two species; one small and the other large. Still, there is another kind called *ya-chiao* mallow."

[186] Literally, *chiao-fang pin-yü* 椒房嬪御, *Chiao-fang* 椒房, rooms with walls coated in ground pepper, were private apartments of the empress and other court ladies. Pepper was used to keep the rooms warm and aromatic; hence the name. For its origin, see *HS* 66/6a Yen Shih-ku's commentary: 椒房, 殿名, 皇后所居也. 已椒和泥塗壁, 取其溫而芳也; "Chiao-fang was a palace name. It was where empresses resided. The wall, painted with a mixture of mud and ground pepper, was intended for warmth and fragrance."

[187] Literally, *i-t'ing mei-jen* 掖庭美人. *I-t'ing* 掖庭 referred to the living quarters of court ladies of lower rank. See *WH* 1/6b 西都賦 quoting *Han-kuan i* 漢官儀: 婕妤以下皆居掖庭, "All those who were below the rank of *chieh-yü* resided in the *i-t'ing*."

[188] The eight correct ways refer to view, thought, speech, deed, occupation, zeal, memory, and meditation.

[189] That is, the One Vehicle, or Mahāyāna, which contains the final or complete law of the Buddha.

[190] According to Ch'en Chung-fan (*Han-Wei Liu-ch'ao san-wen hsüan*, Shanghai, 1956, p. 290), the chignon was a standard hair style of the "barbarians" such as the Northern Wei soldiers, so ordinary males were advised, rather sarcastically, to have the same hairdo in order to win the favor of the nuns. Ch'en Chung-fan's interpretation is different from *CS* (1/56), which asserts that a chignon was a common style for all males of that time.

On the basis of Ch'en Chung-fan's finding, Kenneth Ch'en's translation of this couplet (*Buddhism in China*, p. 160) is perhaps erroneous in assuming that males in Lo-yang were advised to braid their hair into a chignon in order to discourage the nuns from seizing them as husbands.

Gate,[191] which was close to the Chin-yung City [in the southeast corner of Lo-yang]. It was constructed under [Emperor Ming 明帝 regnant A.D. 227–239] of the Wei.[192]

During the Yung-k'ang period 永康 (Eternal Health) (A.D. 300–301) of the Chin, Emperor Hui 惠帝 was imprisoned in Chin-yung City,[193] to the east of which was the Lesser Lo-yang 洛陽小城.[195] It was constructed during the Yung-chia period.[194]

In the northwestern corner of the city was the Pai-ch'ih Tower 百尺樓 (Hundred-foot Tower), which was built under Emperor Wen of the Wei.[196] Despite its age, the structure looked like new. Inside the city was the Kuang-chi Palace 光極殿 (Palace of Ultimate Brilliance) built under Emperor Kao-tsu, who renamed the Chin-yung city gate as Kuang-chi Gate.[197] In addition, [he decreed that more] storied towers and covered walkways be built throughout the highlands or low-lying areas in the city. When viewed from the ground, these buildings looked [to be as high as] the clouds.

The Ching-lo Nunnery 景樂寺 (Nunnery of the Happy View) was founded by [Yüan] I 元懌, Prince of Ch'ing-ho 淸河王 and Grand Tutor (*T'ai-fu*), whose posthumous title was Wen-hsien 文獻 (The Cultured and Dedicated).[198]

[191] The Ch'eng-ming Gate was so named by Emperor Kao-tsu (regnant A.D. 471–499). See the Preface. It was the northwestern gate of the capital city.

[192] *SCC* 16/9b: 魏明帝於洛陽城西北築之, 謂之金墉城.

[193] The imperial imprisonment took place in the first month (January–February), A.D. 301. See *Chin-shu* 4/12a.

[194] Known as Lo-yang Barracks (Lo-yang *lei* 洛陽壘) during the troubled years of Yung-chia (A.D. 307–313). *SCC* 16/10a: 因阿舊城, 憑結金墉, 故向城也. 永嘉之亂, 結以爲壘, 號洛陽壘, "[The barracks] are attached to the old city and connected with the Chin-yung. Therefore they faced the city. During the troubled years of Yung-chia period, they were made into barracks. Hence the name Lo-yang Barracks."

[195] This paragraph, which appears to have been Yang Hsüan-chih's own notes to the main text, is added at the suggestion of Chou Tsu-mo (*CS* 1/56).

[196] *YHNC* 2/20a quoting *Lo-yang chi*: 洛陽城內西北隅有百尺樓, 文帝造, "In the northwestern corner within the city of Lo-yang was the Pai-ch'ih Tower. It was built under Emperor Wen of the Wei (regnant A.D. 220–226)."

[197] Prior to the completion of palace construction, Emperor Kao-tsu took the Chin-yung building as his temporary residence.

[198] This posthumous title is not given in his biography. Both Yüan I and his younger brother, Yüeh, Prince of Ju-nan, were zealous Buddhist devotees. In

> [Yüan] I was the son of Emperor Hsiao-wen and younger brother of Emperor Hsüan-wu.

The nunnery was located to the south of the Ch'ang-ho [Gate] and on the east[199] side of the Imperial Drive, symmetrically facing the Yung-ning Monastery on the opposite side of the Imperial Drive. West of the nunnery was the Office of the Director of Public Instruction, and east of it was Generalissimo Kao Chao's 高肇 residence.[200]

It bordered on the I-ching Ward 義井里 (Ward of the Charitable Well) to the north.

> Outside the northern gate of the I-ching Ward were a number[201] of shrubs.[202] Beneath their luxuriant foliage was a well of sweet water. Stone troughs and metal cans were provided nearby for travelers to drink the water and enjoy the shelter. Many took a rest there.

There was a Hall of Buddha that housed a carriage for the sacred image. The deftness shown in carving it had no parallel at the time. Halls and corridors encircled each other, while inner rooms followed one after another. Soft branches brushed the windows; blooming flowers covered [every inch] of the courtyard. At the time of the "great fast" (six monthly fast days, *posadha*),[203] music performed by

---

addition to the Ching-lo Nunnery, Yüan I also sponsored the construction of the Ch'ung-chüeh Temple 冲覺寺 and Jung-chüeh Monastery 融覺寺 (for the latter two, q.v.) in Lo-yang. For the religious activities of Yüan I and Yüan Yüeh, see Tao-hsüan, *Hsü Kao-seng chuan* 6/474.

In A.D. 515, at the time of Emperor Su-tsung's enthronement, Yüan I was the Grand Tutor in charge of the *Men-hsia sheng* 門下省 (Bureau in Waiting for the Emperor's Service; Teng, *Family Instructions*, p. xxii). He fell victim in A.D. 520 to the conspiracy of Yüan Ch'a and Liu T'eng. See *WS* 22/5a–6b.

[199] The character *tung* 東 is added at the suggestion of T'ang Yen (*Kou-ch'en*, 1/21a).

[200] Kao Chao, the elder brother of Empress Kao-tsu, whose son later became Emperor Shih-tsung (regnant A.D. 499–515), held the office of Generalissimo in A.D. 514. He was murdered the next year by the Prince of Kao-yang after the death of Emperor Shih-tsung. See *WS* 83B/1a–3b.

[201] The text (1/16b) reads "several," but *CT* (1/18b) gives "several tens."

[202] Emending *sang* 桑 ("mulberry") to *ts'ung* 叢 ("bushes") after *YHNC* (3/5b), *YLTT* (13822/9a), and *IS* (1/13a).

[203] That is, the 8th, 14th, 15th, 23rd, 29th, and 30th, the days when the Four Mahārājas (guardians of the universe) take note of human conduct and when evil demons are busy; consequently great care is required to maintain perfect virtue, and nothing should be eaten after noon. See *Yu-p'o-i-to-she-chia ching* (*Taishō* ed.), p. 912.

women artists was often provided: the sound of singing enveloped the beams, while dancers' sleeves slowly whirled in enchanting harmony with the reverberating notes of stringed and pipe instruments. It was rhythmical and breathtaking.

As this was a nunnery, no male visitors were [ordinarily] admitted, but those who were permitted to come in for a look considered themselves as having paid a visit to paradise. After the death of Prince Wen-hsien, restrictions on visitors were less strict, so that people had no trouble in visiting the nunnery.

Later, [Yüan] Yüeh 元悅, Prince of Ju-nan 汝南王[204] had it repaired.

[Yüan] Yüeh was the younger brother of Prince Wen-hsien.

[Yüan] Yüeh summoned a number of musicians to demonstrate their skills inside the nunnery. Strange birds and outlandish animals danced in the courtyards and flew into the sky, and changed into bewildering shapes.[205] They presented a show never seen before in the world. Unusual games and spectacular skills were all performed here. Some magicians would dismember an ass and throw the cut-up parts into a well, only to have the mutilated animal quickly regenerate its maimed parts. Others would plant date trees and melon seeds that would in no time bear edible fruits.[206] Women and men who watched the performance were dumbfounded.

After the Chien-i period (ca. A.D. 528) the capital city repeatedly underwent major military disturbances. [As a consequence], such games disappeared altogether.

The Chao-i[207] Nunnery 昭儀尼寺 (Nunnery of the Exemplar) built by eunuchs, was located to the south of the Imperial Drive and one *li* inside the Tung-yang Gate.

[204] Yüan Yüeh, as noted earlier, was the son of Emperor Kao-tsu and younger brother of Yüan I. He fled to Liang in A.D. 528 and was killed in A.D. 532 after his return to the Northern Wei. See *PS* 19/35a–36a.

[205] According to *CC* (1/53), this is a reference to the various games performed by large animals capable of changing into the shapes of fish and dragons playing in the water. The games were introduced into China from countries in the Western Regions. See *HS* 96B/38 Yen Shih-ku's commentary.

[206] These magical performances, available in China as early as the Former Han, were again introduced from countries in the Western Regions. See *HS* 61/8a Yen Shih-ku's commentary: 眩讀與幻同, 卽今吞刀吐火, 植瓜種樹, 屠人截馬之術皆是也. 本從西域來.

[207] *Chao-i* was one of many titles for palace women close to eunuchs.

To the north of the drive and inside the Tung-yang Gate were the [two] offices of Imperial Granary (*T'ai-ts'ang*)[208] and Grain Sorters (*Tao-kuan*).[209] To the southeast of the offices was the Chih-su Ward 治粟里 (Ward of Grain Management), where officials [of the two government agencies] and their families lived.

When the empress dowager was regent, she showed special favors to the eunuchs, who therefore became extremely wealthy.[210] Consequently, as Hsiao Hsin 蕭忻 described, "All those in draperied high carriages were ladies from the eunuchs'[211] residences, and all those on barbarian horses bejeweled with tinkling jade were none other than eunuchs'[212] adopted sons."

[Hsiao] Hsin, a native of Yang-p'ing 陽平,[213] was fond of literary works and gained fame when young. Seeing that the eunuchs were privileged and prosperous, he wrote these lines, which immediately made him famous. He served the court as Associate Censor in Charge of Drafting.

The nunnery housed statues of one Buddha and two bodhisattvas,[214] splendid sculpture not matched elsewhere in the capital. On the seventh day of the fourth month, [the three statues] were always

[208] The character *pei* 北 between *t'ai* 太 and *ts'ang* 倉 is an interpolation.

[209] *Tao* 導 is a mistake for *tao* 䆃 (Tuan Yü-ts'ai's annotated *Shuo-wen chieh-tzu* [*SPPY* ed.] 7A/34B 禾部䆃字). The office was subordinate to the Grand Minister of Agriculture (*Ta-ssu-nung*) who was charged with the responsibility of selecting rice and supplying other provisions for the emperor. See Tu Yu, *T'ung-tien* (I-wen facsimile ed.) 26/5a. The office was located to the west of the Imperial Granary. See *YHNC* 3/6a.

[210] Literally, *chi-chin man-t'ang*, 積金滿堂, "Halls were filled up with gold that they had amassed."

[211] It was not uncommon for powerful eunuchs of the Northern Wei to have wives and concubines. *WS* 94/17b: 又頗役嬪御,時有徵求,婦女器物,公然受納. Out of sarcasm, "wives" are referred to as "widows" in the text (1/17b).

The text (1/17b) has *li* 嫠, which is a variant of *li* 嫠. *Tso-chuan* Chao 19 48/23a: 初,莒有婦人,莒子殺其夫,已爲嫠婦. Legge 5, p. 675: "At an earlier period, the viscount of Keu had put to death the husband of a woman of Keu, who thenceforth lived as a widow." Tu Yü's commentary: 寡婦爲嫠 Sub-comm.: 嫠, ... 本又作釐.

Adding *chin-shih* 盡是 ("all") after *CT* 1/19b.

[212] Literally, *Huang-men* 黃門 "The Yellow Gate," another name for eunuchs.

[213] According to *WS* 106A/2b, this commandery was a subdivision of Hsiang-chou 相州 (changed to Ssu-chou 司州 during the Northern Ch'i). It corresponded to modern Feng-yang *hsien* 鳳陽縣, Anhui.

[214] During the Northern Wei, it was customary to have a group of three Buddhist statues in any given cave: the Buddha in the center, flanked by two attendants. The

carried to the Ching-ming Monastery 景明寺 (Bright Prospect Monastery) where they were habitually met by three others housed there. [On that occasion] the display of rich music and shows was comparable to that of Liu Teng's [Ch'ang-ch'iu Temple]. In front of the [main] hall were wine-[215] and noodle-[216] trees. In the Chao-i Nunnery was a pond, referred to as the Ti-ch'üan 翟泉 (Fountain of Ti) by literati in the capital.[217]

[Yang] Hsüan-chih's note: According to Tu Yü's 杜預 (A.D. 222–284) notes on the *Tso Commentary to the Spring and Autumn Annals*,[218] the Ti-ch'üan was located southeast of the Imperial Granary of the Chin, inside the Chien-ch'un Gate. Now, the present Imperial Granary was inside the Tung-yang Gate, yet the fountain referred to as the Ti-ch'üan was to the southwest of the present Imperial Granary. Therefore the fountain could not have been the same Ti-ch'üan of the Chin.[219] As the hermit Chao I 趙逸 said later, "This is the private fountain of Shih Ch'ung 石崇, Chief Palace Attendant of the Chin.[220] To the south of the fountain was the Lü-chu Tower 綠珠樓 (Green Pearl Tower)."[221] Thereafter, the literati began to realize that [they were mistaken]. Those who passed this place were able to visualize the beautiful appearance of Lü-chu.

statue of Buddha in such arrangement was referred to as *Pen-tsun* 本尊, "The Most Honored One."

[215] Wine was made out of the flower nectar of the tree. See *Liang-shu* (I-wen facsimile ed.) 54/5b. *CMYS* (10/15a quoting *Chiao-chou chi* 交州記 by Liu Hsin-ch'i 劉欣期), however, refers to coconut juice as a raw material for wine. Lo-yang was perhaps too cold to grow coconut trees.

[216] *CMYS* (10/45a quoting *Wu-lu ti-li-chih* 吳錄地里志) makes mention of *hsiang* trees 欀木, which were native to Chiao-chih 交阯 (North Vietnam), and which contained ricelike grains in the bark. The grains could be powdered, rinsed with water, and made into flour and cakes.

[217] Hsü Kao-juan (*Ch'ung-k'an* 1/9a) classifies this sentence as a note, but I follow *CS* (1/60) in including it in the main text.

[218] See *Tso-chuan* 17/1a Hsi 僖 27 Tu Yü's commentary.

[219] *SCC* lists three reasons why the Ti-ch'üan was not the same one referred to by Lo-yang literati. See *SCC* 16/19b.

[220] Shih Ch'ung (A.D. 249–300), son of Shih Pao 石苞, was a native of Po-hai 渤海. He had been a Cavalier Attendant-in-Ordinary and a Chief Palace Attendant of the Chin, but was killed on order of Ssu-ma Lun 司馬倫, Prince of Chao 趙王. See *Chin-shu* 33/25b–32a.

[221] Name of Shih Ch'ung's favorite entertainer. She was beautiful, elegant, and skillful at playing the flute. See *Chin-shu* 33/30b–31a.

To the southwest of the spring was the Yüan-hui Temple 願會寺 (Temple of the Fulfilled Vow), formerly the residence of Wang Yü 王翊,[222] Squire-attendant of the Central Secretariat (*Chung-shu shih-lang*).[223] In front of the Buddha's Hall was a mulberry tree. At a level five Chinese feet above the ground, the tree had branches and leaves stretching out sideways, taking the shape of an umbrella. This also happened at another level five Chinese feet higher. Altogether there were five such levels, each level having different leaves and berries. In the capital, this was called a sacred mulberry tree by monks and laymen alike. Spectators were as crowded here as in a market place; a great many made donations. But Emperor [Hsiao-wu], hearing of this, was much offended, because he believed that the tree served to delude the people. Consequently, he ordered Yüan Chi 元紀,[224] the Court Secretary (*Chi-shih chung*) and the Attending Secretary within the Imperial Yellow Gate, to have the tree chopped down. The very day became cloudy and dark. From the point where the axe was applied, blood flowed out and down to the ground. Those who saw it all sobbed bitterly.

To the south of the temple was the I-shou Ward 宜壽里 (Deserving Long Life Ward), where the residence of Tuan Hui 段暉, Prefect of Pao-hsin 苞信,[225] was located. Bells were often heard ringing underground, and from time to time five-colored lights shone on the hall. Much amazed, [Tuan] Hui dug a hole at the point where the lights emerged, and there he discovered a golden statue about three Chinese

[222] Wang Yü was the son of Wang Ch'en 王琛 and nephew of Wang Su 王肅 (d. A.D. 501), the latter being a member of the prominent Wang family that was purged by Emperor Wu 武帝 (regnant A.D. 482–493) of the Southern Ch'i dynasty in A.D. 493. Wang Su managed to escape to the Northern Wei, and became a trusted adviser of Emperor Kao-tsu (regnant A.D. 471–499). Wang Ch'en was executed by Emperor Wu in the south. Wang Yü died in A.D. 528. See *WS* 63/7b–8a.

[223] The text (1/18a) is *Chung-shu she-jen*, Drafter of the Central Secretariat. Here I follow *CS* (1/61). *Shih-lang* 侍郎 was two ranks higher than *She-jen*.

[224] Yüan Chi was the son of Yüan Ch'eng 元澄, Prince of Jen-ch'eng 任城王. He fled with Emperor Hsiao-wu to Ch'ang-an in A.D. 534 to avoid possible detention by Kao Huan, founder of the Eastern Wei. See *WS* 19B/27b.

[225] Pao-hsin was a prefecture in the Hsin-ts'ai commandery 新蔡郡 (modern Hsi-hsien 息縣, Honan), a subdivision of Eastern Yü-chou 東豫州. See *WS* 106B/37b.

According to Chou Yen-nien (*Lo-yang ch'ieh-lan chi chu* 1/11b), Tuan Hui, styled Ch'ang-tso 長祚, was a native of Ku-tsang 姑臧 of Wu-wei. However, his assertion cannot be verified since no other information is available.

feet high. In addition,[226] [he discovered] two bodhisattva statues sitting on a stand,[227] bearing the inscription: Made for Hsün Hsü 荀勗 (A.D. ?–289), Chief Palace Attendant and Director of the Central Secretariat (*Chung-shu chien*) on the fifteenth day of the fifth month in the second year of the T'ai-shih period 泰始 (Grand Beginning)[228] (June 24 A.D. 266)." Thereupon [Tuan] Hui donated his residence to be converted into the Kuang-ming Monastery 光明寺 (Monastery of Brightness) which, according to all his contemporaries, was the former residence of Hsün Hsü. Later, when some robbers attempted to steal the golden statue, the statue, joined by the bodhisattva statues, shouted at them in chorus. Alarmed and frightened, the robbers fell to the ground instantly. Having heard the calls of the statues, the monks came out and caught the robbers.

The Hu-t'ung Nunnery 胡統寺 (Nunnery of the Chief of T'o-pa Monks)[229] was founded by an aunt of the empress dowager, who lived here after she had accepted Buddhist teachings and become a nun. It was located slightly more than one *li* to the south of the Yung-ning Monastery. It had a five-storied stūpa, [topped with] a lofty golden steeple. With its many suites of spacious rooms,[230] fitted with symmetrical windows and doors, red pillars and white walls, it was the height of elegance and beauty. The nuns here were among the most renowned and accomplished in the imperial city, skillful at preaching and discussing Buddhist principles. They often came to the palace to lecture on Dharma for the empress dowager, whose patronage of Buddhists and laymen[231] was without equal.

The Hsiu-fan Temple 修梵寺 (Temple for the Cultivation of Goodness) was located to the north of the Imperial Drive and inside the

[226] On the basis of *TPKC* 99/5b and *TPYL* 658/6b, *CS* (1/62) suggests that the character *ping* 幷 be added; hence, the translation.

[227] *Tso* 坐 is added after *IS* (1/14b).

[228] The text reads *t'ai* 太, which is an acceptable substitute for *t'ai* 泰. For Hsün Hsü's biography, see *Chin-shu* 39/13b–21b.

[229] According to Zhou (Chou) Yi-liang, as quoted in *CS* (1/62), *Hu-t'ung* is the abbreviation for *Hu Sha-men t'ung* 胡沙門統, Chief of T'o-pa Monks.

[230] Literally, *tung-fang* 洞房, "deep room." *WH* 11/11a 王延壽魯靈光殿賦: 洞房叫窱而幽邃, "Deep rooms are countless, removed from one another."

[231] Emending *t'u* 徒 to *ts'ung* 從 after *IS* (1/15a).

Ch'ing-yang[232] Gate. To the west of the Hsiu-fan Temple was the Sung-ming Temple 嵩明寺 (Temple of the Sublime and Bright). Both were famous temples, each with sculptured walls, lofty buildings, connected rooms and joined ridges. The Hsiu-fan Temple had a statue of Vajrapāṇi [guarding its gate], where pigeons and doves were not allowed to enter, nor were sparrows or other birds permitted to come to perch. Bodhidharma[233] thought the statue bore a striking likeness [to Vajrapāṇi].

To the north of the temple was the Yung-ho Ward 永和里 (Ward of Eternal Harmony), previously the private residence of Tung Cho 董卓 (A.D. ?–192),[234] Grand Preceptor [of the Han]. In both the south and north end of the ward was a pond constructed on orders of [Tung] Cho. Even today there is still water in the ponds, which do not become dry in winter or summer.

In the ward were the six residences of the following: Chang-sun Chih,[235] Grand Tutor and Chief of Ministers (*T'ai-fu Lu Shang-shu shih*); Kuo Tsu 郭祚,[236] Vice President on the Right, Department of State Affairs (*Shang-shu yu p'u-yeh* 尚書右僕射); Hsing Luan 邢巒,[237] Secretary General of the Ministry of Civil Office (*Li-pu shang-shu*); Yüan Hung-ch'ao 元洪超,[238] Commandant of Justice (*T'ing-wei*

[232] According to *CT* (1/21b), *ch'ing* 淸 is an error for *ch'ing* 靑.

[233] The last character in the transliterated name of Bodhidharma should be *mo* 摩 rather than *mo* 磨, although either character is used loosely.

[234] For Tung Cho's biography, see *HHS* 102/1a–18a. He was a capable but ambitious warlord at the end of the Later Han.

[235] His name has been mentioned before under the Yung-ning Monastery (Chapter 1). See Chen Chi-yun, *Hsün Yüeh*, pp. 3, 41–43, 48–50, 52, 57, 74–76, 79, 113, 134. Grandson of Chang-sun Tao-sheng 長孫道生, he had been a minister of war, in which capacity he accompanied Emperor Kao-tsu in the latter's southward campaign. His name is variably given as *Yu* 幼 (*PS* 22/8b) because of a T'ang taboo (*Chih* 稚 is a homophone of *Chih* 治, the name of Emperor Kao-tsung 高宗, who reigned between A.D. 650 and A.D. 683).

[236] Kuo Tsu served both Emperors Kao-tsu (regnant A.D. 471–499) and Shih-tsung (regnant A.D. 499–515). The highest position he ever obtained was as given in the text. For his biography, see *WS* 64/1a–7a.

[237] The text (1/19b) gives Hsing Luan 邢鸞, *Luan* 鸞 being an error for *Luan* 巒. He was a military as well as a civil leader under Emperor Shih-tsung (regnant A.D. 499–515). Hsing Luan died in A.D. 514. For his biography, see *WS* 65/1a–12b.

[238] In A.D. 517, he sponsored the creation of Ts'ang-chou 滄州 (southeast of modern Nan-p'i 南皮, Hopei) after the pacification of a local uprising. For his

ch'ing); Hsü Po-t'ao 許伯桃,[239] Commandant of the Palace Guards (*Wei-wei ch'ing*); and Wei Ch'eng-hsing 尉成興,[240] Governor of Liang-chou 涼州刺史.[241]

These were all elegant mansions with high gates and spacious halls. The study rooms were imposing and beautiful. Catalpa and locust trees sheltered the street, amidst *wu-t'ung*[242] and willow trees, which were planted in alternation. Contemporaries considered this ward an exclusive area. Here diggers often found such valuables as gold, jade, and other equally precious articles. Once[243] Hsing Luan unearthed at his home some cinnabar and several tens of thousands of coins, along with an inscription that read: "The belongings of Grand Preceptor Tung." One night, later, [Tung] Cho [appeared to Hsing Luan in a dream] and reclaimed these things. [Hsing] Luan,[244] however, refused to yield. A year later, [Hsing] Luan died as a result.

The Ching-lin Monastery 景林寺 (Forest Prospect Monastery) was located to the east of the Imperial Drive and inside the K'ai-yang Gate. Its lecture halls rose one after another; rooms and corridors were closely connected. Red columns gleamed in the sunlight, and painted rafters welcomed the breeze—it was indeed scenic. To the west of the monastery was an orchard, which abounded in rare fruits. Birds sang in the spring and cicadas chirped in autumn—the pleasant sound seemed to be continuous. Inside was a meditation hall,[245]

---

biography, see *PS* 15/33b. His and Chang-sun Chih's mother were sisters. See *PS* 22/10b.

[239] In A.D. 530, he took part in a conference on Buddhist and Taoist teachings. For more information about him, see *Hsü Kao-seng chuan*, 23/624–625.

[240] Ch'eng-hsing was his courtesy name; his name was Yü 聿. A principled man, he defied Yüan Ch'a's authority. See *WS* 26/10a–b.

[241] The text reads Liang-chou 梁州, Liang 梁 being a mistake for Liang 涼. *IS* (1/15a), *YHNC* (3/6a), and *WS* (26/10a–b) all given Liang-chou 涼州.

[242] The *wu-t'ung* (*sterenlia plafamifolia*) tree was believed to be the only species on which the phoenix would perch. See *Shih-ching* 17.4/7b (ode 252, verse 9, line 3) text and Cheng Hsüan's commentary. See also Tjan Tjoe Som, tr., *Po Hu T'ung, the Comprehensive Discussions in the White Tiger Hall* (Sinica Leidensia, no. 6; Leiden, 1949), p. 243.

[243] Emending *ch'ang* 常 to *ch'ang* 嘗 after *YHNC* (3/6a).

[244] The text (1/19b) is *Luan* 鸞, which is a mistake for *Luan* 巒.

[245] Literally, *ch'an-fang* 禪房, a room for cultivation and meditation. *Ta-fang kuang-fo hua-yen-ching yin-i* (chapter A) 大方廣佛花嚴經音義卷上 as quoted in Hui-lin's *I-ch'ieh-ching yin-i* (*Taishō* ed.) 21/439: 禪那, 此云靜慮, 謂靜心思慮也.

within which was an abode of the pure celibate.[246] Small in size, the hall was a matchless design.[247] Furthermore, the meditation pavilions were quiet, and the secluded rooms were hidden from view—fine trees lined the windows, and aromatic *tu[-jo]* 杜[若] (*pollia japonica*) encircled the stairways. Even though the monastery was located in a noisy area, it was as quiet as though it were in a valley or on a cliff. Inside, the monks sat erect, observing ascetic[248] rituals. Feeding on the wind, they were absorbed in Buddhist teachings. Sitting cross-legged, they counted the breaths they took, in order to calm their minds and bodies for meditation.[249]

Inside was a stone monument, the inscription of which was composed by Lu Pai-t'ou 盧白頭, Erudite of the Imperial Academy (*Kuo-tzu po-shih*).[250]

> [Lu] Pai-t'ou, whose style was Ching-yü 景裕, was a native of Fan-yang 范陽. By nature he was fond of tranquillity,[251] enjoying an untrammeled life in the countryside. He had mastered the six classics, and was well-versed in one hundred schools of philosophy. In the early P'u-t'ai years (A.D. 531–532), he started his government career as an Erudite of the Imperial Academy. Even though he was in public service,[252] he engaged himself in writing and in preparing commentaries [for the classics], [including] the commentaries for the *Chou-I* still in circulation.[253]

舊翻爲思維修者, 略也, "Ch'an-na (dhyāna), known in our land as abstract contemplation, refers to meditation in quietude. For the sake of brevity, the old translation is meditation and cultivation."

[246] Literally, *chih-yüan ching-she* 祗洹精舍 (vihāra), *yüan* 洹 being a variant of *t'o* 陀, a park of Srāvasti that was donated to honor Tathāgata. See Hui-chüeh, tr., *Hsien-yü ching* (*Taishō* ed.) 10/418.

[247] Adding the character *pi* 比 after *CT* (1/22b) and *IS* (1/15b).

[248] Changing *ching* 靜 to *ching* 淨 after *CS* 1/65.

[249] This sitting posture and the practice of counting breaths are common among Buddhist monks.

[250] Pai-t'ou was his baby name. For more information about his life, see *PS* 30/26b–27b.

[251] Literally, *hsing ai tien ching* 性愛恬靜, "By nature he was fond of quietude."

[252] Literally *chu men* 朱門, "the red gate," meaning government office.

[253] According to other editions, the Ch'ung-hsü Temple entry appears in Chapter 3, at note 234. *Ch'ung-k'an* (1/11a) gives no convincing reason why this section should be moved to Chapter 1 immediately after the Ching-lin Monastery account. The present translation follows the conventional arrangement, leaving the Ch'ung-hsü Temple entry intact in Chapter 3.

To the south of the Imperial Drive and inside the Chien-ch'un Gate were [three] offices: the office of the Imperial Palace Parks (*Kou-tun*),[254] the Office of Agriculture (*Tien-nung*), and that of the Sacred Field (*Chi-t'ien*).[255] To the south of the Office of the Sacred Field was the Office of Agriculture. To the north of the Imperial Drive was a tract of vacant land originally designated as the site for the palace of the crown prince. It was at the place where the Imperial Granary of the Western Chin had stood. Southwest[256] of the Imperial Granary was the Ti-ch'üan, which was three *li* in circumference. According to the *Spring and Autumn Annals*, Wang Tzu-hu 王子虎 made a covenant at this place with Hu-yen 狐偃 of the Chin [and others].[257] At the present time the water is [still] pure[258] and the bottom clear and calm so that one can distinguish a turtle from a fish hiding under the water.

Emperor Kao-tsu set up [an office] for the Metropolitan Prefect of Honan (Ho-nan *yin* 河南尹) to the north of the Ti-ch'üan. It was known as the Pu-kuang Ward 步廣里 (Ward of Long Strides) during the Western Chin.[259]

To the west of the Ti-ch'üan was the Hua-lin Park 華林園 (Flowering Forest Park).[260] Because the Ti-ch'üan was situated to

[254] A subdivision of *Ta-hung-lu*, the Great Usher in Charge of State Guests. It had the function of taking care of imperial parks during this period. *WH* 3/66 張衡東京賦：奇樹珍果，鉤盾所職, "The Office of Imperial Palace Parks has the responsibility to look after exotic trees and treasured fruits." 薛綜曰：鉤盾，今官，主小苑. Hsüeh Tsung's commentary: "*Kou-tun* is the current name of an official [in charge of the office]. His function is to take care of imperial palace parks."

[255] *Chi-t'ien*, or Office of the Sacred Field, the produce of which was used for imperial ancestral sacrifices. It was customary for the emperor to perform in this field a ceremonial plowing in spring as an example for the people to follow. See Bodde, *Festivals*, p. 223.

[256] Adding the character *hsi* 西 after *YHNC* (3/6b) and *SCC* (16/13a).

[257] *Tso-chuan* Hsi 17/1b–2a: 公會王子虎晉狐偃…盟於翟泉. Legge 5, p. 214: "The duke had a meeting with King Hwuy's son Hoo . . . when they made a convenant at Tieh-ts'euen."

[258] The text (1/20b) and *IS* (1/16a) read *ming ching* 明靜, "glittering and calm." *CS* (1/66) changes *ching* 靜 to *ching* 淨 by following *CT* (1/23a); hence the translation.

[259] Lu Chi's *Lo-yang chi*, as quoted in *SSC* (16/13a), identifies the location of Pu-kuang Ward as to the east of the Lo-yang palaces.

[260] Originally known as Fang-lin Park 芳林園 (Fragrant Forest) under Emperor Ming (regnant A.D. 227–239), it was renamed Hua-lin Park under Ts'ao Fang 曹芳, Prince of Ch'i (regnant A.D. 240–254). See *WH* 20/12b 應貞晉武帝華林園集詩 Li Shan's commentary quoting *Lo-yang t'u-ching*: 洛陽圖經.

the east of the [Hua-lin] Park, Emperor Kao-tsu named it the Ts'ang-lung Lake 蒼龍海 (Lake of Blue Dragon).[261] Inside the Hua-lin Park was a large pond, known as the T'ien-yüan Pond 天淵池 (Heavenly Abyss) during the Han.

In the pond, there was still the Chiu-hua Terrace 九華臺 (Nine Flowers Terrace)[262] [built at the command of] Emperor Wen [of the Wei].[263] Emperor Kao-tsu had a Ch'ing-liang Palace 清涼殿 (Cool, Refreshing Palace) built on the terrace, and Emperor Shih-tsung had a P'eng-lai Hill[264] built in the pond. On the hill was a Hsien-jen Abode 僊人館 (Immortals' Abode), and on the terrace, the Tiao-t'ai Palace 釣臺殿 (Anglers' Tower Palace).[265] The Hung-ni Corridor 虹蜺閣 (Rainbow Corridor) connected the abode and the palace. [One felt himself walking in the void when] visiting these places. At the third day of the third month[266] and again on nice days[267] in the late autumn, the Emperor would come here to ride in a dragon boat, its bow painted with the picture of the fabulous *i* 鷁 bird.[268]

[261] Blue Dragon refers to a group of constellations in the east (*SC* 27/5), hence the name for a lake that was located to the east of the Imperial Park.

[262] *CS* (1/67), on the basis of a *Wei-chih* entry (2/65a), which gives April to May of A.D. 226 as the date of the construction of the Chiu-hua Terrace, adds the character Wei.

[263] The foundation was made of old stone monuments found in Lo-yang. See *SCC* 16/2b.

[264] P'eng-lai was one of the three legendary islands of the immortals in the high seas east of China. Here the concept "east" is again emphasized.

[265] This park was designed very much like the Hsi-yu Park described under the Yao-kuang Nunnery. For the special meaning of an angler's life in the Chinese mind, see note 178.

[266] During the Western Chin, residents of Lo-yang gathered along the Lo River for this festival, but those of royal blood observed the rites on the T'ien-yüan Pond, a site described earlier in the text. Participants would let cups of wine float downstream; others on the receiving line would pick them up and drink. See *Chin-shu* 21C/28b–29a. For information on the lustration festival, see Bodde, *Festivals*, pp. 273 ff.

[267] The exact date is hard to determine: the text reads *ssu-ch'en* 巳辰 (name of a day in a cycle of 60), as against *chiu-ch'en* 九辰 (nine days) in *CT* (1/23b) and *liang-ch'en* 良辰 (nice days) in *IS* (1/16b).

[268] During the Han, the emperor would take a ride in a boat that "had the design of a dragon and a bow painted with the picture of an *i* (a huge bird)." *Huai-nan tzu* 6/4a 龍舟鷁首. Kao Yu's commentary: 龍舟, 大舟也, 刻爲龍文, 以爲飾也. 鷁, 大鳥也, 畫其象著船, 故曰鷁首也, "A dragon boat is a large vessel with the

To the west of the pond was the Ice Storehouse, from which ice was taken out in the sixth month to give to officials. Southwest of the Pond was the Ching-yang[269] Hill 景陽山 (Hill of Bright Sunlight). To the east of the Hill was the Hsi-ho Ridge 羲和嶺,[270] on which was the Wen-feng Chamber 溫風室 (Warm Breeze Chamber). To the west was the Huan-o[271] Peak 姮娥峯, on which was the Lu-han Hall 露寒館 (Hall of Chilly Dew). They were connected by elevated corridors over the hill and valley. To the north of the hill was the Hsüan-wu Pond 玄武池 (Dark Warrior Pond);[272] to the south, the Ch'ing-shu Palace 清暑殿 (Palace to Cool the Summer Heat). To the east of the palace was the Lin-chien Pavilion 臨澗亭 (Pavilion Facing the Brook), to the west, the Lin-wei Tower 臨危臺 (Tower Facing the Danger).[273]

To the south of the Ching-yang Hill was the Pai-kuo Orchard 百果園 (Orchard of the Hundred Fruits) in which each species of fruit was planted in a separate area. Each area had a separate [storage] room.

In the orchard were Immortal's Date Trees, which bore fruit five inches long. When squeezed, the stone, as fine as a needle, would come out from either end. The dates ripened only after frost, and were delicious. The popular belief was that the trees had originated in the K'un-lun Mountains 崑崙山,[274] so they were

design of a dragon carved on it as an ornament. *I* is a huge bird, a painting of which is affixed on the boat. Therefore, it is known as a boat with an *i* bow." During the Sung of the Southern Dynasties (A.D. 420–589), the ceremony was held in late spring. See *Sung-shu* (I-wen facsimile ed.) 15/7b: 暮春天子始乘舟, "In late spring the emperor began to ride in a boat."

[269] After a *SCC* entry (16/2a–b: 穀水枝分,… 歷景陽山北, …其水東注天淵池), *CS* (1/67) suggests that Ching-shan *tien* 景山殿 be changed to Ching-yang *shan* 景陽山. The palace was constructed under Emperor Ming 明帝 of the Wei 魏 (regnant A.D. 227–239) using quartz and multicolored stones as the most important materials. See *SCC* 16/1b and *YHNC* 2/20b.

[270] Hsi-ho 羲和 was the legendary charioteer of the sun, hence the ridge faced the east to welcome the rising sun.

[271] Huan-o was the goddess of the moon, believed to be the wife of I 羿, the archer.

[272] The term Hsüan-wu referred to the one of the five elements, water, associated with the north.

[273] The name was intended as a constant warning to the monarchs who should take everything just as seriously as they would when facing a grave crisis.

[274] The K'un-lun Mountains were a legendary mountain range in the extreme west of China. It was an important source of Chinese mythology.

also known as the Dates of the Queen Mother of the West 西王母棗.[275] In addition, there were Immortals' Peaches of a reddish outside and transparent flesh revealing the meat [tantalizingly] below the surface. The peaches ripened only after frost[276] and they too were known as the Peach [Tree] of the Queen Mother of the West, since they also had their origin in the K'un-lun Mountains.

To the south of the Nai-lin 奈林 (Crab Apple Orchard) was a stone monument erected under Emperor Ming of the Wei, entitled "The Monument of the Thatched[277] [Hall]" 苗茨之碑. [Accordingly,] Emperor Kao-tsu had a Thatched Hall built in the rear of the monument.[278]

In the Yung-an period, Emperor Chuang [practiced] a shooting game on horseback (*ma-she* 馬射) in the Hua-lin Park. When the attending officials read the monument, they suspected that the character *miao* 苗 (of the hall's name) was in error. Li T'ung-kuei 李同軌[279] Erudite of the Imperial Academy, said: "[Emperor] Ming[280] of the Wei was a talented man. [Along with Emperors Wu and Wen], he was known as one of the three [enlightened]

[275] Hsi-wang mu 西王母, Queen Mother of the West, was a legendary goddess. For more information, see Michael Loewe, *Ways to Paradise* (London, 1979), pp. 86–125.

[276] The text (1/21b) is *te shuang chi shu* 得霜即熟, "It ripened as soon as frost fell." *CS* (1/68) emends *chi* 即 to *nai* 乃 after *TPYL* (967/6b).

The Hua-lin Park was already famous for such date and peach trees during the Western Chin. According to *TPYL* (965/5b and 967/5b quoting the *Chin kung-ch'üeh chi* 晉宮闕記), the park had 14 goddess's date trees and 733 different kinds of peach trees. *YYTT* (18/19) gives an identical description of the date tree as the *Ch'ieh-lan chi*.

[277] The text (1/21b), *miao tz'u chih pei* 苗茨之碑, is a source of great controversy. *Miao* 苗, meaning young rice plant, is actually the ancient script for *mao* 茅, "thatch." Scholars among Yang Hsüan-chih's contemporaries as well as of later periods have misinterpreted *miao* 苗 as rice plants, where it should have been considered as a substitute for *mao* 茅, "thatch."

[278] The text (1/2b) names Emperor Kao-tsu as the emperor responsible for its construction, whereas *SCC* (16/11b) names Emperor Wen of the Wei instead. According to *WS* (19b/18a–b), it was actually Emperor Kao-tsu, who, in the company of the prince of Jen-ch'eng, suggested that a thatched hall be built to serve as a constant warning to monarchs in their drive for thriftiness.

[279] Li T'ung-kuei was a scholar who died in A.D. 546. For his biography, see *WS* 84/21a–b.

[280] *Ming* is an error for *Wen*. By Emperor Ming's time, the two scholars mentioned below had already died.

founding ancestors [of the Wei]. Liu Chen 劉楨 and Wang Ts'an 王粲,[281] furthermore, served as his assistants. They might have misunderstood the original meaning, but would certainly not be in error." At the time, in the capacity of a court guest,[282] I[283] then explained: "A hall covered under dried hay[284] is known as 'a thatched hall'. Where is there any error?" All those present approved [this interpretation], considering that I was able to grasp the real meaning.

To the east of the Crab Apple Orchard were the Tu-t'ang 都堂 (Lodging House)[285] and the Liu-shang Pond 流觴池 (Floating-cup Pond).[286] To the east of the House was the Fu-sang Lake 扶桑海.[287]

All the lakes and ponds had underground stone drainage, connected with the Ku River 穀水 (Grain River) to the west and the Yang Canal 陽渠 (Sunlight Canal) to the east. They were also linked with the Ti-ch'üan. At the time of drought,[288] [water] from the Ku River would flow in to keep them from becoming dry. At times of excessive rain,[289] the Ku and Yang would take in

[281] The text reads Tsu Kan Hsüan 祖幹宣, which should have read Kung-kan Chung-hsüan 公幹仲宣. Kung-kan 公幹 is the courtesy name of Liu Chen 劉楨 (d. A.D. 215 or 217), whereas Chung-hsüan is that of Wang Ts'an 王粲 (A.D. 177–217). Both Liu Chen and Wang Ts'an belonged to the "Seven Masters of the Chien-an period" 建安 (A.D. 196–220).

[282] Contrary to what the term may suggest, *Feng ch'ao-ch'ing* simply refers to persons who were summoned or invited to attend social gatherings at the court as occasions demanded. It was not an official title. See Teng Ssu-yü, *Family Instructions*, p. 151 n. 2. See also *T'ung-t'ien* 29/12b: 無員, 本不爲官.

[283] The text (1/21b–22a) reads Hsüan-chih 衒之—the author's given names.

[284] *Kao* 蒿, an alternate for *kao* 藁 or *kao* 槀, meaning dried hay. See *Kuang-yün* 3/35b–36a; *Shuo-wen chieh-tzu*, 7A/33b.

[285] Same as Tu-t'ing 都亭, referred to in the *WS* (21A/30a). It was located in the west part of the Hua-lin Park, which was used as a lodging house for visiting officials. See Iriya, *Rakuyō garan ki* 1/32 n. 16.

[286] Liu-shang Pond was the place where the ceremonies were held on the third day of the third month. See n. 266 above.

[287] Fu-sang Lake was the name of another island of the immortals, said to be located in the east sea. Fu-sang was the residence of the sun after sunset until dawn.

[288] Literally, "When the God of Drought created hardship"—a reference to the *Shih-ching* (18.2/18b: *han pa wei-nüeh* 旱魃爲虐. Mao Heng's 毛亨 commentary: 魃, 旱神也. "*Pa* is the god of drought."

[289] The text (1/22a) is *li Pi p'ang-jun* 離畢滂潤, a reference to the *Shih-ching* (15.3/9a: ode 232, verse 3, lines 3 and 4): 小雅漸漸之石：月離於畢，俾滂沱矣.

water to keep them from overflowing. Rare species of fish and shellfish, along with various kinds of waterfowl, appeared to enjoy nature here, swimming about and [now and then] ducking beneath the surface.

Waley, *Book of Songs*, p. 120: "The moon is caught in the Net/There will be deluges of rain."

Chapter 2

EASTERN SUBURBS
(*Ch'eng-tung* 城東)

The Ming-hsüan[1] Nunnery 明懸尼寺 (Nunnery of Clear Manifestations) was founded by Yüan Hsieh, Prince of P'eng-ch'eng, whose posthumous title was Wu-hsüan 武宣 (Demonstrator of Valor).[2] It was located outside the Chien-ch'un Gate and to the south of the Stone Bridge.[3]

The River Ku circled the walled city, and, after reaching a point outside the Chien-ch'un Gate, flowed eastward into the Yang Canal under the Stone Bridge. The bridge had four stone[4] pillars, on the southern side of the road.[5] On one of the pillars was an inscription that reads: "Built in the fourth year of Yang-chia 陽嘉 (Bright and Auspicious) (A.D. 135) of the Han [under the supervision][6] of Ma Hsien 馬憲, the Palace Internuncio (*Chung-yeh-che*)[7]

[1] A reference to the *I-ching* 7/29a 繫辭上：懸象著明，莫大乎日月. Richard Wilhelm, *I Ching*, 1, p. 343. "Of the images suspended in the heavens, there is none more light-giving than the sun and the moon."

[2] Younger brother of Emperor Kao-tsu. See also Chapter 1 under the Yung-ning Monastery, and *WS* 21B/1a–15a. Yüan Hsieh must have been a devoted Buddhist and well-liked by the monks, for when the news of his death reached the two temples associated with him, more than one thousand monks were so saddened that they decided to fast. See *PS* 19/24b–25a.

[3] Emending *lou* 樓 (tower) to *chiao* 橋 (bridge) after *Kou-ch'en* 2/1a.

[4] Adding *shih* 石 (stone) after *YHNC* 3/9a.

[5] The meaning is not clear. According to *SCC* (16/14b 穀水注), there were two (should read four) stone pillars at one end of the bridge (*chiao shou* 橋首). Could "the end" mean "the entrance"? Were the pillars on or near the bridge? Judging from the statement "on the south side of the road," it seems that the pillars were near rather than on the bridge.

[6] Adding *chien-tso* 監作 (built under the supervision of), after *SCC* 16/14b 穀水注.

[7] This official title is added according to *SCC* 16/14b 穀水注.

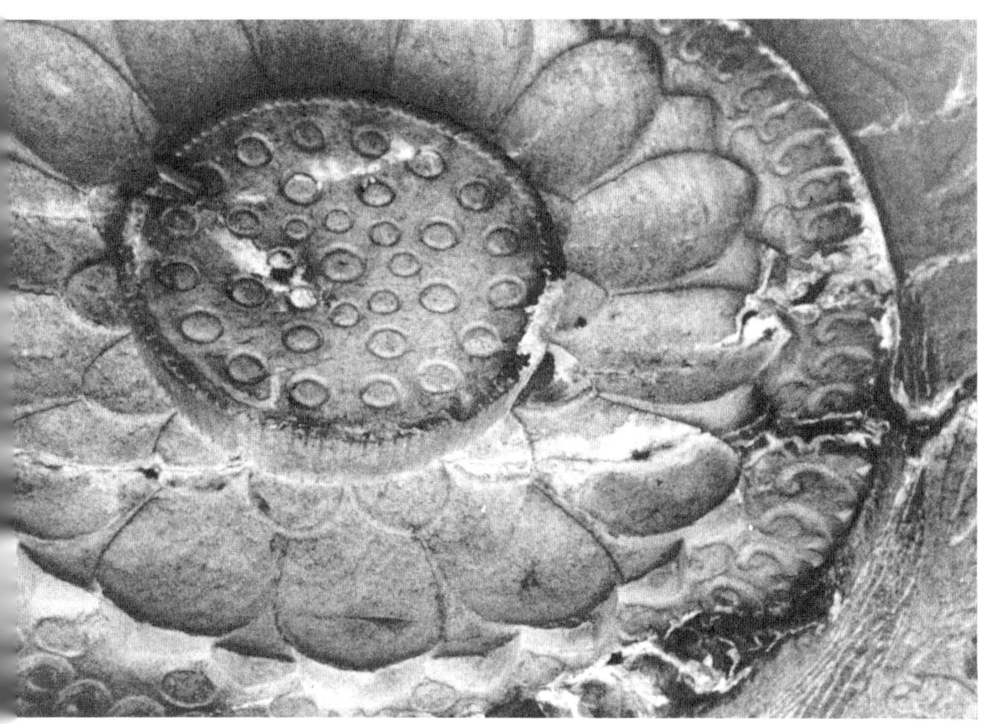

:. 2. Ceiling of the Lotus Flower Cave in Lung-men, Lo-yang, built ca. A.D. 530. Lotus flower
nbolizes purity in Buddhist literature

and currently the Court Architect (*Chiang-tso ta-chiang*)." It was not until[8] the third year of Hsiao-ch'ang (A.D. 527) that a heavy rain damaged the bridge and caused the southern pillars to sink into the water. The [other] two pillars on the northern side of the road, [however], survive even to this day.

[Yang] Hsüan-chih's note: *An Account of Mountains and Rivers, Ancient and Contemporary* 山川古今記[9] by Liu Ch'eng-chih 劉澄之 and *An Account of the Western Expedition* 西征記 by Tai Yen-chih 戴延之[10] both claimed that the bridge was built in the first year of T'ai-k'ang 太康 (Great Peace) (A.D. 280). This is a serious mistake. [Liu] Ch'eng-chih and [Tai] Yen-chih were both[11] born in the Yangtze region and had not traveled in this area.[12] While in military service, they happened to pass through this place. As for the historical events, they were not eyewitnesses. Based on hearsay, [their remarks] were therefore unreliable.[13] For a long time they have misled men of later generations.

In the nunnery was a three-storied stūpa that was not particularly magnificent. To the south of the nunnery was [the site of the] Ever-full Granary (*Ch'ang-man ts'ang* 常滿倉) built during the Western Chin. On order of Emperor Kao-tsu, it was converted into a Tax-Grain Yard[14] where taxes in kind and tributes [collected from every corner] of the nation were stored.

The Lung-hua Temple 龍華寺 (Dragon-flower Temple) founded by *yü-lin* (plumed forest) and *hu-pen* 虎賁 (tiger-rushing) and other palace guards, was situated to the south of the Yang Canal and outside

[8] Literally, *shih* 始.

[9] The full title is *Ssu-chou shan-ch'uan ku-chin chi* 司州山川古今記 (*An Account of Mountains and Rivers, Ancient and Contemporary in Ssu-chou*), 3 *chüan*, by Liu Ch'eng-chih, Minister of Public Works (*Tu-kuan shang-shu*) during the Liu-Sung. (For the function of this office, see *Sung-shu* 39/22a–b 百官志.) See *Sui-shu* (I-wen facsimile ed.) 33/24a 經籍志.

[10] By Tai Tsu 戴祚, styled Yen-chih 延之, 2 *chüan*. See Chang Tsung-yüan, *Sui-shu ching-chi-chih k'ao-cheng* (*Erh-shih-wu-shih pu-pien* ed.) 6/37–44. The title given by the *Sui-shu* (33/24a) is *Sung[-Wu] pei-cheng-chi* 宋[武]北征記 (*An Account of the Northern Expedition by Emperor [Wu] of the* [*Liu-*]*Sung*), 1 *chüan*.

[11] Literally, *teng* 等.

[12] Literally, *chung-t'u* 中土, the Central Land (the Yellow River valley).

[13] Literally, *ch'uan-tso* 穿鑿, "to bore and chisel," that is, illogical or unreasonable.

[14] Literally, *tsu-ch'ang* 租場, Tax-Grain Yard.

the Chien-ch'un Gate. To the south of the temple was the Tax-Grain Yard. To the south of the Yang Canal was the Chien-yang Ward 建陽里 (Welcoming the Sunlight Ward) within[15] which was a mound of [earth]. It rose thirty Chinese feet above the ground, on the top of which were two Buddhist retreats for meditation or study.

> According to Chao I, the mound was the site where the Flag Pavilion (*Ch'i-t'ing* 旗亭)[16] of the Western Chin stood. The pavilion supported a two-storied structure from which a drum was suspended. Someone would strike the drum to mark the end of market [hours].

There was also a bell, which, when struck, could be heard even fifty *li* away. Because it was audible at such a distance, the empress dowager had it moved into the palace and installed in front of the Ning-hsien Hall 凝閑堂 (Hall of Vigilant Leisure).[17] The bell was struck to keep time for those monks lecturing on Buddhist teachings[18] inside [the palace]. In the early years of the Hsiao-ch'ang[19] period, [Hsiao] Tsung 蕭綜, Prince of Yü-chang 豫章王 and son of Hsiao Yen, came over and surrendered (A.D. 525). Impressed by the unusual sound of this bell, he composed three songs entitled "Listening to the Bell"[20] that are presently in circulation.[21]

[15] Adding *nei* 內 after *YHNC* 3/9a.

[16] It occupied a high point of the city, where officials were stationed to regulate business activities. See *WH* 2/8b 張衡西京賦：旗亭五重, 俯察百隧, "Flag Pavilion stood five stories high, overlooking one hundred roads below." Hsüeh Tsung's 薛綜 commentary: 旗亭, 市樓也.

[17] A reference to the life of Confucius, who constantly warned himself against luxurious living and reminded everyone of the ever-present danger even when no danger was visible. See *Li-chi* 51/1a ff. 孔子閒居.

[18] The text (2/2a) gives *chiang nei tien* 講內典. Here the translation follows *IS* 2/1b.

[19] Adding *Hsiao-ch'ang* 孝昌 after *IS* 2/1b.

[20] Adding *chung* 鍾 after *CT* 2/2a.

[21] *Liang-shu* (I-wen facsimile ed.), 55/2b–3a has a complete record of this group of three poems, which reads as follows:

1.

Listening to the ringing bell,
I know the sound comes from the capital city.
Hard to count, since it is struck without rhythm,
But hundreds of worries spring up after so many hardships.
Departing sounds linger with elegance,
An echoing toll whirls in great haste.
Who pities the time keepers

[Hsiao] Tsung, styled Shih-ch'ien 世謙,[22] was the son born to [Hsiao] Pao-chüan 蕭寶卷, the despot of the Ch'i [dynasty] after his death. [Hsiao] Pao-chüan's rule was licentious and catastrophic, which the people in the Wu[23] region found most oppressive. Hsiao Yen, Governor of Yung-chou 雍州,[24] who had enthroned Hsiao Pao-jung 蕭寶融, Prince of Nan-k'ang 南康王, raised an army to march toward Mo-ling 秣陵 [the capital of the Southern Ch'i dynasty]. After the successful campaign, [Hsiao Yen] then murdered [Hsiao] Pao-jung and proclaimed himself the new emperor.[25] Wu Ching-hui 吳景暉, a consort[26] of [Hsiao] Pao-

---

Working so hard at the Chien-chang (To Establish Grandeur) Terrace
建章臺?*

*A major palace built in 104 B.C. after a fire had destroyed the Po-liang (Cypress-beamed) Terrace 柏梁臺.

2.

Listening to the ringing bell,
Listening at many places.
Throwing away such precious stones as *chin* 瑾 and *yü* 瑜 which have been in my possession,
No helping hand for my attempts at ascension.**
Old friends and loves are all scattered, east and west,
Just as fallen leaves are no longer together.
Wild goose, drifting and lonely, where will it perch?
Crane, parting with passion, cries at midnight!

**Literally, to climb up the pine tree and to break cassia branches—to climb up high.

3.

Listening to the ringing bell,
Where is the end of my sorrow?
For more than twenty years,
I have been living aimlessly in the capital.
Looking into the bright mirror:
A sallow countenance.
In vain, I try to suppress
[My sorrows] as thick as the clouds, and
[My thoughts] as vast as an ocean.

[22] *IS* (2.2a) gives his name as *Tsan* 讚, which is in error. The translation follows the *Liang-shu* (55/1a), which reads *Shih-ch'ien* 世謙.

[23] That is, people under his control.

[24] Modern Hsiang-yang 襄陽, Hupeh.

[25] In A.D. 502, Hsiao Pao-jung, then known as Emperor Ho 和帝 of the Ch'i, was murdered by one of Hsiao Yen's confidants. He was then fifteen years *sui*. See *TC* 145/6b–7a.

[26] Literally, *Mei-jen* 美人 "Beauty," one of many titles for palace women.

chüan, who had been pregnant with Hsiao Tsung for several months, had an affair with [Hsiao] Yen. After [Hsiao] Tsung's birth,[27] [Hsiao Yen] then took [the baby] as his own son, renamed him Yüan-chüeh 緣覺 (Enlightened through Reasoning), and ennobled him as the Prince of Yü-chang. [Hsiao] Tsung's manner and appearance bore close resemblance to those of the despot [Hsiao Pao-chüan]. His mother told him the truth [about his origin] and asked him to take any action he saw fit. As a result, [Hsiao] Tsung came to our holy dynasty.[28] He was renamed [Hsiao] Tsuan [蕭]纘,[29] styled Te-wen 德文,[30] [and only until after his surrender to the north was he able to] observe the three-year mourning period for [Hsiao] Pao-chüan. Emperor Ming appointed him Grand Commandant and ennobled him as Prince of Tan-yang 丹陽王. During the Yung-an 永安 period (Permanent Peace) (A.D. 528–530), he was married to Princess Shou-yang 壽陽, styled Chü-li 莒犁, who was Emperor Chuang's elder sister. She was a pretty girl, for whom [Hsiao] Tsung had great respect. In conversation, [Hsiao Tsung] often referred to himself as "your humble servant."[31] He was later promoted[32] to the post of Governor of Ch'i-chou 齊州,[33] with the additional title Palatine Ceremonially Equal to the Three Authorities. When the capital fell into the hands of the rebels (A.D. 530), [Hsiao] Tsung abandoned his provincial post to flee northward.[34] At that time Erh-chu Shih-lung,[35] a man of power at the court, ordered that the princess be escorted to Lo-yang, where he made advances to her. The princess, however, cried out at him, saying, "You barbarian dog! Dare you

[27] He was born seven months after the alleged affair.

[28] Literally *sheng-ch'üeh* 聖闕 "holy tower," that is, the imperial palace.

[29] Emending *Tsan* 讚 to *Tsuan* 纘 after the *Liang-shu* 55/2b.

[30] Emending *Shih-wu* 世務 to *Te-wen* 德文 after the *Liang-shu* 55.2b.

[31] That is, *hsia-kuan* 下官, "subordinate official," a polite term commonly used during the southern dynasties by officials in referring to themselves when addressing their colleagues. See Hsü Shih-ying, "*Shin-shuo hsin-yü* chung ti-i-shen ch'eng-tai-tz'u yen-chiu," *Tan-chiang hsüeh-pao* 2 (1963), 19–21.

[32] The text (2/2b) reads *shou* 授, meaning "appointed as," which is not as precise as the *IS* text (2/2a) *hou ch'u* 後除, "later promoted to." Hence, the translation.

[33] Emending *Hsü* 徐 to *Ch'i* 齊 after *IS* (2/2b) and *WS* (59/20b).

[34] He died soon afterward either of natural causes (*WS* 59/20a) or by execution (*Liang-shu* 55/2b).

[35] Cousin of Erh-chu Jung and Erh-chu Chao, the latter being responsible for the recapture of the capital in A.D. 530. See *WS* 75/1a, 7a.

insult the Heavenly Emperor's daughter?"[36] [Erh-chu] Shih-lung, infuriated, [ordered] her hanged.

The Ying-lu Temple 瓔珞寺 (Necklace Temple) was located inside the Chien-ch'un Gate and to the north of the Imperial Drive. It was in the so-called Chien-yang Ward.

During the Western Chin, the ward was known as the Pai-she 白社 area,[37] where Tung Wei-nien 董威輦[38] lived.

In the ward were ten temples in all: the Ying-lu, Tz'u-shan 慈善 (Temple of the Merciful and Kind), Hui-ho 暉和 (Temple of the Illuminating and Harmonious), T'ung-chüen 通覺 (Temple of Penetrating Enlightenment), Hui-hsüan 暉玄 (Temple of Illuminating the Obscure), Tsung-sheng 宗聖 (Temple of Respect for the Sage), Wei-ch'ang 魏昌 (Temple of Prosperous Wei), Hsi-p'ing 熙平 (Temple of the Prosperous and Peaceful), and Yin-kuo 因果 (Temple of Retribution). A congregation of more than two thousand households (*hu* 戶) lived in the ward, all devoted to Buddhism[39] and serving as provisioners for the temples and monks.[40]

In the Tsung-sheng Temple was an image[41] that was thirty-eight Chinese feet high. Its countenance was unusually grave, and it had all [the thirty-two marks and eighty signs on the body].[42] People held the statue in high esteem and could not take their eyes off it.[43] When-

[36] The monologue is lengthier in *CT* (2/3a), with the following additional couplet: "I would rather be stabbed to death than be despoiled by the rebellious barbarian!"

[37] Emending *ch'ih* 池 to *ti* 地 after *IS* 2/2b.

[38] Emending *pei* 輩 to *nien* 輦 after *IS* 2/2b. Tung Ching 董京, styled Wei-nien 威輦, was a hermit of the Western Chin. He lived as a beggar in Lo-yang. See *Chin-shu* 94/3b–5b; *Pao-p'o-tzu* 抱朴子 (*SPTK so-pen*) *Nei-p'ien* 內篇 15/80 雜應篇.

[39] Literally, *san-pao* 三寶: Triratna or Ratnatraya, "the three jewels or treasures" for taking refuge, include Buddha, Dharma, and sangha. See Fa-yün, *Fan-i ming-i chi* (*SPTK so-pen*) 1/2–3 十種通號 quoting "Fu-t'ien lun-hsü san-pao" 福田論敍三寶：佛也…，法也…，僧也. "They are Buddha . . ., Dharma . . ., and sangha."

[40] Emending *sha-yang* 剎養 to *li-yang* 利養 as given in *IS* 2/2b.

[41] That is, Buddha.

[42] Thirty-two major (*hsiang* 相) and eighty minor (*hao* 好) marks. The Buddha was supposed to have them all. See Ti-p'o-k'o-lo, tr., *Fang-kuang ta Chuang-yen ching* (*Taishō* ed.) 3/557.

[43] Literally, *mu pu chan shun* 目不暫瞬, "without winking, not even for one moment."

ever the statue was on parade, [they would leave their homes or the marketplace to see it, so that] all the homes and marketplaces were virtually empty. The aureole[44] of this statue had no parallel in its time. The skillful games and miscellaneous music performed here were second in excellence only to those in Liu Teng's [Ch'ang-ch'iu Temple]. Men and women living in the eastern section of the city often came to this temple to watch the shows.

Hui-i,[45] a monk of the Ch'ung-chen Monastery, regained life after having been dead for seven days. He was released from [the nether world] by Yama [the God of the Dead] who reviewed his case and found that he had been summoned by mistake in the first place.

Hui-i told [others] what had happened [during the seven-day period]. Five other monks were examined along with him, one among them being Chih-sheng 智聖, a monk of the Pao-ming Temple 寶明寺 (Temple of the Precious and Bright), who was able to ascend to the paradise by practices of meditation[46] and asceticism.[47] Another monk, Tao-p'in 道品 of the Pan-jo Temple 般若寺 (Prajñā Temple) also was able to ascend to the paradise because he had recited the forty-volume Mahāparinirvāṇa sūtra.[48] Another monk, T'an-mo-tsui 曇謨最[49] of the Jung-chüeh Monastery 融覺寺 (Monastery

[44] The translation follows *IS* 2/2b: *yen-kuang hui-ho* 炎光輝赫, "The lights are illuminating and dazzling." The text (2/3a) reads *yen-kuang t'eng-hui ho-ho* 炎光騰輝赫赫, "The lights are soaring, illuminating and extremely dazzling," instead.

[45] The text (2/3b) is Hui-ning 惠凝, but both the *FYCL* (111/1326) and the *Shih-men tzu-ching lu* (*Taishō* ed.; A/811) give Hui-i 慧嶷. The transliteration follows the latter version.

[46] Literally, *tso-ch'an* 坐禪.

[47] Literally, *k'u-hsing* 苦行.

[48] The text (2/3b) reads *ssu-ni-p'an* 四涅槃, but *IS* 2/3a gives *ssu-shih-chüan ni-p'an* 四十卷涅槃. The *Mahāparinirvāṇa sūtra* has two popular editions: the forty-volume version translated into Chinese by Dharmarakṣa (T'an-wu-ch'an 曇無讖) in A.D. 423, generally referred to as the Northern Text (Pei-pen 北本), and the thirty-six volume Southern Text (Nan-pen 南本), the same work translated by Dharmarakṣa, revised in Chien-yeh by Hui-kuan 慧觀 and Hsieh Ling-yün 謝靈運 (A.D. 385–433).

[49] A native of China, he was referred to as "the Buddha of the East" by Bodhiruci (an Indian monk active in Northern Wei in the early sixth century; see Chapter 4 at note 244), and was highly respected by the Wei court around A.D. 520. See *Hsü Kao-seng chuan* 23/624–625 and Chapter 4 at note 244.

of the Harmonious Awakening), had lectured on the Mahāparinirvāṇa and the Avataṁsaka.[50] He was the leader of a group of one thousand persons. Yama said, "Lecturers on Buddhism are inclined to be discriminatory[51] and arrogantly intimidating.[52] This is the most detestable behavior a monk may pursue. Now you should try only to meditate and chant sūtras, paying no attention to lecturing." In reply, T'an-mo-tsui said, "Ever since I became a monk, I have liked lecturing, and indeed I know little about sūtra reciting." Yama then ordered that he be handed over to the proper authority. Immediately ten persons dressed in blue took T'an-mo-tsui toward a gate in the northwest [the direction of death in Taoism], where the rooms were all dark and appeared unpleasant. It did not seem to be a good place.

Another monk who identified himself as Tao-hung 道弘 of the Ch'an-lin Monastery 禪林寺 (Meditation Monastery) said that he, as a fundraiser, gave lectures to all four groups[53] (that is, monks, nuns, male and female disciples) and almsgivers,[54] made [copies] of sūtras, and also duplicated[55] ten life-size images [of Buddha] in gold.[56] Yama said: "To be a monk, one must control his mind and abide by Buddhist teaching, and exert his best in meditating and chanting. He should not be involved in mundane affairs, nor undertake anything that deals with world activities. You made copies of sūtras and duplications of Buddhist images, but your real purpose was to acquire money and things from others. Once you have acquired what you want you will grow greedier, and when you are greedier you will not be free from the three poisons[57] that are sufficient to cause

[50] The popular editions of this sūtra are: 1. the sixty-volume version translated by Buddhabhadra (Fo-t'o-pa-t'o-lo 佛陀跋陀羅) during the Chin; the so-called "Chin sūtra," 2. the eighty-volume edition translated by Śikṣānanda (Shih-ch'a-nan-t'o 實义難陀) about A.D. 700 during the T'ang; the so-called "T'ang sūtra," and 3. the forty-volume edition translated by Prajña around A.D. 810.

[51] Literally, *hsin huai pi wo* 心懷彼我. For the Buddhist, to have the dualistic distinction between one's self and others is bad enough.

[52] Literally, *i chiao ling wu* 以驕凌物, to bully others through arrogance.

[53] Literally, *ssu pei* 四輩, "four groups," that is, the *bhikṣu*, *bhikṣuṇī*, *upāsaka*, and *upāsikā*.

[54] That is, *t'an-yüeh* 檀越, *dānapati*.

[55] The text (2/4a) is *tsao* 造, to make.

[56] Adding *chin* 金 after the *FYCL* 111/1327.

[57] *San tu* 三毒, "three poisons" that is, concupiscence, anger, and stupidity (or greed, hate, and delusion). See Kumārajīva (Chiu-mo-lo-shih), tr., *Ta chih-tu lun* (*Taishō* ed.) 31/286: 釋初品中十八空義：有利益我者貪欲,,違逆我者生瞋恚,

distress." He too was then entrusted to the authority who took him into the black gate in the company of T'an-mo-tsui.

Still another monk, who called himself Pao-chen 寶眞 of the Ling-chüeh Monastery 靈覺寺 (Monastery of Spiritual Awakening) said of himself that he had been the Grand Warden of Lung-hsi 隴西 before leaving home to become a monk. As the Grand Warden, he financed the construction of the Ling-chüeh Monastery, and, upon its completion, he abandoned his official post and became a monk. Although he did not meditate or chant sūtras, he had never been negligent in religious worship. Yama said: "As Grand Warden, you impaired justice, twisted the law, and robbed people's properties. Even if you claim to have built the temple, it is not due to your efforts [because the expenses are from others]. So it is senseless for you to talk about it!" Entrusted to the official in charge, he too was led into the black gate by a person dressed in blue.

Upon hearing of this, the empress dowager sent Hsü Ho, Attending Secretary within the Imperial Yellow Gate, to proceed immediately to the Pao-ming and [other][58] monasteries as Hui-i had said. In the Pan-jo Temple within the city limits, and in the three monasteries [known respectively as] the Jung-chüeh, Ch'an-lin, and Ling-chüeh in the western part of the city, there were indeed such monks as Chih-sheng, Tao-p'in, T'an-mo-tsui, Tao-hung, and Pao-chen [who regained life seven days after their death and whose career during their lifetime verified what Hui-i had said].[59]

The court then resolved: "After death someone may be found guilty, while others may enjoy blessings." Thereupon, one hundred meditating monks were invited to stay inside the palace where they were cared for at public expense. An imperial rescript was issued to prohibit monks from begging [for food and money] on the street while holding Buddhist images and sūtras in hand. Those who used their own money to reproduce sūtras or duplicate images, however,

---

此結使不從智生，從狂惑生故，是名爲癡，三毒爲一切煩惱之根本，悉由吾我. "One is greedy for what benefits him. One hates what stands against him. The root of the trouble does not rise from intelligence; it rises from bewilderment known as delusion. These three poisons are the roots of all perplexities that originate from oneself."

[58] Adding *teng* 等 "others" after *TPKC* 99/2b 釋證部惠凝.

[59] Adding two sentences 死來七日，生時業行如疑所論不差 after *FYCL* 111/1327.

were free to do so. Hui-i, for his part, entered the Pai-lu Mountain 白鹿山 (White Deer Mountain),[60] where he lived in seclusion to practice Buddhism. Thereupon, monks in the capital were [more] devoted to meditating and chanting sūtras than lecturing on them.

More than one *li* beyond[61] the Chien-ch'un Gate is the Tung-shih Bridge 東石橋 (East Stone Bridge). Running from the south to the north, the bridge was built in the first year of T'ai-k'ang of the Chin (A.D. 280). To the south of the bridge was the Horse Market of the Wei,[62] where Hsi K'ang 嵇康 (A.D. 223–262) was executed.[63]

To the north of the bridge was a main street, on the west side of which was the Chien-yang Ward.

On the east side of the main street was the Sui-min Ward 綏民里 (Ward for Comfort of People), which housed the [former] residence of Liu Hsüan-ming 劉宣明, a native of Ho-chien 河間.[64] [Liu] Hsüan-ming was executed in the capital during the Shen-kuei 神龜 period (Sacred Tortoise) (A.D. 518–520) following his submission of a memorial critical of the court. The empress was infuriated and ordered that he be beheaded in the marketplace of the capital. After this was done, his eyes remained open, and his corpse walked one hundred paces. [In private] conversations, his contemporaries deemed him a victim of false accusations.[65] As a youth, [Liu] Hsüan-ming was [already] renowned for his mastery of the classics, but his imprudent conduct led him to his execution.

[60] Northwest of modern Wei-hsien 衞縣, Honan. The mountain resembles a deer; hence the name. See *T'ai-p'ing huan-yü chi* (Wen-hai facsimile of 1803 ed.; Taipei, 1963) 56/8b: 衞州共城縣白鹿山 quoting Lu Ssu-tao's 盧思道 *Hsi-cheng chi* 西征記.

[61] Deleting *nan* 南 after *IS* 2/4a.

[62] To the east of the Chien-ch'un Gate and south of the Yang Canal was the Horse Market, one of the three major markets (the other two were the Sheep Market and the Gold Market) during the Wei-Chin period. See *SCC* 16/15a 穀水注.

[63] Hsi K'ang (A.D. 223–262), one of the "Seven Sages of the Bamboo Grove," was condemned to death by the usurping Ssu-ma family for Hsi K'ang's loyalty to the doomed Wei dynasty. For his biography, see *Chin-shu* 49/16a–26a.

[64] Ho-chien was a subdivision of Ying-chou.

[65] Liu Hsüan-ming was an associate of Yang Yü 楊昱, member of a famous family known for its loyalty to the Wei (*WS* 58/14a–17b). According to an official record (*WS* 9/9b), Liu Hsüan-ming was executed in the ninth month of A.D. 519, for treason discovered in the planning stage. In all probability this was a fabricated charge, from which he was at least partially exonerated here.

The Wei-ch'ang[66] Nunnery 魏昌尼寺 (Nunnery of the Prosperous Wei) was established by the eunuch Li Tz'u-shou 李次壽, Governor of Ying-chou 瀛州.[67] It was in the southeastern corner of the ward, occupying the same site as the Cattle-Horse Market 牛馬市 of the Western Chin.

> The place where Hsi K'ang was executed was located east of the Stone Bridge.[68] Running from the south to the north, the bridge was built in the first year of the T'ai-k'ang period (A.D. 280). It was located to the south of the market under the four reigns of the Western Chin. On the strength of an inscription, which Liu Ch'eng-chih and others might have seen, they thought that the bridge was built in the early T'ai-k'ang years.[69]

On the road to the south of the Stone Bridge was the Ching-hsing Nunnery 景興尼寺 (Flourishing Prospect Nunnery),[70] which was also built by a group of eunuchs as a joint enterprise. There was a gold carriage with an image, which was thirty[71] Chinese feet off the ground. A jeweled canopy was hung above the carriage, from which were suspended gold bells, beads made out of seven varieties of precious materials,[72] and images of Buddhist musicians and entertainers who appeared high up in the clouds.[73] The craftsmanship

[66] The translation follows the *CS* (2/79) in placing the Wei-ch'ang Nunnery under a new paragraph. The *Ch'ung-k'an* (2/14a), on the other hand, treats the Wei-ch'ang entry as part of the foregoing passage.

[67] Li Tz'u-shou, also known as Chien 堅, was a native of Kao-yang. He had been a Court Secretary, Supervisor of the Court of Imperial Stud (*T'ai-p'u-ssu ch'ing*), and Governor of Ying-chou. He was also given the title Earl of Wei-ch'ang 魏昌伯, after which the nunnery was named. For his biography, see *WS* 94/15b.

Ying-chou was created in A.D. 487 (modern Ho-chien, Hopei). See *WS* 106A/13a 地形志.

[68] This passage is repetitious.

[69] *SCC* (16/15a) makes no mention of any inscription, but Yang Hsüan-chih theorized that there might have been one that Liu Ch'eng-chih might have seen.

[70] The *Ch'ung-k'an* (2/14a) includes the nunnery in the preceding passage. The translation follows the *CS* (2/79) and *CC* (2.88) arrangement instead.

[71] Given as *ch'ih* 尺 "one Chinese foot" in a variety of editions. The translation follows the *YLTT* (13823/1b) in emending *ch'ih* 尺 to *chang* 丈, "ten Chinese feet."

[72] That is, gold, silver, glazed material, glass, coral, agate, and sea shells.

[73] The text (2/5b) reads *fei t'ien chi yüeh* 飛天伎樂, "flying musical entertainers in the sky," which, according to the *CS* (2/79), has the same meaning as *chu t'ien shih ts'ung* 諸天侍從, "attendants of heavenly gods." The *CS* assertion is based on a

was so superb it was hard to describe.[74] When the [carriage-held] image was on parade, the emperor as a rule would order one hundred *yü-lin* guards to carry it, with the accompanying music and variety shows all provided for by the court.

To the east of the Chien-yang Ward was the Sui-min Ward, within which, on the bank of the Yang Canal, was Lo-yang City. Outside the city gate was a stone monument dedicated to Yang Chi 楊機,[75] Metropolitan Prefect of Lo-yang (Lo-yang *ling* 洛陽令), in recognition of his exemplary virtues.[76] To the east of the Sui-min Ward was the Ch'ung-i Ward 崇義里 (Ward of Reverence for Righteousness), where the residence of Tu Tzu-hsiu 杜子休, a native of Ching-chao 京兆, was located.[77]

[His residence] faced the Imperial Drive and was spacious and enjoyed an inspiring location. Chao I, a hermit of this time, claimed to be a man [born under the reign of] Emperor Wu (regnant A.D. 265–290) of the Chin. He kept a record of past events that had occurred during the Chin. After his arrival in the capital in early Cheng-kuang period, and after he had seen [Tu] Tzu-hsiu's residence, he said with a sigh: "This residence was the [former] T'ai-k'ang Temple 太康寺 of the Western Chin." Not convinced, his contemporaries then asked him about the history of the temple. [Chao] I

---

similar description of an image-carriage as recorded in the *Kao-seng Fa-hsien chuan* (*Taishō* ed.), p. 851. *T'ien* 天, "heaven," is often translated as *devas*.

[74] Literally, *yang-ch'üeh* 揚推, which originally means "to give a general outline" but now has the meaning "to discuss or to describe." For its origin, see *WH* 4/9a 左思蜀都賦：請爲左右揚推而陳之, "Allow me to discuss and describe them for you." Li Shan's commentary: 揚推, 粗略也 "*Yang ch'üeh* means a sketchy outline."

[75] Yang Chi, styled Hsien-lüeh 顯略, a native of Chi-hsien 冀縣, T'ien-shui 天水, was known for his morality as a youth. He had been acting magistrate of Ho-yin, Senior Administrator in the Office of the General Quelling the West (*P'ing-hsi-fu chang-shih*), before his transfer to the Lo-yang post. In the capital he won respect for his firmness. In the Yung-hsi years he was General of the Guards (*Wei chiang-chün*), Palace Grandee on the Right (*Yu kuang-lu ta-fu*) before his promotion to the position of Minister of Finance (*Tu-chih shang-shu*). Unselfish and impoverished, he could not afford a horse for transportation, but had to rely on a calf-drawn cart. He was thus highly respected for his honesty. Because of his loyalty to the doomed Northern Wei, in A.D. 533 he was executed by the usurper Kao Huan. See *WS* 77/18b–19a.

[76] Literally, *ch'ing-te* 淸德, "pure virtue." Here the term refers to Yang Chi's steadfast virtue in dealing with his powerful colleagues.

[77] The *CC* (2/88) treats the following passage as part of the main text, but I follow the *CS* (2/80) to make this a footnote. No further information about Tu Tzu-hsiu is available.

said: "Wang Chün 王濬, the Dragon-soaring General (*Lung-hsiang chiang-chun*) had this temple built after his conquest of the Wu.[78] Originally it had a three-storied stūpa, which was made of bricks." [Chao I] pointed to [Tu] Tzu-hsiu's garden and said: "This is the site where the stūpa stood." [Tu] Tzu-hsiu dug up the earth in order to verify [his statement], and indeed he found several tens of thousands (*wan*)[79] of bricks. On the eighth day (*hsin-ssu* 辛巳) of the ninth month which began with the *chia-hsü* 甲戌[80] day, [he discovered] at the same place a stone inscription that reads: "In the sixth year of the T'ai-k'ang period of the Chin, which falls in the year-cycle *I-ssu* 乙巳, respectfully built by Wang Chün, Marquis of Hsiang-yang 襄陽侯, Palatine Ceremonially Equal to the Three Authorities."

[At first people could not believe Chao I's statement,] for at the same time, in the garden, fruit [trees] and vegetables were abundant and luxuriant, and the woods were dense. [But with the discovery of bricks underground,] people were convinced by what Chao I had said and therefore referred to him as a sage. [Tu] Tzu-hsiu, for his part, donated his residence and converted it into the Ling-ying Temple 靈應寺 (Temple of Miraculous Response). The bricks that he acquired were used in the restoration of the three-storied stūpa.

Out of curiosity, someone then pressed him,[81] asking how he would measure the Chin capital[82] against the present one.[83] [Chao I] said: "The Chin [capital] was less populous than the capital is today, but residences of princes and dukes were much like those of today." Again he remarked: "From the Yung-chia period to the present,

[78] The campaign was concluded in A.D. 280. In recognition of his accomplishments, Wang Chün was promoted to Generalissimo Aiding the State (*Fu-kuo ta-chiang-chün*) and ennobled as Marquis of Hsiang-yang 襄陽侯. He was given the additional honor of Palatine Ceremonially Equal to the Three Authorities. He died in A.D. 285. See *Chin-shu* 42/9b–23b.

[79] Emending *shu-shih-wan* 數十萬 (*wan* is the equivalent of ten thousand) to *shu-wan* 數萬 after the *TPYL* 658/6b 釋部寺 and *TPKC* 81/22b 異人類趙逸. A three-storied stūpa would not need "several hundred thousand" bricks.

[80] According to Ch'en Yüan's 陳垣 authoritative concordance, the eighth day of the ninth month of A.D. 285 should be *kuei-hai* 癸亥, and the first day of the same month, *ping-ch'en* 丙辰 (rather than *chia-hsü* 甲戌). Accordingly, the eighth day should be October twenty-third in the Gregorian calendar. See Ch'en Yüan, *Erh-shih-shih shuo-jun piao* (I-wen facsimile ed.), p. 50.

[81] Emending *hsün chu-chih* 尋逐之, "then pressed him" to *hsün chu-wen* 尋逐問, "then pressed him with questions" after the *IS* 2/5b.

[82] *IS* (2/5b) reads *ching min* 京民, "people in the capital."

[83] Literally, *hu-jo chin-jih* 何如今日, "how did it compare with today."

during a span of more than two hundred years, there have been sixteen[84] sovereigns who called themselves kings and who [each] founded [their own] dynasties. I visited their capitals and witnessed the things that occurred there. After the downfall of each dynasty, none of the historical works that I read was truthful: they all laid blame on others while claiming credit for themselves. Although Fu Sheng 符(苻)生[85] was bellicose and fond of drink, he was nonetheless humane and not murderous. When one looked at his administration, he was by no means cruel and violent. Yet when one carefully examined the [official] records, [one found that] all evils from every corner of the nation were attributed to him. Fu Chien[86] was on account of this [presented as] as enlightened ruler, but he murdered and replaced his own ruler, and falsely wrote down slander about the latter. In general, all court historians behaved like that. Men are inclined to hold the past in high esteem, but view the present with contempt.[87] Among contemporaries, the living are deemed stupid but the deceased wise. It is indeed very puzzling."

Asked why, [Chao] I said: "In a stele inscription or an epitaph on a

[84] That is:

Name	*Founded by*	*Regnant*
Former Chao 前趙	Liu Yüan 劉淵	A.D. 304–310
Later Chao 後趙	Shih Lo 石勒	A.D. 319–333
Former Yen 前燕	Mu-jung Chün 慕容儁	A.D. 348–360
Former Ch'in 前秦	Fu Chien 苻健	A.D. 351–355
Later Ch'in 後秦	Yao Ch'ang 姚萇	A.D. 384–394
Shu 蜀	Li Hsiung 李雄	A.D. 304–334
Later Liang 後涼	Lü Kuang 呂光	A.D. 386–400
Later Yen 後燕	Mu-jung Ch'ui 慕容垂	A.D. 384–396
Western Ch'in 西秦	Ch'i-fu Kuo-jen 乞伏國仁	A.D. 385–388
Northern Yen 北燕	Feng Pa 馮跋	A.D. 409–431
Southern Liang 南涼	T'u-fa Wu-ku 禿髮烏孤	A.D. 397–399
Southern Yen 南燕	Mu-jung Te 慕容德	A.D. 400–404
Northern Liang 北涼	Chü-ch'ü Meng-sun 沮渠蒙遜	A.D. 401–433
Hsia 夏	Ho-lien Po-po 赫連勃勃	A.D. 407–425
Former Liang 前涼	Chang Kuei 張軌	(fl.. A.D. 301–314)
Western Liang 西涼	Li Sung 李嵩	A.D. 400–420

[85] Reigned A.D. 355–357. He was dethroned and murdered by Fu Chien 苻堅.

[86] Fu Chien (A.D. 338–386) reigned (A.D. 357–386) as the third emperor of the Former Ch'in. For more information about him, see the *Chin-shu* 113/1a–31a, 114/1a–33b.

[87] A reference to Ts'ao P'ei's 曹丕 essay (*WH* 52/5a 典論論文): 常人貴遠賤近, 向聲背實. "All men attach great value to what is remote but belittle what is nearby; they look up to the superficial but turn away from the substantial."

grave for a man who was merely mediocre when alive, he is described as one who had in himself all the great virtues in heaven and on earth, and accomplished the best that any person might have hoped. If a ruler, he is a match for [such legendary ancient] emperors as Yao (trad. d. 2258 B.C.) and Shun (trad. 2317–2208 B.C.); as a minister, he is an equal of I[-yin] (18th cent. B.C.) of the Shang 商 (trad. 1765–1123 B.C.) dynasty and Kao[-yao] 皐[陶] (trad. d. 2204 B.C.) [who served as supreme judge under Emperor Yü 禹 (trad. d. 2197 B.C.)]. As a civic official, [even] tigers, out of respect for his benevolent rule, would cross the river and run away;[88] as a law-enforcement officer, [even] the one who buried his carriage wheels could not compare with his uprightness.[89] This is what we call being equated with the robber Chih 跖[90] when living, but [Po-]i [伯]夷 or Shu[-ch'i] 叔[齊][91] when dead. Dishonest language is harmful to justice, while florid praise beclouds the truth."

Prose writers who heard [Chao] I's remarks were ashamed of themselves.

Li Ch'eng 李澄,[92] Commandant of Infantry (*Pu-ping chiao-wei*), asked: "The shape and structure of the brick stūpa in front of the Office of the Grand Commandant looks very old but remains intact. May I know when was it built?"

[Chao] I replied: "It was built in the twelfth year of the I-hsi 義熙

[88] A reference to Liu K'un 劉昆 of the Later Han, whose benevolent rule as the Grand Warden of Hung-nung 弘農 for three years had been so effective that tigers within his area, with cubs on their backs, crossed the river and ran away. Before his time, however, the tigers had played havoc with travelers along the post roads under his jurisdiction. See *HHS* 109/3b–5a.

[89] In A.D. 142 Chang Kang 張綱 was one of the eight censors appointed by the emperor to investigate conditions of local government. He was the youngest in this group. Although all others took their orders and left for their assigned areas, Chang Kang buried his chariot wheels in a Lo-yang depot and said: "While the [ravenous] wolves stand in our way, what is the use of investigating the [less vicious] foxes?" Accordingly, he submitted a memorial charging Liang Chi 梁冀, generalissimo at the time, with fifteen crimes. See *HHS* 86/2b–6a.

[90] A legendary robber in the state of Lu 魯 during the Ch'un-ch'iu period (722–481 B.C.) who killed innocent people every day and ate their liver and flesh. See *Chuang-tzu* 9/207 盗跖.

[91] Two worthies of the twelfth century B.C. who refused to join the Chou after the downfall of the Shang. They fled into mountains, refrained from eating grain grown under the new regime, and finally died of starvation. They symbolize the loyal and incorruptible official. See *SC* 61/7–17.

[92] No detailed information about him is available.

period (Righteous and Joyful) (A.D. 416) of the Chin by soldiers [who followed] Liu Yü's 劉裕 expedition against Yao Hung 姚泓."[93]

Marveling at his remarks, [Yüan Yüeh], Prince of Ju-nan, took[94] him as an adopted father. Subsequently [the prince] asked him what kind of food or drug he took to secure longevity. [Chao] I said: "I am not familiar with the ways of "sustaining life," but I am naturally long-lived. According to a prophecy Kuo P'u 郭璞 (A.D. 276–324)[95] cast for me, I have a life span of five hundred years. Now I have only passed the half-way mark."

The emperor gave him a vehicle drawn manually.[96] He rode in it across the city, and whatever he passed, he remembered most of its history. Three years later he secretly left [the city], leaving everyone in the dark as to his whereabouts.

To the east of the Ch'ung-i[97] Ward was the Seven-*li* Bridge 七里橋 made of stone. During the Western Chin, Tu Yü stayed here overnight before setting out for Ching-chou 荊州 (A.D. 280).[98]

At a point one *li* from the Seven-*li* Bridge, the city wall had three openings, known as the Three Gates 三門 to contemporaries.

[93] In the eighth month (September–October) of A.D. 416 Liu Yü, founder of the Liu-Sung dynasty (A.D. 420–479), led an army to attack the Later Ch'in (A.D. 384–417) then ruled by Yao Hung. Two months later, Liu Yü captured Lo-yang. See *Chin-shu* 10/20b; *Sung-shu* 2/10b.

[94] Literally, *pan* 拜.

[95] Kuo P'u, a famous occultist and scholar, is best remembered for his commentaries for the *Mu-t'ien-tzu chuan* 穆天子傳, *Shan-hai ching* 山海經, *Erh-ya* 爾雅, and *Ch'u-tz'u*. He was executed in A.D. 324 by the rebel general Wang Tun 王敦 (A.D. 266–324), who was infuriated by Kuo P'u's unfavorable prognostication. See *Chin-shu* 72/1a–16b.

[96] That is, *pu-wan* 步挽 (same as *wan* 輓) *chü* 車. *TC* 112/3a [涼王呂]纂醉乘步輓車, "[The King of Liang Lü] Tsuan took a ride in *pu-wan-chü* while intoxicated." Hu San-hsing's comm.: 步輓車不用牛馬若羊等, 令人步而輓之, "*Pu-wan-chü* did not use such animals as cattle, horses, or sheep, but was drawn by human beings while stepping forward."

[97] Emending *i* 儀 to *i* 義 after *YHNC* 3/9b.

[98] A farewell party in Tu Yü's honor prior to his successful campaign against the Kingdom of Wu in A.D. 280 was held here. See *Shih-shuo hsin-yü* (I-wen facsimile ed.) B/6b–7a; Mather, *New Account*, pp. 155–156. See also the *Chin-shu* 3/29b.

Tu Yü was a renowned general responsible for the conquest of the Kingdom of Wu. He was also an authority on the *Tso Commentary*, which still carries his name as the most distinguished commentator. See the *Chin-shu* 34/18a–29a.

Those who were to participate in farewell gatherings would often say: "I'll send you off outside the Three Gates." As a rule, men of letters in the capital often came here [to attend] farewell or welcome [gatherings].

The Chuang-yen Temple 莊嚴寺 (Temple of the Adornments) was located on the north side of the Imperial Drive, one *li* outside the Tung-yang Gate, in the so-called Tung-an Ward 東安里 (Ward of Eastern Peace). To the north [of the temple] was the Tax-Grain Yard. In the ward were the four residences each of Ssu-ma Yüeh 司馬悅,[99] the Commandant of Attending Cavalry (*Fu-ma tu-wei*); Tiao Hsüan 刁宣,[100] Governor of Chi-chou 濟州; Li Chen-nu 李眞奴,[101] Governor of Yu-chou 幽州; and Kung-sun Hsiang 公孫驤, Governor of Yü-chou 豫州.[102]

The Ch'in[103] T'ai-shang-chün Monastery 秦太上君寺 (Monastery of the Grand Duchess of Ch'in) was established by order of Dowager Empress Hu.[104]

At the time, Empress Dowager [Hu] was given the official title

[99] Emending *huang* 恍 to *yüeh* 悅 after *YHNC* 3/9b.

Ssu-ma Yüeh was the grandson of Ssu-ma Ch'u-chih 司馬楚之, who deserted the Liu-Sung to the Northern Wei. See *WS* 37/6a–7b. The title Commandant of Attending Cavalry was reserved for the husband of a princess, but his biography makes no mention of such a marriage. [Ssu-ma] Yüeh's son Fei 朏, however, was married to the younger sister of Emperor Shih-tsung. See *WS* 37/7b.

[100] Emending *fen* 分 to *Tiao* 刁 after *YHNC* 3/9b. Tiao Hsüan was defeated by, and subsequently surrendered to, Ch'en Ch'ing-chih following the latter's victorious entry into Lo-yang (A.D. 529). He was married to the younger sister of Yüan Lüeh 元略, Prince of Tung-p'ing 東平王. See *Liang-shu* 32/4a; *WS* 38/7b.

[101] The name of Li Hsin 李訢 as a youth. He was a native of Fan-yang who had been governor of Hsiang-chou and Hsü-chou. See *WS* 46/4b–8b.

YHNC (3/9b) mistakenly gives *Chih-nü* 直奴 for *Chen-nü* 眞奴.

[102] *YHNC* (3/9b) gives *jang* 讓 for *hsiang* 驤. No detailed information about him is available.

[103] Hu Kuo-chen had been acting governor of Yung-chou 雍州, which lay in a general area known as Ch'in. Hence, he was ennobled as the Duke of Ch'in.

[104] The following passage (thirty-two characters in all) appears in the middle of the next paragraph. Designed as an explanation of the Empress Dowager Hu's motive in deciding to build this monastery, this paragraph should be moved up. *Chi-cheng* (24b) and *CS* (2/84) are in agreement with this arrangement.

Ch'ung-k'an treats this passage as part of the main text.

Ch'ung-hsün(-mu)[105] 崇訓(母), [meaning that she was] setting a motherly model[106] for the whole nation to follow. Her father was honored as the Grand Duke of the Ch'in (Ch'in T'ai-shang-kung 秦太上公),[107] and her mother, as the Grand Duchess of the Ch'in (Ch'in T'ai-shang-chün 秦太上君). The monastery was built as a means by which posthumous blessings could be offered to the empress dowager's mother;[108] hence the name.

[This monastery] was located on the north side of the Imperial Drive, two *li* outside[109] the Tung-yang Gate, within the so-called Hui-wen Ward 暉文里 (Ward of Resplendent Culture).

Inside the ward were the four residences of Ts'ui Kuang 崔光,[110] the Grand Guardian (*T'ai-pao*); Li Yen-shih 李延寔,[111] the Grand Tutor; Li Shao 李韶,[112] Governor of the Chi-chou 冀州; and Cheng

[105] The text (2/8b) has an additional character *mu* 母, which is an obvious interpolation.

In A.D. 394, Lady Li of the Chin, Emperor Hsiao-wu's 孝武帝 mother, was honored as the empress dowager and her palace was known as Ch'ung-hsün (*Chin-shu* 9/24b). The Wei followed this precedent and used the same name, Ch'ung-hsün, for the empress dowager. In fact, Ch'ung-hsün appears in another source as part of her official title. See *MCCS* plate 40.2 魏故胡昭儀墓誌銘.

[106] Adding *i* 儀 after the *CT* 2/9b.

[107] Chang P'u-hui 張普惠, an authority on ancient rituals, argued in a lengthy memorial that there had never been such titles conferred on any empress's father in the past, but his objection was brushed aside by a reviewing board. See *WS* 78/9b–11b.

[108] She died in A.D. 502, sixteen years before her husband's death (May 7, 518 A.D.). See *WS* 83B/5b–6b. A separate temple was built in his honor. See Chapter 3 below.

[109] Adding *wai* 外 after *YHNC* 3/9b.

[110] Ts'ui Kuang was a native of Eastern Ch'ing-ho 東清河 (east of modern Shang-hsien 商縣, Honan) and a member of the famous Ts'ui clan of Po-ling 博陵 (east of modern Po-yeh 博野, Hopei). He had been an Erudite of the Central Secretariat (*Chung-shu po-shih*), Archivist (*Chu-tso lang*), Chief Palace Attendant, and Minister of Public Instruction, and finally the Grand Guardian (A.D. 522). He was a leading supporter of Buddhism. For his biography, see *WS* 67/1a–14b.

[111] The text (2/8b) gives 寔 instead of 實; 實 is as given in his biography (*WS* 83B/8b–9a). A native of Lung-hsi 隴西 (modern Lin-t'ao 臨洮, Kansu) Li Yen-shih was the eldest son of Li Ch'ung 李沖, Vice President, Department of State Affairs (*Shang-shu p'u-yeh* 尚書僕射). He was appointed as the Grand Tutor after Emperor Chuang's ascension.

[112] Emending *Chao* 詔 to *Shao* 韶 after *YHNC* 3/9b. The eldest son of Li Pao 李寶, Li Shao had been Governor of Yen-chou and Chi-chou. See *WS* 39/2a–3b.

Tao-chao 鄭道昭,[113] the Supervisor of Archives (*Mi-shu chien*). All [residences had] numerous elevated halls rising abruptly [with] lofty, cavernous openings of high gates.

According to Chao I, the Hui-wen Ward was formerly the Ma-tao Ward 馬道里 (Horse-path Ward) of the Chin, and [Li] Yen-shih's residence was formerly that of Liu Shan 劉禪 (regnant A.D. 223–263), ruler of the Kingdom of the Shu. To the east of [Li] Yen-shih's residence was that of Hsiu-ho 修和,[114] which formerly belonged to the ruler[115] of the Kingdom of the Wu, Sun Hao 孫皓 (regnant A.D. 264–280). Li Shao's residence was formerly that of Chang Hua 張華 (A.D. 232–300), the Grand Minister of Public Works of the Chin.[116]

In the monastery was a five-storied stūpa, with a tall steeple piercing the clouds and a high gate facing the street. [The excellence of] the sumptuous Buddhist decorations matched that of the Yung-ning Monastery. Chanting rooms and meditation halls were laid out one after another. Flowers, shrubs, and aromatic plants were luxuriant everywhere, filling in the stairways. Always [there were] monks of great virtue and fame lecturing here on the canon.

Those śramaṇa disciples who came to study [also] numbered more than one thousand.

Li Yen-shih, the Grand Tutor, was Emperor Chuang's maternal uncle.[117] During the Yung-an period (A.D. 528–530),[118] he was appointed Governor of Ch'ing-chou. Shortly before setting out

[113] Cheng Tao-chao, son of Cheng Hsi 鄭羲, was a native of Yung-yang 滎陽 (southeast of modern Yung-tse 滎澤, Ho-nan), where the Cheng clan had been particularly influential. He served as an archivist before his transfer to the position of Supervisor of Archives. He died in A.D. 516. See *WS* 56/3b–6b.

[114] No further information is available for this man.

[115] Emending *wang* 王 to *chu* 主 after the *CT* 2/9b. It is a scribal error.

[116] Chang Hua was a statesman of the Western Chin (A.D. 265–316) and author of the *Po-wu-chih* 博物志, *Record of the Investigation of Things*. For his biography, see the *Chin-shu* 36/27b–40b and also Anna Straughair, *Chang Hua: A Statesman-poet of the Western Chin Dynasty* (Canberra, 1973).

[117] Emperor Chuang's mother was the daughter of Li Ch'ung and the younger sister of Li Yen-shih. See *MCCS* plate 186: 彭城武宣王[勰]妃李氏墓誌銘.

[118] According to Wu T'ing-hsieh 吳廷燮 (*Yüan-Wei fang-chen nien-piao* A/10, column C 青州; *Erh-shih-wu-shih pu-p'ien* ed.), the exact date for this event is the tenth month (November–December) A.D. 529.

for his new post, he came to court to bid farewell. The emperor said to [Li Yen-]shih: "It is commonly known that [the people of Ch'ing-chou] are difficult to handle because of their habits of carrying bricks with them. "You should exert your best efforts in order to reciprocate the trust of the court."

In reply, [Li Yen-]shih said: "Your subject is approaching old age[119] and my vitality [diminishes as fast as the evaporating] morning dew. Gradually I am retreating from the world of activities, and with every passing day I am approaching closer to the pine mound [the grave]. For many years your subject has requested retirement, but Your Majesty, [aroused by the affection that] exists between a nephew and his maternal uncle,[120] has extended your imperial favor to this old subject, making it possible for one who should have retired[121] to learn how to run a local government.[122] Respectfully I accept your order and dare not fail you."

[119] Literally, *sang-yü* 桑榆, "mulberry and elm," referring to the fact that the sun's last rays can be seen only in the tops of these trees. Hence, "late." *HHS* 47/6a 馮異傳：可謂失之東隅，收之桑榆. "This can be said that what is being lost at sunrise has been restored at sunset." Li Hsien's 李賢 (A.D. 651–684) commentary: 桑榆，謂晚也，"*Sang-yü* means 'late.'"

[120] Literally, *Wei yang* 渭陽, "north of the Wei River," which alludes to a nephew's intimate feeling toward his maternal uncle, particularly after the death of his mother. When this conversation took place (A.D. 529), the emperor's mother had been dead for more than five years (she died on February 4, A.D. 524; see *MCCS* plate 186). For the origin of *Wei yang* 渭陽, see the *Shih-ching* 6.4/11a (ode 133, verse 1, lines 1 and 2): 秦風渭陽：我送舅氏，曰至渭陽. Waley, *Book of Songs*, p. 197: "I escorted my mother's brother/As far as the north of the Wei."

[121] Literally, *yen hsing tsui jen* 夜行罪人, "a criminal who walked at night." This is a reference to T'ien Yü 田豫 of the Three Kingdoms who declined to stay on as the Commandant of the Palace Guards (*Wei-wei* 衛尉), arguing, "For me, over seventy years old, to occupy this position is the same as to walk endlessly when the day bell has struck (a signal to stop) and the clepsydra has dropped all its water (another signal to stop). This will make me a criminal!" See *Wei-chih* 26/11b.

It should be noted that during the Han, a bell was struck during the daytime as a signal to stop, whereas a drum was beaten during the night as a signal to rise. *HHS* 5/9a 禮儀志中 quoting Ts'ai Yung's 蔡邕 (A.D. 133–192). *Tu-tuan* 獨斷：鼓以動衆，鐘以止衆. 故夜漏盡鼓鳴則起，晝漏盡鐘鳴則息，"A drum is beaten to signal people to advance, whereas a bell is struck to signal people to withdraw. Therefore when in the night the clepsydra has dropped all its water and when the drum is beaten, [people] should rise; when in the daytime the clepsydra has dropped all its water and when the bell is struck, [people] should rest." The same custom seems to have been carried into the Wei. (*Wei-chih* 26/11b quoting Chao I-ch'ing 趙一清

At the time, Yang K'uan 楊寬, Attending Secretary within the Imperial Yellow Gate, was at the side of the emperor,[123] and privately asked Wen Tzu-sheng 溫子昇, Drafter of the Central Secretariat,[124] about the meaning of "carrying bricks," which [Yang K'uan] did not understand. [Wen] Tzu-sheng said: "I have heard that when the emperor's elder brother, [Yüan Shao 元劭], Prince of P'eng-ch'eng, was the Governor of the Ch'ing-chou, he learned from the advisors[125] who had accompanied him to Ch'ing-chou: 'The customs of the people of Ch'i are quite frivolous. They talk big but superficially, and care only for their own glory and benefit. When a governor is about to enter [the Ch'i] territory, all come out

---

[1710?–1764?].) No one was permitted to walk on the street during the curfew hours. Referring to this basic idea, T'ien Yü implied that one should not seek government position after the attainment of old age.

[122] Literally, *ts'ai chin wan li* 裁錦萬里, "to cut brocade and rule a district of 10,000 *li*." A reference to *Tso-chuan* Hsiang 襄 31 40/20b–21a. Tzu-p'i 子皮 wanted to appoint Yin-ho 尹何 as a magistrate. Tzu-ch'an 子產 (sixth cent. B.C.), the minister of the state of Cheng 鄭, however, objected, saying: "This can not be done. Now you have a piece of fine brocade and you are unwilling to let someone cut it. People are seeking protection under the rule of a high government official in a large district, yet you are asking some [ordinary person] to run it. How much more care you have for the brocade than [for the people]!" Also see Legge 5, p. 566.

Such expressions as *sang-yü* 桑榆, *chao-lu* 朝露, *sung-ch'iu* 松丘, and *yeh-hsing* 夜行 used in this paragraph all mean "old age." They often appear in the works of contemporaries, such as Yü Hsin 庾信 (A.D. 513–581) (*Yü Tzu-shan chi chu*, *SPPY* ed., 14/32a): 周柱國楚國公岐州刺史慕容公神道碑銘：鐘鳴夜漏，晞露朝陽, "It's like the ringing of a bell [in the daytime] and the dropping out of water in a clepsydra at night; it is also like the morning dew under morning sunlight"; Yu Ming-ken 游明根 (*WS* 55/2b 游明根傳): 臣桑榆之年，鍾鳴漏盡, "Your subject, at his declining years, is like the ringing of a bell and the dropping out of water in a clepsydra"; Hsü Ling 徐陵 (A.D. 507–583) (*Hsü Hsiao-mu chi chien-chu*, *SPPY* ed. 1/15b 爲王儀同致仕表): 鐘鳴漏盡，史有夜行之戒, "History has warned those who walk at night: it is the same as ringing of a bell and the drain of a clepsydra"; and Liu Yü 柳彧 (d. A.D. 606) (*Sui-shu* 62/10a 柳彧傳): 其人年八十，鍾鳴漏盡, "That man is eighty years old, same as a ringing bell and draining clepsydra."

[123] Yang K'uan 楊寬 was at the time the Attending Secretary within the Imperial Yellow Gate. He escaped to the Liang after the fall of Lo-yang into the hands of rebels in A.D. 530, but returned to Wei after the restoration of peace. For his biography, see *PS* 41/43b–45b.

[124] The text (2/9a) reads *She-jen* 舍人, which is an abbreviation for *Chung-shu she-jen* 中書舍人. His biography (*PS* 83/7b–10b) verifies that he had held this position for some years.

[125] This is a free translation of *pin-k'o* 賓客.

to flatter him by lying prostrate and touching [their foreheads] to bricks that they had carried with them. When a governor returns home at the end of his tenure, they throw the same bricks at him.' The change from loyalty to betrayal is said to be faster than turning one's own palm. As a result, there is a song in the capital as follows:

With no inmates in the jail,
With no man of Ch'ing-chou in your house,
Even if your family fortune declines,
You will have no worries in your mind.[126]

This is where the term 'carrying bricks' originated."

Hsün Chi 荀濟 of Ying-ch'uan 潁川,[127] a famous gentleman with a cultivated lifestyle, enjoyed a commanding position among his contemporaries for his acute discernment and profound insight. When Ts'ui Shu-jen 崔叔仁 of Ch'ing-ho 清河 spoke[128] highly of gentlemen from Ch'i, [Hsün] Chi[129] retorted: "The people of Ch'i outwardly pretend benevolence and righteousness, but inwardly they entertain mean and covetous desires. They are as weightless as feathers, yet as sharp as awls. They like to promote empty fame [of others], and, by association and by the exercise of flattery, make a name for themselves. Wherever power lies, there they are, shoulder to shoulder, struggling to get in.[130] Dedicated

[126] *IS* (2/7b) and *CT* (2/10b) reads *fu-chung* 腹中, "inside the belly" rather than *ch'ang-chung* 腸中, "inside the intestine." This is a free translation.

The classical compound *huai-chuan* 懷磚, "carry brick," originates from this passage.

[127] Hsün Chi, born and raised in Chien-k'ang, was a close friend of Emperor Wu of the Liang (regnant A.D. 502–549), who was a fervent Buddhist devotee. Hsün Chi, however, attacked Buddhism in a memorial. Infuriated by this document, the emperor decided to have him arrested and executed. As a consequence, Hsün Chi ran to the Northern Wei, where he plotted with Yüan Chin 元瑾 to try to murder Kao Ch'eng 高澄, a powerful minister disloyal to the Wei. Instead, Hsün Chi was killed after the disclosure of the plan. See *PS* 83/10a–b. For his memorial denouncing Buddhism, see *Kuang Hung-ming chi* 7/74–79.

[128] Ts'ui Shu-jen was the son of Ts'ui Hsiu 崔休 and younger brother of Ts'ui Ling 崔㥄. It was in the house of Ts'ui Ling that Hsün Chi stayed after his flight from the Liang. Ts'ui Shu-jen had been General of the Whirling Cavalry (*Piao-ch'i chiang-chün*) concurrently Governor of Ying-chou. See *WS* 69/3a.

[129] The important character Chi 濟 is added at the suggestion of *CC* 2/98. Without this addition, the whole dialogue would be meaningless.

[130] Literally, *ts'e-chien* 側肩, "to turn the shoulder sideways," that is, for speedy entry.

to the search for glory and gain, they enjoy their sweet and affluent life.[131] By comparison[132] [with people] of all other regions,[133] they are by far the most opportunistic."

He then labeled the Ch'i literati as opportunistic gentlemen.

Knowing that they were labeled as "brick carriers" and opportunists, officials of Lin-tzu 臨淄[134] residing in different[135] parts of the capital all felt ashamed, except for Ts'ui Hsiao-chung 崔孝忠,[136] the only person who did not mind. When asked why, [Tsui] Hsiao-chung replied: "Customs of Ying-ch'iu 營丘[137] are the remnant heritage of T'ai-kung 太公.[138] Confucian scholars at Chi-hsia [Academy] 稷下[139] were creators of such practices and ideas as rituals and righteousness. Even though they have deteriorated somewhat at present, they are still good enough to be taken as national models. Hsün Chi [as a man] is no Hsü Shao

[131] The text (2/10a) has only three characters *t'ien jan nung* 甜然濃, which do not constitute a balanced sentence. The fourth character *hou* 厚 is added after the *YLTT* (7328/27b) quotation.

[132] Adding *pi* 比 after *YLTT* 7328/27b.

[133] Literally, *ssu-fang* 四方, "four directions," that is, everywhere in the nation.

[134] Lin-tzu, the name of the provincial capital of Ch'ing-chou, is used figuratively to refer to the entire area of Ch'ing-chou.

[135] Emending *yu* 有 to *pu* 布 after *IS* 2/8a.

[136] The text implies that Ts'ui Hsiao-chung was a native of Ch'ing-chou, but actually he was from the An-p'ing 安平 district of the Po-ling area, where a major branch of the famous Ts'ui clan originated. Son of Ts'ui Hsiu-ho 崔修和, he had been an Attendant Censor (*Shih-yü-shih*) and archivist. See *WS* 57/16a. For more information about the Ts'ui clan, see Patricia Buckley Ebrey, *The Aristocratic Families of Early Imperial China*, Cambridge, 1978.

[137] Ying-ch'iu, "encircled mound" is so named because in the inner city of Lin-tzu, a mound, three hundred paces (1,500 Chinese feet) in circumference, was surrounded by the Tzu 淄 River. See *SCC* 26/13b–14a 淄水注.

[138] T'ai-kung Wang 太公望 received Ying-ch'iu as a fief from King Wu of the Chou (regnant 1027–1005 B.C.). T'ai-kung is known otherwise as Lü Wang 呂望 and Chiang T'ai-kung 姜太公. He was the chief minister of King Wu of the Chou. See *SC* 32/2–10 齊太公世家 and Hsiao Kung-ch'üan, *A History of Chinese Political Thought*, tr. F. W. Mote (Princeton, 1979) 1, 49, 73 ff.; also pp. 167–169 for King Wu.

[139] Name of a city gate in the western section of Lin-tzu in the state of Ch'i underneath which scholars met and held discussions. Later, an academy was built by King Wei 齊威王 in about 357 B.C. on its site. See *SC* 46/31 田敬仲完世家: [宣王時,] 是以齊稷下學士復盛, 且數百千人, "Subsequently, once again scholars came to Chi-hsia [Academy] of the Ch'i in increasing numbers, ranging from several hundred to one thousand." See also Hsiao, *History of Chinese Thought*, 1, 5n.

許劭[140] or Kuo T'ai 郭泰,[141] and he fails to recognize [the presence of Confucius to the] east of his house.[142] It would be improper [for us] to feel either honored or disgraced by listening to the ugly remarks[143] he uttered."

The Cheng-shih Monastery 正始寺 (Monastery of the Beginning of Justice) was founded [through the contributions of] various government officials. It was built during the Cheng-shih period; hence the name. [The monastery] was located on the south[144] side of the Imperial Drive and outside the Tung-yang Gate, in the so-called Ching-i Ward 敬義里 (Ward of Respect for Righteousness).

In the ward was the Office of Imperial Parks[145] and Ponds.

Its splendid and spotless rooms and eaves were even more beautiful than those of the Ching[146]-lin Monastery. In front of the monks' compartments, tall trees faced the windows. Branches of blue pines and green willows were in close contact, gleaming in alternation. [The monastery] had quite a few *chih* 枳 trees,[147] the fruits of which tasted bad. There was also a stone monument, on the back of which was an inscription [listing donations by various officials]: Ts'ui

[140] Hsü Shao (A.D. 153–198), a person renowned for his skillful appraisal of other men. He and his associates held characterization sessions known as "first-of-the-month critiques" (*yüeh-tan p'ing* 月旦評), the outcome of which might be fatal or beneficial to those being reviewed. See *HHS* 98/7b–8b and Chen Chi-yun, *Hsün Yüeh*, p. 146.

[141] Kuo T'ai (A.D. 128–169), better known by his style Lin-tsung 林宗, was the leader of these literati skilled at characterization. See *HHS* 98/1a–3a.

[142] A reference to a fool who lived to the west of Confucius' house, and, in complete ignorance of the importance of Confucius, called the latter "my eastern neighbor Ch'iu" (*tung chia Ch'iu* 東家丘). See *WH* 41/18b.

The counterpart of this parable is "a fool in the western house" *hsi chia yü fu* 西家愚夫. See *Wei-chih* 11/26a 邴原傳, commentary quoting 邴原別傳.

[143] *Shih-ching* 12.1/10a (ode 192, verse 2, line 6) 小雅正月：莠言自口. Bernhard Karlgren, *The Book of Odes* (Stockholm, 1950), p. 135: "bad words come from mouths." Mao Heng's commentary: 莠, 醜也, "*Hsiu* means ugly."

[144] Emending *hsi* 西 to *nan* 南 after the *IS* 2/8a and *YLTT* 13823/3a.

[145] That is, *Tien-yü ts'ao* 典虞曹, a subdivision of the Court of Imperial Stud (*T'ai-p'u ssu*) during the Chin. See the *Chin-shu* 24/23b 職官志.

[146] The text (2/10b) reads *ts'ung-lin* 叢林, but both the *IS* (2/8a) and *YLTT* (13823/3a) give *ching-lin* 景林. *Chi-cheng* (6b) prefers the latter; hence, the translation.

[147] Oranges planted north of the Huai River would change into this variety. See *Chou-li* 39/5a 考工記總目：橘踰淮而北爲枳.

Kuang 崔光,[148] the Chief Palace Attendant, contributed four hundred thousand coins; Li Ch'ung 李崇, Marquis of Ch'en-liu 陳留侯, two hundred thousand coins,[149] and contributions by other officials in amounts appropriate to their rank. Still, the smallest amount came to no less than five thousand coins. The inscription was engraved by someone of a later period.

To the south of the Ching-i Ward was the Chao-te Ward 昭德里 (Ward of the Manifestation of Virtue), in which were located the residences of Yu Chao 游肇 (A.D. 452–520), Vice President, Department of State Affairs;[150] Li Piao 李彪 (A.D. 444–501), the Chief Censor;[151] Ts'ui Hsiu 崔休 (d. A.D. 523), Minister of the Seven Forces;[152] Ch'ang Ching, Governor of Yu-chou;[153] and Chang Lun 張倫, Minister of Agriculture (*Ssu-nung* 司農).[154]

[Li] Piao and [Ch'ang] Ching, who came from a family of Confucian scholars, led a simple and frugal life. But [Chang] Lun, unlike

[148] Ts'ui Kuang was a great Buddhist devotee, even more so in his old age. He used to hold discussion sessions for monks and court dignitaries. For his official career, see Chapter 2 at note 110 under the Ch'in T'ai-shang-chün Monastery.

[149] Li Ch'ung (A.D. 455–525) was the nephew of Emperor Wen-ch'eng. He inherited the title Marquis of Ch'en-liu from his father and had been Generalissimo Governing the West. In his later years he was demoted to Marquis of Ch'en-liu, General Pacifying the East. See *WS* 66/1a–11a.

[150] Son of Yu Ming-ken 游明根, Yu Chao had been Attending Secretary within the Imperial Yellow Gate, and concurrently Chief Palace Attendant, and finally Vice President on the Right, Department of State Affairs. See *WS* 55/3b–6b.

[151] Emending *Yü-shih wei* 御史尉 *to Yü-shih chung-wei* 御史中尉 after *YHNC* 3/10a. As Chief Censor, Li Piao was noted for his stern and merciless rule. See *WS* 62/1a–20b.

[152] Emending *Ping-pu shang-shu* 兵部尚書 to *Ch'i-ping shang-shu* 七兵尚書 after *YHNC* 3/10a; emending Ts'ui Lin 崔林 to Ts'ui Hsiu 崔休 after *WS* 69/1a–3a.

Ts'ui Hsiu started his career as a major and, concurrently, Ministrant of the Imperial Yellow Gate (*Chi-shih huang-men shih-lang*) under Emperor Kao-tsu, but was promoted to the Minister of Seven Forces (*Ch'i-ping shang-shu*) and Minister within the Palace (*Tien-chung shang-shu*). The seven forces refer to the left middle and right middle, left external and right external, cavalry, special, and metropolitan forces. Minister of Five Forces (*Wu-ping shang-shu*) was an old Wei-Chin institution, but that of Seven Forces was a Northern Wei innovation.

[153] See Chapter 1 at note 16 under the Yung-ning Monastery.

[154] Chang Lun, a native of Shang-ku 上谷 (west of modern Kuang-ling 廣靈, Hopei), was the son of Chang Pai-tse 張白澤. He served Emperor Hsiao-chuang (regnant A.D. 528–531) as the Grand Minister of Agriculture, in which office he died. See *WS* 24/9a–11a.

them, was extremely extravagant and given to luxury. His study and house were bright and beautiful, and his costumes and curios were the choicest and rarest. The carriages and horses that he used for travel were superior to those of the state rulers. The excellence of his park, shrubbery, mountain and pond could not be matched by those of the princes.

He had a Ching-yang Hill 景陽山[155] built, which took on a natural appearance. On the hill were cliff after cliff, summit after summit, [all seemingly] connected at a high altitude.[156] Deep valleys and open ravines were linked with one another. High forests and huge trees were sufficient to shut out the light of the sun and the moon, and the hanging creepers and drooping vines let the wind and mist in and out. The rugged stone path, seemingly blocked off, was actually passable, and the deep creeks, winding at first, were straight later on. Therefore those with a feeling for mountain or wilderness life would enjoy themselves here and forget [the time] to return. Chiang Chih 姜質,[157] a native of T'ien-shui 天水 (southwest of modern Hsi-ho *hsien*, 西河縣 Kansu), was a nonconformist by conviction and in temperament. Clad in a hemp garment and wearing a turban of coarse cloth, he had the principles of a hermit. He could not help but fall in love with [Chang] Lun's [garden] when he saw it. Consequently he wrote a piece of rhymed prose entitled T'ing-shan 庭山賦 ("Rhymed prose on Courtyard and Mountain"),[158] which has been in circulation. It reads: "Now[159] those who are biased[160] are

[155] There was another mountain bearing the same name in the Hua-lin Park. Possibly Chang Lun's garden was an imitation. See Chapter 1 at note 269 under the Ching-lin Monastery.

[156] Literally, *ch'in yin* 嶔崟, descriptive of a state of loftiness.

[157] Chiang Chih is mentioned in the biography of Ch'eng Yen 成淹 (*WS* 79/7b). He is reported as a friend of Ch'eng Hsiao 成霄, son of Ch'eng Yen, and both liked to write poems and rhymed prose, which were not highly regarded by their contemporary literati. Nevertheless, they were popular among the less educated. This Chiang Chih was identified as a native of Ho-tung (modern An-i 安邑, Shansi), not T'ien-shui as recorded in the *Ch'ieh-lan chi*. See *WS* 79/5b.

[158] Emending *t'ing* 亭 to *t'ing* 庭 after *YHNC* 3/10a.

[159] The text (2/11a) reads *chin* 今, but on the basis of an ancient manuscript of the *Ch'ieh-lan chi*, *Ch'üan Hou-Wei wen* (54/9a) gives *fu* 夫 instead. Both characters can be translated as an introductory "now," however.

[160] The text gives *p'ien chung* 偏重, meaning personal preference.

especially[161] fond of ancient people for their simplicity and purity. It is therefore obvious that such elements as simplicity and purity serve as a bridge[162] [between men] and the Creator. Both the visitor to the Hao River[163] and the historian under the pillar[164] filtered their minds through nonactivity, which they comprehended,[165] and upheld the principle of spontaneity to fulfill their will. As a rule, they attached great value to mountains and rivers, but held official posts[166] in low esteem. Trusting to nature to float or sink, [their life] appears to be without taste or flavor.[167]

Now Master Chang, Minister of Agriculture, really follows in

[161] Deleting a repetitious *chung* 重 after the *CHWW* 54/9a.

[162] Emending *chin mien* 津勉 to *chin liang* 津梁 after *IS* (2/9a) and *CHWW* (54/9a). *Chin* 津 rhymes with *ch'un* 純; hence, a more logical choice.

[163] That is, Chuang-tzu, who on one occasion engaged himself in a dialectic argument with his friend Hui-tzu 惠子 (or Hui Shih 惠施, fourth cent. B.C.) at a dam near the Hao River. Chuang-tzu, a leader of the Taoist teaching, asserted the freedom that the swimming fish enjoyed in the water, whereas Hui-tzu, a logician philosopher, questioned the ability of Chuang-tzu, not a fish himself, to know how and what fish enjoyed. *Chuang-tzu* 6/128 秋水：莊子與惠子遊於濠梁之上. Burton Watson, tr., *The Complete Works of Chuang Tzu* (New York, 1968), p. 188, "Autumn Floods": "Chuang Tzu and Hui Tzu were strolling along the dam of the Hao River. . . ."

[164] That is, Lao-tzu (ca. 300 B.C.; believed to be the founder of the Taoist school of philosophy). *SC* 63/2–3 老子韓非列傳： 老子者， … 周守藏室之史也, "Lao-tzu . . . was a historian who took care of the archive room of the Chou [dynasty]." Commentary: 按藏室史, 周藏書室之史也. 又張蒼傳：老子爲柱下史, 蓋即藏室之柱下，因以爲官名, "The historian of the archive room was the one who took care of the archive room for the Chou [dynasty]. Again, according to the 'Biography of Chang Ts'ang' [in the *Shih-chi*], Lao-tzu was a Historian under the Pillar, that is, the pillar of the archive room. Hence, he took this as his official title."

[165] Emending *wo* 臥 to *wu* 悟 after *IS* 2/9a.

[166] Literally, *chang-fu* 章甫, ceremonial caps of the Yin dynasty. *Li-chi* 59/1a 儒行：孔子對曰：長居宋, 冠章甫之冠, "In reply Confucius said: 'When I grew up and stayed in Sung, I wore a *chang-fu* cap.'" Commentary (59/1b): 章甫, 殷冠也. "*Chang-fu* is the name of a Yin cap."

[167] *Lao-tzu tao-te ching* 老子道德經 (*SPTK so-pen*, B/12) 仁德第三十五：道之出口, 淡乎其無味. Wing-tsit Chan, tr., *The Way of Lao Tzu* (New York, 1963), p. 162, "But the words uttered by Tao/How insipid and tasteless!." Actually, the opposite is true. See *Ch'üan Han wen* 全漢文 (Taipei, 1961, 53/4b) 揚雄解難：大味必淡, 大音必希 "Great flavors are necessarily tasteless; big sounds are necessarily inaudible."

their footsteps. His great capacity for tolerance stands out above all others, and [a sense of] self-satisfaction helps him to enjoy life to the fullest. No dark green pine is cleaner; no white jade more precious. He rests his mind on Nothing but leads an actual life of Something; his feelings enter the past as if they were the present.

Obsessed neither with secluded life[168] nor excessive formality, settled between activity and tranquility, he never loses interest in mountains and rivers. He built a courtyard between hills and valleys, where he lets his eyes and mind wander about. Stepping forward, he seeks neither fame nor glory; stepping back, he wants no seclusion where one may speak with greater freedom.

Then stones were broken to make way for the creek water to flow, and mountain tops were made to appear just in front of the eaves. Slanting against the treacherous clouds, ledges meet with the ridge of a curved beam.[169] Here the mist rising high in the Constellation of the Heavenly Ford[170] is tempted to descend, and the distant smoke of the Eastern Sea[171] is harbored. Its delicate tracery appears to be ancient, and the hazardous conditions indicate that it is one thousand years old.

As for the cut-off ridge and hanging slope, [hikers find it easy to] go amiss or to lose balance. The rapids, winding and sometimes slow-flowing, sometimes rise sharply in waves; mountain rocks, high and low, present further hazards. For forty Chinese feet, one hundred ascents;[172] [within] ten paces, a thousand hops. We know

[168] Literally, *yin fang* 隱放, which is a contraction of *yin-chu fang-yen* 隱居放言. See *Lun-yü* (I-wen facsimile *SSCCS* ed., 18/6b), 微子. Arthur Waley, *The Analects of Confucius* (London, 1938), p. 222: "... lived in seclusion and refrained from comment."

[169] The text (2/11b) reads *ch'ü-tung* 曲棟, a curved beam in a roof or ridgepole. Probably it is used here figuratively for the ridge of a mountain.

[170] *T'ien-chin* 天津, also known as *T'ien-han* 天漢 or *T'ien-chiang* 天江, a group of nine stars. See *Chin-shu* 11A/31a 天文志. See also Ho Peng-yoke, *The Astronomical Chapters of the Chin-shu*, Paris, 1966.

[171] Literally, *Ts'ang hai* 滄海, "Black Sea." It was supposedly in the north but was actually in the east. *Hai-nei shih-chou chi* (*IS* ed.) 8a–b, has a mention of it.

[172] Literally, *wu hsün* 五尋, "five *hsün*." Each *hsün* is equal to eight Chinese feet (*Shuo-wen chieh-tzu* 3B/21a) 度人兩臂爲尋, 八尺也, "In measuring a person, [the combination of] two arms' length is a *hsün*, or eight [Chinese] feet"; *Shih-ching* 20.2/15b (ode 300, verse 9, line 4) 魯頌閟宮：是尋是尺. Commentary: 八尺也. Translated by Arthur Waley as "cubits"; *Book of Songs*, p. 273.

Wu Mountain 巫山[173] does not measure up, but what about P'eng-lai 蓬萊?[174]

Here in the valley are flowers in mist and grasses under dew, some slanting, some falling; trunks [covered] with frost and branches [sweeping] in the wind, half erect and half drooping. Jade leaves and gold stems are scattered around the stairways. The color [of flowers] dazzles one's eyes, and the pleasant aroma penetrates one's nose. [Blooming all year long], not only do they flourish like the sunny spring; they are also as pure as the white snow. Some say they are the bones of the gods, or the essence of *yin* and *yang*.[175] But, since even Heaven and Earth are unaware of having produced these, how can human beings recognize their names?

Fowls of all kinds alight here.[176] Their colors vary from blue green to yellow. Green heads [ducks], purple necks [storks], in the company of bright green [kingfishers], present a picture of mingled beauty.[177] White storks[178] are born in other districts, and red-legs [birds] from alien lands. All come to gather here from afar, or to fly [high above] the water and [near] the trees. They forget to return to the [northern] desert in spring, or to fly southward in autumn. Unless attracted by this man, how could these migrating birds lose [their sense of] direction?

[173] A reference to the treacherous Wu Gorges 巫峽 in the Upper Yangtze, where, in an area of seven hundred *li*, both banks of the river are continuous cliffs and precipices that so completely block the sky and shut off the sun that one can hardly see any light except at noon or midnight. *SCC* 34/3b 江水注：自三峽七百里中, 兩岸連山, 略無闕處, 重巖叠嶂, 隱天蔽日, 自非停午夜分, 不見曦月.

[174] One of the three legendary and inaccessible islands in the high seas to the east of China, where immortals are supposed to live. The other two islands are Fang-chang 方丈 and Ying-chou 瀛州. See *SC* 28/24 封禪書.

[175] *Yin* and *yang* are two cosmic forces whose interaction produces all patterns, ideas, systems, and culture of the Chinese society. See Needham, *Science and Civilisation*, I, 153–154.

[176] *Fen-po* 紛泊, a bound form, means "to alight and settle." See *WH* 4/15a 左思蜀都賦：羽族紛泊. Liu K'uei's 劉逵 commentary: 紛泊, 飛薄也.

[177] The text (2/12a) reads *hao ts'ui lien fang* 好翠連芳, "bright green is blended with fragrance." Although *fang* 芳, "fragrance," rhymes with *huang* 黃 in the couplet immediately preceding, it can hardly be used to describe a bird. The meaning is therefore unclear; the text may be in error.

[178] The text (2/12a) gives 䴏, a character not listed in any dictionary. *CS* (2/93) suggests that it may be a variant of 鶴, which is another name for *ho* 鶴, "stork;" hence the translation.

How could it be the work of a man of little intelligence; indeed,[179] it is the marvel of the gods. He who can create needs to write poems; anyone who dares to go, will compose *fu*. Some choose a windy place, others go to a cloudy point. Sitting on[180] a chrysanthemum-ridge or a peak with plum trees, one writes in spring or autumn according to whatever inspiration he may have received.

Afar, appreciated by immortals; nearby, be known to court officials. Seeking to leave aside my official duties, I participate in this mountain gathering. Tzu-ying 子英 flew to heaven on the back of a fish in jade;[181] Wang Ch'iao 王喬 tied his crane to the branches of a pine tree.[182] The Fang-chang [Immortal Isle][183] is no more spectacular than this, on which subject [people] will chant and sing. Upon hearing [such chanting voices], [Juan] Ssu-tsung's [阮]嗣宗[184] spirit will be agitated and [Hsi] Shu-yeh's [嵇]叔夜[185] soul will be stunned. They regret their inability to

[179] Sun Hsing-yen 孫星衍, *Hsü Ku-wen yüan* (Yeh-ch'eng shan-kuan ed., 1812, 2/25a) has the additional character *shih* 實; hence, the translation.

[180] *Hsü Ku-wen yüan* (2/25a) suggests that one character is missing. I speculate that the missing character must be a verb; hence the translation.

[181] Tzu-ying was a skilled fisherman. Once he caught a carp, took it home, and let it grow in his pond. In one year it grew to more than ten Chinese feet, with a horn and wings. Much surprised, Tzu-ying bowed to it. The fish then asked Tzu-ying to ride on its back, and ascended to heaven. See *Lieh-hsien chuan* (*IS* ed.) B/7b–8a.

The text (2/12b), which reads *Tzu-ying yu-yü yü yü chih* 子英游魚於玉質 may be in error.

[182] Prince Ch'iao (sixth cent. B.C.) was the son of Emperor Ling 靈 (regnant 571–545 B.C.) of the Chou. He was a skillful pan-pipe (*sheng* 笙) player. At the invitation of the Taoist monk Fou-ch'iu kung 浮丘公, he went into the Sung Mountains, where he stayed for more than thirty years. Eventually he took a ride on the back of a white stork and soared into the sky. See the *Lieh-hsien chuan* A/12b–13a.

The text (2/12b) reads 王喬繫鵠於松枝, which may again be in error.

The two legends concerning Tzu-ying and Prince Ch'iao are introduced in the work of rhymed prose to dramatize the fabulous splendor of Chang Lun's garden of hills and streams, where similar things might be expected to happen.

[183] One of the three major islands in the Eastern Sea. See note 174 above. *Ch'ung-k'an* (2/17a) is perhaps in error in punctuating this couplet.

[184] Style of Juan Chi (A.D. 210–263), a famous poet and whistler and one among the "Seven Sages of the Bamboo Grove." For his biography, see *Chin-shu* 49/1a–8b; for a study of his poetry, see Wang Yi-t'ung, "The Political and Intellectual World in the Poetry of Juan Chi," *Renditions* 7 (Hong Kong, 1977), 48–61.

[185] Style of Hsi K'ang (A.D. 223–262), a renowned lute player and poet and

break out of their earthen [graves], and to become intoxicated in this mountain [resort].

Other noblemen and dignitaries who prefer seclusion now set out together in carriages, thinking of the mountains and remembering the water. Meeting with a ridge, they delight in its curve; seeing a boulder, they admire its slanting [edge]. This courtyard[186] is fertile ground[187] for benevolence and wisdom; and so there can be planted[188] here this rock mountain.

Luxuriant, the grass and trees,
Ever-generating, the wind and mist,
A lonely pine may keep off age,
Half a rock will also prolong your life.
If you do not sit or sleep by its side,
[Neither] walk in, nor ascend to the mountains in spring and summer—
Bleached bones will only rot by themselves,
What would even be left in your heart[189] to remember?"

The P'ing-teng Monastery 平等寺 (Monastery of Equanimity)[190] was established at the former residence of [Yüan] Huai [元]懷, the Wu-mu[191] 武穆 (Martial and Solemn) Prince of Kuang-p'ing 廣平王. It was on the north side of the Imperial Drive, two *li* outside the Ch'ing-yang Gate, and within the so-called Hsiao-ching Ward (Ward of the Filial and Reverent). The halls and rooms were vast and

another member of the "Seven Sages of the Bamboo Grove." See *Chin-shu* 49/16a–26a; Donald Holzman, *La vie et la pensée de Hi K'ang (223–262 A.P. J.C.)* (Leiden, 1957); and Robert H. van Gulik, *Hsi K'ang and His Political Essay on the Lute* (Tokyo, 1968).

[186] Adding the key character *t'ing* 庭, "courtyard", after the *IS* (2/10a) and *YLTT* (13823/4a).

[187] Literally, *t'ien* 田, "land, field." This is a loose translation.

[188] Literally, *chung* 種, "to plant." Possibly it is an error.

[189] Deleting the redundant character *hsin* 心, which appears after *fang-ts'un* 方寸.

[190] *P'ing-teng*, or *samtá*, refers to Budda's universal, impartial, and equal attitude toward all beings.

[191] Yüan Huai (A.D. 488–517), son of Emperor Hsiao-wen, had been Generalissimo of the Whirling Cavalry, Minister of Public Work, Grand Guardian, and Acting Minister of Public Instruction (September 11, A.D. 515). His biography in the *WS* (22/6b) is by no means complete, but a rubbing of a stele inscription erected in his honor is available in the *MCCS* (plate 193).

beautiful, [sheltered by] stately trees that presented a solemn atmosphere. Its [raised] foundation and covered passageway were outstanding structures of the time.[192] Outside the gate of the monastery was a [gilt] bronze image[193] that was twenty-eight Chinese feet high, whose physiognomy and marks [conveyed] dignity. Often there was mysterious proof of its spiritual efficacy. When the nation was due to receive good or bad fortune, the image would first manifest [appropriate] signs.

In the twelfth month of the third year of the Hsiao-ch'ang period (January–February A.D. 528), the face of the image had a sorrowful expression. Both eyes shed tears, and the entire body was wet. Called by contemporaries the Buddha's sweat, [these tears] attracted all[194] men and women from every marketplace and every ward of the capital to come and view it. A monk took a piece of clean silk floss to wipe away the tears, but in an instant the floss was drenched. Another piece of floss was used, but in no time it was wet also. The sweating persisted for three days before it came to an end. In the fourth month of the next year (May–June A.D. 528), Erh-chu Jung entered Lo-yang, and many officials were executed. The dead covered the ground [in the capital]. In the third month of the second year of the Yung-an period (March–April A.D. 529), the image again sweated; literati and commoners of the capital again came to look. In the fifth month (May–June), the Prince of Pei-hai entered Lo-yang, forcing Emperor Chuang to retreat to the north. In the seventh month (August–September A.D. 529), the prince of Pei-hai suffered a smashing defeat. All of the five thousand soldiers from the Yangtze and Huai regions under his command were captured. Not a single one could return home [alive]. In the seventh month of the third year of the Yung-an period (August–September A.D. 530), this image wept bitterly as before. With the [previous] prognostications proven true,

[192] According to a monument inscription written in A.D. 572 to consummate major repair work, this temple enjoyed a spectacular view. "With the lofty Mang Mountains in the back, it faced the clear Lo River. On the right was the parapet of the city wall; on the left, a vast lake. The Sung Mountains stood attentively in the front, while the holy [Yellow (?)] River floated in the rear." See Wang Ch'ang, *Chin-shih ts'ui-pien* (Ching-hsün-t'ang ed.) 34/30b 馮翊王修平等寺碑.

[193] *Chin-shih ts'ui-pien* (34/28b) supplies this additional bit of information.

[194] Literally, *k'ung shih-li wang erh kuan chih* 空市里往而觀之, "The exodus was such that the market places and wards were emptied."

[people] were frightened day and night. [An imperial order then] prohibited viewing [the image]. In the twelfth month (January–February A.D. 531), Erh-chu Chao entered Lo-yang and captured Emperor Chuang, who was subsequently murdered in Chin-yang. Palaces in the capital (that is, Lo-yang) were deserted; for one hundred days there was no ruler.[195] Only Erh-chu Shih-lung, President of State Affairs, Governor of Ssu-chou, and Prince of Lo-p'ing, stationed [his troops] in the capital [to insure] the unimpeded commercial transactions and prevent [city] robbery and thievery.[196].

In the second year of the Chien-ming period (A.D. 531),[197] the Prince of Ch'ang-kuang left Chin-yang for the capital. Upon arrival in the suburbs,[198] [Erh-chu] Shih-lung forced him to abdicate in favor of [Yüan] Kung [元]恭, Prince of Kuang-ling 廣陵王, giving as his reason that Ch'ang-kuang was distantly related to the imperial household[199] and his administration unremarkable.

> [Yüan] Kung[200] was Emperor Chuang's cousin. An Attending Secretary within the Imperial Yellow Gate during the Cheng-kuang period (A.D. 520–524), Yüan Kung witnessed Yüan Ch'a's exercise of power, [as] the government fell into the hands of deceitful and insinuating officials. [For the sake of security, therefore, Yüan Kung] pretended to be dumb and he did not participate

[195] In late A.D. 530, after the downfall of Emperor Chuang, Yüan Yeh 元曄, Prince of Ch'ang-kuang 長廣王, was enthroned with the support of Erh-chu Shih-lung and Erh-chu Chao. Soon afterward, however, the new emperor was forced to abdicate in favor of the Prince of Kuang-ling, who was later known as Ch'ien-fei ti 前廢帝 ("The Former Dethroned Emperor"). On January 6, A.D. 531, Erh-chu Chao entered Lo-yang, but Erh-chu Tu-lü and Erh-chu Shih-lung were the two generals actually responsible for security in the capital. The Prince of Ch'ang-kuang, then in Chin-yang, did not arrive in Lo-yang until April first of the same year (the twenty-ninth day of the second month), *TC* 155/2a. (*WS* 11/1b is mistaken in giving the "third month" instead.) This explains why "for one hundred days there was no ruler" in the capital. See *WS* 10/14b–15a 孝莊紀, 11/1a–2a 前廢帝紀 and 75/9a 爾朱世隆傳.

[196] *TC* 155/1b quotes this passage in full.

[197] The name of the Prince of Ch'ang-kuang's regnal period changed into P'u-t'ai (A.D. 531–532) when the Prince of Kuang-ling became emperor.

[198] An area south to the Mang Mountain and outside the east gate of the capital city, where an abdication ceremony later took place. See *WS* 11/1b.

[199] The prince was the great-grandson of Emperor Ching-mu 景穆 (d. A.D. 451), therefore only indirectly related to the reigning emperor.

[200] Adding *Kung* 恭 after the *IS* 2/11a.

in contemporary affairs. During the Yung-an years, (A.D. 528–530), he fled into the mountains of Shang-lo 上洛.[201] Governor Ch'üan Ch'i 泉企[202] arrested him and had him sent [to the capital]. Suspecting that [Yüan] Kung might be deceiving him, Emperor Chuang ordered someone to rob his clothing during the night. The man drew a sword [as if] to kill him, but Yüan Kung merely opened up his mouth and pointed to his tongue, never saying a word at all. Convinced that [Yüan Kung's] dumbness was genuine, Emperor Chuang permitted him to return to his residence. [Yüan] Kung stayed most of the time in the Lung-hua Monastery[203] until Erh-chu [Shih-lung] forced the [Prince of] Ch'ang-kuang to abdicate in his favor.

The abdication decree read:

"Greetings from the Emperor to [Yüan] Kung, the prince of Kuang-ling:

"Ever since the conquest of the nation by our Great Wei, one sage emperor after another rules the nation with enlightenment, doubling the basis and expanding the rulership, until we have become master of a myriad countries[204] and gloriously taken possession of all the land within the four seas. As a result, the way [we adhere to] is superior to that of all preceding kings,[205] and our virtue extends to all corners of the empire.[206]

"Nevertheless, with Emperor Hsiao-ming's demise, both the gods and men [were deprived of] a ruler.

[201] A commandery of Lo-chou 洛州 (*WS* 106C/18b–19a); modern Shang-hsien 商縣, Shensi.

[202] *PS* 66/11b gives his personal name as *Hsien* 仚 (an immortal) rather than *Ch'i* 企 (to hope for). An influential general in the Western Wei dynasty, he was captured in A.D. 534 by the rival Eastern Wei dynasty. See *PS* 66/116–13a 泉仚傳.

[203] A temple founded by his family, possibly by his father Yüan Yü 元羽. It was located in the southern suburbs of Lo-yang. For the Lung-hua Monastery, see Chapter 3 after note 110.

[204] Literally, *yen yu wan pang* 奄有萬邦, "to cover and possess myriad countries." For the origin of *yen-yu* 奄有, see the *Shih-ching* 20.2/1b (ode 300, verse 1, line 12) 魯頌閟宮:奄有下國. Waley, *Book of Songs*, p. 269. "He took possession of all lands below." Cheng Hsüan's comm.: 奄猶覆也, "'*Yen*' means 'to be possessed of.'"

[205] Literally, *tao i pai wang* 道溢百王, "Our principle brims over [the level set by] the Hundred Kings," that is, we are much superior to all of them.

[206] Literally, *te chien wu wai* 德漸無外, "No [place] lies outside [the area] imbued with our virtue," that is, all are within the realm of our benevolent influence.

"The late Pillar of the State, Generalissimo, Prime Minister, Prince of T'ai-yüan [Erh-chu] Jung, who [was responsible for the security of an area] on both the east and west side of Shan [as were the Duke of Chou (d. 1105 B.C.) and the Duke of Shao (d. 1053 B.C.) in the past],[207] acted as a prime minister outside the capital.[208] Sincerely loyal to the imperial household and greatly fearful of national collapse, he supported the ascension of [Yüan] Tzu-yu, Prince of Ch'ang-lo, to reestablish the broken imperial sovereignty. [He had high hopes] that the mandate [symbolized by] the nine tripods[209] with each passing day would prosper, and that the seven huudred year's reign would last forever. Yet the numerous flying [birds] were restless,[210] and inundations

[207] A reference to the Duke of Chou and Duke of Shao, who, as prime ministers, ruled to the east and west of the Chou metropolis, respectively. See *Ch'un-ch'iu Kung-yang chuan* (I-wen facsimile *SSCCS* ed.); Yin 隱 5 3/4a: 天子三公者何？天子之相也. 天子之相何以三？自陜而東者, 周公主之; 自陜而西者, 召公主之. 一相處乎內, "Who are the three lords of the Son of Heaven? They are his ministers. Why are ministers of the Son of Heaven three? [The area] from the Shan eastwards is under the jurisdiction of the Duke of Chou; west of the Shan is under the jurisdiction of the Duke of Shao. An additional minister takes his position between them."

[208] T'ao K'an 陶侃 (A.D. 259–334), a powerful Eastern Chin general-governor was concurrently prime minister from his post outside the capital. *Chin-shu* 66/29a 陶侃傳論：超居外相, 宏總上流, "He was promoted, rather unconventionally, to the position of a prime minister outside of the capital, enjoying an usual position in the upper [Yangtze] River."

[209] According to one source, nine tripods were cast under the sage-king Emperor Yü of the Hsia dynasty (trad. 2205–1766 B.C.) to symbolize the nine provinces. According to another, these nine tripods were moved to the capital of the Shang following the downfall of Hsia, and to the Chou capital after the downfall of the Shang. By tradition, Chou rule lasted for seven hundred years because of the tripods in its possession. *HS* 25A/29b 郊祀志：禹收九牧之金, 鑄九鼎, 象九州, 皆嘗鬺享上帝鬼神, "Emperor Yü collected metals from the governors of nine provinces, which were cast into nine tripods as a symbol of nine provinces. The contents of the nine tripods were all presented as offerings to gods, ghosts, and spirits." *Tso-chuan* Hsüan 3 21/16b: [王孫滿曰]：商紂暴虐, 遷鼎於周. …成王定鼎於郟鄏, 卜世三十, 卜年七百, 天所命也. Legge 5, 293: "[Wang-sun Mwan replied]: Chow of Shang proved cruel and oppressive, and they (that is, the tripods) were transferred to Chow. . . . King Ch'ing fixed the tripods in Këah-juh, and divined that the dynasty should extend through thirty reigns, over seven hundred years."

[210] A reference to contenders struggling for power. *Ch'u-tz'u* 3/58 天問：會鼂爭盟, 何踐吾期, 蒼鳥羣飛, 孰使萃之. David Hawkes, *Ch'u Tz'u*, p. 53: "On the morning of the first day we took our oath. How did we all arrive in time? When the geese came flocking together, who was it made them gather?"

were about to reach [everywhere].[211] Like wolves with heads turned, like owls wide-eyed [at their prey],[212] [the wicked were] unmoving as mountains, and stalemated as in chess.[213] But with one stroke of the prime minister, peace was restored to all parts of the nation. [Yüan] Tzu-yu,[214] unmindful of the national welfare and envious of [those who were] meritorious and virtuous, gathered the unprincipled and murderous men around him and picked flatterers as attendants.[215] As a result, the emperor was a greater tyrant than he who cut out the heart [of Pi-kan].[216] The [resultant] pain was like applying pincers to one's teeth.[217] Indeed, [the emperor's crime] deserved more protest than the one inscribed on the golden tablet,[218] and [the deed of the

[211] "Inundation" is analagous to "troubled world." Fan Ning, *Ch'un-ch'iu Ku-liang-chuan chi-chieh hsü* (I-wen facsimile *SSCCS* ed.; 4b): 孔子觀滄海之橫流，廼喟然而歎曰：文王既沒，文不在茲乎？ "After viewing the inundation of the vast sea, Confucius said with a sigh: 'Now that Duke Wen has died, could culture still be here?'"

[212] *WH* 44/8a 陳琳檄吳將校部曲文：其餘鋒捍特起，鸇視狼顧，爭爲梟雄者，不可勝數，"Many others sprang up spiritedly. Like owls wide-eyed, wolves with heads turned and struggling for hegemony, they are simply countless." Commentary quoting the *Huai-nan-tzu* 淮南子：鴟視虎顧，"Peeping like owls and turning back their heads like tigers."

[213] Emending *yüeh-li chi-chih* 岳立基趾 to *yüeh-li chi-chih* 岳立棊峙，"Unmoving as mountains and stalemated as in chess" after *Chi-cheng* 2/7a. The latter is based on a contemporary passage written by Li Ch'ien 李騫 (*WS* 36/11a 李騫釋情賦)：既雲擾而海沸，亦岳立而基峙，"Not only are they like scurrying clouds and embroiling seas, they are also like unmoving mountains and stalemated chessmen."

[214] That is, Emperor Hsiao-chuang (regnant A.D. 528–531).

[215] Literally, *jen jen* 壬人, which is the same as *ning-jen* 佞人. See *HS* 9/7b 元帝紀：是故壬人在位，"Therefore flatterers are in authority." Fu Ch'ien's 服虔 (A.D. 2nd cent.) commentary: 壬人，佞人也，"*Jen-jen* is the same as *ning-jen*."

[216] Pi-kan (12th cent. B.C.) reprimanded his nephew, Emperor Ch'ou, the last wicked king of the Shang dynasty, for his use of cruel tortures. Infuriated by this, Emperor Ch'ou had Pi-kan killed, then opened up his heart to find out whether there were indeed seven apertures, as a good-hearted man was supposed to have. See *SC* 3/32 殷本紀.

[217] The source of this allusion is unknown. It might refer to Fan Chü 范雎 (early third cent. B.C.), also known as Marquis of Ying 應侯, who was so badly beaten by his suspicious superiors that his ribs and teeth were broken. See *SC* 19/3 范雎蔡澤列傳.

[218] Following the execution of Lung-feng 龍逢 (minister of the ancient tyrant Chieh 桀, d. 1763 B.C.), on the *keng-tzu* 庚子 day, an inscribed golden tablet emerged from the ground as a proof of his innocence. See *WH* 40/18b 任彥昇百辟勸進今上牋：金版出地，告龍逢之怨.

late prime minister was more noble than] what the great bird should be grateful for.[219] Thereupon the hopes of the nation were shattered in an instant. I am of the humble opinion that the palaces should not be deserted for long[220] and the throne[221] should by no means be without an occupant. As a matter of expediency, I therefore have followed the suggestions of the many [officials] to reign temporarily over the masses. Now the six armies, in marching toward the south, have reached the bank of the Yellow River. With the capital in sight, I have a sense of regret and shame. After self-examination, I found myself deficient[222] in virtue, [and only] remotely related to the imperial household. Thus how could I look for[223] heavenly favor above, and defy people's wishes below?

"The virtue of Your Highness is well known to the masses, and your fame is far greater than that of rulers of the past myriad years.[224] In your past, [beset with] great worries and confronted with[225] the manifold hardships of the time, you have for many years kept silent and lived in seclusion aloof from national affairs. Now heaven blesses the one with bright virtue, and people adhere to an august leader[226] destined for the mandate, and your praises are sung in unison. [I beg that Your Highness], by words and deeds,[227] with dignity and favorable consideration, respond to our wishes, which are being offered with anxious expectations.[228]

[219] Yang Chen 楊震, the Grand Commandant under Emperor An 安帝 (regnant A.D. 107–125) of the Later Han, was slandered by the powerful eunuch Fan Feng 樊豐 and subsequently dismissed from office. Yang Chen poisoned himself. More than ten days prior to his burial, a huge bird came to the funeral site, calling bitterly and shedding tears to such a degree that the ground was soaked. After Emperor Shun's 順帝 ascension, an order was issued to the local government that a magnificent banquet be offered to Yang Chen's shrine and all charges hitherto brought against him be dismissed. See *HHS* 84/6b–7a.

[220] Emending *i* 以 to *chiu* 久 after *IS* 2/12a.

[221] Literally, *shen-ch'i* 神器, "a divine utensil." For its origin, see *Lao-tzu A/11* 無爲第二十九:天下神器, 不可爲也. Chan, *The Way of Lao-tzu*, p. 151, "The Empire is a spiritual thing, and should not be acted on."

[222] Reversing *po kua* 薄寡 to *kua po* 寡薄 after *IS* 2/12a.

[223] Emending *i* 異 to *chi* 冀 after *IS* 2/12a.

[224] Literally, *wan ku* 萬古, "10,000 past generations."

[225] Adding *tsao* 遭 after *IS* 2/12a.

[226] That is, *ao-chu* 奥主. *Tso-chuan* Chao 13 46/12a: 共有寵子, 國有奥主. Legge 5, p. 650: "There is [another] favourite son of [King] Kung; there is [another] lord more honoured in the state." Commentary: 奥主, 國內之主.

[227] *I-ching* 7/17ab 繫辭上:言行, 君子之樞機, 樞機之發, 榮辱之主也.

With reverence I am now sending you the Great Seal, and at the same time I am retiring to my private lodging.[229] Let you, O king, pursue the established task [of our ancestors] with respect, and be impartial.[230] When praised, do not think you are praiseworthy.[231] Be cautious, and be increasingly cautious with each passing day. Have respect for this!"

[Yüan] Kung declined, saying:

"The heavenly mandate is of the utmost seriousness and the destiny should not be accepted lightly. Unless someone is familiar with the Three Ways[232] [those of heaven, earth, and mankind], and has accomplishments [beneficial to all] within the four seas, he should not be selected as one fit for the imperial line of succession.[233] Nor is he justifiably acceptable as the leader of the masses.[234] Your subject is without aid, dull, and wanting prescience and farsightedness. Even now that a great order has been handed down to me, I dare not accept it. I beg that you rescind your order so as to satisfy my inner feelings."

Again said the Prince [of Ch'ang-kuang]:

"Since the virtue of Your Highness agrees with what has been recorded in the sacred maps and charts,[235] and since you have won the hearts of all the people, you should hold on to the middle (that is, exercise supreme power) and ascend the throne. You should not

---

[228] Literally, *chu-chu* 竚屬, "to stand on tiptoe and hope for acceptance", that is, to hope for prompt acceptance.

[229] Literally, *pieh-ti* 別邸, "other lodging house"; that is, to vacate the main palace for the emperor.

[230] *Shu-ching* 4/8b 大禹謨：惟精惟一, 允執其中. Legge 3, pp. 61–62, "The Counsels of the Great Yu: Be discriminating, be undivided, that you may sincerely hold fast the mean."

[231] *Shu-ching* 19/25a 呂刑：雖畏勿畏, 雖休勿休, "Being respected, do not think you are respectable; being praised, do not think you are praiseworthy."

[232] Literally, *san tsai* 三才. *I-ching* 8/22a 繫辭下：有天道焉, 有人道焉, 有地道焉. 兼三材而兩之, 故六六者非它也, 三材之道也. Richard Wilhelm, *I Ching*, 1, 377: "The tao of heaven is in it, the tao of earth is in it, and the tao of man is in it. It combines these three primal powers and doubles them; that is why there are six lines. The six lines are nothing other than the ways (tao) of the three primal powers."

[233] *Ti t'u* 帝圖, that is, *ti wang p'u lu* 帝王譜錄 as translated.

[234] *Shih-hsi* 師錫, "all." *Shu-ching* 2/24a 堯典：師錫帝曰. Legge 3, p. 26, "The Canon of Yaou:" "All *in the court* said to the emperor."

[235] *T'u-lu* 圖籙, maps and charts in which a legitimate ruler is supposed to have a recorded place.

overly trouble yourself by being humble, lest you offend both the people and spirits."

Altogether [Yüan] Kung declined three[236] times before finally ascending the throne and changing the name of the regnal period to P'u-t'ai. Hsing Tzu-ts'ai 邢子才,[237] Attending Secretary within the Imperial Yellow Gate, was ordered to prepare a document granting a [general] amnesty,[238] which included a description of how Emperor Chuang unjustifiably killed the Prince of T'ai-yüan. The Prince of Kuang-ling said: "Yung-an (that is, Emperor Chuang, Yung-an being the name of his regnal period) cut down a powerful minister with his own hand. This was not due to a loss of virtue [on the emperor's part or on the Prince of T'ai-yüan's part]. It was simply that heaven was not yet satiated with disorders that [the emperor] met with the same misfortune as was caused by Ch'eng Chi 成濟."[239] Calling his attendants, the prince said: "Give me a piece of paper for a script. I am going to prepare an essay myself."

He then dictated as follows:

"A directive to the Men-hsia 門下:[240]

"Of little virtue, We nonetheless meet an auspicious moment in winning your voluntary support. We would like to share this joyous occasion with the masses. Let the established practice be followed and an amnesty be granted to all who are found guilty."[241]

[236] Emending *erh* 二 to *san* 三 after *IS* 2/12b. *San* 三 agrees with tradition, whereas *erh* 二 does not.

[237] *Ming Shao* 劭, which was taboo during the Wei (*Shao* 劭 being the name of the prince of P'eng-ch'eng); therefore he was known by his style. He and Wen Tzu-sheng 溫子昇 were the best-known essayists in the closing years of the Wei. See *PCS* 36/1a–5b.

[238] Customarily, a general amnesty was granted at the ascension of a new emperor or on other equally important occasions.

[239] Ch'eng Chi, Chamberlain of the Crown Prince (*T'ai-tzu she-jen*) was the murderer of a Wei emperor (Duke of Kao-kuei hsiang 高貴鄉公). He committed this crime at the instigation of Ssu-ma Chao 司馬昭, who soon after usurped the Wei. See *Wei-chih* 4/57b–58a.

[240] Literally, *men-hsia* 門下, "[a bureau] underneath the palace gate," that is, a bureau for instant service of the emperor. Along with the *Shang-shu sheng* (Department of State Affairs) and *Chung-shu sheng* 中書省 (Central Secretariat), it exercised overwhelming authority in China's traditional political system.

[241] *Ssu-sheng* 肆眚, "to grant pardon for past offenses." For the origin of this term,

The Prince of Kuang-ling, silent for eight years, did not talk until this moment. Without exception, literati and commoners[242] called him a sage ruler.

Thereupon he named the Prince of Ch'ang-kuang as Prince of Tung-hai 東海王; conferred on [Erh-chu] Shih-lung the additional titles of Palatine Ceremonially Equal to the Three Authorities, President of State Affairs, and Prince of Lo-p'ing. [Erh-chu] Shih-lung was to keep all other titles without change. [The Prince of Ch'ang-kuang] gave the Prince of T'ai-yüan such posthumous titles as Prime Minister and Prince of Chin, and also the Nine [Privileged] Bestowals.[243] A shrine was built in his honor in the Shou-yang 首陽 section of the Mang Mountains. There had been in the mountains a shrine for the Duke of Chou, and next to it [Erh-chu] Shih-lung established this [new] shrine in order to imply a comparison between the Prince of T'ai-yüan's achievements and those of the Duke of Chou. After its completion, the shrine was destroyed by a fire, leaving a damaged pillar, which, in a thunderstorm three days later, was struck and broken into several segments. The foundation stones and shrine tiles of the pillar were all scattered at the foot of the mountain.

Officials were further ordered to discuss [with which emperor] the Prince of T'ai-yüan should be a coadjutor in the sharing of sacrificial honors. Liu Chi-ming 劉季明,[244] Director of Uprightness (*Ssu-chih* 司直), asserted that there was none for the Prince [to

see *TC* 155/2b Hu San-hsing's commentary quoting the *Ch'un-ch'iu* (Chuang 莊 22; not available in modern ed.): [春王正月], 肆大眚. 注:赦有罪也.…放赦罪人. 盪滌衆故, 以新其心. "[In the first month of the spring], a pardon was granted for serious offenders." Commentary: "This was to pardon criminals. . . . Criminals were pardoned to eradicate their various offenses and renew their life [literally, heart]."

[242] Reversing *shu shih* 庶士 to *shih shu* 士庶 after *Kou-ch'en* 2/15b.

[243] *Chiu-hsi* 九錫, symbols of imperial authority, customarily awarded by the captive emperor to successful usurpers during the Wei-Chin period. They are: 1. chariots and horses, 2. ceremonial costumes, 3. musical instruments, 4. a vermilion gate, 5. a raised dais for stairways, 6. one hundred *hu-pen* guards (palace guards), 7. bows and arrows, 8. axes and halberds, and 9. special wine for ancestral sacrifices. For its origin, see *Ch'un-ch'iu Kung-yang-chuan* (6/5b). Chuang 1, Ho Hsiu's 何休 commentary. See also Mather, *New Account*, p. 644.

[244] Not much information about Liu Chi-ming is available, but there is a mention of his name in the "Treatise on Rituals" of the *WS* (108.4/16b–17a). An Erudite of the Four Gates near the end of A.D. 518, he participated in a court discussion about

share sacrificial honors with]. Asked why, [Liu] Chi-ming replied:

"If he is a coadjutor of [Emperor] Shih-tsung, he really did not accomplish anything in the cause of the emperor in question.

"If he is a coadjutor of [Emperor] Hsiao-ming, however, he was personally responsible for the death of the emperor's mother. [245]

"If he is a coadjutor of Emperor Chuang, as a minister he was not [entirely faithful] toward the end. [On the contrary], he was killed by Emperor Chuang for his questionable loyalty.

"To draw a conclusion on this basis, he should not share sacrificial honors with any emperor."

In an outburst of anger, [Erh-chu] Shih-lung replied:

"You indeed deserve death!"

In reply [Liu] Chi-ming said:

"Your [humble] subordinate is a minister whose responsibility it is to deliberate. I speak in terms of the rites. If it does not accord with your sage mind,[246] imprison or execute me as you please!"

All critics admired [Liu] Chi-ming for speaking against the powerful, and, without exception, all sighed and bowed [to his courage]. Despite [Erh-chu] Shih-lung's harsh words, [Liu] Chi-ming managed to be free from trouble in the end.

Previously, when [Erh-chu] Shih-lung led his rebels northward, Emperor Chuang dispatched Shih Wu-lung 史仵龍, General Pacifying the East (*An-tung chiang-chün*) and Yang Wen-i 楊文義, General Quelling the North (*P'ing-pei chiang-chün*), each in command of three thousand soldiers, to guard the T'ai-hang Range 太行嶺,[247] and Yüan Tzu-kung, the Chief Palace Attendant, to safeguard Ho-nei. When later Erh-chu Chao headed for the south,

---

mourning costumes to be worn by officials at the burial ceremony of Empress Dowager Wen-chao 文昭皇太后.

According to *TC* (155/3a), Liu Chi-ming at this time took charge of the discussion. According to the same source (155/2a quoting the *T'ung-tien*), ten such posts were created in A.D. 530 under the Commandant of Justice to review cases of impeachment brought before him by the censors.

Among the three brothers Erh-chu Chung-yüan, Erh-Chu Yen-po, and Erh-chu Shih-lung, the first named was the most vicious. See *WS* 75/7a.

[245] That is, Empress Dowager Hu.

[246] The literal translation of *sheng hsin* 聖心.

[247] The T'ai-hang Range is in the borderland of Honan, Hopei, and Shansi provinces.

[Shih] Wu-lung and [Yang] Wen-i and others led their troops to surrender prior [to battle]. [Yüan] Tzu-kung, seeing that [Shih] Wu-lung and [Yang] Wen-i and the others had surrendered, for his part, saw which way the wind was blowing and dispersed [without a fight].[248] Consequently, [Erh-chu] Chao was able to utilize a favorable position, chase after the defeated, and march straight into the capital. His soldiers reached the [palace] watch-tower, their arrows flooding the imperial apartments. Now, when their contributions were reviewed, Shih Wu-lung and Yang Wen-i were each to receive a fief of one thousand households. To this the Prince of Kuang-ling objected, saying: "[Shih] Wu-lung and [Yang] Wen-i served the interest of the Prince [of Lo-p'ing], but not that of the nation." [The emperor] to the end refused [to listen]. His contemporaries commended the emperor for his uprightness and steadfastness.

Erh-chu Chung-yüan 爾朱仲遠, Prince of P'eng-ch'eng and the elder brother of [Erh-chu] Shih-lung, stayed with his army in Hua-t'ai 滑臺.[249] He memorialized the emperor, requesting that his Subordinate Inspector ([*Pu-*]*hsia tu-tu* [部]下都督), I[250] Yüan 乙瑗, be appointed Governor of Western Yen-chou 西兗州. I Yüan already served in that capacity before [Erh-chu Chung-yüan submitted his request] in the memorial. In reply, the Prince of Kuang-ling said: "Since you are able to fill [the post] with someone close, why bother notifying me from a distance?"

When [Erh-chu] Shih-lung waited on the emperor at banquets, the emperor often said: "The Prince of T'ai-yüan was greedy enough to take credit for Heaven's accomplishments as his own. For this crime alone[251] he deserved death," [a remark that] shocked [Erh-chu] Shih-lung and others.[252]

From that point onward, [Erh-chu] Shih-lung dared not attend court audiences. He often exercised dictatorial power, becoming all the more arrogant and abusive. He gave directives from his

[248] Literally, *wang-fen k'uei-san* 望風潰散, "dispersed at the sign of the wind."

[249] Modern Hua-hsien 滑縣, Honan.

[250] The text (2/17b) gives no surname. *WS* 44/5b–6a makes a mention of I Yüan 乙瑗, grandson of I Huai 乙瓌, who was married to Princess Huai-yang 淮陽 (daughter of Emperor Kao-tsu) and held the same post.

[251] Emending *yu* 有 to *i* 亦 after *IS* 2/13b.

[252] Literally, *teng* 等, "and others."

seat[253] for the operation of various government departments,[254] and managed all national matters[255] at home. Every item of business—important or trifling—was referred to [Erh-chu] Shih-lung's residence prior to implementation. The emperor merely folded his hands[256] without interfering.

Only in the first year of the Yung-hsi (A.D. 532) period, upon the ascension of the Prince of P'ing-yang [as the successor to the Prince of An-ting], was a five-storied stūpa built.

The Prince of P'ing-yang[257] was the youngest son [the third son] of the Prince of Kuang-p'ing.

Wei Shou 魏收,[258] Squire-attendant of the Central Secretariat, and others were ordered to compose an inscription for the monastery. On the fifth day of the second month of the second year [of the Yung-hsi period] (March 15 A.D. 533), the construction was completed, on which occasion the emperor led various officials [to preside over] a meeting of the myriad monks (*pañca pariṣad*).[259] On that day the stone statue outside the monastery gate moved by itself, for no reason, lowering and lifting its head for a whole day before it [finally] stopped. The emperor, coming in person to pay his respects, found it strange. Lu Ching-hsüan 盧景宣,[260] Drafter of the Central Secretar-

[253] Literally, *tso* 坐, "a seat; to sit." *WS* (75/9b) reports that, as President of the Department of State Affairs, Erh-chu Chung-yüan ordered his subordinates Sung Yu-tao 宋遊道 and Hsing Hsin 邢昕 (both secretaries in the same department) to perform their official duties in his private residence; hence, the translation "at home."

[254] Literally, *t'ai-sheng* 臺省, "tribunals and departments."

[255] Literally, *wan-chi* 萬機, "a myriad matters."

[256] Literally, *kung-chi nan-mien* 拱己南面, "to fold both hands on the breast and face the south"—descriptive of an effortless imperial sway. For the origin of *kung-chi*, see *HS* 3/8a 高后紀贊:故惠帝拱己, "Therefore Emperor Hui held both hands on the breast"; for the origin of *nan-mien*, see *Tso-chuan* Hsiang 26 37/15a: 鄭於是不敢南面, "On this Cheng no longer ventured to turn its face to the south."

[257] He was later known as Emperor Hsiao-wu.

[258] Wei Shou (A.D. 506–572) was a famous man of letters and the author of the *Wei-shu*. For his biography, see *PCS* 37/1a–14b.

[259] A similar gathering was held in A.D. 518 under the empress dowager to honor her deceased father. The attending "myriad monks" (*wan-seng* 萬僧) were given free meals and invited to participate in scriptural discussions. See *WS* 83B/6b.

[260] Also known as Lu Pien 盧辯, younger brother of Lu Ching-yü 盧景裕. Lu Pien served as a Drafter of the Central Secretariat around A.D. 531, but became more influential in later years. He was most responsible for institutional reforms during the Northern Chou dynasty. See *PS* 30/27b–32b.

iat, explained: "There were cases in high antiquity where stones stood upright and the shrine to the god of the soil moved.[261] Why should Your Majesty find this strange?" The emperor then returned to the palace. In the seventh month of the following year, the emperor was forced by Chief Palace Attendant Hu-ssu Ch'un to flee to Ch'ang-an. By the end of the tenth month,[262] the capital had been moved to Yeh.[263]

The Ching-ning Temple 景寧寺 (Temple of Peaceful Prospect) was established by Yang Ch'un 楊椿[264] (A.D. 453–531), Grand Guardian and Grand Minister of Public Works (*Ssu-t'u kung*). It was located on the south side of the Imperial Drive three *li* outside the Ch'ing-yang Gate, in the so-called Ching-ning Ward 景寧里 (Peaceful Prospect Ward).

After Emperor Kao-tsu moved the capital to Lo-yang, [Yang] Ch'un sponsored the construction of this ward, in which he lived. He also donated part of his residence as the [temple], which was named after the ward. The design and ornamentation of the temple were very beautiful, [with] carved pillars and draperies strung with pearls. Yang Ch'un's younger brother, [Yang] Shen [楊]慎[265] (A.D. 465–

[261] This is a reference to an *HS* entry (27.B.A./29a) which indicates that when a stone stands up by itself, there will be a new emperor rising to power from the rank of commoner.

[262] The text (2/18a) gives no exact date. According to *WS* (11/19b), this occurred on August 21, A.D. 534 (*TC* 156/23a gives August 22), which marks the beginning of the Western Wei.

[263] Emperor Hsiao-ching (Yüan Shan-chien) left Lo-yang on the twenty-seventh of the tenth month (November 18, A.D. 534; *WS* 12/1b) and arrived at Yeh on December 2, 534 (*TC* 156/29a).

[264] A native of Hua-yin 華陰 of Hung-nung commandery (south of modern Ling-pao 靈寶, Honan), Yang Ch'un was the younger brother of Yang Pu 楊播, another member of this famous Yang family. He was a general and governor under six emperors before his execution by Erh-chu Shih-lung in A.D. 531. See *WS* 58/7a–14a.

According to his biography (*WS* 58/13b), he was then seventy-seven *sui*. He was therefore born in A.D. 453, not 455 as claimed by Iriya Yoshitaka (*Rakuyō garan ki*, p. 55 n. 121).

[265] *WS* 58/18a gives his name as *Shun* 順 rather than *Shen* 慎 as recorded in the *Ch'ieh-lan chi*. These two characters were often mixed up by scribes of the T'ang. Yang Shun was Governor of Chi-chou, carrying at the same time a military title,

531), Governor of Chi-chou, and [Yang] Shen's[266] younger brother [Yang] Chin [楊]津[267] (A.D. 467–531), Minister of Public Works were both by nature tolerant, refined, and attached great value to principles, taking riches lightly. A household of four generations living together, the family included great granduncles, granduncles, and uncles.[268] There had never been any at court as principled and as willing to live together as they were.[269] During the P'u-t'ai period (A.D. 531–532),[270] [Yang Ch'un] was executed by Erh-chu Shih-lung. Later, his house was set aside for the Chien-chung Temple.

Three *li* outside the Ch'ing-yang Gate and on the north side of the Imperial Drive was the Hsiao-i Ward 孝義里 (Ward of the Filial and Righteous). In the northwestern section of the ward was the tomb of Su Ch'in 蘇秦,[271] which bordered on the Pao-ming Monastery 寶明寺 (Monastery of the Precious and Bright). Monks often saw [Su] Ch'in coming into and going out from the tomb. His horses, carriages, and other plumed insignia[272] were very much like those used by the current prime ministers.

To the east of the Hsiao-i Ward was the Little Market of Lo-yang (*Lo-yang hsiao-shih* 洛陽小市),[273] to the north of which was the

---

General Quelling the North (*P'ing-pei chiang-chün*) (*WS* 58/18a). Iriya (*Rakuyō garan ki*, p. 56 n. 122) gives his dates as A. D. 467–531. According to his biography, however, Yang Shun died in A.D. 531 at the age of sixty five; hence, he was born in A.D. 465.

[266] *Shun* 順 should read *Shen* 慎. See note above.

[267] Iriya (*Rakuyō garan ki*, n. 123) gives his dates as A.D. 469–531. His biography (*WS* 58/22b–23a) reports that he died in A.D. 531 at the age of sixty-three. Therefore, he was born in A.D. 467 instead of 469.

[268] Literally, *San-ts'ung* 三從, defined as brothers of one's great-grandfather, grandfather, and father in *Erh-ya* (I-wen facsimile *SSCCS* ed.) 4/14b–15a 釋親.

[269] In the biography of Yang Yüan-jang 楊元讓 (Yang Ch'un's nephew), the author speaks very highly of the generosity and congeniality of the Yang brothers. There were one hundred males and females in the household who lived together and shared meals prepared in the same kitchen. During the Wei, only the Lu Yüan 盧淵 brothers could compete with the Yangs in this respect. See *WS* 58/25a–26a.

[270] The exact date is the seventh month (July–August), A.D. 531.

[271] Su Ch'in (d. 317 B.C.) was a leading statesman during the period of Warring States. He was the chief advocate for a "vertical alliance" of six states against the state of Ch'in in the west. He died in 317 B.C.

[272] That is, *yü-i* 羽儀. See Robert des Rotours, *Traité des fonctionaires et de l'armée* 1, 362.

[273] Emending *ssu* 寺 to *shih* 市 after *YHNC* 3/10a and *IS* 2/14b.

residence of Chang Ching-jen 張景仁, the General of Chariots and Cavalry.[274]

[Chang] Ching-jen was a native of Shan-yin 山陰 in K'uei-chi [commandery] 會稽[郡]. In the early years of the Cheng-kuang period (A.D. 520–524),[275] he accompanied Hsiao Pao-yin 蕭寶夤 to surrender to the Wei, whereupon he was appointed Commander of the Plumed Forest Guards and given a residence in the Kuei-cheng Ward 歸正里 (Ward of the Return to Legitimacy), known as part of the "Southerners' District" (*Wu-jen fang* 吳人坊). The majority of the southern people who surrendered to the Wei lived here. Located close to the two rivers, the I and the Lo, the inhabitants were allowed [to maintain] their own customs. Within this block were more than three thousand families[276] who created their own lanes and maintained their own marketplace.[277] The things on sale were for the most part seafood; hence contemporaries called this area the Fish and Turtle Market.[278] Ashamed of living here, [Chang] Ching-jen moved to the Hsiao-i Ward instead.

At this time the court, desirous of encouraging people in distant areas[279] to immigrate, treated the southerners with generosity. Anyone who pulled up his skirt and crossed the [Yangtze] River[280] would be given a [high] post [without the usual process of grading]. Without any military merits,[281] [Chang] Ching-jen

[274] His biographical sketch is not available elsewhere.

[275] The text (2/19a) is in error; the date should be A.D. 501 (the second year of Ching-ming 景明)—the year Hsiao Pao-yin deserted his native Ch'i dynasty to join the Wei. See *WS* 59/7b.

[276] *YHNC* 3/8a gives 30 (*san-shih* 三十) instead of 3,000 (*san-ch'ien* 三千).

[277] Emending *ssu* 寺 to *shih* 市 after *YHNC* 3/8a and *YLTT* 13823/4a.

[278] Emending *ssu* 寺 to *shih* 市 after *YLTT* 13823/4a and *IS* 2/15a.

[279] Literally, *chao huai huang-fu* 招懷荒服, "to give inspiration to, and show care for those in outlying regions [within three thousand *li* from the national capital]." For the origin of *huang-fu* 荒服, see *Chi-chung Chou-shu* (*SPTK so-pen*) 7/42 王會解:[方]三千里之內爲荒服, "Within three thousand [square *li* from the capital] is *huang-fu*."

[280] Literally, *ch'ien-ch'ang tu yu Chiang che* 褰裳渡於江者, "to cross the river by pulling up the lower garments," that is, those deserters from the south who had made no contributions to the Northern Wei.

[281] Literally, *wu han-ma chih lao* 無汗馬之勞, "without the toil of causing the horse to sweat"; that is, without military merit.

occupied a high and very distinguished post. In the second year of the Yung-an period (A.D. 529), Hsiao Yen dispatched [the Prince of] Pei-hai, escorted by the clerk Ch'en Ch'ing-chih 陳慶之,[282] to Lo-yang to usurp the throne. As a reward for this mission, [Ch'en] Ch'ing-chih was promoted to the post of Chief Palace Attendant.

When [Chang] Ching-jen was in the south, [Ch'en] Ch'ing-chih had been his old acquaintance. Consequently, [Ch'en] Ch'ing-chih [was invited] to come to [Chang] Ching-jen's home for a drinking feast. Hsiao Piao 蕭彪,[283] Minister of Agriculture, and Chang Sung 張嵩,[284] Secretary on the Right, Department of State Affairs (*Shang-shu yu-ch'eng*) both[285] southerners, also attended the banquet. [Among those present], Yang Yüan-shen 楊元愼,[286] the Palace Grandee (*Chung ta-fu*) and Wang Hsün 王眗,[287] the Ministrant and Palace Grandee (*Chi-shih chung ta-fu*), were the only two from prominent clans in the North China plain. Because he was intoxicated, [Ch'en] Ch'ing-chih spoke to Hsiao, Chang, and the others:

"The Wei, though flourishing, are still referred to as [one of] the five barbarians.[288] Legitimacy[289] of course rests in the Southern

[282] Ch'en Ch'ing-shih, a confidant of Emperor Wu of the Liang, was charged with the responsibility of escorting the Wei refugee, the Prince of Pei-hai, to return to the capital city Lo-yang. At the time Ch'en Ch'ing-chih was given the title Commissioner Holding Imperial Credentials, General of Whirlwindlike Bravery (*Chia-chieh piao-yung chiang-chün*). See *Liang-shu* 32/3a.

[283] No biography or any other information is available.

[284] No biography or any other information is available.

[285] The text (2/19b) reads Piao 彪, which is probably an erroneous interpolation. First, the following sentences define Yang and Wang as the only northerners present at the banquet, implying that both Hsiao and Chang were southerners. Second, another sentence reads that "Ch'en Ch'ing-chih . . . talked with Hsiao and Chang" as a group, suggesting once again that both were migrants from the south. The translation therefore does not follow the text as given.

[286] No biography or any other information is available.

[287] No biography or any other information is available.

[288] The T'o-pa tribesmen were traditionally classified as a branch of the Hsien-pei 鮮卑, one of the "Five Barbarians," *Wu-hu* 五胡. For a study of the "Five Barbarians," see Wang Yi-t'ung, "Wu-hu t'ung-k'ao," *Chung-kuo-wen-hua yen-chiu-so hui-k'an* 3 (Chengtu, 1943), 57–79.

[289] Literally, *cheng shuo* 正朔 refers to the official calendar (*cheng* 正, meaning the first day of a year; *shuo* 朔, the first day of a month). The term is taken as a symbol of a legitimate and sovereign government.

Court.[290] The Grand Jade Seal of the Ch'in dynasty[291] is now in the possession of the Liang dynasty." With a stern countenance, [Yang] Yüan-shen retorted:

"The Southern Court, breathing a stolen breath, lives in seclusion in an out-of-the-way corner [of China]. Its land for the most part is low-lying and damp, where insects and ants swarm and breed. Its domain is infected with a malarial epidemic, where frogs and turtles share the same cave and where men and birds are of the same flock. The ruler, with his hair cut short, does not appear to have that elongated head [we associate with good breeding];[292] the people, with tattooed bodies, are by nature small and vile. Floating in the three rivers[293] and boating in the five lakes,[294] they

[290] Literally, Chiang-tso 江左, "on the left bank of the Yangtze." In Chinese historical geography, the region is variably referred to as Chiang-tso 江左, Chiang-yu 江右, Chiang-nan 江南, and Wu 吳.

[291] The seal carried an eight-character inscription handwritten by Li Ssu 李斯 (d. 208 B.C.), the man most responsible for the unification of China by the Ch'in, which reads *shou-ming yü t'ien, chi-shou yung ch'ang*, 受命於天, 旣壽永昌, "Receiving the mandate from heaven, [the Ch'in] will enjoy both longevity and prosperity." It had been passed on from the Ch'in to the Han, then to Wang Mang 王莽 (regnant A.D. 9–23), Emperor Kuang-wu of the Later Han (regnant A.D. 25–57), through the Wei and Chin courts to Liu Ts'ung 劉聰 (regnant A.D. 301–318) of the Former Chao 前趙, Shih Lo 石勒 (regnant A.D. 319–333) of the Later Chao 後趙 (A.D. 319–352), and again Emperor Mu 穆帝 (regnant A.D. 344–361) of the Eastern Chin in A.D. 352. From the Eastern Chin, in turn, the seal was passed on to the the Sung 宋 (A.D. 420–479), Ch'i 齊 (A.D. 479–502), and now the Liang 梁 courts (A.D. 502–557), as noted by Ch'en Ch'ing-chih. It was considered that any dynasty in possession of the seal was the one recognized as legitimate by heaven. For more information about the history of its transmission, see Ts'ui Yü 崔彧, "Ch'uan-kuo-hsi chien" 傳國璽牋, as quoted in *Nan-ts'un cho-keng lu* (Yü-lan ts'ao-t'ang [Ming] ed.) 26/1a–9b.

[292] *WH* 6/17b 左思魏都賦：巷無杼首，里罕耆耋, "In the streets, there are no elongated heads; in the wards, no elderly gentlemen." Commentary: 方言曰：燕記曰：豐人杼首. 杼首，長首也. …交益之人，率皆弱陋，故曰無杼首也, "The *Yen-chi* as quoted in the *Fang-yen* reads: 'Healthy persons have elongated heads. *Shu-shou* means elongated heads.' People in the Chiao[-chou] and I[-chou] are generally weak and ill-developed; hence, there are no persons with elongated heads."

[293] Among the many possible interpretations of the "three rivers," *san-ho* 三河, the one dealing with the Lou 婁, Tung 東, and Sung 松 (all in modern Kiangsu) Rivers seems to have more direct bearing on the Wu region, from where Ch'en Ch'ing-chih came to Lo-yang. See *Shu-ching* 6/12a 禹貢：三江旣入. K'ung An-kuo's commentary quoting the *Wu-ti chi* 吳地記：松江東北行七十里得三江口，東北入海爲婁江，東南入海爲東江，並松江爲三江, "The Sung River runs

are neither accustomed to[295] rituals and music, nor are they governed by statutes and laws. As fugitives from the Ch'in and Han, although their spoken language has an admixture of standard Chinese, [in the main] it is the difficult dialect of Min 閩 (Fukien) and Ch'u 楚 (Hupeh), which can never be changed. Even when they set up rulers and subjects, the superiors are insolent and the subordinates violent. That is why first Liu Shao 劉劭 killed his own father[296] and second [Liu] Hsiu-lung [劉]休隆 committed incest with his mother.[297] They violated the principles governing human relationships, and acted no differently from birds and beasts. In addition, [the princess] of Shan-yin 山陰公主,[298] in disregard of her husband's dignity, asked for more consorts. As a group, they behaved licentiously at home and ignored the scorn and ridicule directed against them. Reared in this tradition and unexposed to our cultural refinement, [southerners are like] the so-called man of Yang-ti 陽翟, who fails to realize that goiters are ugly.[299]

"Having received an appointment from heaven through the holy maps,[300] our Wei selected [an area between] the Sung Mountain and the Lo [River] as the site of our capital. Safeguarded

---

seventy *li* northwesterly before it reaches a point where three rivers meet. Flowing northeasterly to the sea is the Lou River, southeasterly is the Tung River. Together with the Sung River, they are known as the 'Three Rivers.'"

[294] Possibly, the "five lakes" refer to the Ke 滆, T'ao 洮, She 射, Kuei 貴, and T'ai 太, all in the Wu region, the general area of modern I-hsing 宜興 and Wu-hsi 無錫 prefectures in Kiangsu. See *HHS* 58/8b 馮衍傳 commentary quoting Yü Fan 虞翻.

[295] Emending *ku* 沽 to *chan* 沾 after *IS* 2/15b.

[296] Liu Shao (d. A.D. 454), son of Emperor Wen of the Liu-Sung (A.D.420–479), committed regicide when he noted that the emperor was about to hold him accountable for treasonous acts. See *Sung-shu* 99/1a–5a.

[297] Styled name of Liu Chün 劉駿 (A.D. 426–464), who reportedly had illicit relations with his own mother, Empress Dowager Lu 路 (Emperor Wen's wife). See *Sung-shu* 41/14b–17a.

[298] In a request to her brother, the emperor, for consorts, the princess argued that, while the emperor had ten thousand ladies in the harem waiting on him, she herself had only one husband in her household. It was therefore totally unfair. As a result, the emperor gave her thirty male companions for compensation. See *Sung-shu* 7/7b.

[299] A disease said to be common among the people of Yang-ti 陽翟 (modern Yü-hsien 禹縣, Honan). See *Yün-yü yang-ch'iu* (in *Li-tai shih-hua*, I-wen facsimile ed., 10/2b).

[300] For "holy maps," see Yang Hsüan-chih's Preface and Chapter 2 under the P'ing-teng Monastery.

by the [Sacred] Five Mountains,[301] we treat all within the four seas as one family. The statutes regulating reforms in customs and tradition are comparable to those of the Five Emperors,[302] and the richness of rituals, music, and institutions dwarfs that of the hundred kings preceding us. Now how can you, one of a band of fish and turtles, desire righteousness and come to [our] court [to pay homage], drinking water from our pond and pecking rice grains [provided by] us, and be so insolent?"

[Overpowered by Yang] Yüan-shen's torrential and rapid-flowing phrases and sentences, which were both beautiful and elegant, [Ch'en] Ch'ing-chih and all the others closed their mouths, their sweat flowing, and swallowed their words.[303]

Several days thereafter, [Ch'en] Ch'ing-chih fell ill with acute heart pains. He sought someone to cure him by exorcism. [Yang] Yüan-shen claimed to be one capable of expiating [the evil] spells. [Ch'en] Ch'ing-chih then relied on [Yang] Yüan-shen for treatment. [Yang] Yüan-shen immediately took and held a mouthful of water, which he then spat at [Ch'en] Ch'ing-chih, saying:

"You ghost of the Wu region who lived in Chien-k'ang 建康![304] Wearing a small cap and short garment, you call yourself 'A-nung' 阿儂[305] and call others 'A so and so.'[306] You eat *ku* 菰[307] seeds and darnel[308] for meal, drink slops as your bev-

[301] That is, Mountains T'ai 泰 (in modern Shantung), Hua 華 (in modern Shansi), Huo 霍 (in modern Shansi), Heng 恒 (in modern Shansi), and Sung 嵩 (in modern Honan), all lying within the Wei domain.

[302] Emending *wu-ch'ang* 五常 to *wu-ti* 五帝 after *YLTT* 13823/4b.

[303] Emending *ho* 合 to *han* 含 after *IS* 2/16a.

[304] Another name for Chien-yeh 建業, Pai-hsia 白下, Mo-ling 秣陵, and Chin-ling 金陵 (modern Nanking). Chien-yeh was the capital of Wu, Eastern Chin, and four other dynasties in the south.

[305] "A" 阿, now pronounced in the fifth tone in the Wu dialect, was pronounced in the first tone during the Southern Dynasties period and used as a prefix for surnames, given names, and even in addressing the second and third person. See *Jih-chih lu* 日知錄 (*SPPY* ed.) 32/11b–12a under 阿.

[306] For the phrase *yu tse ah p'ang* 語則阿傍, the translation is speculative, since the exact meaning is unclear.

[307] *Ku* 菰, also known as *chiang* 蔣, the seeds of which are edible. *Kuang-ya* 廣雅 (*SPPY* ed.) 10A–44b 釋草:蔣也, 其米謂之雕胡. "The seeds of aquatic grass (*chiang*) are known as *tiao-hu* 雕胡." *Tiao-hu* is translated as "bog rhubarb" by Burton Watson. See his *Chinese Rhyme-prose, Poems in the Fu Form from the Han and Six Dynasties Periods*, (New York 1971), p. 32.

[308] *Pai* 稗, a weed that looks like a rice plant. *Shuo-wen* 7A/30a: 禾別也. "*Pai* is

erage,[309] sip *ch'un* 蓴[310]-plant stew and suck[311] crab spawn.[312] You roll nutmeg[313] in your hand and chew betel nuts.[314] Having just arrived in Central China,[315] you are homesick. Hurry, hurry to leave here, leave here for your [native] Tan-yang 丹陽![316]

"Now perhaps you are a ghost from a family of humble origin, ...[317] Like a fish in a net or a turtle in a trap you are fond of munching waterchestnuts and lotusroots, collecting chicken-heads,[318] and savoring frog and oystersoup. Wearing cloth garments and straw sandals, you may enjoy riding a buffalo backward. Or you may like to be driven aimlessly in a boat through the Yüan 沅, Hsiang 湘, Yangtze, and Han 漢 Rivers,[319] following

---

different from *ho* (rice plant)." Tuan Yü-ts'ai's comm.: 謂禾類而別於禾也, "It belongs to the rice family but is a different species."

[309] *Chiang* 漿, "thick fluid." The meaning is not clear.

[310] *Ch'un* 蓴, an edible water-lily (*brasenia purpurea*) which was a southern delicacy.

[311] Literally *ch'ieh-sou* 唼嗍, descriptive of the noise of waterfowls when feeding. 嗍 is also written as 敕. *Chi-yün* 集韻 (*SPPY* ed.) 9/12a.

[312] A southern delicacy when seasoned with spices. See *TPYL* 942/8b 鱗介部蟹 quoting the *Ling-piao lu-i* 嶺表錄異:蟹殼內有膏如黃蘇, 加以五味, 和殼煿之, 食亦有味 (passage not available in modern version of the same work), "Inside of the crab carapace is a paste that looks like *huang-su*, 'yellow crisp,' that is, crab spawn. Blended with five spices and roasted in the carapace, it is also tasty."

[313] The aromatic seeds of *myristica fragrans*, which were used as spices. Hsi Han 嵇含, *Nan-fang ts'ao-mu chuang* (Facsimile ed., Shanghai, 1955) A/2: 豆蔻花, 其苗如蘆, 其葉似薑, 其花作穗, 嫩葉卷之而生, "*Myristica fragrans* has stalks like those of reeds, leaves like those of ginger, flowers like the ears of grains. When it grows, it is rolled inside of tender leaves."

[314] *Nan-fang ts'ao-mu chuang* 檳榔樹:實大如桃李, …出林邑, 彼人以爲貴, "The fruits are as big as peaches and apricots, ... [and] are produced in Lin-i (in modern Vietnam).... People over there treasure them."

[315] Literally, *chung-t'u* 中土. See n. 12 above.

[316] Tan-yang 丹陽, southeast of Chien-k'ang, is used here to mean the region south of the Yangtze River.

[317] The text (2/21a) ? *t'ou yu hsiu* ?頭猶脩 "? head is oblong," with the first character missing. The meaning of the sentence is not clear.

[318] *Ch'i-t'ou* 雞頭, same as *ch'ien* 芡. *Fang-yen shu-cheng* (with commentaries by Tai Chen, *SPPY* ed.) 3/4a: 葰, 芡, 雞頭, …南楚江湘之間謂之雞頭, "*I, ch'ien, chi-t'ou* ... are known as *chi-t'ou* in Southern Ch'u, and along the Chiang and Hsiang Rivers." *Chi-t'ou* 雞頭 was also a colloquialism in the central Yangtze during the Southern Dynasties.

[319] All in the central Yangtze area.

the waves or running against the current, surfacing,[320] sinking or floating, as do the fish. Wearing garments of coarse white fabric,[321] you may like to stand up and dance, or beat the waves and burst into song. Hurry, hurry to leave here, leave here for your [native] Yang-chou 揚州!"[322]

Lying against a pillow, [Ch'en] Ch'ing-chih said: "Master Yang, you have deeply humiliated me!"

From this time on, southerners never again dared to speak of spells.[323]

Soon afterwards, [the Prince of] Pei-hai was executed. As for [Ch'en] Ch'ing-chih, he rushed back to Hsiao Yen, who appointed[324] him Governor of Ssu-chou 司州,[325] [in which capacity Ch'en Ch'ing-chih] showed unusual respect for northerners. Chu I 朱异[326] found this strange and asked him why. [In reply, Ch'en Ch'ing-chih] said: "Since the time of the Chin and the Sung, Lo-yang has been labeled a piece of deserted land, and we in our area categorically refer to those [living] to the north of the Yangtze as barbarians. After my recent visit to Lo-yang, I began to realize that cultured clansmen are [all] in the Central China plain where rituals and etiquette flourish and people are rich and prosperous. There were things that I did not know when I saw them, neither can I give a verbal account of what I have seen. That is what we call:

[320] Literally, *yen-yung* 噞喁, descriptive of a school of fish surfacing for air. *WH* 5/3b 左思吳都賦：泝洄順流，噞喁沈浮, "This fish swim against or with the current, surfacing or submerging in the water."

[321] *Chu-i ch'ih-fu* 紵衣絺服, common attire worn by the Wu people (*WH* 5/9b); also title of a popular song prevailing during the Chin (Kuo Mou-ch'ien, *Yüeh-fu shih-chi*, *SPTK so-pen*, 55/411).

[322] The passage consists of two sections, with four characters for each line and rhyming at the end of alternate lines. The key rhyme word in the first half (eight couplets) is *yang* 陽; the second half (nine couplets), *yu* 尤.

[323] As a result of this insult, those from Wu were reluctant to ask for spells.

[324] Adding *ch'i* 其 after *IS* (2/16a) and *YLTT* (13823/5a).

[325] Actually there had been two provinces of Ssu-chou, the southern and the northern, which bordered on the Wei. Ch'en Ch'ing-chih was governor of both (*Liang-shu* 32/6a). For more information, see Hsü Wen-fan, *Tung-Chin Nan-Pei-ch'ao yü-ti piao* (*Erh-shih-wu-shih pu-pien* ed.) 7/119.

[326] A scholar well-versed in classics, history, and literature, Chu I (A.D. 483–549) was denounced in the standard histories for his role in aggravating Hou Ching's 侯景 rebellion between the years A.D. 548 and 552. See *Liang-shu* 38/1a–4b.

'Splendid, splendid is the capital city,
A model for the whole nation to follow.'[327]

"Insofar as one who has ascended the [sacred] Mountain T'ai would despise a small mound, and one who has traveled on the Yangtze River and seas would look down upon the Hsiang and Yüan [Rivers], how can we afford not to hold northerners in great respect?"

Thereupon [Ch'en] Ch'ing-chih imitated the Wei patterns for his insignia and costumes, which were quickly followed by literati and common people of the south.[328] Loose garments and wide girdles caught the fancy of Mo-ling.[329]

[Yang] Yüan-shen, a native of Hung-nung 弘農, was the sixth-generation direct descendant of [Yang] Ch'iao [楊]嶠, Governor of Chi-chou during the Chin. His great-grandfather, [Yang] T'ai [楊]泰, accompanied Emperor Wu of the Sung to march through [T'ung-]Pass [潼]關 [in the latter's successful campaign against the Later Ch'in in A.D. 417,] and for seven years he had been Grand Warden of Shang-lo 上洛 before he deserted the illegitimate [Lin-Sung] to surrender[330] to the Wei. [Because of this], Emperor Ming-yüan[331] enfeoffed him as the Marquis of Lin-chin 臨晉侯. He had been Grand Warden of Kuang-wu commandery 廣武郡 and Ch'en commandery 陳郡, and was honored posthumously as Governor of Liang-chou 涼州 and Marquis of Eminence 烈侯. [Yang] Yüan-shen's grandfather, [Yang] Fu [楊]撫, holder of a

[327] A paraphrase of the *Shih-ching* 20.4/12b (ode 205, verse 5, lines 1 and 2) 商頌殷武：商邑翼翼，四方之極. Waley, *Book of Songs*, p. 280: "Splendid was the capital of Shang/A pattern to the peoples on every side."

[328] Actually this style of ceremonial garments had been worn ever since the Han (*HS* 雋不疑傳：褒衣博帶，盛服至門上謁). Also popular during the Liang dynasty, when a big hat and high clogs were added, it was not necessarily the result of Ch'en Ch'ing-chih's sponsorship. See Yen Chih-t'ui, *Yen-shih chia-hsün* (*SPPY* ed.) 4/21a 涉務篇; Teng, *Family Instructions*, p. 116.

[329] Another name for Chien-yeh (modern Nanking).

[330] In early A.D. 423, in the wake of the death of Emperor Wen of the Liu-Sung, the Wei general Shu-sun Chien 叔孫建 led his troops across the Yellow River to conquer Sung lands such as Ch'ing-chou and Yen-chou, whereas many Liu-Sung generals then surrendered to the Wei. Yang T'ai's desertion might have taken place in conjunction with this. See *WS* 3/13b–14a.

[331] Emperor Ming-yüan 明元, otherwise known as Emperor T'ai-tsung 太宗. Here the character Yüan 元 is missing in the text (2/21b).

Ming-ching 明經 (Clearly Understanding the Classics) degree, was an Erudite.[332] [Yang] Yüan-shen's father, [Yang] Tz'u [楊]辭, was content with nature and uninterested in serving kings and marquises. [Yang Yüan-shen's uncle, Yang] Hsü [楊]許,[333] was a metropolitan prefect of Ho-nan 河南令 and Grand Warden of Shu commandery 蜀郡. For generations, [the Yangs] were renowned for scholarship and [good] conduct; their fame was great within their own locality.

[Yang] Yüan-shen had aesthetic tastes. [Even] as a youth, he had high principles, goodheartedness, and no regard for contemporary restraints. Fond of mountains and rivers, he took pleasure in wandering among forests and marshes. Widely learned in the field of literature and nearly godlike in the art of "pure conversation," he was matchless for quick and impromptu responses in colloquy. He studied *Lao* [*-tzu*] and *Chuang* [*-tzu*], and was skilled at discussing the primal principles. Fond of wine, he could drink up to one *shih*[334] without it affecting his composure. He often bemoaned [his cruel fate], with a sigh, that he had not been born at the same time as Juan Chi. He was unwilling to be involved with politics, so during his tenure as a Palace Attending [Grandee] (*Chung-san* [*ta-fu*] 中散[大夫]) he often claimed to be ill and lived in seclusion, neither paying courtesy visits to dignitaries nor being sociable with his relatives and acquaintances.[335] He was strict in choosing friends, so his contemporaries did not know him well. Sometimes there would be men who, out of admiration for his noble principles, came to his gate and left visiting cards, but [Yang] Yüan-shen pretended to be sick, reposing on a raised bed.

In addition, he was pensive, imaginative, and skillful at interpreting dreams. In the early Hsiao-ch'ang years,[336] when Yüan Yüan 元淵,[337] Prince of Kuang-yang 廣陽王,[338] had just been

[332] The text (2/22a) is *Chung po-shih* 中博士, a rare title. Its exact function is unclear. The character *Chung* probably means "palace," and *Chung po-shih* is probably an abbreviation for *Chung-shu po-shih* (Erudite of the Central Secretariat).

[333] *Shu* 叔, that is, Yang Tz'u's younger brother.

[334] The equivalent of 24.50 liters.

[335] Literally, *i pu ch'ing-tiao ch'in-chih* 亦不慶弔親知, "without offering congratulations or condolences to his relatives and acquaintances."

[336] The exact date is the fifth month (May–June), A.D. 526. See *WS* 9/24a.

[337] Because of a T'ang taboo, his name is variably given as *Yüan* 淵 or *Shen* 深.

[338] The text (2/22b) mistakenly gives Prince of Kuang-ling 廣陵王.

installed as Palatine Ceremonially Equal to the Three Authorities with command of an army of ten thousand to fight [the rebel] Ko Jung 葛榮,[339] he dreamed that he wore a ceremonial garment and stood leaning one night against a locust tree—a dream he thought auspicious. He requested [Yang] Yüan-shen's interpretation. [Yang] Yüan-shen[340] said: "This is an omen indicating that you will be [one of the] Three Lords." [Yüan] Yüan was very pleased [with this remark]. After [Yang] Yüan-shen went home, he confided in someone, saying: "The prince of Kuang-yang[341] will soon die—the character *huai* 槐 (locust tree) [consists of] a ghost (*kuei* 鬼) to the side of a tree (*mu* 木). He will become [one of the] Three Lords [only] after death."

Indeed, the Prince was killed by Ko Jung and awarded the posthumous title of Grand Minister of Public Instruction.[342] In the end, the prediction turned out to be true.

In the early[343] Chien-i period, when Hsüeh Ling-po 薛令伯, Grand Warden of Yang-ch'eng 陽城[344] learned that the Prince of T'ai-yüan had killed many officials[345] and enthroned Emperor Chuang, he left his post and fled eastward. Suddenly he dreamed of having shot down a wild goose, so he asked [Yang] Yüan-shen [for an interpretation]. [Yang] Yüan-shen said: "[For gift-giving], ministers present lambs; grandees present wild geese.[346] You will be appointed to the post of grandee." Soon afterward [Hsüeh] Ling-po was installed as Grandee Remonstrant (*Chien-i ta-fu*).

[339] Ko Jung was a follower of Hsien-yü Hsiu-li 鮮于脩禮, who started a rebellion in A.D. 526.

[340] Adding the two characters *Yüan-shen* 元慎 after *YYTT* 8/49 夢.

[341] The text (2/22b) is Kuang-ling 廣陵, which is an obvious mistake for Kuang-yang 廣陽.

[342] The text (2/22b) reads *Ssu-k'ung kung* 司空公, which is a mistake for *Ssu-t'u kung* 司徒公. His son's stele inscription ("Yüan Chan mu-chih" 元湛墓誌, *MCCS* plate 96.2) as well as other sources (*PS* 16/30a and *YYTT* 8/49) all give *Ssu-t'u* 司徒; hence, the translation.

[343] Adding *ch'u* 初 after *IS* 2/17b and *YLTT* 12823/5b.

[344] Modern Huang-ch'uan *hsien* 潢川縣, Honan.

[345] See Chapter 1 under the Yung-ning Monastery at note 59.

[346] This is a reference to the *Chou-li*. The lamb symbolizes faithful adherence to the herd, whereas the wild goose stands for punctuality. *Chou-li* 18/23b 春官大宗伯; sub-commentary: 云羔, 小羊, 取其羣而不失其類者; …云鴈, 取其候時而行者, "By *kao*, it means lamb that adheres faithfully to the herd and will not part with it. By *yen*, it means wild goose that migrates according to schedule."

Hsü Ch'ao 許超 of Ching-chao 京兆 (the capital district), dreamt that he was jailed for the theft of a sheep. So he asked [Yang] Yüan-shen, who explained: "You will be appointed Prefect of Ch'eng-yang 城陽令."[347] Later, for his merit he was enfeoffed as the Marquis of Ch'eng-yang.

[Yang] Yüan-shen had myriad[348] ways of interpreting dreams, adjusting his ideas in each case to a given situation as he saw fit. Without exception, he was miraculously accurate. Although there was a slight discrepancy between "prefect" and "marquis," now "prefect" means "a lord who rules one hundred *li*." The term *pai-li* 百里 is equivalent to the feudal lord in olden days. Judging from this, this was also a superb interpretation. Contemporaries likened him to Chou Hsüan 周宣.[349]

After Erh-chu Chao entered Lo-yang, he gave up his post and, with Wang T'eng-chou 王騰周, a hermit of Hua-yin 華陰,[350] went to the Shang-lo Mountain.

To the north of the market and east of the Hsiao-i Ward was the Chih-huo Ward 殖貨里 (Ward of Market Transactions), where Liu Hu 劉胡 and his three brothers, all bound servants to [the Ministry of] Grand Ceremonies (*T'ai-ch'ang* [*ssu*]),[351] were butchers by profession. During the Yung-an period (A.D. 528–530), while [Liu] Hu was killing a pig, the animal suddenly shouted "Spare my life!" Its cries reached to neighbors in all directions, who, suspecting that the [Liu] Hu brothers might be fighting against each other, came to see. [They found that] it was the pig [that had cried]. [Liu] Hu[352] then gave up his house, which was converted to the Kuei-chüeh Temple 歸覺寺

[347] Sheep (*yang* 羊) is a homophone of *yang* 陽.

[348] The text (2/23a) is *fang* 方, which is an obvious mistake for *wan* 万 (same as 萬).

[349] Chou Hsüan, a renowned dream-diviner of the Three Kingdoms period, (A.D. 221–280) was the author of the *Chan-meng shu* 占夢書 (1 *chüan*), which is listed in the *Sui-shu* "Treatise on Literature." See *Wei-chih* 29/18a–19a 方技傳; Yao Chen-tsung 姚振宗, *Sui-shu ching-chi-chih k'ao-cheng* (*Erh-shih-wu-shih-pu-pien* ed.) 36/582 子部五行家.

[350] In modern Shang-hsien 商縣, Shensi.

[351] The text (2/23a) has three additional characters, *T'ai-ch'ang min* 太常民, which, according to T'ang Ch'ang-ju, *Wei-Chin Nan-pei-ch'ao shih lun-ts'ung hsü-pien* (Peking, 1959), p. 50 n. 1, means persons held in bondage under the Ministry of Grand Ceremonies. See also Yi-t'ung Wang, "Slaves and Other Comparable Social Groups during the Northern Dynasties," *HJAS* 16 (1953), 293–364.

[352] *TPKC* 439/5a 畜獸豕 has an additional character *Hu* 胡.

(Temple of the Return to Enlightenment), and with the members of his family became a Buddhist devotee.

In the first year of P'u-t'ai (A.D. 531), hair grew on the golden image in the temple; the eyebrows and the hair on the head were complete. Wei Chi-ching 魏季景,[353] Secretary on the Left, Department of State Affairs (*Shang-shu tso-ch'eng*) confided to his friends, saying: "Previously, the same thing happened [under the reign] of Chang T'ien-hsi.[354] As a consequence, his kingdom was overthrown. This too is inauspicious." The next year the Prince of Kuang-ling[355] was deposed, and subsequently murdered.

[353] Wei Chi-ching, an uncle of Wei Shou, was a famed man of letters. He had been a Secretary on the Right, not on the Left, as reported here. See *PS* 56/21b.

[354] Chang T'ien-hsi, the youngest son of Chang Chün 張駿, became the king of Former Liang in A.D. 363. His kingdom, founded by his grandfather Chang Kuei 張軌, was conquered by Fu Chien 苻堅 in A.D. 376. See *Chin-shu* 86/42a–45a.

The event under discussion here occurred in A.D. 365 under Chang T'ien-hsi, eleven years before his downfall. See T'ang Ch'iu, *Shih-liu-kuo ch'un-ch'iu chi-pu* (Kuang-ya shu-chü ed., Canton, 1895) 73/1b 前涼錄.

[355] The Prince of Kuang-ling was deposed in A.D. 532 and murdered on June 21 the same year. See *PS* 5/8a–b.

Chapter 3

SOUTHERN SUBURBS
(*Ch'eng-nan* 城南)

The Ching-ming Monastery was established by Emperor Hsüan-wu[1] during the Ching-ming period (A.D. 500–503); hence, the name. Located on the eastern side of the Imperial Drive and one *li* outside the Hsüan-yang Gate, the monastery [compound], in length and breadth,[2] was five hundred *pu*[3] square. [The monastery] faced the western range of the Sung Mountains[4] and had the capital at its back. It was shaded by green woods, and girdled by azure streams. It commanded an area unmatched in scenic beauty, altitude, and dry[5] atmosphere. With Sung Mountain in the foreground,[6] the monastery consisted of more than one thousand rooms, [subdivided into]

[1] Emperor Hsüan-wu, otherwise known as Shih-tsung, was the second son of Emperor Kao-tsu, also known as Hsiao-wen. He reigned from A.D. 499 to A.D. 515.

[2] Literally, *tung nan hsi pei* 東南西北, "from east to west and from south to north," that is, length and breadth.

[3] A measure of length variably determined at eight Chinese feet; six Chinese feet four inches (*Li-chi* 13/25a–b 王制：古者以周尺八尺爲步, 今以周尺六尺四寸爲步. "in ancient times eight Chou feet was the equivalent of one *pu*, but now six Chou feet and four inches equal to one *pu*"); or six Chinese feet (*Kuo-yü* 3/29 周語下：不過步武尺寸之間, "the difference is no more than one *pu*, *wu*, *ch'ih* and *ts'un*.) Comm.: 六尺爲步. "Six Chinese feet equal to one *pu*."

[4] The Sung Mountains were the Sacred Mountains of the Center (中嶽) in ancient China. Its eastern range was called the T'ai-shih 太室; the western range, the Shao-shih 少室—the two ranges were seventeen *li* apart. Here the text (3/1a) is Shao-shih. *WH* 22/14a 沈約鍾山寺應西陽王教：少室邇王城, "Shao-chih was close to the king's capital." Li Shan's commentary quoting the *Hsi-cheng chi* (by Tai Yen-chih): 嵩, 中嶽也. 東謂太室, 西謂少室, 相去十七里. 嵩高, 總名也, "Sung is the Central Sacred Mountain. Its eastern range is known as T'ai-shih, and western range, Shao-shih. 'Lofty Sung' is the collective name."

[5] *Tso-chuan* Chao 3 42/12b: 請更諸爽塏者. Comm.: *shuang* 爽, *ming* 明. Subcommentary: *K'ai* 塏, *tsao* 燥.

[6] Different editions give different readings, but none makes good sense. The text

groups of halls and suites of compartments, with carved windows on opposite sides[7] and [ornamental] gutters facing one another.[8] Elevated passageways connected the blue platforms and purple pavilions. Although outside [the monastery building] there were [changes in] the four seasons, within there was no winter or summer. Beyond the eaves[9] there was nothing but hills and ponds. Bamboo and pines, orchids and *chih*-iris 芷 trailed along the stairways, their pervasive fragrance wafted by the wind or through the evaporated dewdrops deposited therein.

Not until the Cheng-kuang period (A.D. 520–524) did the Empress Dowager [Hu] order the construction of a seven-storied stūpa, which reached eight hundred Chinese feet[10] above the ground. This is why Hsing Tzu-ts'ai's stone inscription reads: "[One can] hear the flashing thunder below, [and see] the shooting stars on either side." It was indeed so. The splendor of the ornaments was comparable to that of the Yung-ning Monastery,[11] with the golden plates and precious bells glittering in the low rosy clouds.

In the monastery [compound] were three ponds, where reeds, rushes, water chestnuts, lotus roots, and water creatures grew. At times, [fish with] yellow shells or purple scales surfaced through or submerged themselves under duck-weed and aquatic grasses; at other times blue-green ducks and white wild geese floated on or dived into the green water. [In all grain processing such as] rolling,[12] grinding,

---

(3/1a) reads: *shan hsüan t'ang kuang kuan sheng* 山懸堂光觀盛; the *IS* (3/1a), *shan hsien t'ai kuan kuang sheng* 山縣臺觀光盛, and the *YLTT* (13822/11b): *shan hsien t'ang kuan kuang sheng* 山縣堂觀光盛. The translation is based on conjecture rather than textual evidence.

[7] Literally, *chiao shu* 交疏. *WH* 29/2b 古詩：交疏結綺牕，阿閣三重階，"Silk-covered windows stand on opposite sides; pavilions with four raised roof-corners have a stairway of three steps."

[8] *Shih-ming* 釋名 (*SPTK so-pen*) 5/24 釋宮室：霤，流；水從屋上流下也；"*Liu* equals *liu*, into which water drops from the roof." *Li-chi* 8/18a 檀弓上：池視重霤. Cheng Hsüan's commentary: 承霤以木爲之，用行水，亦宮之飾也，"*Ch'eng-liu* is made of wood, into which water flows. It is another ornament of the palace."

[9] *Fang yen* 房簷, "eaves."

[10] Literally, *pai jen* 百仞, "one hundred *jen*." Each *jen* is eight Chinese feet high.

[11] *WS* 114/20b 釋老志：［永寧寺］佛圖九層，高四十餘丈. … 景明寺佛圖，亦其亞也. "The stūpa in [the Yung-ning *ssu*] has nine stories at a height of more than four hundred Chinese feet. . . . The stūpa in the Ching-ming *ssu* is next to it in height."

[12] The text (3/1b) reads 䃅, a rare character not found in dictionaries. In modern Chinese it is replaced by *nien* 碾, "rolling."

pounding, and winnowing that was powered by water,[13] the wealth[14] of the monastery was unequaled.

At the time, the nation liked to pray for happiness, [so] on the seventh day of the fourth month all images in the capital were assembled in this monastery, numbering more than one thousand, according to the records of the Office of Sacrifices,[15] Department of State Affairs. On the eighth day,[16] the images [were carried] one by one into the Hsüan-yang Gate, where the emperor would scatter flowers in front of the Ch'ang-ho Palace 閶闔宮.[17]

At this moment, gold-colored flowers reflected the dazzling sunlight, and the bejeweled canopies [over the carriages] for the images floated in the clouds. Banners were [as numerous as trees] in a forest, and incense smoke was [as thick as] a fog. Indian music and the din of chanted Buddhist scriptures moved heaven and earth alike. Wherever variety shows [were performed], there was congestion. Renowned monks and virtuous masters, each carrying a staff, formed a throng. The Buddhist devotees and their "companions in the law" holding flowers resembled a garden in bloom. Carriages and horses

[13] A very lucrative industry since the end of the Western Chin, water mills were owned almost exclusively by privileged individuals or groups, including Buddhist temples. They were used as an important source of power to produce flour by grinding and sifting the wheat. For a discussion of this matter, see Yang Lien-sheng, "Notes on the Economic History of the Chin Dynasty" in *Studies in Chinese Institutional History* (Cambridge, Mass., 1961), p. 130 and n. 59. See also Nishijima Sadao, "Tenkai no kanata" in his *Chūgoku keizaishi kenkyū* (Tokyo, 1966), pp. 235–278.

[14] The text (3/1b) reads *miao* 妙, a character with a wide range of possible meanings. Following the previous sentence that deals with water mills and the like, I suggest "riches" or "wealth" as the most appropriate and logical translation.

[15] *Tz'u-pu ts'ao* 祠部曹, *"Office of Sacrifices."*

[16] The text (3/1b) reads *pa-yüeh chieh* 八月節 "eighth-month festival," but *IS* (3/1b) gives *pa-jih* 八日 "eighth day." The eighth day of the fourth month is generally accepted as Buddha's birthday.

[17] It is so recorded in the *WS* (114/8a) 釋老志：世祖初即位，亦遵太祖太宗之業，…於四月八日輿諸佛像，行於廣衢，帝親御門樓，臨觀散花，以致禮敬，"Soon after Emperor Shih-tsung's ascension to the throne (A.D. 499), he also followed the precedent of Emperors T'ai-tsu (regnant A.D. 386–409) and T'ai-tsung (regnant 409–424).... On the eighth day of the fourth month, when the various Buddhist statues were placed in carriages and paraded on main streets, Emperor [Shih-tsung] would ascend the watchtower of the palace [facing the street], and scatter flowers in person so as to show his respect for [the Buddha]." To worship the Buddha on his birthday is therefore an obvious tradition of the Wei.

choked [traffic][18] and jostled each other.[19] A foreign monk from the Western Regions saw it, and he chanted and said it was [the same as the Buddha's land as he had witnessed it].

Not until the Yung-hsi period did Hsing Tzu-ts'ai,[20] Libationer of the Imperial Academy (*Kuo-tzu chi-chiu*), receive a court order to prepare a stone inscription for the monastery.

> [Hsing] Tzu-ts'ai was a native [of Mo 鄚, a subdivision of] Ho-chien 河間 commandery. Intelligent[21] and refined,[22] he concentrated on his studies by living in seclusion,[23] and acquired new knowledge by reviewing the old.[24] A man of letters and a savant, he distinguished himself by matching Pan [Ku] 班[固] and [Ssu-] ma [Ch'ien] [司]馬[遷].[25] A distinguished model [for his contemporaries],[26] he attained a unique position superseding that of

[18] Literally, *chü-ch'i t'ien-yen* 車騎塡咽. *WH* 5/9a 左思吳都賦：冠蓋雲蔭, 閭閻闐噎, "caps and canopies formed a shade like a cloud; lanes and streets were congested [with people]." Liu K'uei's 劉逵 comm.: 閭閻闐噎, 言人物遍滿之貌, "*Lü-yen t'ien-i* describes the overcrowded conditions."

[19] *WH* 4/14a 左思蜀都賦：輿輦雜沓, 冠帶混幷, 累轂疊跡, 叛衍相傾, "Carriages moved on tumultuously; caps and belts [of officials] were intermixed in disorder. The carriages, one after another, left piles of tracks, spreading out one atop the other." Li Shan's commentary quoting Ssu-ma Piao's 司馬彪 commentary for the *Chuang-tzu*: 叛衍, 猶漫衍也, "*P'an-yen* is the same as *man-yen*—spreading out."

[20] Style of Hsing Shao 邢邵, son of Hsing Ch'iu, who had been Superintendant of the Imperial Household (*Kuang-lu ch'ing*). Hsing Shao's other name was Chi 吉. He used his style because his name 邵, a homophone of 劭, was taboo under the Wei dynasty. For Hsing Shao's biography, see *PCS* 36/1a–5b; see also Chapter 2, at note 237.

[21] Literally, *chin-hsing t'ung-min* 志性通敏, "by nature penetrating and sagacious," referring to his natural endowment.

[22] Literally, *feng-ch'ing ya jun* 風情雅潤, "an elegant and broad air," referring to his acquired qualities.

[23] Literally, *hsia wei tan ssu* 下帷覃思, "to pull down the curtain and think hard." This is a reference to Tung Chung-shu 董仲舒 (179?–104? B.C.), who, as an Erudite, studied for three years in his library behind closed curtains, without venturing once outside to the garden. See *HS* 56/1a–b Tung Chung-shu's biography.

[24] *Lun-yü* 2/4a 爲政 comm.: 溫, 尋也; 尋繹故者, 又知新者, 可以爲人師矣, "*Wen* (to refresh) means search. To search and understand what one has already heard, and to know what is yet new—one can be a teacher of others by so doing."

[25] Pan Ku (d. A.D. 92) is the author of the *History of the Former Han* and the famous rhymed prose of the Western and Eastern Capitals. Ssu-ma Ch'ien (ca. 145–ca. 86 B.C.) is the author of the first general history of China, the *Shih-chi*.

[26] Literally, *ying-kuei sheng-fan* 英規勝範, "an excellent pattern and a distinguished example."

Hsü [Shao] and Kuo [T'ai].[27] As a result, well-educated men[28] congregated at his door, and visitors versed in [Confucian] teachings, now coming, now going, filled his room. For those who ascended his inner hall, it was like ascending to Confucius' door,[29] and for those who received his praise, it was like listening to the remarks of Tung-wu 東吳.[30] Renowned among his contemporaries, his fame reached far and near.

When entering government service[31] for the first time toward the end of the Cheng-kuang period, [Hsing Tzu-ts'ai] was appointed *wan-lang* (pallbearer)[32] for Emperor Shih-tsu, and Court Guest. Later, he was promoted to Squire-attendant of the

[27] For Hsü Shao, see Chapter 2 at note 140 under the Ch'in T'ai-shang-chün Monastery; for Kuo T'ai, see Chapter 2 at note 141.

[28] Literally, *i-kuan chih shih* 衣冠之士, "literati wearing [ceremonial] robes and caps," that is, officials.

[29] Literally, *jo teng K'ung-tzu chih men* 若登孔子之門, "same as entering Confucius' door," that is, to receive Confucius' teaching in person. See *Lun-yü* 11/5a–b 先進：門人不敬子路. 子曰：由也, 升堂矣, 未入於室也. Arthur Waley, *The Analects of Confucius*, p. 156: "Whereupon the disciples ceased to respect Tzu-lu. The Master said, The Truth about Yu is that he has got as far as the guest-hall, but has not entered the inner rooms." Hence, Yang Hsiung 揚雄 (53 B.C.–A.D. 18) of the Former Han (206 B.C.–A.D. 5) classified Confucius' disciples into two categories: (1) "those who had entered the guest-halls," that is, those who were accepted but not favored by the Master; and (2) "those who were in the inner rooms," that is, those closer to Confucius and therefore favored. See *Fa-yen* 法言 (*SPPY* ed.) 2/1b 吾子：如孔子之門用賦也, 則賈誼升堂, 相如入室矣, "If rhymed prose had been a subject taught by Confucius, then Chia I would have been an accepted disciple and [Ssu-ma] Hsiang-ju a favored one."

[30] Source of the subject, "Tung-wu" 東吳 (Eastern Wu), is unclear. Chou Yennien (*Lo-yang ch'ieh-lan chi chu*, 3/1b) suggests Lu Su 魯肅 (A.D. 172–217), who commented favorably on Lü Meng 呂蒙 (A.D. 178–219), a famous general of the Kingdom of Wu (A.D. 222–280), as the source, but Fan Hsiang-yung (*CC* 3/137–138) believes "Tung-wu" refers to K'ung Jung 孔融 (A.D. 153–208) instead. K'ung Jung once spoke very highly of Yü Fan's 虞翻 (A.D. 164–233) *Commentaries for the Book of Changes*. For Lü Meng, see *Wu-chih* (in *San-kuo chih chi-chieh*) 9/23b; for Yü Fan, see 12/5b.

PC (114–115) believes that "Tung-wu" 東吳 is an abbreviation for Tung-wumen 東吳門, who was not emotionally affected by the death of his own son (*Lieh-tzu* 列子 6/12a–b 力命, *SPPY* ed.). Although Hsing Shao maintained his composure when his nephew Hsing Shu 邢恕 died, this is not relevant here: this reference is to hearing a person's comments, not to something he might have done.

[31] Literally, *shih ho* 釋褐, "to get rid of a nonofficial garment of coarse fabric." For its origin, see *WH* 45/6a 揚雄解嘲：或釋褐而傅.

[32] That is, *wan-lang* 挽郎. This is a Chin institution. In A.D. 341, for example, sixty

Central Secretariat and [Attending Secretary within][33] the Imperial Yellow Gate. A man of great learning and profound insight, there was no subject that [Hsing] Tzu-ts'ai did not master, so he was always consulted on matters relating to military [affairs] and political institutions. In the face of the turmoil that swept the nation, academic pursuits[34] were almost completely abandoned. When [Hsing] Tzu-ts'ai was later promoted to Libationer of the Imperial Academy, he [was determined] to provide the best possible education for the students. He fined those who were lazy and rewarded the industrious, directing all his efforts to encouraging and guiding them. As a consequence, those wearing blue collars[35] competed with each other in embracing "the fine arts,"[36] and Confucian teachings[37] once again flourished there. Toward the end of the Yung-hsi period, he submitted his resignation [because he wished to wait on] his aged mother, but the emperor rejected his request. [Hsing] Tzu-ts'ai begged with great sincerity and earnestness, with an outburst of words and tears at the same time. Only then did the emperor accept his request. An edict authorized him to

youngsters were selected from among the children of officials with sixth rank to serve as pallbearers for the deceased Empress Tu. See *Chin-shu* 20/25b 禮志. No record of this post is available in the *WS* chapter on Government Officials, which is chapter 113.

[33] The text (3/2b) has only *huang-men* 黃門. The remaining part of his title is added according to his biography in *PCS* (36/2b).

[34] That is, *Hu-men yeh-fei* 虎門業廢, a reference to the White Tiger Hall, where a meeting of scholars was convened by Emperor Chang of the Eastern Han in A.D. 79 to discuss different texts of the classics. See *HHS* 3/6b 章帝本紀. See also Tjan Tjoe Som, tr., *Po Hu T'ung*.

[35] *Ch'ing-chin* 青衿, blue collar worn by literati. *Shih-ching* 4.4/6a (ode 91, verse 1, line 1) 鄭風子衿:青青子衿. Sun Yen's 孫炎 commentary: 衿與襟音義同. 衿是領之別名, 故曰青衿; 青領也, "Pronunciation and meaning of *chin* 衿 and *chin* 襟 are alike. *Chin* 衿 is another name for *ling* 領 (collar). Therefore it is known as *ch'ing-chin*, meaning a blue collar." Waley, *Book of Songs*, p. 49: "Oh, You with the blue collar." *Yen-shih chia-hsun* 6/6b 書證篇:古者斜領不連於衿, 故謂領爲衿, "In ancient times the sloping collar (*ling*) was not connected with the lapel (*chin*), and thus *ling* and *chin* could be used alternatively." See Teng, *Family Instructions*, p. 162.

[36] *Ya-shu* 雅術.

[37] *Chu Ssu* 洙泗, names of two rivers in the ancient state of Lu (modern Shantung), where Confucius gave instructions to his disciples. *Li-chi* 7/8b 檀弓上: (Tseng-tsu 曾子 spoke to Tzu-hsia 子夏): 吾與女事夫子於洙泗之間, "You and I had waited upon our Master between the Chu and Ssu Rivers."

wait on his mother with the official title Imperial Household Grandee (*Kuang-lu ta-fu*). At his residence, he was to have five servants provided [by the government], and he was to come to court once every year to fulfill his duty as consultant. At the time of his departure,[38] dukes and marquises bade him farewell, in the same manner as the Han court sending the two Shus 二疏.[39]

After the imperial seat was moved to Yeh, litigation among the people became all the more frequent. Early ordinances and later edicts contradicted one another. Records[40] of unsolved cases before judicial officials piled up like mountains. The emperor therefore ordered [Hsing] Tzu-ts'ai and Wen Tzu-sheng, the Cavalier Attendant-in-Ordinary (*San-ch'i ch'ang-shih*) to compile a "New Code of the Lin-chih" (Unicorn's Hoofprint 麟趾新制) in fifteen chapters.[41] Government departments in the capital used this new code to settle disputed cases, while local governments looked upon it as a guiding manual.

In the Wu-ting period, he was appointed Generalissimo of the Whirling Cavalry (*Piao-ch'i ta-chiang-chün*) and concurrently Governor of Western Yen-chou. Free from corruption,[42] his administration pleased both officials and the people. Later, he was summoned [to the court] and installed as President of the Imperial Secretariat.

At the time, fighting was everywhere[43] and the court was confronted with all sorts of trouble. Such matters as state cere-

[38] Literally *tsu-tao* 祖道, sacrifices offered to the god of the road for a pleasant journey.

[39] A reference to Shu Kuang 疏廣 and his nephew Shu Shou 疏受, who jointly asked for voluntary retirement. At the time they left the capital (58 B.C.), court officials in "several hundred chariots" rode to see them off. Spectators also sighed and sobbed at the scene. See *HS* 71/4a Shu Kuang's biography.

[40] *Pu-ling* 簿領. *WH* 29/8b 劉楨雜詩:沈迷簿領書, "Busily engaged in official records." Li Shan's commentary: 簿領, 謂文簿而記錄之, "*Pu-ling* means to keep records of official documents."

[41] Many officials participated in the codification of the laws that took place in the Lin-chih Pavilion; hence the name. The resultant law code was promulgated on November 19, A.D. 541. See *WS* 12/8b.

[42] According to his biography, he was an effective administrator who watched over his subordinates vigilantly to guard against possible corruption. For this reason, people within his jurisdiction remembered him fondly at the end of his tenure. See *PS* 43/24a.

[43] Literally, *jung ma tsai chiao* 戎馬在郊, "war horses were in the suburbs."

monies and court rituals were all determined by [Hsing] Tzu-ts'ai. His writings—poetry, rhymed prose, rescripts, memorials, stone inscriptions, epitaphs, comments, and accounts—which numbered five hundred "chapters," are in circulation today.[44] Neighboring states[45] respected him as an excellent model, whereas people, whether in or out of court, took him as an inspiring topic of conversation.

The Ta-t'ung Temple 大統寺 (Temple of the Great Unification) was located to the west of the Ching-ming Monastery in the so-called Li-min Ward 利民里 (Ward of Benefit to the People).[46] To the south of the temple was the residence of Kao Hsien-lüeh 高顯略,[47] Foreman Clerk [Assigned to] the Three Lords (*San-kung ling-shih*).[48] [At the mansion], always at night, there would appear a red light moving before the hall—a scene that appeared more than once. When the earth was dug to a depth of more than ten Chinese feet in the spot illumined, one hundred[49] catties of gold was found. An inscription read: "The gold belongs to Su Ch'in's family. The finder must perform meritorious deeds on my behalf [in the cause of Buddhism]."[50]

[Kao] Hsien-lüeh subsequently had the Chao-fu Temple 招福寺

[44] Altogether the collection of his writings came in thirty *chüan*, "rolls." See *PCS* 36/5b.

[45] On one occasion when the Wei envoys arrived in the rival Liang dynasty, they were asked why such a talented man as Hsing Tzu-ts'ai was not sent over as a goodwill delegate. See *PS* 43/23a–b.

[46] Also known as Li-jen *li* 利仁里, Ward of Benefit and Benevolence, (*T'ai-p'ing huan-yü chi* 3/14b 河南道洛陽縣 quoting the *Chün-kuo chih* 郡國志).

[47] Kao Hsien-lüeh's name is alternately given as Kao Hsien-lo 高顯洛 (*TPKC* 391/1b 銘記部高顯洛) and Kao Hsien-yeh 高顯業 (*T'ai-p'ing huan-yü chi* 3/10b 河南道洛陽縣.) The *Ch'ieh-lan chi* refers to his name later in the paragraph as "Lo," suggesting that his correct name might have been Kao Hsien-lo, or that later editors changed it. Kao Hsien-lo was active in A.D. 520.

[48] According to the *T'ung-tien* (22/19b 職官四令史), the Foreman Clerk is a Later Han institution. From eighteen to twenty-one clerks were selected from among officials in the Orchid Terrace (*Lan-t'ai* 蘭臺) (Bureau of Archives) to keep official papers. With some modification, this institution was followed in the southern and northern dynasties.

[49] *IS* (3/3a) reads *i ch'ien* 一千, "one thousand."

[50] Literally, *tsao kung te* 造功德. Mine is a free translation.

Su Ch'in (d. 317 B.C.) was an active statesman long before the introduction of Buddhism into China. The statement here is therefore quite fictitious.

(Summoning Good Fortune Temple) built. People claimed it was the old residence of Su Ch'in. At the time Yüan Ch'a was in power, and, when he heard about the discovery of gold, he went to [Kao Hsien-] lüeh[51] for the gold. [Kao Hsien-lüeh] gave him twenty catties.

> [Yang] Hsüen-chih's note: At Su Ch'in's time there was no Buddhist teaching [in China]. The statement about "meritorious deeds" did not necessarily mean [the construction of] a temple, but rather [the preparation of] a stone inscription in praise of [Su Ch'in's] achievements.

To the east of the Ta-t'ung Temple and one *li* south of the Ching-ming Monastery two monasteries [were constructed] in honor of the Father of the Supreme Empress.[52] The one on the west was established by the empress dowager, whereas the one on the east was founded by her younger sister.[53] Both were dedicated to the posthumous happiness of their father; hence, the name. Contemporaries, however, called them the Shuang-nü Monasteries 雙女寺 (Monasteries of Two Sisters).

The gates of both monasteries approached the Lo River, where the branches of luxuriant trees spread out in all directions,[54] with the foliage casting shadows beneath. Each monastery had a five-storied stūpa that rose five hundred Chinese feet above the ground, decorated with undyed colored paintings comparable to those in the Ching-ming Monastery. When the [six monthly] great fasts[55] were

[51] The text (3/3b) gives Lo 洛. For an explanation, see n. 47 above.

[52] The text (3/3b) reads *T'ai-shih* 太師 (Grand Preceptor), which had never been the official title of Hu Kuo-chen 胡國珍 (d. A.D. 518), the empress dowager's father, at any time of his career (*WS* 83B/5a ff). *T'ai-shang-kung* 太上公, "Grand Father of the Empress" was his title. *IS* (3/3a) gives *T'ai-shang*; hence, the translation.

Liu T'eng 劉騰 (d. A.D. 523) supervised the construction; see *WS* 94/17a. For the T'ai-shang-chün Monastery, see Chapter 2 at note 103 ff.

[53] Literally *huang i* 皇姨, "the emperor's aunt," that is, the empress dowager's younger sister, who was married to Yüan Ch'a. She was at first enfeoffed as the Duchess of Hsin-p'ing commandery 新平郡君 (in modern Honan; no exact identification available), but later was renamed the Duchess of P'ing-i 馮翊 (modern Kao-ling 高陵, Shensi). See *WS* 16/15a 元乂傳.

[54] Literally, *fu-shu* 扶疎. *Fu* 扶 is a variant of *fu* 枎, meaning "spread out in all directions." *Shuo-wen chieh tzu* 6A/17b 枎:扶疏, 四布也.

[55] See Chapter 1 under the Ching-lo Nunnery at note 198.

due, a [eunuch] attendant within the Yellow Gate (*Chung huang-men* 中黃門) would always be sent to supervise the monks' quarters, and take care of provisions and donations.[56] No other monasteries enjoyed this privilege.

To the east of the monasteries was the Imperial Observatory,[57] the foundation of which, although in ruins, was still more than fifty Chinese feet in height. This was indeed the one constructed under Emperor Kuang-wu (regnant A.D. 25–57)[58] of the Han. To its east was the Hall of the Circular Moat[59] (Pi-yung 辟雍 Hall), which was constructed under [Emperor] Wu of the Wei (A.D. 155–220). During the Cheng-kuang period of our dynasty, a Hall of Illumination (Ming-t'ang 明堂) was built to the southwest of the Pi-yung Hall. It

[56] *Ch'en shih* 襯施. Tao-ch'eng, *Shih-shih yao-lan* (*Taishō* ed.) A/276 嚫錢：梵語達嚫拏 (dakṣiṇā)，此云財施，今略達拏，但云嚫. 五分律云：食後施衣物，名達嚫; "In Sanskrit it is known as *ta-ch'en-na*, abbreviated now as *ta-na*. In our [land] it is called donation of valuables, or simply called *ch'en*. According to the *Wu-fen lü*, '*Ta-ch'en*' means to provide [monks] with clothing and other articles after meals."

[57] The original observatory was sixty Chinese feet high with a foundation twenty paces (*pu* 步) square. *SCC* 16/22b 穀水注：穀水又逕靈臺北，望雲物也. 漢光武所築，高六丈，方二十步; "The Ku River passed by the north of the Imperial Observatory, which was designed to view astronomical phenomena. [The observatory] was constructed [during the reign of Emperor] Kuang-wu of the [Later] Han, at a height of sixty Chinese feet and a foundation of 20 *pu* square." The *Han kung-ko shu* 漢宮閣疏 as quoted in the *YHNC* 2/15a, however, asserts that the Han Observatory was thirty Chinese feet high, with twelve gates. For a historical study of the Imperial Observatory, see Hashimoto Masukichi, "Reidaikō," *Shigaku* 13:4 (1934), 1–23. For recent archaeological discoveries of the Ling-t'ai remains of the Han-Wei periods, see Chung-kuo K'o-hsüeh-yüan K'ao-ku-yen-chiu-so Lo-yang kung-tso-tui, "Han-Wei Lo-yang-ch'eng nan-chiao ti Ling-t'ai i-chih," *K'ao-ku*, 1 (1978), 54–57.

[58] Emending Han Wu-ti 漢武帝 (140–87 B.C.) to Han Kuang-wu 漢光武 (regnant A.D. 25–57) after *IS* 3/3b. Han Wu-ti had his capital in Ch'ang-an, whereas Han Kuang-wu had his in Lo-yang, where the Ling-t'ai was located. The Imperial Observatory of the Later Han was built in A.D. 56. See *HHS* 1B/22a.

[59] *Pi-yung*, also known as Imperial Academy (*T'ai-hsüeh* 太學) was the place where rituals and music were performed as part of education. It had circular walls to resemble heaven and a circular moat to symbolize the flow of education. See Pan Ku, *Po-hu-t'ung te lun* (*SPTK so-pen*) 4/39–41; see also Tjan, *Po Hu T'ung* 2, 482–488.

Construction of a *P'an-kung* 泮宮 (same as *Pi-yung*, but *P'an-kung* was for an emperor whereas *P'an-kung* was for a feudal lord) in A.D. 217 is mentioned in *Wei-chih* (1/118b). It was located, however, in Yeh, not Lo-yang.

had a round top on a square base, with eight windows and four gates.[60] [Yüan Yüeh,] the Prince of Ju-nan,[61] added a brick stūpa atop the Imperial Observatory.

In the early Hsiao-ch'ang period (A.D. 525), heretical rebels raided from all directions, overthrowing local governments in provinces and commanderies.[62] The court set up a recruiting office to the north of the Hall [of Illumination], conferring such ranks as the General of the Wilderness (*K'uang-yeh chiang-chün*)[63], Generals on the Flanks (*P'ien chiang-chün*), and Adjunct Generals (*Pei chiang-chün*)[64] on those who enlisted. At the time, [the unit of] soldiers in armor were named the Regiment of the Hall of Illumination (*Ming-t'ang tui*). There was then a *hu-pen* (tiger-rushing) guardsman, Lo Tzu-yüan 駱子淵,[65] who claimed to be a native of Lo-yang. While he was stationed in P'eng-ch'eng during the Hsiao-ch'ang years,[66] his comrade-at-arms Fan Yüan-pao 樊元寶

[60] Four gates were intended to welcome each of the four seasons, whereas eight windows were designed to give passage for eight different winds. The round top resembled heaven. See *WS* 32/15a–16a 封軌明堂辟雍議; J.J.M. de Groot, *Universismus, die Grundlage der Religion und Ethik, des Staatswesens und der Wissenschaften Chinas* (Berlin, 1918), pp. 263 ff.; Otto Franke, *Geschichte des chinesischen Reiches*, 5 vols. (Berlin and Leipzig, 1930–1952), 1, 74; and Joseph Needham, *Science and Civilisation in China*, 4:3, p. 70.

[61] See Chapter 1 at note 198 under the Ching-lo Nunnery.

[62] *CC* (3/144) has prepared a long list of such disturbances.

[63] The text (3/4b) gives *K'uang-yeh* 曠掖; both *IS* (3/3b) and *YLTT* (13822/12b) give *K'uang-yeh* 曠夜 instead. *WS* (113/30a) reads *K'uang-yeh* 曠野, which is more conventional and is therefore followed in the translation.

An imperial rescript was issued on January 13, A.D. 526 regarding the recruitment. See *WS* 9/22a–b 肅宗紀.

[64] The General of the Wilderness was the ninth rank according to the Wei scale, whereas the Flanks and Adjunct Generals were Quasi-Ninth. See *WS* 113/30a–31b 官氏志.

[65] The *Chün-kuo chih*, as quoted in the *T'ai-p'ing huan-yü chi* (3/13a), reads Lo 洛 instead of Lo 駱, and gives his official title as *Hu-pen chung-lang-chiang* (Commandant of Tiger-rushing Squires). The story given there is about the same as that given here, but he was later enshrined as god of the Lo River. The official title is a later embellishment, for, according to the *Ch'ieh-lan chi*, he was no more than an ordinary soldier stationed (*hsü* 戌) in P'eng-ch'eng (modern *Hsü-chou* 徐州, Kiangsu).

[66] The text (3/4b) has an additional character *hsi* 昔, which does not appear in the *FYCL* (113/1340 酒肉篇), nor in the *TPKC* (292/4a 神類洛子淵). The translation follows the latter two versions.

returned to the capital on leave. [Lo] Tzu-yüan, entrusting him with a sealed letter for home, said: "My home is located to the south of the Imperial Observatory and close to the Lo River. You, sir, have only to go there—my folks will undoubtedly come out to meet you." As instructed, [Fan] Yüan-pao went to the south of the Imperial Observatory, where there was not a single household at which to make inquiries. Pacing back and forth[67] and preparing to leave, [Fan] Yüan-pao suddenly saw an old man coming in his direction, inquiring where he came from and [why he was] wandering here. [Fan] Yüan-pao told him all [that had happened]. The old man said, "This is my son." So he took the letter and led him into [the house]. There appeared spacious buildings and beautiful rooms. After they were seated, [the old man] asked a maid to serve wine. Shortly afterward [Fan Yüan-pao] saw the maid holding a dead boy [in her arms] and passing in front of him. At first he felt quite puzzled. Soon afterward, wine was brought, deep red in color and with an unusual aroma and flavor. In addition, fine dishes were provided, including all delicacies from sea and land. After the dinner was over, [Fan] Yüan-pao bade him goodbye. The old man escorted [Fan] Yüan-pao out, saying, "It is difficult to calculate when we shall meet again, so I [find our parting] sorrowful and regrettable." He was very attentive [at the time of] farewell. When the old man returned to his house, [Fan] Yüan-pao could no longer see the gate and lane; he could see only an embankment high above the water, and the green waves [of the Lo River] spilling[68] toward the east. There he saw a boy about fifteen years old, drowned shortly before, whose nose was bleeding. Only then did he realize that the wine he had drunk was the boy's blood. When he returned to P'eng-ch'eng, [Lo] Tzu-yüan had already

[67] Literally *hsi i* 徙倚, which comes from the *Ch'u-t'zu* (5/87) 遠遊:步徙倚而遙思兮. Hawkes, *Ch'u Tz'u*, p. 81: "Restless I paced, with my mind on distant things." Commentary: 彷徨東西, 意愁憤也. "Wandering aimlessly eastward and westward is the state of mind when one is worried and vexed." Compare with Hsien-yi and Gladys Yang's translation in *The Man Who Sold a Ghost* (Hong Kong, 1974), p. 133.

[68] The text (3/6a) read *tung ch'ing* 東傾, "pouring toward the east." *IS* (3/4a) and *YLTT* (13822/12b) both give *lien-i* 漣漪, "rippling." The former expression connotes a far more powerful flow of water, which would be fatal to a boy fifteen years old; hence the translation.

disappeared. For three years [Fan] Yüan-pao and [Lo] Tzu-yüan had been stationed together as recruits, but [Fan Yüan-pao] had never known that [Lo Tzu-yüan] was the god of the Lo River.

The Pao-te Temple 報德寺 (Temple of Repayment of Virtue) was established by Emperor Hsiao-wen, [otherwise known as] Kao-tsu, and dedicated to his grandmother Empress Feng[69] for her posthumous happiness. It was located three *li* outside the K'ai-yang Gate and to the east of the Imperial Drive. [At the K'ai-yang Gate] was the Academy for the Sons of the Noblemen of the Han,[70] in front of which were the "stone classics" on twenty-five slabs in three different scripts. Engraved on both sides were the two classics, the *Spring and Autumn Annals* and the *Book of Documents*. The three scripts were: seal, *k'o-tou* 科斗, and *li* 隸,[71] which were the calligraphic relics of Ts'ai Yung 蔡邕, the Right Commandant of Palace Squires (*Yu chung-lang chiang* 右中郎將) of the Han.[72] Eighteen slabs [of his] still survived, but all the others were either damaged or destroyed.

In addition, there were forty-eight [other] slabs engraved in *li*-script on both sides, on which were written the four classical works [known respectively as] the *Chou-I*, the *Book of Documents*, the *Kung-yang Commentary*, and the *Book of Rites*. Along with an additional

69 The temple was built on the old site of the *Ying-shih ts'ao* (Office of Hawks' Trainers), which had been abolished to show the emperor's concern for life. See *WS* 13/7a 文成文明皇后傳 and 114/16a 釋老志.

70 The lecture hall of the academy was built in A.D. 51, according to the *SCC* (16/25a 穀水注 quoting a Yang-chia 陽嘉 stone inscription; the *YHNC* (2/15a) gives the date as A.D. 29 instead). It was one hundred Chinese feet long and thirty Chinese feet wide. As the title suggests, the Imperial Academy for the Sons of the Noblemen was reserved for members of the nobility, whereas the Imperial Academy (*T'ai-hsüeh*) was open to other candidates.

71 The three-script "stone classics" were cut during the Wei, not the Eastern Han. In the latter case, Ts'ai Yung's (A.D. 132–192) calligraphy executed between A.D. 175 and 183 was confined to one script. It has been suggested that Yang Hsüan-chih, a learned scholar, could not have confused the two distinctly different sets of stone inscriptions. The *CC* (3/151 n. 3) therefore suggests that an interpolation might exist in the text: the sentence about Ts'ai Yung's calligraphy should have followed "the four classical works: the *Chou-i* . . . and the *Book of Rites*" in the next paragraph.

TC (148/28a–b) also has a mention of the stone classics.

72 For Ts'ai Yung's biography, see *HHS* 90B/1a–20b; for his role in stone inscription, see *HHS* 90B/7b.

Fig. 3. Sample of the Three-Script Inscription from the chapter "To-shih" (the "Numerous Officers") in the *Book of Documents*

monument, "Tsan Hsüeh" 讚學, "In Praise of Studies",[73] they were all erected in front of the hall. Of the six[74] slabs mentioned in the *Tien-lun* 典論 (*Treatise on Writing*) composed by Emperor Wen of the Wei,[75] four still survived in A.D. 493.

In the fourth year of the Wu-ting period (A.D. 546), [Kao Ch'eng 高澄] had all the "stone classics" moved to Yeh.[76]

Emperor Kao-tsu labeled [this area] Ch'üan-hsüeh (Exhortation to Study) Ward. [In][77] the ward were three temples: the Ta-chüeh 大覺寺 (Great Awakening),[78] the San-pao 三寶寺 (the Three Precious Ones),[79] and Ning-yüan 寧遠寺 (To Quell the Distant Regions), surrounded by an orchard that produced such valued fruits as Ta-ku 大谷 (Great Valley)[80] and Ch'eng-kuang 承光 (To Accept Light) apricots.

[73] Emending *Tu-shu pei* 讀書碑 to *Tsuan-hsüeh pei* 讚學碑 after *YHNC* (3/7a). *YLTT* (589/7a 文部碑 quoting the *Hsi-cheng chi*) gives *T'ai-hsüeh tsuan* 太學讚 (In Praise of the Imperial Academy) instead. It was also Ts'ai Yung's calligraphy.

[74] Emending *yün* 云 (so said) to *liu* 六 (six) after *IS* 3/4b.

[75] Ts'ao P'ei 曹丕 (A.D. 187–226), the eldest son of Ts'ao Ts'ao and the first monarch of the Kingdom of Wei as Emperor Wen (regnant A.D. 200–226) was the author of many essays, poems, and the *Tien-lun*, a work of literary criticism.

[76] The text (3/6a) attaches this sentence of twelve characters to the next paragraph, but *Chi-cheng* (92) suggests that it be moved here; hence the translation. The text (3/6a) also gives *Ying* 穎, which is an obvious error for *Yeh* 鄴. The move took place in the eighth month of A.D. 546 (*TC* 159/15b; *PCS* 6/4b 孝昭紀). Fifty-two monuments were involved. See *PCS* 4/11b 文宣紀; *TC* 159/15b.

The stone inscription of both the Han and the Wei has been a subject of extensive studies, among which one may list the following:

Chang Kuo-kan, *Li-tai shih-ching k'ao* (Peiping, 1930).

Chang Ping-lin, "Hsin-ch'u san-t'i shih-ching k'ao," in *Chang-shih i-shu hsü-pien* (Peiping, 1933), vol. 3.

Liu Ch'uan-ying, *Han-Wei shih-ching k'ao* (T'un-ch'eng, 1886).

Liu Wen-hsien, *Han shih-ching I-li ts'an-shih chi-cheng* (Taipei, 1969).

Pai Chien, *Wei shih-ching ts'an-shih chi* (Shanghai [?], 1930).

Sun Hai-po, *Wei san-tzu shih-ching chi-lu* (I-wen facsimile ed., Taipei, 1975).

Sun Hsing-yen, "Wei san-t'i shih-ching i-tzu k'ao," in *P'ing-chin-kuan ts'ung-shu*, vol. 6, Lan-ling, 1806.

Wang Kuo-wei, "Wei shih-ching k'ao," in *Kuan-t'ang chi-lin* (I-wen facsimile ed., Taipei, 1956), 16/12–12b.

Wu Wei-hsiao, *Hsin-ch'u Han-Wei shih-ching k'ao* (Shanghai, 1927).

[77] Adding *nei* 內 after *CT* (3/6b).

[78] Emending *Wen-chüeh* 文覺 to *Ta-chüeh* 大覺 after *IS* (3/4b) and *CT* (3/6b).

[79] That is, Buddha, the Law, and Monastic Dicipline.

[80] *CT* (3/6b) gives more information about this special variety of pear. They were

The Ch'eng-kuang Temple also produced many other fruits, but the apricots were the most delicious and without equal in the capital.

To the east of the Ch'üan-hsüeh Ward was the Yen-hsien Ward 延賢里 (Ward of Invitation to the Worthy), in which was the Cheng-chüeh Nunnery 正覺寺 (Perfect Enlightenment Nunnery). It was established by Wang Su 王肅 (A.D. 463–501), President of the Department of State Affairs.

[Wang] Su, styled Kung-i 恭懿,[81] a native of Lang-yeh, was the son of [Wang] Huan [王]奐, Governor of Yung-chou of the Ch'i.[82]

Learned and versatile, [Wang] Su was a man with superb skill at letters. In the eighteenth year of the T'ai-ho period (A.D. 494),[83] while serving the Ch'i as Assistant Archivist (*Mi-shu ch'eng*), he deserted the illegitimate and surrendered to the legitimate. At the time, Emperor Kao-tsu was building a new capital in Lo-yang, where many reforms[84] were carried out. [Wang] Su, vastly knowledgeable of past events, was tremendously helpful. Emperor Kao-tsu held him in high esteem and always called him Master Wang. The name of Yen-hsien was adopted because of [Wang] Su.

When [Wang] Su was in the south of the Yangtze, he was married

---

also known as "han-hsiao" 含消 (hold in the mouth and melt away) pears. It is said that each weighed ten catties (roughly equivalent to 2.22 kilograms), although if such a pear dropped to the ground, it changed into juice. The character for "ten" (*shih* 十) is perhaps a mistake for "six" (*liu* 六), as is given in *TPYL* (969/3b) 果部梨 and *YYTT* 10/56.

[81] The text (3/6a) gives *kung* 公, which is an error for *kung* 恭.

[82] *Ch'ung-k'an* (3/23a) treats this sentence as a separate note, but I prefer to consider it a continuation of the statement immediately preceding.

Wang Huan, General Governing the North (*Chen-pei chiang-chün*) and concurrently Governor of Yung-chou, was killed by Emperor Wu of the Ch'i in A.D. 493, along with four other sons. At the time Wang Su was twenty years old. See *Nan-Ch'i shu* (I-wen facsimile ed.) 49/1a–6a.

[83] The text gives A.D. 494 as Wang Su's surrender to the Wei. It should be A.D. 493. See *Nan-Ch'i shu* 3/17a and *WS* 63/1a.

Emperor Kao-tsu received Wang Su at Yeh following the latter's desertion from the South. See *WS* 63/1a–b.

[84] The text gives *tsao-chih* 造制, of which *chih* 制 is equivalent to *chih* 製 (*CT* 3.5a). After *chih* there is another character *lun* 論, which is deleted after *IS* 3/5a and *CT* 3/5a.

to a daughter of a Hsieh family.[85] After his arrival in the [Wei] capital, he was married again to a princess.[86] Later, Lady Hsieh became a nun. She too came to join [Wang] Su. [Knowing that Wang Su had a wife who was a princess,[87] his first wife Hsieh] wrote a five-character poem for [Wang] Su as a gift, which reads:

Hitherto a silkworm on a bamboo stand,
Now silk in the loom.
Attached to the spinning wheel[88] and following the spindle,[89]
"Don't you recall the days of intimate relationship [between
the silk and worm]?"

The Princess wrote a poem in reply for [Wang] Su, saying:

The needle lets the thread pass through.
In its eye it always takes in the silk.
Now sewing a new piece of fabric,
How can it accept[90] [the thread] of the past?[91]

[85] Daughter of Hsieh Chuang 謝莊, Palace Grandee on the Right. See "Wang Shao mu-chih" 王紹墓誌 (*MCCS* plate 218) and "Shih-tsung Kuei-hua Wang P'u-hsien mu-chih" 世宗貴華王普賢墓誌 (*MCCS*, plate 22).

Wang Shao (A.D. 492–515) was the son of Lady Hsieh.

[86] Younger sister of Emperor Kao-tsu, who was first enfeoffed as Princess of P'eng-ch'eng but later as Princess of Ch'en-liu 陳留. See *WS* 63/4b 王肅傳. She was married to Liu Ch'eng-hsü 劉承緒, son of Liu Ch'ang 劉昶 (A.D. 435–497), who, like Wang Su, was a deserter from the south. After Liu Ch'eng-hsü's death, she was remarried to Wang Su. See *WS* 59/5b 劉承緒傳.

[87] The translation is based on a *TPKC* (493/1b 雜錄) quotation from the same passage of the *Ch'ieh-lan chi*, which contains the following sixteen characters: 其後謝氏入道爲尼, 亦來奔肅, 見肅尙主.

[88] The text (3/5b) reads *lu* 路, which should have been *lo* 絡, the spinning wheel. *Lo* 絡 is used here for *lu* 路 as a pun. See *Ch'üan Pei-Wei shih* 全北魏詩 10b 王肅妻謝氏贈王肅[詩].

[89] *Sheng* 勝, a spindle, also has the meaning "to win, to have the upper hand." It is used as a pun here. A free translation of this line is: "Now you have found a way to better yourself."

On the basis of a *Shih-ming* (5/21 釋首飾) entry, the *CC* (3/155 n. 19) defines *sheng* 勝 as a type of barrette for women. This, however, is unrelated to spinning, silk, and other ideas expressed in the lines, and therefore does not fit.

[90] *Na* 納 "to accept," another pun. It means the same loom would not take back the silk that was finished and removed.

[91] The rhyming characters of both poems are identical (*ssu* 絲 and *shih* 時).

Chiao Hung, in his *Chiao-shih pi-cheng hsü-chi* 焦氏筆乘續集 (Taipei, *Kuo-hsüeh chi-pen ts'ung-shu* ed., 1968; 3/193), believes this to be the beginning of the *tz'u-yün*

Greatly embarrassed by this, [Wang] Su built the Cheng-chüeh Nunnery for her to live a secluded life.[92]

Remembering that his father had been killed without due cause, [Wang] Su always entertained the idea of taking revenge as Wu Tzu-hsü 伍子胥 had done in the case of Ch'u.[93] He wore undyed cloth for life[94] and refrained from music. For this he won praise among his contemporaries.

When [Wang] Su first came to the state of [Wei], he did not take such food as lamb and goat's milk. He often ate carp soup; when thirsty he drank tea. Literati in the capital said that he drank one *tou* 斗[95] at a gulp; for this he was nicknamed "Leaky Goblet." Several years later, at a palace banquet [hosted by] Emperor Kao-tsu, [Wang] Su partook of a large amount of lamb and milk curd.

次韻 style (poems exchanged between friends or married couples using the same rhymes) that became very popular during the T'ang, particularly between Po Chü-i 白居易 (A.D. 772–846) and Yüan Chen 元稹 (A.D. 779–831). Chiao Hung says: 次韻非始唐人：世傳詩人次韻，始於白樂天元微之，號元和體．然楊衒之洛陽伽藍記，載王肅入魏，舍江南故妻謝氏而娶元魏帝女，其故妻贈之詩曰．… 繼妻代答，亦用絲詩兩韻，是次韻非始元白也，"It has been accepted by contemporaries that the *tz'u-yün* style was started by Po Lo-t'ien (style of Po chü-i) and Yüan Wei-chih (style of Yüan Chen), a literary style also known as the Yüan-ho (name of regnal period, A.D. 807–820). But according to Yang Hsüan-chih's *Lo-yang ch'ieh-lan chi*, which records that when Wang Su went to Wei, and when he deserted his former wife Lady Hsieh of Chiang-nan, and when he was remarried to the daughter of the Yüan-Wei Emperor, his former wife presented him a poem, which read. . . . In reply to her, his new wife wrote [a poem] for him, using the same rhymes *ssu* and *shih*. From this, [we know] the *tz'u-yüan* did not begin with Yüan [Chen] and Po [Chü-i]."

[92] *WS* (63/6b Wang Li's 王理 biography) states Wang Su's first wife came to meet with Wang Su in Shou-ch'un 壽春 shortly before his death. This information appears to be in disagreement with the *Ch'ieh-lan chi* account. Actually, this is not the case. The wife of the Hsieh clan came to the Wei at an earlier date, but was ordered by Wang Su to stay in Lo-yang while he lived with his new wife in Shou-ch'un. Accompanied by two daughters and a son, Wang's first wife came to Shou-ch'un from Lo-yang, not from the Southern Dynasty Ch'i, to join her dying husband.

[93] Both Wu Tzu-hsü's father, Wu She 伍奢, and elder brother, Wu Shang 伍尚, were killed by King P'ing of the Ch'u 楚平王 (regnant 6th cent. B.C.). Wu Tzh-hsü then fled to the kingdom of Wu, where he raised an army and successfully avenged himself against Ch'u in 506 B.C. See *SC* 66/2–12 Wu Tzu-hsü's biography.

[94] The text (3/6b) reads *pei shen* 卑身, "to debase oneself," but *IS* (3/5b) and *CT* (3/7b) both give *pi shen* 畢身 (where *shen* 身 "self" means *sheng* 生, "life"), "throughout his life" when he was in mourning.

[95] One *tou* during this period measured around 2.45 liters.

Emperor Kao-tsu found it strange and asked: "Among Chinese dishes,[96] how does lamb compare with fish soup and tea with milk?" In reply, [Wang] Su said: "Lamb is the best of land produce, while fish leads among seafood. Depending on one's preference, both are considered delicacies. In terms of taste, there is a difference between the superior and inferior. Lamb is comparable to such large states as Ch'i and Lu 魯; fish, such small kingdoms as Chu 邾 and Chü 莒.[97] Only tea is no match; it is a slave of milk." Emperor Kao-tsu laughed heartily, and, lifting his wine cup, said:

Three horizontal strokes, thrice;
Two vertical strokes, twice.
He who is able to solve this riddle
Will be given this golden wine cup!

Li Piao,[98] the Chief Censor (*Yü-shih chung-wei*), said:

An old barmaid pours wine from a jar into a long-necked pitcher 甿 (*ɣrung*),
A butcher, cutting meat [to fill an order] is as exact 同 (*dung*) as a scale.

Chen Ch'en 甄琛, Assistant President on the Left,[99] Department of State Affairs, said:

Swimmers of the Wu region call themselves experts 工 (*kung*),
The throws of female entertainers end in the void 空 (*khung*).

[96] Literally, *ch'ing chung-kuo chih wei yeh* 卿中國之味也, "you of the Chinese taste," which may contain some interpolation. *IS* (3/5b) gives *chi* 即 for *ch'ing* 卿, after which one character such as *wei* 謂 should be added. The whole sentence may be translated as "This is what you call Chinese taste."

Fish and tea were at this time exotic products of the south and popular only among the southerners.

[97] Ch'i, Lu, Chu and Chü were all states in North China. Chu and Chü were two small states neighboring Ch'i and Lu.

[98] For Li Piao, see Chapter 2 under the Cheng-shih Monastery at note 151. I am grateful to Dr. Ting Pang-hsin 丁邦新 of the Academia Sinica (Taiwan) for the ancient phonetics that appear in parentheses.

[99] The text (3/7a) reads *Yu ch'eng* 右丞, Assistant President on the Right, but the *TPKC* (174/7b–8a) gives *Tso ch'eng* 左丞, Assistant President on the Left instead. Chen Ch'en had been an Erudite of the Central Secretariat (*Chung-shu po-shih*), Grandee Remonstrant, and General of Chariots and Horsemen. For his biography, see *WS* 68/1a–9b.

It should be noted that the verses exchanged between Emperor Kao-tsu, Li Piao, and Chen Ch'en also used the same rhymes: 橫, 縱, 鍾, 甿, 同, 工, 空. Therefore they constitute another early example of the *tz'u-yün* style.

The Prince of P'eng-ch'eng, [Yüan] Hsieh [元]勰, said: "Your subject now understands that this is the character *hsi* 習 (to be accustomed to)."[100] Thereupon Emperor Kao-tsu gave [Li] Piao the golden wine cup. Court officials admired [Li] Piao for his intelligence and knowledge, and Chen Ch'en for his quick response.

To [Wang] Su the Prince of P'eng-ch'eng said, "You have no regard for such large states as Ch'i and Lu, yet are fond of such small kingdoms as Chu and Chü?" In reply, [Wang] Su said: "What is admired in my native land, I have to like." The Prince of P'eng-ch'eng then spoke again, "Come to see me tomorrow; I will prepare the food of Chu and Chü for you. I shall provide a 'milk slave.'" From then on, tea was known as milk slave.

At the time Liu Kao 劉縞, Court Secretary and an admirer of [Wang] Su, concentrated on learning to drink tea. The Prince of P'eng-ch'eng spoke to him, saying, "You do not admire the eight delicacies[101] of dukes and marquises, but are fond of 'the water peril'[102] of those servants.[103] On the high seas are men who seek offensive odors;[104] within the ward are women who 'imitate the frowns' [of other ladies].[105] You indeed belong to such a cat-

[100] The couplets of Li Piao and Chen Ch'en both emphasize the idea of constant practice; hence the answer *hsi* 習, "accustomed to."

[101] For an interpretation of *pa chen* 八珍, "the eight delicacies," see the *Chou-li* 4/1b 天官膳夫, Cheng Hsüan's commentary.

[102] The term *shui e* 水厄, "water peril," was coined by Wang Meng's 王濛 (A.D. 309–347) visitors, who were often forced to drink tea against their will. See *Kan-chu chi* (1137 Manuscript in the Harvard-Yenching Library), vol. 4: 王濛好茶. 人至輒飲, 士大夫甚以爲苦, 每欲候濛, 必云:今日有水厄. "Wang Meng liked tea. As a rule he forced his visitors to drink it. Greatly annoyed by this, each time literati who wanted to visit with him would say: 'Today we will have water peril.'" I am indebted to Mr. Pao-liang Chu, who made this entry available to me.

[103] Literally, *ts'ang t'ou* 蒼頭, "black-haired." It means masses or skilled servants. It is also used as a derogatory term. See Chapter 1 at note 48.

[104] A reference to an anecdote about a man with offensive odor. None of his relatives, brothers, sisters, wife, or concubines could stand him, so he withdrew into the seas. There, however, some people who were particularly fond of his odor followed him day and night in order the enjoy the smell. See *Lü-shih ch'un-ch'iu* (*SPTK so-pen*) 14/88 孝行覽遇合篇.

[105] A reference to Hsi-shih 西施, a famed ancient beauty who frowned as a result of heart pain. An ugly woman in the same block so admired the beauty that she too held her hands against her breast and frowned. Rich men closed their doors and stayed inside so as to keep themselves away from such an ugly sight, and poor people even took their families and fled. See *Chuang-tzu* 5/110 天運.

egory." The Prince of P'eng-ch'eng had in his household a slave from the south, so he made fun of [Liu Kao] with this remark. From then on, at the banquets, court dignitaries all were ashamed of taking tea, although it was provided. Only those destitute refugees from the south, who came to surrender from a distance, liked it.

Following the surrender of Hsiao Cheng-te 蕭正德,[106] the Marquis of Hsi-feng 西豐侯 and [adopted] son of Hsiao Yen, Yüan Ch'a wanted to set out tea for him, [but] first inquired how much "water peril"[107] [Hsiao Cheng-te would like]. Not understanding what [Yüan] Ch'a meant, [Hsiao] Cheng-te replied: "Although your humble servant[108] was born in a land of water, he never has had any trouble with the God of Water[109] as an adult." Yüan Ch'a and his visitors in attendance all laughed.

[106] He was the third son of Hsiao Yen's half brother, Hsiao Hung 蕭宏 (d. A.D. 526), who was adopted by Hsiao Yen prior to the birth of Crown Prince Hsiao T'ung 蕭統 in A.D. 501. Hsiao Cheng-te deserted to the Wei in A.D. 522, but returned to the Liang court the following year when he became dissatisfied with the treatment he received in the Wei. See *Liang-shu* 55/6a–7a and *Nan-shih* (I-wen facsimile ed.) 51/20a–23a; see also *TC* 149/28b–29a.

[107] The custom of drinking tea began in the period of Three Kingdoms. *Nan-ch'uang chi-t'an* 南窗紀談 (Anonymous, *Hsüeh-hai lei-pien* 學海類篇 ed.) 9a–b 飲茶:飲茶或云始於梁天監中, 事見洛陽伽藍記, 非也. 按吳志韋耀傳:孫皓時每宴饗, 無不竟日. 坐席無能否, 飲酒率以七升爲限. 雖不入口, 皆澆灌取盡. 曜所飲不過二升, 初見禮異時, 爲或裁或減. 或賜茶, 即以當酒. 如此言則三國時已知飲茶, 但未能如後世之盛. "Some said the custom of drinking tea began with the T'ien-chien period (A.D. 502–521) of the Liang [dynasty] as was recorded in the *Lo-yang ch'ieh-lan chi*. This is untrue. According to the 'Biography of Wei Yao' (same as Wei Chao, A.D. 204–273) in the *Wei-chih*, when Sun Hao (regnant A.D. 264–280) hosted a feast, the feast would last a whole day. Among those present, regardless of their capacity to drink, they were as a rule given a quota of seven *sheng* of wine. They might not drink it up, but they [pretended] to finish it by pouring it [on the ground]. [Wei] Yao could drink no more than two *sheng*, so when he was at first received [by the emperor] with unusual kindness, his [quota of drink] was either eliminated, reduced, or [he was] given tea as a substitute for wine. According to the statement, then, people of [the period of] Three Kingdoms (A.D. 220–265) already knew how to drink [tea], but drinking tea was not as popular as in later times."

[108] Literally, *hsia-kuan* 下官. See Chapter 2 at note 31 under the Lung-hua Temple.

[109] The term Marquis of Yang 陽侯 refers to an ancient nobleman drowned in a river whose spirit was able to stir up waves. See *HS* 87A/6a Yang Hsiung's biography, commentary quoting Ying Shao 應劭 (ca. A.D. 140 – ca. 206).

The Lung-hua Monastery was established by the Prince of Kuang-ling;[110] the Chui-sheng Monastery 追聖寺 (Monastery in Memory of the Sage [Buddha]) by the Prince of Pei-hai[111]—both were located to the east of the Pao-te Temple.[112] Here religious activities and monks' rooms were [as flourishing and beautiful as those of] the Ch'in T'ai-shang-kung Monastery. Fruit trees were planted in all the temples of the capital, but none could compare with the orchards of these three monasteries.

Four *li* outside the Hsüan-yang Gate was built a Floating Bridge[113] (*Fou-ch'iao* 浮橋) above the Lo River.[114] It was the so-called Yung Bridge 永橋 (Eternal Bridge).[115]

> In the Shen-kuei period (A.D. 518–519), Ch'ang Ching wrote an epitaph in praise of the [Lo][116] Bend, which reads: "Turbulent, the great river; impetuous, the clear Lo. Its origin is in the Hsiung-erh 熊耳 [Mountain],[117] and it controls the tributaries rushing from the gullies. It takes in the Ku [River] and discharges into the I [River], threading through the Chou[118] and draining the Po 亳.[119] Unimpeded to the nearby Yellow River Progenitor,[120]

[110] That is, Yüan Yü 元羽, younger brother of Emperor Kao-tsu. For his biography, see *WS* 21A/13b–20a. Yüan Yü's son, Yüan Kung, was also enfeoffed as Prince of Kuang-ling. He pretended to be dumb for eight years while living here. See Chapter 2 after note 200 under the P'ing-teng Monastery.

[111] That is, Yüan Hsiang 元詳, younger brother of Emperor Kao-tsu. For his biography, see *WS* 21A/27b–32b.

[112] The text (3/8a) reads *Pao-en ssu* 報恩寺, *en* 恩 being an obvious error for *te* 德.

[113] Known as *fou-hang* 浮航 (a floating ferry) in *WS* 79/5a Ch'eng Yen's 成淹 biography, it was constructed in about A.D. 495 under the auspices of the Office of Waters 都水. The bridge connected Lo-yang proper and the four lodging houses of "barbarians" who had abandoned their own land to settle in the Northern Wei.

[114] The Lo River 洛水 was situated seven *li* south of the city. See Yang Ch'üan-ch'i's 楊佺期 *Lo-yang chi* 洛陽記, as quoted in the commentary for P'an Yüeh's "Hsien-chü fu" 閑居賦 (*WH* 16/3a).

[115] According to another source, the bridge was five *li* south of the city. See commentary for "Hsien-chü fu," quoting *Ho-nan chün-hsien ching-chieh pu*.

[116] Should read "*Lo jui sung*" 洛汭頌; *jui* 汭 means a bend. See *WS* 82/8b 常景傳.

[117] *Shu-ching* 6/28b 禹貢:導洛自熊耳. Legge 3, p. 139, "The Tribute of Yu": "He surveyed the Lo from Heung-erh." Hsiung-erh 熊耳 is southwest of modern Lu-shih 盧氏, Honan.

[118] *Chou* 周 refers to *Ch'eng-chou* 成周, another name for Lo-yang.

[119] Po 亳 refers to Hsi Po 西亳, the old capital of Shang situated west of modern Yen-shih 偃師, Honan. The River Lo passed by both ancient cities.

[120] Literally, *chin ta Ho tsung* 近達河宗. *Ho tsung* 河宗 means "to take the Yellow

then paying court to the distant God of the Sea.[121] It responds to the good omens of the Lo,[122] and is indeed located in the central lands.[123] It corresponds to the constellations Chang 張 and Liu 柳 above,[124] and is based in the [Yellow] River and the Sung [Mountain] below, pleasant in summer and winter, bright under either sun- or moonlight. The glorious home of generations of emperors,[125] its influence, like wind, sweeps the whole empire.[126] In the front it approaches the Shao-shih [Range],[127] and backs on the T'ai-hang [Range].[128] It enjoys the strategic Chih 制,[129] its eastern city; and the precipitous Yao 崤 [Mountain],[130] its west-

---

River as its master."

[121] *Hai-jo* 海若, God of the Sea. See *Chuang-tzu* 6/119 秋水篇. See Watson, tr., *Chuang-tzu*, p. 96.

[122] A reference to the *Shu-ching* 15/13b 洛誥: 予惟乙卯, 朝至于洛師, 我卜河朔黎水, 我乃卜澗水東, 瀍水西, 惟洛食. 我又卜瀍水西, 亦惟洛食. Legge 3, pp. 436–437, "The Announcement Concerning Lo": "On the day Yih-maou, in the morning, I came to the city of Lŏ. I *first* divined concerning *the country about* the Le water on the north of the Ho. I then divined concerning the east of the Këen water and the west of the Ch'en water, when the *ground near the Lo* was indicated." K'ung An-kuo's comm. (15/16a): 卜先墨畫龜, …然後灼之, 求其兆順食, 此墨畫之處.

[123] *Shu-ching* 15/8b 召誥: 王來紹上帝, 自服于土中. *HS* 28B/56a 地理志: 昔周公營雒邑, 以爲在于土中. 諸侯蕃屏四方, 故立京師.

[124] *HS* 28B/55b–56a 地理志: 柳七星, 張之分野也. 今之河南雒陽, 穀成, 平陰, 偃師, 鞏, 緱氏, 是其分也. "[It lies in the domain of Chou], bordered by the seven stars in the Liu constellation and the Chang constellation. Lo-yang, Ku-ch'eng, P'ing-yin, Yen-shih, Kung, Hou-shih of the present-time Honan are all within its domain."

[125] *Shu-ching* 2/4a 堯典序: 昔在帝堯, 聰明文思, 光宅天下 K'ung An-kuo's comm.: 言聖德之遠著.

[126] The text (3/8b) reads ? *han hsia feng* □函下風, but *IS* (3/7a) gives *han hsia ? feng* 函夏□風. Sun Hsing-yen's *Hsü Ku-wen yüan* 續古文苑 (1812 ed.) 14/10b is *han hsia t'ung feng* 函夏同風, which the translation follows. *Han-hsia* means "all China," hence, *t'ung-feng* (to have similar influence everywhere) is more meaningful.

[127] See Chapter 3 at note 4 under the Ching-ming Monastery.

[128] The T'ai-hang range originates in Chi-yüan *hsien* 濟源縣, Honan, and runs northward into Shansi. It is located to the north of Lo-yang; hence, the expression "backs on" 却負.

[129] *Tso-chuan* Yin 隱 1 2/16a: 制, 巖邑也. 虢叔死焉. Legge 5, p. 5: "It (that is, the city of Chih) is *too* dangerous a place," was the reply. "The Younger of Kwoh died there...." The site lies west of modern Fan-shui *hsien* 氾水縣, Honan.

[130] Both *CC* (3/165, n. 18) and *CS* (3/129) suggest *ch'iao* 峭 as a mistake for Yao 崤.

ern stronghold. The key point for all four directions, the grand [hub][131] of six thoroughfares. [The dynasty] is safe if it relies on virtue,[132] but perishes if it loses the Way. A careful examination of past events and consultation with ancient texts[133] [shows] now abdications, now "changes of mandate." Sometimes [emphasizing] simplicity, sometimes cultivation. In the remnant Chou, the nine splits:[134] by the end of the Han, three parts.[135] The fortunes of the Wei declined, then came the twilight of the Chin. Heaven and earth emitted bright rays; [with the delivery of] the Map and Books by dragons and turtles from the Yellow River and the Lo River as [an obvious sign],[136] the mandate was conferred. Thus was founded the august [Wei], whose godlike achievements are without peer. Wei has receipt of the heavenly Appointment; magic charms in its possession shine [everywhere].[137] Fit into the heavenly cycle, it prospers; [Heaven's] mandate has been conferred through the Dragon Map.[138] The standardization of [the width] of carriage axles and the styles of script[139] is an assurance of eternal stability.[140] Let our accomplishments be further expanded and let our excellent pattern[141] pass down to posterity. Let our ceremonial caps be adopted [by other states]. Let our godlike rule

[131] *Erh-ya* B.1/9a 釋宮：六達謂之莊. Hao I-hsing's 郝懿行 (1757–1825) comm.: 按莊之言壯, 壯亦大也.

[132] A reference to Wu Ch'i 吳起 (d. 378 B.C.), who advised Duke Wu of Wei to rely on virtue, not physical impregnability, for national security. *SC* 65/14 吳起傳：在德不在險.

[133] The translation follows the *Hsü Ku-wen yüan* (14/10b) version: 詳觀古昔, 列見丘墳. For *ch'iu-fen* 丘墳, see *Tso-chuan* Chao 12 (45/37a: 是能讀三墳五典, 八索九丘; see also Yang Hsüan-chih's Preface at note 1.

[134] *Chiu-lieh* 九裂, that is, splits (*lieh*) within the nine (*chiu*) provinces.

[135] *San-fen* 三分, that is, Han was divided into Three Kingdoms after A.D. 220.

[136] *WH* 3/5a 張衡東京賦：龍圖授羲. 龜書畀姒.

[137] *Ch'üan Liang wen* 全梁文, *Ch'üan Shang-ku San-tai Ch'in-Han San-kuo Liu-ch'ao wen*, edited by Yen Ko-chün 嚴可均 (Taipei facsimile ed., 1961), 15/1b 梁元帝玄覽賦：粤我皇之握鏡, 實乃神而乃聖.

[138] According to *Hsü Ku-wen yüan* (4/10b), this couplet *hsi-yün hui-ch'ang* 璽運會昌, *lung-t'u shou-ming* 龍圖受命 is redundant.

[139] A reference to the first Emperor of the Ch'in, who is given credit for the standardization of carriage axles, measurements, and scripts. See *SC* 6/29.

[140] Emending *pao* 寶 to *pao* 保 after *IS* (3/7a). *Shih-ching* 9.3/7b (ode 166, verse 1, lines 1 and 2) 小雅天保：天保定爾, 亦孔之固. Waley, *Book of Songs*, p. 175: "May Heaven guard and keep you / In great security."

[141] Emending *hung mo* 洪謨 to *hung mo* 洪模 after *IS* 3/7a.

be recognized as [the only] legitimate one. [Lo-yang] is a hub of water and land transportation, the intersection of main roads leading to Chou and Cheng 鄭.[142] An epitaph on the Bend of Lo is therefore inscribed herewith in order to inform those living in Central China."

On each of the northern and southern banks was a [stone] pillar that rose to a height of two hundred Chinese feet. On top of the pillar was a figure of a [golden][143] phoenix seemingly poised to fly high into the sky.

To the south of the Yung Bridge and north of the Huan-ch'iu 圜丘 (Circular Mound), between the I and Lo Rivers, was the Imperial Drive with buildings[144] on both sides. On the eastern side were the Four Barbarians' Lodging Houses: (1) Chin-ling 金陵 [south], (2) Yen-jan 燕然[145] [north], (3) Fu-sang 扶桑 [east], and (4) Yen-tzu 崦嵫 [west].[146] On the western side were the Four Barbarians' Wards: (1) Kuei-cheng, (2) Kuei-te 歸德 (Return to the Virtuous), (3) Mu-hua 慕化 (Admire the Refined), and (4) Mu-i 慕義 (Admire the Righteous). Deserters from the Wu region were housed in the Chin-ling Lodge[147] [at first], but given residences in Kuei-cheng Ward three years later.

In the early Ching-ming period (A.D. 500–503), Hsiao Pao-yin,[148] Prince of Chien-an 建安王 of the illegitimate Ch'i [dy-

[142] Lo-yang lies between the capital of Western Chou (trad. 1122 or 1027–771 B.C.) to the west and the state of Cheng to the east; hence its geographical importance.

[143] Adding *chin* 金 "golden" after *YHNC* 3/7b. The same source gives four pillars instead of two.

[144] Literally, *hsia* 夾, "sandwiched." Actually the text strongly implies that on each side of the drive were four houses and wards in symmetrical arrangement.

[145] Yen-jan is the name of a mountain in the land of the Hsiung-nu. Tou Hsien 竇憲 (d. A.D. 92) of the Later Han erected a slab monument on the mountain to commemorate his victory over the Southern Hsiung-nu in A.D. 89. Hence it is a term loosely referring to the northern lands.

[146] Twelve characters are left out in the text (3/9a). The translation follows *YHNC* 3/7b.

[147] Chin-ling is another name for Chien-yeh, the national capital for all Southern Dynasties.

[148] Hsiao Pao-yin 蕭寶寅 (寅 also written as 夤) of the Ch'i court surrendered to the Wei in A.D. 501, but later rose against it in the wake of his repeated failures to crush the rebel Mo-ch'i Ch'ou-nu 万俟醜奴. He was defeated by the Wei and ordered to commit suicide in A.D. 530. See *WS* 59/7a–19b.

nasty], surrendered. He was then ennobled as Duke of K'uei-chi 會稽公, and given a residence in Kuei-cheng Ward. The residence was specially built for him. Later, he was promoted to be Prince of Ch'i, and married to the Senior Princess of Nan-yang 南陽長公主.[149] Ashamed of living among[150] the barbarians, he entrusted the princess with a request to Emperor Shih-tsung that he be permitted to live in the city. Emperor Shih-tsung granted his request and gave him a residence in the Yung-an Ward 永安里 (Ward of Permanent Peace).

In the fourth year of the Cheng-kuang period (A.D. 523), Hsiao Cheng-te, Marquis of Hsi-feng and son of Hsiao Yen, came [to Lo-yang] to surrender. He was housed in the Chin-ling Lodge. In addition, a residence was built for him in the Kuei-cheng Ward, which was later[151] donated by [Hsiao] Cheng-te as the Kuei-cheng Temple.[152]

Northern barbarians who had surrendered were assigned to the Yen-jan Lodge, and given houses three years later in the Kuei-te Ward.

In the first year of Cheng-kuang (A.D. 520), when the chieftain of Ju-ju 蠕蠕主, Yü-chiu-lü A-na-hung 郁久閭阿那肱[153] came to pay tribute, officials in charge of [his visit] did not know [according to protocol] which place [among ranking officials] he should be assigned to. Ch'ang Ching, Drafter of the Central Secretariat, advised:

"During the Hsien-ning period 咸寧 (All at Peace) (A.D. 275–280) when the Shan-yü 單于[154] came to the court,[155] the Chin

[149] Senior Princess of Nan-yang was Emperor Hsüan-wu's (regnant A.D. 499–515) elder sister.

[150] Adding *lieh* 列, "among" after *IS* (3/7b) and *CT* (3/11a).

[151] Adding *hou* 後, "after," after *YHNC* 3/8a.

[152] This passage dealing with Hsiao Cheng-te is treated as main text in the *Ch'ung-k'an* (3/24a), but my translation reclassifies it as a footnote, like the Hsiao Pao-yin passage.

[153] His name is variably given as ? ? chih Tu-chiu-lü a-na-hung □□至都久閭阿郁紘 (3/9b of our text), Jui ? chu Yü-chiu-lü-ho-na-hung 芮□主郁久閭河那肱 (*IS* 3/8a), Ju-ju chu Yü-chiu-lü a-na-hung 蠕蠕主郁久閭阿郁紘 (*CT* 3/10b), and Pei-i Yü-chiu-lü a-na-hung 北夷郁久閭阿郁紘 (*YHNC* 3/8a). Ju-ju is name of a tribe. For his domestic troubles and his eventual surrender to the Wei, see *WS* 103/10b–17b 蠕蠕傳 and 9/11a–b 肅宗紀.

[154] Shan-yü was the leader of the Hsiung-nu 匈奴.

[155] This occurred in A.D. 279. See *Chin-shu* 3/29b–30a 武帝紀.

government assigned him to a place below that of princes, dukes, and the Specially Advanced (*T'e-chin*).[156] It is therefore proper to place [A-]na-hung[157] between vassal kings and Palatines Ceremonially Equal to the Three Authorities."

The court followed [Ch'ang Ching's] advice.[158]

The chieftain was assigned to the Yen-jan Lodge and given a residence in the Kuei-te Ward.

In order to avoid the hot weather in China, the sons of northern barbarian chieftains who were sent to wait [on Chinese emperors][159] always came in autumn and returned to their own land in spring. They were thus called "wild goose subjects"[160] by their contemporaries.

Eastern barbarians who came to surrender were assigned to the Fu-sang Lodge[161] and [later] given residences in the Mu-hua Ward.

Western barbarians who had surrendered were assigned to the Yen-tzu Lodge[162] and [later] given residences in the Mu-i Ward.

Of the hundred kingdoms and thousand cities [in the area extending] from west of Ts'ung-ling Range 葱嶺 (the Green Onion Range)[163] to Ta-Ch'in 大秦 (the Byzantine Empire), none did not accept China's suzerainty with gratitude.[164] Tradesmen doing business with barbarians and peddlers rushed to China's border every

[156] A special honor granted to meritorious generals, dukes, and high-ranking officials. It carried no real power.

[157] The text (3/10a) reads *na hung* 郍紘, which is incomplete.

[158] This advice is also recorded in his biography. See *WS* 82/7b.

[159] Literally, *ju shih* 入侍, "to enter to serve." The term refers to a sort of hostage system by means of which China controlled her vassal kingdoms. See Yang Lien-sheng, "Hostages in Chinese History," pp. 43–59.

[160] Literally, *yen ch'en* 鴈臣, "migrating goose subjects." This seasonal migration was a common practice among the T'o-pa and the Ch'ih-le 敕勒 peoples. See *WS* 15/10b Yüan Hui's 元暉 biography, and *PS* 54/22b Hu-lü Chin's 斛律金 biography.

[161] Fu-sang 扶桑, name of a tree in which the sun rises. The term also loosely refers to any place to the east of China. See *Shan-hai ching* 山海經 (*SPTK so-pen*) 9/54 海外東經.

[162] The place where the sun sets. The term also loosely refers to any place to the west of China. See *Ch'u-tz'u* (1/15) 離騷：吾令羲和弭節兮，望崦嵫而勿迫. Hawkes, *Ch'u Tz'u*, p. 28: "I ordered Hsi-ho to stay the sun-steeds' gallop change, to/To stand over Yen-tzŭ mountain and not go in." Comm.: 崦嵫，日所入山也. 下有蒙水，水中有虞淵, "Yen-tzu is the mountain into which sun sets. Underneath [the mountain] is the Meng River, in which is the Yü-yüan."

[163] The "Green Onion Range" generally refers to the present-day Pamirs.

[164] Emending *huan fu* 歡附 to *k'uan fu* 款附 after *IS* 3/8a.

day[165]—indeed, China was the axis mundi of the whole universe. Those who took delight in China's customs and who had consequently taken residence [in China] were too numerous to count. At any rate, more than ten thousand households surrendered, and adapted to Chinese culture. Wards and lanes were orderly and well kept, [subdivided into] rows after rows of [houses] and countless gates. Green locust trees cast shadows over the streets; green willows drooped in the courtyards. Rare commodities from every corner of the world were all available here.

A separate marketplace established to the south of the Lo[166] River, known as the Ssu-t'ung Market, was popularly referred to as the Market of the Yung Bridge.[167] Fish from the I and Lo Rivers were sold here. Literati and commoners [in the city] desirous of fish fillets all came here to get them. They were delicious. In the capital there was a saying:

Carp of the Lo,
Bream of the I,
Costlier than
Beef and lamb!

East of the road and to the south of the Yung Bridge were two wards known respectively as White Elephant (*Pai-hsiang* 白象) and Lion (*Shih-tzu* 獅子).[168]

A white elephant was presented by the barbarian king of Ch'ien-t'o-lo 乾陀羅國 (Gandhāra, in the north of modern Punjab)[169] in the second year of Yung-p'ing (A.D. 509). A five-colored screen[170] and a "seven precious"[171] sedan chair were

[165] A paraphrase of *HHS* (118/26b) 西域傳論:商胡販客, 日款於塞下, "Barbarian tradesmen and peddlers daily came to pay tribute at our frontier lookouts."

[166] The text (3/10a) mistakenly gives *le* 樂 for *lo* 洛.

[167] The text (3/10b) is *wei Yung ch'iao shih* 謂永橋市, whereas *IS* (3/8b) gives *wei Yung ch'iao shih* 爲永橋市. The translation combines both versions to make better sense.

[168] Here "lion" may be used figuratively to refer to a tiger, which Majursi usually rides on.

[169] The text (3/10b) reads Ch'ien-lo 乾羅, but *YHNC* (3/8b) is Ch'ien-t'o-lo 乾陀羅, a country then (A.D. 509) occupied by Yen-ta 嚈噠 (*WS* 8/17a). It is also transliterated as Chien-t'o-lo 健馱羅 (*Ta-T'ang Hsi-yü chi*, *SPTK so-pen*) 4/40 under 傑迦國.

[170] Emending *wu-ts'ai* 五綵 to *wu-ts'ai* 五采 after *YHNC* 3/8b.

[171] See Chapter 2 at note 72 under the Ching-hsing Nunnery.

[carried on] its back. The chair would accommodate several persons. Truly it was an unusual animal. Kept ordinarily in the Bureau of Imperial Carriages,[172] it frequently destroyed houses and walls [in the bureau]. When running out [of the bureau compounds], it uprooted whatever trees it encountered and felled whatever walls it came across. Out of terror, people ran about in great confusion. Empress Dowager [Hu] therefore had the elephant moved and confined in this ward.

A lion to be presented by the barbarian king of Po-ssu 波斯[173] was captured and retained by the rebel Mo-ch'i Ch'ou-nu while on its way to the capital.[174] Toward the end of Yung-an (A.D. 530), with the downfall of [Mo-ch'i] Ch'ou-nu, [the lion] finally reached the capital. Emperor Chuang said to Li Yü,[175] the Chief Palace Attendant: "We have heard that when a tiger sees a lion, it will always lay prostrate.[176] Let's get a tiger and try to find out whether this is true."

Accordingly, commanderies and prefectures in districts close to the mountains[177] were ordered to capture tigers and then send them on to the capital. Kung-hsien[178] 鞏縣 and Shan-yang[179]

[172] For the Sheng-huang Stable, see Chapter 1 at note 153, Chien-chung Temple.

[173] It is otherwise known as Po-chih 波知 (in a hilly area between modern Zebak and Chetral). See *WS* 102/20b.

[174] To commemorate this event, Mo-ch'i Ch'ou-nu changed the name of his regnal period into Shen-shou 神獸, "The Holy Animal." See *TC* 152/18a–b. For the correct pronounciation of Mo-ch'i, see Yao Wei-yüan, *Pei-ch'ao Hu-hsing k'ao*, p. 248.

[175] The text (3/11a) reads Li Huo 李或, *Huo* 或 being an error for *Yü* 彧. Li Yü, son of Li Yen-shih 李延寔, was married to the elder sister of Emperor Chuang. He held a variety of high offices, including those of Chief Palace Attendant, Palace Grandee on the Left, Director of the Central Secretariat, Generalissimo of the Whirling Cavalry, Palatine Ceremonially Equal to the Three Authorities, and Governor of Kuang-chou 廣州刺史. See *WS* 83B/9a (in Li Yen-shih's biography).

[176] A dog-sized beast is recorded to be as frightening to other animals as a lion would be. It was shipped to China from the Western Regions for the first time during the reign of Emperor Wu of the Han (140–87 B.C.). Emperor Chuang might have referred to this animal. See *Po-wu chih* 博物志 (*IS* ed.) 3/1a–b 異獸.

[177] The text (3/11a) reads *chin shan chün hsien* 近山郡縣. This is a free translation.

[178] During the Wei, it was a subdivision of Ch'eng-kao 成皐 commandery of the Northern Yü province. It corresponds to modern Kung-hsien, Honan. See *WS* 106B/16b–17a.

[179] A subdivision of Chi commandery (modern Hsiu-wu *hsien* 修武縣, Honan) of Ssu-chou. See *WS* 106A/3b–4a.

山陽 both shipped two tigers and one leopard, which the emperor watched in the Hua-lin Park.[180]

Then, as soon as the tigers and leopard saw the lion, all of them closed their eyes and dared not to look upward. In the park there had been a blind bear which was very tame. The emperor ordered them to fetch it to test [its reaction]. When the keeper led the blind bear in, as soon as it smelled the odor, it became terrified and agitated, and ran away dragging its chain. The emperor burst into laughter.

In the first year of the P'u-t'ai period (A.D. 531), upon the ascension of the Prince of Kuang-ling,[181] an edict was issued which reads: "It is against the nature of birds and animals to be caged. It is therefore appropriate to release them back into mountains and forests."

The lion, too, was ordered to be taken back to its country of origin. The barbarian who had received the order to take the lion home, thinking that Po-ssu was too far away and inaccessible, killed it en route and returned. The authority in charge suggested in a reprimand that the man be punished for the crime of violating an imperial order. The Prince of Kuang-ling said: "How can a human creature be punished because of a lion?" Thereupon the man was pardoned.

The P'u-t'i Temple 菩提寺 (Bodhi Temple) was established by barbarians of the Western Regions. It was in the Mu-i Ward.

The śramaṇa Ta-to 達多, in digging out a tomb to seek bricks, found a man [alive underground] and sent him to the court. At the time the empress dowager [neé Hu 胡] and the emperor were in the Tu-t'ang[182] of the Hua-lin Park and thought this a weird omen. They asked Hsü Ho,[183] Attending Secretary within the Imperial Yellow Gate: "Has there been anything like this since antiquity?" He replied: "Formerly during the Wei [of the Three Kingdoms] when a tomb

[180] For the Hua-lin Park, see Chapter 1 at note 260 under the Chien-ch'ün Gate.

[181] For the Prince of Kuang-ling, see Chapter 2 after note 198 under the Ping-teng Monastery.

[182] The text (3/11b) reads Hua-lin Tu-t'ang 華林都堂. There is a mention of Tu-t'ang 都堂 in Chapter 1 under the Chien-ch'un Gate. *TPKC* (375/2a 再生部崔涵) gives Hua-lin t'ang 華林堂, without the character *tu* 都.

[183] For Hsü Ho, see Chapter 1 at note 50 under the Yung-ning Monastery.

was opened up, there was found a slave of Fan Ming-yu 范明友,[184] the son-in-law of Huo Kuang 霍光.[185] The slave talked about the events [leading to the forced] abdication [of the King of Ch'ang-i 昌邑王] and the ascension [of Emperor Hsüan 宣帝]. [His verbal account] agreed with the historical records. [The present case] is not [unusual] enough to be counted as [a heaven-sent] portent."

The empress dowager ordered [Hsü] Ho to ask [this man] his name, how long he had been dead, and what he took for drink and food.

The dead man said: "Your subject's surname is Ts'ui 崔, given name is Han 涵, and style, Tzu-hung 子洪. I am a native of An-p'ing 安平 of Po-ling.[186] My father's name is [Ts'ui] Ch'ang [崔]暢; my mother's maiden name, Wei 魏. My residence was in the Fu-ts'ai Ward 阜財里 (Ward of the Wealthy) in the western suburb. Dead at the age of fifteen, I am now exactly twenty-seven. While underground for the past twelve years, I have slept as if in a stupor, and had no need of food. At times I roamed around and perhaps came upon food or drink [I happened to find]. But all this was like a dream and I am hazy about the details."

The empress dowager then dispatched Chang Chün 張雋,[187] Clerk of the Palace Gate (*Men-hsia lu-shih*), to proceed to the Fu-ts'ai Ward for an interview with [Ts'ui] Han's parents. There he [indeed]

[184] This is also referred to in the *Po-wu chih* (7/4a–b 異聞), but the time given is the "end of Han" (*Han mo* 漢末) rather than the Wei. Perhaps the story began to prevail in the Chien-an period, when for all practical purposes it was already Wei though still known as Han.

Fan Ming-yu was Commandant of the Wei-yang (Boundless) Palace Guards (*Wei-yang[-kung] wei-wei* 未央[宮]衞尉). He was executed in 67 B.C. along with many members and relatives of the Huo family. See *HS* 8/10b and 68/14b.

[185] Huo Kuang was a powerful minister of the Western Han (206 B.C. – A.D. 5). After the death of Emperor Chao in 74 B.C., Huo Kuang enthroned Liu Ho 劉賀, King of Ch'ang-i 昌邑王, as the new ruler, but a rift soon developed between them. Huo Kuang then deposed Liu Ho in favor of Emperor Hsüan 宣帝 as the new ruler (regnant 73–49 B.C.). See *HS* 68/4b ff.

[186] Modern An-p'ing 安平, Hopei.

[187] The text (3/12) reads Chang Hsiu-hsi 張秀攜, but *FYCL* (116/1386) gives Chang Chün 張儁 and *TPKC* (375/2a 再生類崔涵), Chang Chün 張雋. The translation follows the latter for three reasons: (1) it was unconventional to have two-character given names at this time, (2) *hsi*, meaning "hold," has seldom been used as a given name, and (3) *hsiu* means *chün*, therefore Chang Chün is preferable to Chang Hsiu-hsi.

found Ts'ui Ch'ang [and Ts'ui Ch'ang's] wife whose maiden name was Wei.

[Chang] Chün asked: "Did you have a son who died?"

[Ts'ui] Ch'ang replied: "I have a son [Ts'ui] Tzu-hung[188] who died at fifteen."

[Chang] Chün said: "[His tomb] was excavated. He is presently alive and in the Hua-lin Park. [Because of this], Her Majesty[189] sent me over to make inquiries."

After hearing this, [Ts'ui] Ch'ang was terrified, saying: "I really do not have this son. What I have said was false."

Upon [Chang] Chün's return, he related the truth to the Empress Dowager, who ordered him to take [Ts'ui] Han home. Learning about [Ts'ui] Han's arrival, [Ts'ui] Ch'ang, before the front door, lit a fire outside, grasped a knife, and, while his wife held peach branches,[190] said to [Ts'ui Han]: "You need not come. I am not your father and you are not my son. Hurry, hurry[191] to leave here so you may get away unhurt!"

Consequently, [Ts'ui] Han left and wandered about in the capital, often sleeping under the gates of temples. The Prince of Ju-nan[192] gave him a set of saffron garments. By nature [Ts'ui] Han was afraid of sunlight, so he dared not look up [at it]. Furthermore, he was afraid of such things as water, fire, knives, weapons, and the like. He often ran in the main streets, stopping only when tired; never did he walk at a slow pace. His contemporaries still called him a ghost.

To the north of the main market of Lo-yang was the Feng-chung Ward, most of the residents of which sold funeral articles and coffins.

[188] The text (3/12a) gives *han* 涵, which is an error for *hung* 洪.

[189] Emending *chu jen* 主人 to *chu shang* 主上 after *FYCL* (116/1386).

[190] Peach-tree branches were believed to have the power of warding off evil spirits. *Chou-li* 32/13b 夏官戎右：贊牛耳，桃茢. "Cut off a bull's ear and let it bleed into a container; then stir the blood with a peach broom." For the mythological power of peach trees in warding off evil demons, see Bodde, *Festivals*, pp. 127–129. *Tso-chuan* Chao 4 42/23b: 桃弧棘矢，以除其災. Legge 3, p. 596: "a bow of peach wood and arrows of thorn were employed to put away calamitous influences."

[191] *Chi-shou* 急手, a popular colloquialism during the Northern Wei. See also Chapter 2 after note 315, before note 322, under the Ching-ning Temple.

[192] That is, Yüan Yüeh, son of Emperor Kao-tsu. A great believer in Taoism, he therefore gave Taoist garments to Ts'ui Han. For his biography, see *WS* 22/7a; see also Chapter 1 after note 204.

To them [Ts'ui] Han said: "In making cypress-wood coffins,[193] do not use mulberry wood for liners." When asked why, [Ts'ui] Han replied: "When underground, I noticed one[194] [of the ghosts] levying ghost soldiers. One ghost protested, 'Mine is a cypress-wood coffin so I should be exempted.' The officer then said: 'Although yours is a cypress-wood coffin, the liner is made of mulberry wood.' So he was not exempted in the end."

When people in the capital heard about this, the price of cypress wood soared. It was suspected that coffin sellers bribed [Ts'ui] Han to invent this kind of story.

The Temple of the Prince of Kao-yang 高陽王寺 was originally the private residence of [Yüan] Yung, Prince of Kao-yang. It was located on the west side of the Imperial Drive and three *li* outside the Chin-yang Gate. Following [Yüan] Yung's violent death caused by Erh-chu Jung,[195] his residence was given away as a temple.

In the Cheng-kuang period (A.D. 520–524), [Yüan] Yung, as Prime Minister, was awarded [the right to have] feathered curtains for his carriages, a band, and one hundred *hu-pen* (tiger-rushing) guards, each carrying painted swords.[196] His position was the highest that any subject could possibly attain; his wealth encompassed [everything] on land and sea. His retreat and residence were a match for imperial palaces. White walls and red pillars stretched elegantly for a considerable length; overhanging eaves[197] and upsweeping roof-edges were intricately interconnected.[198] Male servants num-

[193] It was customary to use large coffins of cypress wood, a symbol of longevity, during the Northern Wei. The coffins were often decorated with bronze rings on each end, for rings were believed to have a magical function. See *YYTT* 13/70 尸穸篇.

[194] Literally, *jen* 人, "someone." For a translation of the same story, see Yang and Yang, *The Man Who Sold a Ghost*, pp. 129–130.

[195] Yüan Yung was killed at Ho-yin (east of modern Meng-chin, Honan) in A.D. 528. See Chapter 1 at note 59 under the Yung-ning Monastery.

[196] The text (3/13b) reads *pan-chien* 班劍, meaning wooden swords painted in patterns. For his luxurious life, see also *WS* 9/11a–b 肅宗紀 and 21A/21a–b Yüan Yung's biography.

[197] *WH* 2/7a 張衡西京賦：反宇業業, 飛檐巘巘, "With lofty elevated eaves and magnificent gutters."

[198] Ibid., 3/11a 張衡東京賦：闟戟轇輵. Hughes, *Two Chinese Poets*, p. 58: "A mass of halberds." Hsüeh Tsung's comm.: 轇輵, 參差縱橫也, "*Chiao-ke* means unmatched and disorderly."

bered six thousand, and female entertainers,[199] five hundred. Fabulous pearls[200] lustered in the sun; robes of gauze fluttered in the wind. Since the time of the Han and Chin, no other princes had [led a life] so extravagant and luxurious. When going out, he had the street cleared by mounted guards in his company, while his honor guards formed a column. Hand-bells jangled sharply, and reed whistles sounded mournfully. When one entered his house, singing girls and dancers played flutes and blew pan-pipes. String and pipe instruments were played in succession, day in and day out. His bamboo forest and fish ponds matched those in the forbidden quarters [of the emperor]. Fragrant grasses looked like a pile [carpet],[201] while rare trees formed an unbroken shadow.

A gourmet, [Yüan] Yung spared himself nothing. For each meal[202] he regularly spent as much as several ten-thousand coins, with the result that he had delicacies from land and sea, [covering] a space ten square Chinese feet[203] before him. Li Ch'ung,[204] Marquis of Ch'en-liu,[205] told someone: "Each meal[206] of Kao-yang is the equivalent of my meals for one thousand days."

[Li] Ch'ung, President, Department of State Affairs and

[199] Hui-lin, *I-ch'ieh-ching yin-i* (*Taishō* ed.) 21/438 quoting Hui-yüan's 慧苑 *Ta-fang kuang-fo Hua-yen-ching yin-i* 大方廣佛花嚴經音義:妓, 女樂也…妓, 美女也. "*Chi* is a female musician. . ., *chi* is a beautiful girl."

[200] Literally, *Sui-chu* 隋珠, which refers to a large pearl presented to Marquis Sui 隋侯 by a grateful snake whose life he saved. *Huai-nan-tzu* 8/40 覽冥訓 Kao Yu's comm.: 隋侯見大蛇傷斷, 以藥傅之. 後蛇於江中, 銜大珠以報之, 因曰隋侯之珠, 蓋明月珠也, "Seeing that a large snake was wounded, Marquis Sui applied a coat of medicine [on its wounds]. Later in the river the snake repaid him with a large pearl held in its mouth, so it was since known as 'the Pearl of Marquis Sui,' 'It was a pearl [as lustrous as] the moon.'"

[201] The text (3/13b) and *YLTT* (13822/13a) read *fang ts'ao ju chi* 芳草如積. *WH* 2/4b 張衡西京賦:嘉木樹庭, 芳草如積, "Splendid trees are planted in the courtyard; aromatic grasses are as luxuriant as a carpet." Li Shan's comm.: 韓詩曰:綠蓄如簀. 簀, 積也. 薛君曰:簀, 綠蓄, 盛如積也. 蓄音竹.

[202] Emending *i-jih* 一日 to *i shih* 一食 after *YLTT* 13822/13a and *IS* 3/11a.

[203] Literally, *fang chang* 方丈, "ten square Chinese feet." See *Meng-tzu* 14B/6a 盡心下:食前方丈, 侍妾數百人. Lau, *Mencius*, p. 201: "Their (that is, men of consequence) tables, laden with food, measure ten feet across, and their female attendants are counted in the hundreds." Chao Ch'i's comm.: 極五味之饌食, 列於前, 方一丈.

[204] For Li Ch'ung, see Chapter 2 after note 149 under the Cheng-shih Monastery.

[205] East of modern Shang-ch'eng 商城, Honan.

[206] See n. 202 above.

Palatine Ceremonially Equal to the Three Authorities, was also one of the wealthiest in the nation. [The master of] one thousand servants, but by nature a miser, [he allowed for himself only] shabby clothing and poor food. At meals, he was usually a vegetarian, eating only [fresh] leeks, vegetables, salted and preserved leeks.[207] Li Yüan-yu 李元祐,[208] one of his retainers, told others: 'Lord Li[209] had eighteen varieties for each meal." When asked what he meant, [Li] Yüan-yu said: "Two *chiu* 九 (nine)[210] makes eighteen." Those who had heard about it burst into laughter. Because of this, [Li Ch'ung] was ridiculed by his contemporaries.

After [Yüan] Yung's demise, all his female entertainers were ordered to enter nunneries, except those few who married. Hsü Yüeh-hua 徐月華,[211] a beauty, was skillful at playing the harp (*k'ung-hou* 箜篌)[212] and able to sing the song of "Lady Ming Leaving the Border [for the Hsiung-nu Land]" 明妃出塞之歌.[213]

[207] The text (3/14a) reads *chih-yu chiu-chü* 止有韭菹, but *TPYL* (976/8a 菜茹部韭), *TPKC* (165/8a 吝嗇部李崇) and *YLTT* (13822/13a) all give *chih yu chiu-ju chiu-chü* 止有韭茹韭菹, "There are only leeks and preserved cut leeks." The character *chiu* 韭 should be repeated in order to fit into Li Yüan-yu's sarcasm as recorded in the following text.

Chü 菹 is a mixture of cut vegetables, which contains leeks. See *Chou-li* 6/3b 天官醢人:七菹 Cheng Hsüan's commentary.

[208] The text (3/14a) is Li Yüan-yu 李元祐, but *IS* (3/11a) gives Yu 祐 instead of Yu 佑. No other information about him is available.

[209] Literally, Li Ling-kung 李令公, "The Venerable President Li" (*Ling* is an abbreviation for his official title, *Shang-shu ling* 尚書令 (President of the Department of State Affairs). Kao Yung 高允 (A.D. 389–487), as the President of the Department of State Affairs, established a precedent when he was addressed as "Ling-kung" (Venerable President) by Emperor Kao-tsu. See *WS* 51/12a Kao Yung's biography.

[210] The text (3/14a) is *chiu* 九, "nine," which should be *chiu* 韭, "leek," a homophone of 九 "nine." Here Li Yüan-yu is using it as a sarcastic pun.

A parallel can be drawn with Yü Kao-chih 庾杲之 of the Southern Ch'i Dynasty, whose food often contained three kinds of leeks: *chiu-chü* 九菹, *yüeh-chiu* 瀹韭, and *sheng-chiu* 生韭 (preserved cut leeks, pickled leeks, and fresh leeks). For this Jen Fang 任昉 made fun of him, saying, "Who would say that Master Yü is poor? When eating he often has twenty-seven (3 × 9) varieties [of food]!" See *NCS* 34/9a and *Nan-shih* 49/1b Yü Kao-chih's biography.

[211] She is unidentifiable.

[212] A twenty-three-string lute plucked with both hands. Hsü Yüeh-hua's talent is also referred to in *YYTT* 6/41 樂篇.

[213] A song composed during the Chin by Shih Ch'ung 石崇 (A.D. 249–300) in honor of Wang Chao-chün 王昭君 (Chao 昭 was changed to Ming 明 because of a

Everyone who heard it was moved. In the Yung-an years (A.D. 528–530), she became concubine to Yüan Shih-k'ang 原士康, General of the Guards (*Wei chiang-chün*), whose residence was close to the Ch'ing-yang Gate. While playing the harp, she sang with a mournful voice that pierced the clouds. Passersby who listened [to her singing] suddenly formed a throng. Hsü [Yüeh-hua] often told [Yüan] Shih-k'ang, "The prince had two beautiful ladies, one named Hsiu-jung 脩容 and the other Yen-tzu 艷姿. Both had moth-eyebrows and white teeth. Their fresh, pure appearance conquered the whole city. Hsiu-jung, for her part, could sing [well] 'Green-water Song' (*Lü shui ko* 綠水歌),[214] and Yen-tzu had mastered the 'Flaming Phoenix Dance' (*Huo-feng wu* 火鳳舞).[215] Most beloved in the harem, their favor surpassed that of the other ladies."

After having learned about this, [Yüan] Shih-k'ang often asked Hsü [Yüeh-hua] to play the "Green-water" and "Flaming Phoenix" songs for him.

To the north of Kao-yang's residence was the Chung-kan Ward 中甘里 (Ward of Inner Sweetness), where Hsün Tzu-wen 荀子文 of Ying-ch'uan lived.[216] At the age of thirteen, he was precociously intelligent, of godlike discernment—even Huang Wan 黃琬[217] and [K'ung] Wen-chü [孔]文舉[218] could not surpass him. In the early Cheng-kuang period, P'an Ch'ung-ho 潘崇和[219] of Kuang-tsung 廣宗[220] lectured on Fu [Ch'ien's] 服

Chin taboo), a concubine of Emperor Yüan of the Han (regnant 48–33 B.C.), who was given away to the Hsiung-nu chieftain as his wife. She never had a chance to see the emperor until she was about to go. See *WH* 27/15a 石季倫王昭君辭; *YFSC* 29/256–257 quoting *Ku-chin yüeh-lu* 古今樂錄.

[214] One of the five songs attributed to Ts'ai Yung 蔡邕 of the later Han, the other four being "Yu-ch'un" 遊春, "Yü-chü" 幽居, "Tso-ch'ou" 坐愁, and "Ch'iu-ssu" 秋思. See *YFSC* 59/437 quoting *Ch'in-li* 琴歷.

[215] The text (3/14b) is *huo-feng* 火鳳, but both *IS* (3/11b) and *YLTT* 13822/13a) give *yao-feng* 么鳳, "a young phoenix."

[216] Emending Hsün Ying Tzu-wen 荀穎子文 to Ying-ch'uan Hsün Tzu-wen 潁川荀子文 after *IS* 3/11b.

[217] Grandson of Huang Ch'iung 黃瓊 (A.D. 86–164), Huang Wan (A.D. 140–192) was known as a prodigy. He was opposed to the warlord Tung Cho's decision to move the capital to Ch'ang-an, so eventually he was killed by Tung Cho's associates in A.D. 192. See *HHS* 91/19a–21a Huang Wan's biography.

[218] Style of K'ung Jung 孔融 (A.D. 153–208), one of the seven master writers of the Chien-an period (A.D. 196–220). For his biography, see *HHS* 100/3a–15a.

[219] *Kou-ch'en* (3/14a), on the basis of *PS* (81/7a–b 儒林傳序), suggests Ch'ung-ho

[虔][221] version of the *Ch'un-ch'iu* in the Chao-i Ward 昭義里 (Ward of Manifest Righteousness) of the eastern suburb of Lo-yang.[222] [Hsün] Tzu-wen held up his robe,[223] acknowledged himself a student,[224] and received [P'an Ch'ung-] ho's instruction. At the time Li Ts'ai 李才 of the Chao commandery 趙郡 asked [Hsün] Tzu-wen: "Master Hsü, where do you live?" In reply, [Hsün] Tzu-wen said: "Your servant lives in Chung-kan Ward." Li Ts'ai pursued [the matter], "Why should you live in the southern suburb of the city?" [Li] Ts'ai jeered at him since the Four Barbarians' Lodges were in the same location.[225] [Hsün] Tzu-wen retorted: "The southern suburb of the capital is a splendid location—why should you, sir, find it strange? Speaking of waterways, there are the prestigious I and Lo; of historic sites, there are the Imperial Observatory and the Stone Classics. Of beautiful temples,[226] there are the Pao-te and Ching-ming. Among contemporary men of high position, [there we have the Prince of] Kao-yang and [the Prince of] Kuang-p'ing.[227] There is represented there regional customs from every corner [of the empire], of myriad nations and one thousand cities. As for a man of talents, there is myself, not you!"[228]

崇和 as the *ming* of P'an Shu-ch'ien 潘叔虔, a well-known scholar in the Fu Ch'ien 服虔 (A.D. 2nd cent.) tradition of the *Ch'un-ch'iu*. The style, Shu-ch'ien (literally, "Ch'ien the Junior") suggests that P'an Ch'ung-ho was a great admirer of Fu Ch'ien and therefore seems to verify the *Kou-ch'en* theory.

[220] A subdivision of Ssu-chou (west of modern Hsin-hsien 忻縣, Shansi). See *WS* 106A/4a.

[221] For Fu Ch'ien (A.D. 2nd cent.), see *HHS* 109b/12a–b 儒林傳. His work on the *Tso-chuan* was as popular in the north as was Tu Yü's 杜預 (A.D. 222–284) commentaries for the same work in the south. See *PS* 81/7b.

[222] Literally, *ch'eng tung* 城東, "to the east of the city."

[223] Literally, *she ch'i* 攝齊, "to pull up the lower part of the robe" as a way to show respect for the teacher. See *Lun-yü* 10/3a 鄉黨：攝齊升堂, 鞠躬如也. Sub-comm. (10/3b): 衣下曰齊, 攝齊者, 摳衣也.

[224] Literally, *pei mien* 北面, "to face the north" in the subordinate position, the opposite direction from the teacher, who faces the south.

[225] Literally, *ch'eng nan* 城南, a phrase repeated twice in as many sentences.

[226] Literally, *chao-t'i* 招提.

[227] That is, Yüan Huai 元懷. For his biography, see *WS* 22/6b.

[228] This passage consists of fourteen sentences, each with four characters. Except for the first two sentences, the remaining twelve are couplets, which rhyme at the end of alternate lines. The rhyming characters are: 嶸 (*jung*), 經 (*ching*), 明 (*ming*), 平 (*p'ing*), 城 (*ch'eng*), and 卿 (*ch'ing*).

[Li] Ts'ai could not find any answer.

[P'an] Ch'ung-ho said: "[The tongues of] literati in Ju[-nan] 汝[南][229] and Ying[-ch'uan] 潁[川][230] are as sharp as awls; the ones of people in Yen 燕[231] and Chao 趙,[232] as dull as hammers.[233] This is indeed a truthful statement."

All the students in the academy laughed.

The Ch'ung-hsü Temple 崇虛寺 (Temple of Respect for the Void)[234] was located in the western[235] suburb of the city, occupying the Han site of the Cho-lung Yüan 濯龍園 (Dragon-washing Park).[236]

In the ninth year of Yen-hsi (A.D. 166), Emperor Huan [of the Han] offered sacrifices to Lao-tzu in the Cho-lung Park,[237] [including such rites as] setting up[238] a floral canopy[239] and performing a special type of music [normally] reserved for the suburban sacrifices.[240] This was the site. Immediately after Emperor Kao-tsu [of

[229] Southwest of modern Shang-ts'ai 上蔡, Honan.

[230] East of modern Yen-hsien 偃縣, Honan.

[231] Name for a general area in the northern part of modern Hopei.

[232] Name for general area in the southern part of modern Hopei.

[233] 錐 (*chui*, awl) rhymes with 錘 (*'ch'ui'*, hammer).

A Six Dynasties colloquialism; 錐 is also written as 槌. Similar remarks were exchanged between Tsu Na 祖納 (late 3rd cent. A.D.) and Chung Ya 鍾雅 (d. A.D. 328 or 329). See *TPYL* 466/5b 人事部嘲戲 quoting P'ei Ch'i's 裴啟 *Yü-lin* 語林.

[234] *Ch'ung-k'an* (3/26b) moves this section to the end of Chapter 1, a suggestion with which *CC* (3/183) concurs. The translation follows the original textual order.

[235] *CS* (3/141) suggests that the text should perhaps be amended to read "southwest."

[236] Emending Yo-lung *ko* 躍龍閣 to Cho-lung *yüan* 濯龍園 after *YLTT* 13822/1a. According to de Crespigny, "The Harem of Emperor Huan: A Study of Court Politics in Later Han," in *Papers in Far Eastern History* 12 (Canberra, 1975), p. 21, n. 28, the Cho-lung Palace—not Pavilion or Park, as it appears in my translation—was built to house an increasing number of imperial concubines.

[237] See *HHS* 7/14b 桓帝紀.

[238] Emending *shih* 室, "room," to *she* 設, "setting up" after *IS* 3/12a and *YLTT* 13823/1a.

[239] *Ku-chin chu*, A/4a 輿服篇：華蓋，黃帝所作也. 與蚩尤戰於涿鹿之野，常有五雲氣，金枝玉葉，止於帝上，有花葩之象，故因而作華蓋也. "A floral canopy was made [on the order of the] Yellow Emperor. When he fought Ch'ih-yu in the countryside of Cho-lu, there were always clouds in five colors above the emperor. They were shaped like gold branches and jade leaves, resembling a flower. As a result, a floral canopy was made."

[240] The suburban sacrifice (*chiao-t'ien* 郊天) to heaven was normally performed

the Northern Wei] moved the capital to Lo-yang, he gave away parcels [of adjoining] land to the people. Those who took rest here often saw weird and unusual [apparitions]. As a result, all the people deserted [this area] and built a temple there.[241]

---

by the emperor at an open-air altar south of the capital. It took place around the winter solstice. See Bodde, *Festivals*, pp. 213–214.

[241] *CS* (3/141) questions the accuracy of this statement. The Dragon-washing Park of the Han was inside the city walls (*HHS* 18/8b), whereas in all probability the Wei temple was outside the city. Hence, the temple could not occupy the same Han site.

For Emperor Huan's motivation and participation in this ceremony, see de Crespigny, "The Harem of Emperor Huan," p. 40.

Chapter 4

WESTERN SUBURBS

(*Ch'eng-hsi* 城西)

The Ch'ung-chüeh Temple 冲覺寺 (Temple of Full Enlightenment), established by [Yüan] I, the Prince of Ch'ing-ho and Grand Tutor, was located on the north side of the Imperial Drive one *li* outside the Hsi-ming Gate. It had been [Yüan I's private] residence [prior to his death].

[Yüan] I was the best-known and best-mannered of all the princes. Consequently, of all his younger brothers, Emperor Shih-tsung loved [Yüan] I most. In the fourth year of the Yen-ch'ang period (A.D. 515), at Emperor Shih-tsung's death, [Yüan] I, along with the Prince of Kao-yang [Yüan] Yung and the Prince of Kuang-p'ing [Yüan] Huai, received the testamentary edict to assist and protect Emperor Hsiao-ming, who was at the time only six years old, and in his name the empress dowager [née Hu] took care of myriad affairs of state.[1] Because of [Yüan] I's reputed virtues and close relationship [with the emperor], and also because he embodied the Way and was just, there was no matter big or small on which he was not repeatedly consulted. As a result, during the Hsi-p'ing (A.D. 516–517) and Shen-kuei (A.D. 518–519) periods, his authority overshadowed that of the monarch, and his residence was even grander and more splendid than that of [the Prince of] Kao-yang.[2] In the northwest corner of his home site was a tower, which was higher than the Ling-yün Tower,[3]

[1] Emperor Hsiao-ming (Su-tsung) ascended the throne on January 31, A.D. 515. Yüan I, uncle of the new emperor, was promoted to Grand Tutor on March 10 of the same year. See *WS* 9/1a–b.

[2] The Prince of Kao-yang was known for his wealth and extravagance; hence, one would expect his residence to be unexcelled. See also Chapter 3 after note 195.

[3] For the Ling-yün Tower, see Chapter 1 at note 177 under the Yao-kuang Nunnery.

from which one could see the market below, and gaze into all corners within the capital city. Indeed, it was like the two lines of the [anonymous] Ancient Poems[4] which read:

In the northwest was a lofty tower
Equal [in height] with the floating clouds.[5]

Under the tower were the Ju-lin *kuan* 儒林舘 (Scholar's Mansion) and Yen-pin *t'ang* 延賓堂 (Hall of Welcome),[6] which resembled the Ch'ing-shu Palace[7] in style. The [man-made] hills and fishing ponds [there] were the most outstanding of the time. [Views of] slanting cliffs projected into the windows; curved ponds encircled the hall. From the trees[8] sounded the flying birds' calls; at the stairs,[9] clustered the flowering herbs. [Yüan] I was fond of visitors and had great respect for literature. As a result, all the talented men within the empire made their way [to his place]. From among those who were outstanding he selected his subordinates and assistants.

In the early morning, against the background of attractive scenery,

[4] For the Nineteen Ancient Poems, see *WH* 29/1b–5b. These two lines appear in Poem 5 (29/2b). As a group, the Nineteen Ancient Poems are believed to be the earliest examples of the five-character verse. For English translation, see Arthur Waley, *170 Chinese Poems* (London, 1918), pp. 59–68.

[5] Because of this quotation, the author was criticized by the compilers of the prestigious *Ssu-k'u ch'üan-shu tsung-mu t'i-yao* (I-wen facsimile ed.) 70/9b–10a 史部地理類四. Actually the criticism itself is not well-grounded. Yang Hsüan-chih quotes the existing poem to prove the spectacular height of the tower; he did not mean that the poem was written to describe this particular Northern Wei tower. Furthermore, the criticism mistakenly attributes the tower to the Prince of Kao-yang instead of the Prince of Ch'ing-ho. See also Yü Chia-hsi, *Ssu-k'u t'i-yao pien-cheng* (I-wen facsimile ed.) 8/427–431 史部地理類三.

[6] Emending *T'ui-pin* 退賓 to *Yen-pin* 延賓 after the *YHNC* 3/10b. The following text emphasizes the prince's hospitality, so it is logical to call it "Hall of Welcome."

[7] In the Hua-lin Park. See Chapter 1 after note 260 under the Chien-ch'ün Gate.

[8] See the *Shih-ching* 9.3/1b (ode 165, verse 1, line 2) 小雅伐木：鳥鳴嚶嚶. Waley, *Book of Songs*, p. 204: "Ying, ying, cry the birds." Cheng Hsüan's comm.: 嚶嚶, 兩鳥聲也, "Ying, ying are the cries of two birds."

[9] These four lines, in two couplets, are yet another good example of the parallel prose style that demonstrates the symmetrical placing of each component character according to its phonetics and semantics. They read as follows:

First couplet: *hsíeh fēng jù yǔ* 斜峯入牖, *ch'ü chǎo húan t'áng*; 曲沼環堂;

Second couplet: *shù hsiǎng fēi yīng* 樹響飛嚶, *chīeh ts'úng hūa yào*. 堦叢花藥.

Note that the second characters in the second couplet function as verbs.

he would gaze at his ease from the high terrace.[10] The rare delicacies were all set out, the lute and pan-pipes played together. Aromatic wine filled the pitchers. Distinguished guests crowded every mat. [By comparison], the Prince of Liang would have been ashamed of his retinue at the Rabbit Park (*T'u-yüan* 兎園)[11] and Prince Ssu of Ch'en, of his feasts at the [Bronze] Sparrow Tower ([*T'ung-*]*ch'üeh t'ai* [銅]雀臺).[12]

In the early years of the Cheng-kuang period, Yüan Ch'a was in power. He imprisoned the empress dowager in the rear of the palace, and slew [Yüan] I in the Bureau in Waiting (*Hsia-sheng* 下省).[13] In the first year of the Hsiao-ch'ang period (A.D. 525), the empress dowager[14] returned to power to take charge of myriad affairs of state, giving [Yüan] I the posthumous title of Grand Preceptor of the Grand Heir, Marshal, Inspector-General of Internal and External Military Affairs (*Tu-tu chung-wai chu chün-shih*). [For his funeral service], he was given an axe of gold (*huang-yüeh* 黃鉞),[15] nine fringes for his banner (*chiu-liu* 九旒),[16] a carriage equipped with bells (*luan-lu* 鸞輅),[17] a carriage lined with yellow silk (*huang-wu* 黃屋), a

[10] Emending *nan-t'ai* 南臺 to *kao-t'ai* 高臺 after the *YLTT* 13823/6a.

[11] The Rabbit Park was built on the order of the Filial Prince of Liang 梁孝王 of the Han, and he entertained his guests there every day. See, *Hsi-ching tsa-chi* 2/8.

[12] Upon the completion of the tower in A.D. 210, Ts'ao Ts'ao ordered each of his sons to compose a piece of rhymed prose to commemorate the occasion. Ts'ao Chih 曹植, posthumously known as the Prince Ssu of Ch'en 陳思王, promptly finished one, which impressed his father greatly. See *Wei-chih* 1/78a–b and 19/4b–6a.

[13] *Hsia-sheng* is the abbreviation for *Men-hsia-sheng*, Bureau in Waiting for the Emperor's Service.

He was killed at the age of thirty-four. See Chapter 1 at note 198 under the Ching-lo Nunnery.

[14] The text reads *T'ai-tzu* 太子, which is an obvious mistake for *T'ai-hou*; hence, the translation.

[15] Axes of gold were normally reserved for imperial use. He who received such an axe would have the same authority as the emperor himself in administering martial law. See *Ku-chin chu* A/2a 輿服篇.

[16] *Chou-li* 37/13a 秋官大行人:上公之禮,…建常九斿, "The rites for high-ranking dukes . . . called for the provision of nine fringes for their banner." Cheng Hsüan's comm. (37/14a): 常, 旌斿也. 斿其屬, 幓垂者也, "Fringes were those attached to and drooped from the banner."

[17] *Chou-li*, 22/3b 春官冢人:及葬, 言鸞車象人, "By the time of funeral, [the official would give] words that the bell-equipped carriage and the figure of a man [made of straw be moved toward the tomb]." Chia Kung-yen's 賈公彥 sub-comm.:

feathered pennant hoist on the left carriage rail (*tso-tu* 左纛),[18] with windows to control temperature (*wen-liang-chü* 轀輬車),[19] two marching bands, one in the front and the other in the rear, to play *yü-pao* 羽葆 songs[20] in praise of him, one hundred *hu-pen* (tiger-rushing) guards, each with painted swords, and two troupes playing funeral songs.[21] The funeral rituals were to be conducted according to the precedent set for [Ssu-ma] Fu [司馬]孚, Prince of An-p'ing 安平王 under the Chin.[22] [Yüan] I was honored with the posthumous name of Wen-hsien 文獻 (The Cultured and Dedicated), and his portrait was prepared for display in the Chien-shih Palace. Han Tzu-hsi

---

[鄭注云:]亦設鸞旗者, 以其遣車有鸞和之鈴, 兼有旌旂, "By 'the equipment of *luan-ch'i*,' it meant the dispatched carriage was equipped with bells ringing as harmoniously as the cry of phoenix, and also with banners."

[18] *HS* 1A/36a 高祖紀:紀信乃乘王車, 黃屋左纛, "Chi Hsin then rode the king's carriage lined with yellow silk and feathered pennant hoisted on the left carriage rail." Homer H. Dubs, tr., *The History of the Former Han Dynasty by Pan Ku*, 1 (Baltimore, 1938), 85 n. 1 gives: "the emperor's chariot had a yellow silk lining to its roof, and the 'plumes' 纛 were a bunch of feathers or of yak tail hair attached to the left end of the yoke at the end of the chariot tongue or attached to the left outer horse of the quadriga." A similar passage translated in Burton Watson's *Records of the Grand Historian of China* (New York, 1961, 1, 64) reads: "Chi Hsin then rode forth in the yellow canopied royal carriage with its plumes attached to the left side." Comm.: 李斐曰: 天子車以黃繒爲蓋裏. 纛, 毛羽幢也, 在乘輿車衡左方上注之, "The carriage of the Son of Heaven is lined with the yellow silk from the top [of the cabin]. *Tu* is a feathered pennant planted above the left arm rest of the carriage."

[19] *SC* 87/15–16 李斯傳:[始皇崩], 置始皇居轀輬車中, "[After the death of the first Emperor (of the Ch'in, regnant 221–208 B.C.)], he was placed in a windowed hearse." *Chi-chieh* comm.: 如衣車, 有牕牖, 閉之則溫, 闢之則涼, 故名之轀輬車也, "It was like a lined carriage with windows. When the windows were closed, the hearse became warm [inside], and when open, it became cool. It was therefore known as a 'warm and cool' hearse."

[20] *WH* 58/16a 王儉褚淵碑文:給節羽葆鼓吹, 班劍爲六十人, "[He was given a marching] band to play the *yü-pao* music, [accompanied by] sixty persons each bearing a sword." *YFSC* 16/174–175: 鼓吹曲辭:唯羽葆諸曲備敍功業, 如前代之制, "Only the songs like *yü-pao* that narrated details of past meritorious achievements, [were played] in the same way as they were done in previous dynasties."

[21] For *wan-ko* 挽歌, "hearse-puller's songs" see Chapter 3 at note 32 under the Ching-ming Monastery.

[22] Ssu-ma Fu 司馬孚 was the younger brother of Ssu-ma I, founder of the Chin. He died in A.D. 272 at the age of ninety-three. At the time of his funeral, he was treated with signal honors by the reigning emperor. See *Chin-shu* 37/6a–7a.

韓子熙,[23] formerly Prefect [of the Palace Squires] ([*Lang-chung*] *ling*)[24] in the Kingdom of Ch'ing-ho, was promoted to the post of Attending Secretary within the Imperial Yellow Gate. Three other officials in his former principality were called in[25] to serve as halberd-bearers. [Treatment such as this] was unprecedented in recent times.

A five-storied stūpa was erected to offer posthumous blessings to Wen-hsien. The workmanship was comparable to the one in the Yao-kuang Nunnery.[26]

The Hsüan-chung Temple 宣忠寺 (Temple of Manifest Loyalty) established by [Yüan] Hui 元徽,[27] Prince of Ch'eng-yang 城陽王, Chief Palace Attendant and Governor of Ssu-chou,[28] was located on the south side of the Imperial Drive, one *li* outside the Hsi-yang Gate.

In the Yung-an[29] years, the prince[30] of Pei-hai entered Lo-yang,[31] [forcing] Emperor Chuang to flee northward. The remaining princes assumed a position of neutrality, except [Yüan] Hui, the only [prince] who accompanied Emperor Chuang to the city of Ch'ang-tzu.[32] At the time, the rival military forces faced each other across the [Yellow] River, with the eventual victor as yet undecided. [Yüan] Hui vowed

23 Han Tzu-hsi, a former subordinate of Yüan I, submitted a moving memorial to the empress dowager asking for the immediate exoneration of the prince. This memorial, now available in his biography, was instrumental in bringing down Yüan Ch'a, the man responsible for Yüan I's tragic death. See *WS* 60/3b–7a.

24 The text has *chung* 中. [*Lang-*]*chung* [郎]中 is added after *IS* 4/2a and *YLTT* 13823/6a.

25 Literally, *hsi* 徙, "moved" (the text 4/2a gives *ts'ung* 從, "follow," which is emended to *hsi* 徙 after *IS* 4/2a) *wang-kuo san ch'ing* 王國三卿, "to transfer three ministers of [the former] principality."

26 For the Yao-kuang Nunnery, see Chapter 1 at note 174 ff. The Yao-kuang Nunnery stūpa rose five hundred feet from the ground.

27 Adding *Hui* 徽 after *IS* 4/2a.

28 Son of Yüan Luan 元鸞 and great grandson of Kung-tsung 恭宗 (Ching-mu 景穆; Crown Prince of Emperor Shih-tsu; died in A.D. 451). He had been President, Department of State Affairs prior to the post mentioned in the *Ch'ieh-lan chi*. See *WS* 19C/19b–21b.

29 Emending *Yung-k'ang* 永康 to *Yung-an* 永安 after *IS* 4/2a.

30 Adding *wang* 王, "prince," after *YHNC* 3/10b.

31 That is, Yüan Hao, the Prince of Pei-hai, who was supported by the Liang to recapture Lo-yang on June 17, A.D. 529. See Chapter 1 after note 66 under the Yung-ning Monastery.

32 West of modern Ch'ang-tzu *hsien* 長子縣, Shansi. See Chapter 1 at note 96 under the Yung-ning Monastery.

that if he should ever return to Lo-yang, he would have his residence converted to a temple. After the defeat of Pei-hai and the rout [of his army] the fortunes of the dynasty brightened again.[33] [Yüan Hui] then donated his residence as promised.

Toward the end of the Yung-an period, Emperor Chung planned to kill Erh-chu Jung. Worried about possible failure, he asked [Yüan] Hui for advice. [Yüan] Hui said: "Use the birth of the crown prince as a pretense. Your Majesty could invite [Erh-chu] Jung to come to court. He certainly will come, and can then be done away with." Emperor Chuang said: "The empress has not yet been[34] pregnant [for her term of] ten months—she has been pregnant now for nine months only—can this be done?" [Yüan] Hui said: "When a woman delivers a child, sometimes it is overdue, while at other times it is premature. He won't give it a second thought." The emperor accepted his advice and made it widely known that a crown prince had been born. He dispatched [Yüan] Hui to make a special visit[35] to the residence of the Prince of T'ai-yüan, informing the latter about the birth of an heir-designate.[36]

At that time [Erh-chu] Jung was gambling with [Yüan] T'ien-mu, the Prince of Shang-tang.[37] [Yüan] Hui took off [Erh-chu] Jung's hat, whirling about and dancing joyfully. [Yüan] Hui had been known for his unusual forbearance; heretofore neither delight or anger showed in his countenance. [But this time] he shouted merrily, while circling both in and out of Erh-chu [Jung's] palace. So [Erh-chu] Jung, believing him, set out to the court in the company of [Yüan] T'ien-mu.

Learning of [Erh-chu] Jung's arrival, Emperor Chuang unwittingly turned pale. Wen Tzu-sheng, Drafter of the Central Secretariat, said: "Your Majesty has changed color!" The emperor repeatedly asked for [more] wine to drink. Subsequently, he carried out his plot.

33 Literally, *kuo tao ch'ung hui* 國道重輝, "The way of the court shines again."

34 Emending *yü* 於 to *wei* 有 after the *Ho-chiao* 4/2a and *Kou-ch'en* 4/2b.

35 The wording varies from *t'e chih* 特至, "specially to go [visit]" (our basic text 4/2b), *ch'ih chih* 馳至, "rush to" (*YLTT* 13823/6b), *ch'ih chao chih* 馳詔至, "to rush an imperial edict to" (*IS* 4/2b) to *ch'ih ch'i chih* 馳騎至, "to gallop to" (*TC* 154/13a). As always, the *CC* (4/191) follows the *TC*. The translation follows the basic text.

36 Literally, *kao yün huang-ch'u tan-yü* 告云皇儲誕育, "to inform him about the birth of an heir-designate." Emperor Chuang was the son-in-law of Erh-chu Jung.

37 Modern Ch'ang-chih *hsien* in southeastern Shansi.

After [Erh-chu] Jung and [Yüan] T'ien-mu were duly executed, [Yüan] Hui was appointed Grand Preceptor[38] and Marshal, along with his previous posts. He was put in charge of imperial guards, and enjoyed full confidence [of the emperor].

After Erh-chu Chao's capture of Emperor Chuang, [Yüan] Hui fled [to the house] of K'ou Tsu-jen,[39] the former metropolitan prefect of Lo-yang.[40] In the household of [K'ou] Tsu-jen there were [three][41] governors, all of whom had been [Yüan] Hui's [former subordinate] generals or colonels.[42] Because of these past ties, Yüan [Hui] went there for sanctuary. K'ou Tsu-jen spoke to the younger members of his family, saying: "Now I have heard that Erh-chu Chao has set a high price [on the head of] the Prince of Ch'eng-yang: the captor will be enfeoffed as a marquis of one thousand households. Now riches and honor have arrived!" As a result, he beheaded [Yüan] Hui[43] and sent his head to [Erh-chu] Chao.

[38] The text (4/3a) reads *T'ai-shih ssu-ma* 太師司馬, meaning Sergeant-at-Arms in the Office of Grand Preceptor, a position too low for such an imperial confidant as Yüan Hui. I suggest the character 大 (*Ta*) be added to *Ssu-ma*; hence, the translation.

[39] Albert E. Dien translates the same story from a *Yüan-hun chih* entry, which is believed to have been based on the *Ch'ieh-lan chi*. However, there are obvious textual variants. See Dien, "*The Yüan-hun Chih* (*Account of Ghosts with Grievances*): A Sixth-Century Collection of Stories," *Wen-lin* 文林, *Studies in the Chinese Humanities*, edited by Chow Tse-tsung (Madison, Wisc., 1968), pp. 220–221, and n. 27 on p. 270.

Possibly, K'ou Tsu-jen was the style of K'ou Mi 寇彌, the son of K'ou Chen 寇臻. K'ou Chen had three sons, whose style all had the character *tsu* 祖 "ancestor" in common: K'ou Kuei 寇軌, Tsu-hsün 祖訓; K'ou Chih 寇治, Tsu-li 祖禮; and K'ou Mi, Tsu-jen. Mi was also written as 禰. See *Tzu-chih t'ung-chien k'ao-i* 資治通鑑考異 (*SPTK so-pen* 7/47). For K'ou Mi's biography, see *WS* 42/8b.

[40] *CS* (4/147) suggests that the text might have mistaken K'ou Tsu-jen for his elder brother K'ou Chih, who had been prefect of Lo-yang, whereas K'ou Tsu-jen had not.

[41] *TC* (154/21a) sets the number at three, and *CC* (4/193, n. 9) enumerates them as the following:

K'ou Chih, Governor of Eastern Ching-chou and Ho-chou;
K'ou Fei-chih 寇朏之, son of K'ou Chih, Governor of Eastern Ching-chou;
K'ou Tsun-kuei 寇遵貴, son of K'ou Kuei 寇軌 (K'ou Kuei was the eldest son of K'ou Chen), Governor of Kuang-chou 光州.

CC (4/193) bases its information on *WS* 42/8a–b, 42/9a, and "K'ou Yin-che mu-chih" 寇胤哲墓志 (*MCCS* plate 355).

[42] Adding *chiao* 校, "colonel," after *IS* (4/2b).

[43] There are two versions as to how Yüan Hui was killed. According to Yüan

When [Yüan] Hui went into hiding at [K'ou] Tsu-jen's house, he had had in his possession fifty horses and one hundred catties of gold. To benefit from Yüan [Hui's] wealth and property, [K'ou] Tsu-jen acted as he did. He [then] divided the horses and gold evenly among all his paternal cousins of the past five generations.[44] This is indeed an instance of "One is not guilty, but to possess a piece of jade [as does Yüan Hui] makes him guilty.[45]

Upon the receipt of [Yüan] Hui's head, [Erh-chu] Chao gave no reward to [K'ou] Tsu-jen. [On the other hand], [Erh-chu] Chao saw [Yüan] Hui in a dream saying: "I have two hundred catties of yellow[46] gold and one hundred horses at [K'ou] Tsu-jen's place. You may have them."

When [Erh-chu] Chao awoke, he thought to himself: "The Prince of Ch'eng-yang, with a high position and salary,[47] was not known to be destitute. I have often searched his house in person,[48] but have found no gold or silver at all. This dream may come true."

Early next morning he had [K'ou] Tsu-jen seized, and demanded the gold and horses. [K'ou] Tsu-jen thought that someone had secretly reported [the matter to Erh-chu Chao]; seeing which way the wind was, he immediately confessed that he had actually

---

Hui's biography (*WS* 19A/21b), K'ou Tsu-jen advised Yüan Hui to leave his house on the pretense that police were about to come and arrest the latter. He then sent someone to kill [Yüan] Hui after the latter's departure. According to K'ou Mi's biography (*WS* 42/8b), however, he never admitted [Yüan] Hui into his house, but ordered someone else to kill him.

Yüan Hui's stele inscription (*MCCS* plate 145) gives January 9, A.D. 531 as the date of his death.

[44] Literally, *ssu-fu chih nei* 緦服之內, that is, the coarse mourning garments worn by one's distant relatives for a period of three months.

[45] A common saying of the Chou dynasty as recorded in the *Tso-chuan* (Huan 10). Tu Yü's comm. (7/7b): 人利其璧, 以璧爲罪, "As people are greedy for his jade, he who is possessed of jade constitutes a crime."

[46] This is, *huang chin* 黃金, "gold." *YLTT* (13823/6b) and *IS* (4/3a) give only *chin* 金, "metal."

[47] Literally, *lu-wei lung-chung* 祿位隆重, "high position and rich salary." *YLTT* (13823/6b) and *IS* (4/3a) both read *wei-wang lung-chung* 位望隆重, "occupied a prestigious position."

[48] Literally, *ch'ang tzu ju ch'i chia ts'ai-lüeh* 常自入其家採掠, "Often went to his house in person to plunder." The last character, *lüeh* 掠, "plunder," is perhaps in error. *IS* (4/3a) reads *chi* 跡, which also seems erroneous.

acquired one hundred catties of gold and fifty horses. Suspecting that K'ou [Tsu-jen] had hidden something from him, [Erh-chu] Chao demanded of him as much as he had dreamed. In other rooms of [K'ou] Tsu-jen's household, there were thirty catties of gold and thirty[49] horses, all of which he presented to [Erh-chu] Chao. This, however, was still less than the figure [shown in the dream]. As a result, [Erh-chu] Chao, in a fit of anger, had [K'ou] Tsu-jen arrested, and hung by the head from a high tree, [torturing him still further by] suspending a large stone from his foot, and whipping him until he died.[50] Contemporaries called this a reciprocal punishment.

Yang Hsüan-chih would say: "'A family that upholds decency will have happiness to spare; in a household that has accumulated evil deeds, troubles will collect.'[51] Turning against his benefactor and biting the hand that fed him,[52] [K'ou] Tsu-jen killed [Yüan] Hui because of his greed. [Yüan] Hui then in a dream increased the amount of gold and horses, prompting [Erh-chu] Chao to kill [K'ou] Tsu-jen in return. In the process, Yüan [Hui] subjected [K'ou] Tsu-jen to whipping and beating, and condemned him to unutterable misery.[53] [By comparison,] even the whipping of T'ien Fen 田蚡 by Wei Hou 魏侯[54] and the stabbing of Yao Ch'ang 姚萇[55] by the ruler of Ch'in were no harsher!"

[49] Emending *wu-shih p'i* 五十疋 to *san-shih p'i* 三十疋 after *YLTT* (13823/7a) and *IS* (4/3a).

[50] According to his biography (*WS* 42/8b), K'ou Tsu-jen died a natural death in the Western Wei. But *FYCL* (84/1009 怨苦篇 quoting *Yüan-hun chih*) gives a story similar to the *Ch'ieh-lan chi* version. The *Yüan-hun chih* account is believed to have been based on the *Ch'ieh-lan chi*. See Introduction.

[51] A paraphrase of the *I-ching* (1/26a 坤文言): 積善之家, 必有餘慶; 積不善之家, 必有餘殃. Richard Wilhelm, *I Ching*, 2, 26–27, hexagram no. 2 "K'un—The Receptive"; "A house that heaps good upon good is sure to have an abundance of blessings. A house that heaps evil is sure to have an abundance of ills."

[52] Literally, *fu-en fan shih* 負恩反噬, "to betray the favors of someone and bite him instead."

[53] Literally, *ch'iung ch'i t'u-t'ai* 窮其塗炭, "tasting mire and charcoal to the fullest" that is, to suffer great distress. For the origin of *t'u-t'ai* 塗炭, see the *Shu-ching* 8/6b 仲虺之誥: 民墜塗炭. Legge 3, p. 178, "The Announcement of Chung-hwuy: ... and the people were *as if they were* fallen amid mire and charcoal." K'ung Ying-ta's 孔穎達 (A.D. 574–648) sub-comm.: 民之危險, 若陷泥墜火, 無救之者, "People faced the perils as if they had fallen into mud and fire and had no one to save them."

[54] The text (4/4a) is Wei-hou *chih ch'ih* T'ien Fen 魏侯之笞田蚡, Wei-ch'i Hou

The Wang Tien-yü Monastery 王典御寺 (Monastery of Wang the Imperial Chef)[56] located to the east of the Hsüan-chung Temple, was founded by the eunuch[57] Wang T'ao-t'ang 王桃湯.[58] At the time, all temples founded by eunuchs were nunneries; only this one established by [Wang] T'ao-t'ang was for monks. It was [therefore] called[59] "a hero" [rather than "a heroine"] by contemporaries. Near the gate was a three-storied stūpa, the workmanship of which was more superb than that of the Chao-i [Nunnery].[60] Of all religious

---

(Marquis of Wei-ch'i) being Tou Ying's title of nobility. T'ien Fen, (d. 131 B.C.), as the prime minister, had a grudge against Tou Ying and Kuan Fu 灌夫 (d. 131 B.C.), both of whom were executed as a result of T'ien Fen's slander. When T'ien Fen fell ill, he hired a witch to ward off the evils, but the witch saw the spirits of Tou Ying and Kuan Fu coming to demand T'ien Fen's death. See *SC* 107/27 魏其侯武安侯列傳, Burton Watson, tr., *Records of the Grand Historian of China* 2, 107–129, and *Yüan-hun chih* as quoted in *FYCL* 87/1049–1050.

[55] The text (4/4a) is *Ch'in chu chih tz'u* Yao Ch'ang 秦主之刺姚萇. The term *Ch'in-chu* (the Ch'in ruler) refers to Fu Chien 苻堅, a former superior of Yao Ch'ang. After Fu Chien's defeat at the Fei River in A.D. 383, Yao Ch'ang turned against Fu Chien and committed regicide. As a further expression of his hatred, he exhumed Fu Chien and disrobed and beat his remains. When Yao Ch'ang fell ill, he saw Fu Chien in a dream, leading an army of ghosts chasing after him. Holding spears in hand, Yao Ch'ang's ladies in waiting came out to stab the ghosts, but by mistake they hit Yao Ch'ang instead. The ghosts said to each other, "Good, they have hit the right and fatal spot." Consequently the ghosts pulled out the spearhead, causing Yao Ch'ang to bleed. When he awoke, he had a swollen scrotum. A physician operated on him, causing him to bleed in the same way as did the ghosts. He therefore died. See *Chin-shu* 116/18a and *Yüan-hun chih* as quoted in *FYCL* 87/1050–1051. See also *Shih-liu-kuo ch'un-ch'iu chi-pu* 38/4b 前秦錄 and 50/8a–b 後秦錄.

[56] *Ch'ung-k'an* (4/29a) treats the Wang Tien-yü Monastery as a continuation of the previous entry. My translation, however, starts with this monastery in a new paragraph.

[57] Between "the eunuch" and "Wang T'ao-t'ang," the text (4/4b) has another character Yang 楊, which bears an orthographic resemblance to T'ang 湯 and was thus inserted by mistake. It is deleted in the translation.

[58] Wang T'ao-t'ang served both Emperors Kao-tsu (regnant A.D. 471–499) and Shih-tsung (regnant A.D. 499–515). For his biography, see *WS* 94/20a–b. He was killed in A.D. 528 at Ho-yin along with a great number of court officials.

[59] The text (4/4b) has a blank between *ch'eng* 稱, "called," and *ying hsiung* 英雄, "hero," but both *YLTT* (13823/7a) and *IS* (4/3b) give *chih* 之, "it," as the direct object. Hence the translation. "Hero" here perhaps means "outstanding" or "unusual."

[60] *Chao i* 昭儀. The second character is erroneously given as I 義 in the text (4/4b). For the Chao-i Nunnery, see Chapter 1 after note 207.

shrines[61] established by eunuchs, this was by far the most splendid. At the time of the six [monthly Great][62] Fasts there were always dancing and drum-beating [ceremonies].

The establishment of the Pai-ma Temple 白馬寺 (Temple of the White Horse) by Emperor Ming (A.D. 58–75) of the Han marked the introduction of Buddhism[63] into China. The temple was located on the south side of the Imperial Drive, three *li* outside the Hsi-yang Gate.

The emperor dreamt of the golden man sixteen Chinese feet tall, with the aureole of sun and moon radiating from his head and his neck.[64] A "golden god," he was known as Buddha. The emperor dispatched envoys to the Western Regions in search of the god, and, as a result, acquired [Buddhist] scriptures[65] and images. At the time, because[66] the scriptures[67] were carried into China on the backs of white horses, [White Horse] was adopted as the name of the temple.

After the emperor's death, a hall for meditation[68] was built on his tomb. Thereafter stūpas were sometimes constructed [even] on the graves of the common people.

The scripture cases housed in the temple have survived until this day; to them incense was often burned and good care was given. At times, the scripture cases gave off light that illuminated the room and

[61] The text (4/4b) reads *chao-t'i* 招提 (*catur-deśa*). See Preface, note 17.

[62] For *liu chai* 六齋 see Chapter 1 at note 203 under the Ching-lo Nunnery.

[63] Emending *Fo* 佛 "Buddha" to *Fo chiao* 佛教 "Buddhism" after *TPYL* 658/6a 釋部寺.

The text (4/4b) is *Fo ju Chung-kuo chih shih* 佛入中國之始, "the beginning of Buddha's entry into China." This is a loose translation.

[64] Literally, *hsiang-pei jih-yüeh huang-ming* 項背日月光明, "as bright as the sun and the moon around the neck and on the back." *IS* (4/4a) mistakenly writes *chieh* 皆, "all," for *pei* 背, "back." For "neck," see Yang Hsüan-chih's Preface at notes 7 and 8.

[65] That is, *ching hsiang* 經像, "scriptures and images." The envoys, Ts'ai An (or Yin) 蔡愔 and Ch'in Ching 秦景 were reported as having acquired *The Sūtra in Forty-two Sections* 四十二章經 and a statue of the Buddha that they took home in A.D. 67. See *WS* 114/1b 釋老志 and *Mao-tzu*'s "Li-huo-lun" 牟子理惑論 as quoted in Seng-yu's *Hung-ming chi* (*Taishō* ed.) 1/4–5.

[66] Adding *i* 以 after *TPYL* 658/6a 釋部寺.

[67] Adding *ching* 經, "scriptures," after *TPYL* 658/6a 釋部寺 and *IS* 4/4a.

[68] *Jetavana*—a term that derives from a garden donated by Prince Jeta for the orphaned and helpless. See *Hsien-yü ching* (*Taishō* ed.) 10/418 須達起精舍品第四十.

Fig. 4. The Pai-ma (White Horse) Temple stūpa in Lo-yang, supposedly the stūpa of the first Buddhist temple ever built in China

hall. As a result, both laymen and Buddhist devotees reverently worshiped as if they were facing the real Buddha.

In front of the stūpa were pomegranate trees[69] and grapevines that were different from those grown elsewhere: they had luxuriant foliage and huge fruits. The pomegranates [each] weighed seven catties, and the grapes were bigger than dates. The taste of both was especially delicious, superior [to all others] in the capital.[70] At harvest

[69] The text (4/5a) reads *nai lin* 奈林 (crabapple orchard), but *CS* (4/151), on the basis of a *TPYL* (972/2b 果木部蒲萄) quotation, suggests *t'u-lin* 茶林, otherwise known as *t'u-lin* 塗林. *T'u-lin* 塗林, or *an shih-liu* 安石榴 (pomegranate), was imported into China on Chang Ch'ien's 張騫 return (126 B.C.) from the Western Regions (*CMYS* 4/13a). *CC* (4/196), however, maintains that *nai* 奈 should stand unchanged; *nai* 奈 and *liu* 榴 belong to the same generic family.

[70] Literally, *chung ching* 中京, "the central capital," meaning Lo-yang, as compared to K'ai-feng to the east and Ch'ang-an to the west. On the basis of a *Li-chi* (10/24a 檀弓下釋文) entry that considers *ching* 京 "capital" as a possible mistake for *yüan* 原, "plain," *CC* (4/99 n. 4) suggests *chung ching* 中京 as a variant of *chung yüan* 中原, "Central Plain."

5. Figure of a white horse in front of the main entrance of the Pai-ma (White Horse) Temple
.o-yang

time[71] the emperor often came in person to pick them. Sometimes he would give [some] to ladies in the harem, who in turn would present them as gifts to their relatives. They were considered rare delicacies. The recipients often hesitated to eat them; instead, the fruits would be passed on and on to several households. In the capital there was a saying:

Sweet pomegranates of the White Horse,
Each fruit is as valuable as an ox.[72]

Pao-kung 寶公, a śramana[73] whose native place nobody knew,

[71] Literally, *chih shu shih* 至熟時, "at the time of ripening."

[72] The couplet rhymes at the last (the fourth) character of each line (that is, *liu* 榴, "pomegranate," and *niu* 牛, "ox").

[73] This monk remains unidentified. Some suggest he is to be identified with Pao Chih 寶誌 of the Liang dynasty, a famous Buddhist prophet who died in A.D. 514 at ninety-seven *sui*, but no visit of this monk is recorded. Others believe the monk to be the same hermit of the Sung Mountains referred to in Hou Chün-su's 侯君素 *Ching-i chi-lu* 旌異記錄 (quoted in *FYCL* 109/1301).

was ugly in appearance but brilliant in intelligence. He had an insight into the "three periods":[74] past, [present], and future. Whatever he said was just like a prophecy, incomprehensible [at the time] but verifiable later when the event he had foretold really took place. Hearing of this, Empress Dowager Hu asked him about current affairs. Pao-kung said:

Handful of husked rice to give to the chickens,
And call "chu, chu!"[75]

Contemporaries could not understand what he meant. Only in the first year of the Chien-i period (A.D. 528), after the murder of the empress by Erh-chu Jung, was his prophecy fulfilled.

At that time there was a Chao Fa-ho 趙法和,[76] a native of Lo-yang who asked for his prognostication as to whether in the course of time [Chao Fa-ho] could expect some position in the government. Pao-kung said:

A large bamboo arrow does not await feathers,
Hurry, hurry to build the eastern chamber!

Contemporaries [again] failed to understand his meaning. A little more than ten days later [Chao] Fa-ho lost his father. By "a large bamboo arrow" [Pao-kung] meant a bamboo staff [held by the chief mourner], and "an eastern chamber" denoted the lean-to [where the mourners stayed].

He also composed songs for the twelve-*ch'en* 十二辰歌[77]—the songs were to the end his words.[78]

The Pao-kuang Temple 寶光寺[79] (Temple of Precious Radiance) was located on the north side of the Imperial Drive outside the Hsi-yang Gate. There was a three-storied stūpa built on a stone founda-

[74] Literally, *san shih* 三世, "three ages."

[75] "Chu, chu" is descriptive of the sound used to call chickens. Here "chu" is doubled, possibly referring to both Erh-*chu* Jung and his Erh-*chu* associates.

[76] No other information is available for this man.

[77] *Ch'en* 辰 is the equivalent of two hours. A twenty-four-hour cycle of day and night is divided into twelve *ch'en*. Consult also Jao Tsong-yi and Paul Demiéville, eds., *Airs de Touen-Houang* (Paris, 1971), pp. 72 and 301.

[78] The exact implication of this sentence, *chung ch'i yen yeh* 終其言也, is not clear.

[79] The text (4/5b) and *CT* (4/6b) reads *Pao-kuang ssu* 寶光寺, but *IS* (4/4b) and *YLTT* (13823/15a–b) give *Kuang-pao ssu* 光寶寺 instead.

tion. It followed an ancient style, adorned with artistic carvings.[80]

When the hermit Chao I saw this temple, he sighed: "The [site of] the Shih-t'a Temple 石塔寺 (Temple of the Stone Stūpa) of the Chin is where the Pao-kuang Temple now stands." People asked him why. [Chao] I said: "The forty-two[81] temples of the Chin were all ruined, excepting this sole survivor." Pointing to a place in the garden, he said: "This used to be the site of a bathing room. There should be a well five paces in front of it." Some monks dug into it, and just as he said they found a room and a well. Although the well had been blocked up, the brick opening was as before. Underneath the bathing room, several scores of stone still remained. In former years the ground of the garden[82] was level, and vegetables and fruit trees were abundant.

[Spectators at the site] all sighed and lamented.

In the garden there was a lake known as Hsien-ch'ih 咸池 (Pool of Heaven.)[83] Young bulrushes and reeds blanketed its banks, while water chestnuts and lotus covered [the surface of] the water. Row after row of dark green pines and green bamboo grew on its shore. On pleasant days and festivals, or when off duty,[84] literati of the capital would invite their friends and associates to visit this temple with them. As a result, the thundering[85] chariots followed one after

[80] The text (4/5b) is *hua-kung tiao-k'e* 畫工雕刻, after which another sentence seems missing.

[81] *WS* 114/5a 釋老志 and the preface to the *Ch'ieh-lan chi* both give forty-two as the number of temples in the Chin capital. Thus thirty-two is perhaps a mistake for forty-two. Hence, the translation.

[82] Emending *yüan ch'ih* 園池, "garden pool," to *yüan ti* 園地, "garden land" after *IS* 4/5a and *YLTT* 13823/15b.

[83] Hsien-ch'ih is identified either as the name of a constellation or of a pond where the sun bathes, *Ch'u-tz'u* 1/15 離騷：飲余馬於咸池兮. David Hawkes, *Ch'u Tz'u*, p. 29: "I watered my dragon steeds at the Pool of Heaven." Comm.: 咸池，日浴處也. …咸池，星名.

[84] Han officials in the capital took every fifth day off as a holiday. *TC* 23/5a: [霍]光每休假出. Hu San-hsing's comm.: 漢制：中朝官五日一下里舍休沐，三署諸郎亦然, "According to the Han regulation, court officials took every fifth day off so as to go home for rest and to bathe. The various grandees in the *San-shu* 三署 (Three Bureaus, that is, *Wu-kuan shu* 五官署, *Tso-shu* 左署 and *Yu-shu* 右署, each under the jurisdiction of a *Chung-lang-chiang* 中郎將, that is, Commandant) had the same privilege." See also Yang Lien-sheng, "Schedules of Work and Rest in Imperial China," in *Studies in Chinese Institutional History*, p. 19.

[85] Literally, *lei chü* 雷車, "thundering carriages." *WH* 4/16a 左思蜀都賦：車馬雷駭, "[The noise of running] horses and carriages was as frightening as thunder."

another[86] and the feathered canopies [of their carriages] formed [man-made] shade. [Some visitors] would set out wine in the woods or near the springs, write poems in the flower gardens, pick lotus roots or float melons [in the pool]—thus each of them enjoyed the festivity and moments of relaxation.

By the end of the P'u-t'ai period (A.D. 531–532), Erh-chu T'ien-kuang,[87] Prince of Lung-hsi 隴西王 and the Governor of Yung-chou 雍州刺史, gathered his army and horses in this temple. Soon afterward, all the gates in the temple collapsed.[88] [Erh-chu] T'ien-kuang, seeing this, hated it [as a bad omen]. That year he was defeated in a battle and subsequently executed in the eastern marketplace [of Lo-yang].

The Fa-yün Monastery 法雲寺 (Monastery of the Dharma-cloud) was established by T'an-mo-lo 曇摩羅,[89] a śramaṇa from the Kingdom of Wu-ch'ang 烏場國 (Udyāna)[90] in the Western Regions of Central Asia. It was located to the west of the Pao-kuang Temple.[91] Separated by a wall, their [main] gates stood side by side.

[T'an-]mo-lo was intelligent, possessed of keen senses, and had exhausted the limits of Buddhist learning. Upon his arrival in China, he soon understood the Chinese language and the *li* script. He comprehended thoroughly whatever he heard or saw. As a result, both laymen and Buddhist devotees recognized [his abilities] and looked up to him. He had a shrine[92] built, which was splendid in design and workmanship.

[86] *Chieh chen* 接軫, "touched bumpers," *chen* 軫 being the horizontal wooden bar attached to the back of a vehicle.

[87] Erh-chu T'ien-kuang, cousin of Erh-chu Jung, was defeated in A.D. 532 at the famous Battle of Han-ling 韓陵 by Hu-ssu Ch'un 斛斯椿, another general who was disloyal to the Northern Wei; Erh-chu T'ien-kuang was subsequently captured and executed at the age of thirty-seven *sui*. See *WS* 80/5b 斛斯椿傳 and 79/15b 爾朱天光傳.

[88] The text (4/6b) reads *peng* 崩, "to fall with a booming sound." Here the exact condition of the collapse is not clear.

[89] The text (4/6b) reads Seng-mo-lo 僧摩羅, but *TPYL* 655/7a and *IS* (4/5b) both give T'an-mo-lo, the first two characters being a transliteration of Dharma.

[90] Also written as Wu-yang 烏陽 (*IS* 4/5b) and Wu-ch'ang 烏萇 (*WS* 102/20b 西域傳). See Chapter 5 at note 113.

[91] *IS* (4/5b) gives *Kuang-pao ssu* 光寶寺 instead.

[92] The text (4/6b) reads *Chih-yüan ssu* 祇洹寺. *Chih-yüan* (see note 68 above) is a retreat or abode of Buddhist saints, not the name of a temple. Therefore the character *ssu* 寺 is not warranted (*IS* 4/5b reads *Chih-yüan* 祇垣 without *ssu* 寺).

All the ornamentation in the Buddhist halls and monks' cloisters were in the barbarian style, [painted in] dazzling colors of red and blue,[93] [adorned with] glittering [articles of] gold and jade. A reproduction of "the Sixteen-Footer"[94] portrait looks like the god [Buddha] as he appeared at the Lu-yüan 鹿苑 (the Deer Park),[95] and the imposing beauty of its countenance was just like [the scene] when the Buddha[96] presented himself in the grove of sāla trees.[97] Within the monastery, flowers and fruits proliferated, aromatic grasses interlaced, and pleasant trees covered the courtyard. Those śramaṇas of the capital who preferred the ways of Central Asia came to receive his teachings. It is hard to elaborate on how strictly the Buddhist rules were enforced here. The effectiveness of their charms, well proven here, could not be found elsewhere on earth.[98] By charms, they were able to grow branches and leaves on withered trees; by curses, to change human beings into donkeys and horses, the sight of which was sufficient to frighten all viewers. The *śarīra*,[99] the Buddha's teeth, scriptures, and portraits, given by countries in the Western Regions, were all housed here.

To the north of the monastery was the residence of Yüan Yü, the Chief Palace Attendant, President of State Affairs, and Prince of Lin-huai 臨淮王.[100]

[93] Emending *tan-su* 丹素, "red and white," to *tan-ch'ing* 丹青, "red and blue," after *CT* (4/7b).

[94] *Chang liu* 丈六, "one *chang* six *ch'ih*" = 16 [Chinese] feet, that is, Buddha. See Chia-liu-t'o-ch'ieh, tr., *Fo-shuo shih-erh yu ching* (*Taishō* ed.), p. 146: 佛身長丈六尺.

[95] Lu-yüan, or Mṛgadāva, is the name of a park northeast of Varanasi where Śākyamuni is reported to have preached his first sermons and converted his first five disciples. See *Shih-shih yao-lan*, A/262.

[96] Literally, *chin-kang* 金剛, the diamond indestructible body. See *Fan-i ming-i chi* 3/92 七寶篇.

[97] Literally, *shuang lin* 雙林, a grove of sāla trees where the Buddha is reported to have attained complete extinction of individual existence (parinirvāṇa). Fa-hsien, tr., *Ta-pan nieh-p'an ching* (*Taishō* ed.) B/198: 汝今當知, 我於今昔, 後夜分盡, …沙羅雙樹間, 入般涅槃, "You should know now that I shall attain the state of complete extinction in the grove of sāla trees at midnight day after tomorrow."

[98] Literally, *Yen fou* 閻浮, Jambu-dvīpa. See Chapter 1 at note 27 under the Yung-ning Monastery.

[99] *Śarīra* means Buddha's bone. See *Fan-i ming-i chi* 5/153 名句文法篇.

[100] Southeast of modern Lin-pi *hsien* 臨壁縣, Anhui.

Along with Yüan Yen-ming, the Prince of An-feng, and Yüan Hsi, Prince of Chung-shan, they were known as the trio of scholars of the imperial household.

[Yüan] Yü was well-versed in classics, discerning and refined. He was punctilious in his carriage, and admirable in his manner. On the auspicious New Year's[101] day, when [envoys of][102] a multitude of states or kingdoms attended[103] [the court], he would put on a cap brightly decorated with a carving of a cicada in gold, and a sash with pieces of tinkling jade, and holding a *hu* 笏[104] tablet before his breast, would proceed elegantly along the covered passageway. All those who watched him would forget their fatigue, and not a one but sighed in admiration. [Yüan] Yü by nature was fond of woods and fountains. Further, he loved the company of visitors. At the time when spring breezes gently blow and flowering trees are like brocade, he would take his morning meal in the southern hall and roam at night in the rear garden. With his subordinates in a throng and gifted men[105] filling the mats, [he would listen to] the sounding lute as the winged[106] wine cups were passed around. When he presented poems and rhymed prose, or suddenly took up "pure conversation," everyone [in attendance] would drink in its profundity and overlook its [possible] shortcomings. As a result, those who were accepted into [Yüan] Yü's inner circle said they had ascended as immortals.

Yüan Yü had been Chief Palace Attendant, General of the Guards, and Vice President on the Right, Department of State Affairs. In A.D. 528, following Erh-chu Jung's execution of many in the aristocracy, he took refuge with the Liang dynasty, but soon returned to wait on his old mother. In A.D. 530, he was murdered during Erh-chu Chao's uprising. See *WS* 18/2b–6a.

[101] Literally, *san yüan* 三元, "three firsts": the beginning of the first day of the first month of the new year.

[102] A Han tradition. See *WH* 1/16a 班固東都賦：是日也，天子受四海之圖籍，膺萬國之貢珍, "On that day, the Son of Heaven accepted the maps and documents [from countries] in the four seas, and [also] tributary treasures from myriad states."

[103] Emending *chen* 珍, "rarities," to *chen* 臻, "assemble," after *IS* 4/6a.

[104] The *hu* 笏 was a tablet about three Chinese feet long, made of different materials according to the rank of the holder. Notes were written on its back when the holder had an imperial audience. Possibly because of its size, the text (4/7b) reads *fu* 負, "to carry," *ho* 荷, "to shoulder," and *chih* 執, "to hold."

[105] *Chün min* 俊民, "outstanding people."

[106] Literally, *yü-shang liu-hsing* 羽觴流行. For *yü-shang* 羽觴, see *HS* 97B/9a 孝成班倢伃傳：酌羽觴之消憂, "Drink from winged goblets to dispell worries." Meng K'ang's comm.; 羽觴，爵也，作生爵形，有頭尾羽翼, "A winged goblet is one that looks like a live bird. It has head, tail, and feathered wings."

Chang Fei 張斐,[107] a talented man of Ching-chou 荊州, once wrote a poem in the style of five characters per line; the two best lines read:

From different woods,[108] flowers are uniform in color;
On separate trees, birds share the same melody.

[In return for] Chang [Fei's] poem, [Yüan] Yü gave him a brocade with dragon designs. He also gave others red or purple silk. Only P'ei Tzu-ming 裴子明 of Ho-tung was unskilled at writing poems, so he was forced to drink one *shih*[109] of wine as punishment. [P'ei] Tzu-ming drank eight *tou*[110] and fell asleep intoxicated. For this his contemporaries likened him to Shan T'ao 山濤.[111]

When Erh-chu Chao entered the capital, [Yüan] Yü was slain by unruly soldiers. Both those in and out of power were grieved [at his death].

On the south side of the Imperial Drive and four *li* outside the Hsi-yang Gate was the main marketplace of Lo-yang, which was eight *li* in circumference. To the south of the marketplace[112] was the Princess' Tower (Huang-nü *t'ai*) 皇女臺 founded by Liang Chi 梁冀, Generalissimo of the Han.[113] Even today the tower still rises more

[107] The text (4/7b) reads *Ch'ang P'ei-ch'ang* 張裴裳, *P'ei* 裴 being a mistake for *Fei* 斐 and *Ch'ang* 裳 for *Ch'ang* 常. *IS* (4/6a) has an additional character *Ch'ang* 常 after *Ch'ang* 裳. *YHNC* 3/11a reads *Chang Fei* 張斐; hence the translation.

[108] Emending *ch'iu* 秋, "autumn," to *lin* 林, "forest," after *IS* 4/6a and *YHNC* 3/11a.

[109] *Shih* or *tan* 石, a measurement for both weight and capacity. It is the equivalent of ten *tou* when used for capacity (each *tou* is the equivalent of about 2.45 liters).

[110] Emending *pa-jih* 八日, "eight days," to *pa-tou* 八斗, "eight *tou*" after *IS* 4/6b. *Pa-tou* agrees with the story of Shan T'ao referred to in the next line.

[111] A high-ranking official (A.D. 205–283) of the Chin in charge of civil service. One of the Seven Sages of the Bamboo Grove, he was known for his ability to drink up to eight *tou* of wine. He died in A.D. 283 at the age of seventy-nine *sui*. See *Chin-shu* 43/9a.

[112] The text (4/8b) reads *shih nan* 市南, "south of the market," but *IS* (4/6b) gives *shih tung-nan* 市東南, "southeast of the market." The *SCC* (16/20b–21a) makes mention of P'ing-lo *kuan* 平樂觀, which is believed to be identifiable with the Princess' Tower.

[113] Liang Chi was a dictator of the Later Han who hand-picked three emperors (Ch'ung 冲, Chih 質, and Huan 桓) at will (*HHS* 64/10b). *SCC* (16/20b–21a) and

than fifty Chinese feet tall. [On a site] above the tower the monk Tao-heng 道恒[114] had the Ling-hsien Temple 靈僊寺 (Temple of Efficacious Immortals) built during the Ching-ming period (A.D. 500–502). To the west of the tower was the prefecture of Ho-yang; to its east, the residence of Hou Kang 侯剛,[115] the Chief Palace Attendant.

To the northwest of the marketplace were a mound and a fish pond, also constructed by [Liang] Chi. This is referred to in a *Han-shu*[116] account as follows: "Earth was collected to make a mound, which had nine slopes within ten *li*, resembling the twin cliffs of the Yao Mountain 崤山."[117]

To the east of the market place were the two wards, T'ung-shang 通商里 (Ward of Conducting Trade) and Ta-huo 達貨里 (Ward of Shipping Merchandise). All residents were shrewd, making a living as butchers or tradesmen. They were wealthy, owning thousands [of coins].

> There was one Liu Pao 劉寶 who was the wealthiest. He maintained ten[118] horses at each of his residences located in the major cities of various provinces and commanderies. He set up a uniform price for salt and rice [that he handled] in all these places. He would buy and sell merchandise in any place if it was within the reach of boats and carriages or human beings.[119] As a result, commodities within the [four] seas were all stored in his courtyards. His wealth was comparable to the Copper Mountain 銅山 [of Teng T'ung 鄧通],[120] and he [seemed to] store a gold mine.[121] [The structure

YHNC (3/11a) make no mention of Liang Chi as the one responsible for the construction.

114 See also *Lo-yang chih* 洛陽志 as quoted in *YLTT* 13823/7a.

115 Emending Hou Chao 侯釗 to Hou Kang 侯剛 after *IS* (4/6b). Hou Kang worked his way up as a chef, but later in his life he was a powerful minister, largely due to his association with Yüan Ch'a. He died in A.D. 526. See *WS* 93/18a–20b; *MCCS* plate 249.

116 This is, *HHS*. See n. 113 above.

117 The Yao Mountain is sixty *li* north of the modern Lo-ning *hsien* 洛寧縣, Honan.

118 Emending from *i* 一, "one," to *shih* 十, "ten," at the suggestion of *CC* (4/157).

119 Literally, *tsu-chi so-lü* 足跡所履, "wherever there were footprints."

120 Teng T'ung, a fabulously rich man and a male favorite of Emperor Wen (regnant 179–157 B.C.) of the Former Han, was given a copper mine by the emperor and given the special privilege to mint coins for circulation throughout the empire.

121 Kuo K'uang 郭況, the younger brother of Empress Kuo, the first consort of

and size] of his house exceeded the sumptuary regulations, and his terrace and towers rose loftily into the clouds. His chariots, horses, dresses, and ornaments were comparable to those of princes.[122]

To the south of the marketplace were the two wards T'iao-yin 調音里 (Ward of Musical Tones) and Yüeh-lü 樂律里 (Ward of Musical Notes), the residents of which were [mostly] musicians and singers. The most skillful [performing] artists of the empire came from here.

One of them was T'ien Seng-ch'ao 田僧超 (d. A.D. 525),[123] who was skillful at playing the reed whistle and singing such songs as the "Chuang-shih" 壯士歌 ("Song of the Warriors")[124] and "Hsiang Yü" 項羽吟 ("Song of Hsiang Yü").[125] He was much liked by Ts'ui Yen-po 崔延伯, General of the Western Expedition (*Cheng-hsi chiang-chün* 征西將軍).[126] Near the end of the Cheng-kuang period (A.D. 520–525), [the district] Kao-p'ing 高平[127] fell into the hands of rebels, and avaricious officials[128] were everywhere. In the face of plunder and raids staged by the rebel leader

---

Emperor Kuang-wu (regnant A.D. 25–57), received lavish gifts of money and silk from the emperor, who frequently paid him visits. He became so rich that people in the capital referred to his home as a "gold mine." See *HHS* 10A/4b 郭皇后傳.

[122] The text (4/8b) reads *wang che* 王者, "princes," which is followed in the translation. *YHNC* (3/12a) gives *hou-wang* 侯王, "marquises and princes," instead.

[123] No additional information about him is available.

[124] A song dedicated to Ch'en An 陳安 for his bravery. Ch'en An, a general of the Western Chin (A.D. 265–316), was defeated by insurgent forces of Liu Yao 劉曜 (ruler of the Former Chao, regnant B.C. 318–329) at Lung-ch'eng 隴城. Hence, the song is also known as "Lung-shang ko" 隴上歌. See *YFSC* 85/584.

[125] The same famous song dedicated to Lady Yü 虞姬 shortly before the downfall of Hsiang Yü 項羽 (232–202 B.C.). The song contains the three characters *li-pa-shan* 力拔山, so it is also known as "li-pa-shan ts'ao" 力拔山操. *YFSC* 58/438.

T'ien Seng-ch'ao's musical talent is also recorded in *YYTT* 6/41 樂篇, whose account is perhaps based on the *Ch'ieh-lan chi* entry.

[126] Ts'ui Yen-po was a general noted for his fortitude and strategy. Ts'ui Yen-po was at one time a subordinate of Hsiao Pao-yin (for Hsiao Pao-yin see Chapter 2 under the Ching-ning Temple and Chapter 3 at note 148 under the Pao-te Temple). He was likened to Kuan Yü 關羽 and Chang Fei 張飛, two renowned generals of the Three Kingdoms period (A.D. 220–265). For his biography, see *WS* 73/8b–11b.

[127] Modern Ku-yüan *hsien* 固原縣, Kansu.

[128] Emending *nüeh-li* 虐吏, "cruel officials," to *hu li* 虎吏, "tiger-like officials," after *IS* 4/7a.

Mo-ch'i Ch'ou-nu[129] between the Ching 涇 and Ch'i 岐 areas, the court postponed meals,[130] [hard-pressed as it was to cope with the worsening situation]. [Accordingly], [Ts'ui] Yen-po was ordered to lead an armed force of fifty thousand infantry and cavalry soldiers to launch a punitive expedition against him. [Ts'ui] Yen-po mobilized his army at the Chang Fang Bridge 張方橋[131] in the western suburb of Lo-yang, which was also the site of the Hsi-yang Pavilion 夕陽亭 (the Sunset Pavilion) of the Han.[132]

At the time, dukes and ministers of all ranks congregated to offer sacrifices to the god of the road[133] with their carriages and cavalry [attendants] lined up [according to rank]. With his jaunty hat and long sword,[134] [Ts'ui] Yen-po himself dazzled with martial appearance in the front, while [T'ien] Seng-ch'ao performed the "Chuang-shih" flute-song[135] in the rear. Hearing this, cowards became brave men and swordsmen longed for combat.

[Ts'ui] Yen-po, a man of unusual courage, had long enjoyed awesome fame. For more than twenty years he had exerted his best efforts for the country: no cities could withstand his attacks, and in

[129] Emending 万侯 to 万俟 (pronounced Mo-ch'i). *Hou* 侯 is an obvious scribal error.

[130] Literally, *kan-shih* 旰食, "to take a late meal" because of the pressure of business. For the origin of *kan-shih* 旰食, see *Tso-chuan* Chao 20 49/4a [伍]奢聞[伍]員不來, 曰:楚君大夫其旰食乎 . Legge 5, p. 680: "and when Woo, [that is, Wu] Ch'ay heard that [Woo] Yun had not come, he said, 'The ruler of Ts'oo and his great officers will [now—Legge's own addition] take their meals late.'" Tu Yü's comm.: 將有吳憂, 不得早食, "Because of the pending Wu invasion (literally, worried), he will be unable to have meals served on time."

[131] For the Chang Fang Bridge, see Chapter 4 at note 296 under the Yung-ming Monastery.

[132] In the western suburb of Lo-yang. The official send-off for Chia Ch'ung 賈充 (A.D. 217–282), father-in-law of Emperor Hui (regnant A.D. 290–306) of the Western Chin, occurred in this pavilion when he was about to set out to assume his new post in Ch'ang-an. The farewell gathering lasted from dawn to sunset; hence the name. See *YHNC* 2/14b.

[133] The term *tsu-tao* 祖道 also appears in Chapter 3 at note 38 under the Ching-ming Monastery.

[134] *Wei-kuan ch'ang-chieh* 危冠長解, "jaunty cap and [unbuckled] long [sword]." *Chuang-tzu* 9/210 盜跖篇:使子路去其危冠, 解其長劍, 而受教於子. Burton Watson, tr., *The Complete Works of Chuang-tzu*, p. 328, "Robber Chih"; "(With your honeyed words) you persuaded Tzu-lu to become your follower, to doff his jaunty cap, unbuckle his long sword, and receive instruction from you."

[135] *Ti* 笛, "flute." This character is not given in *YHNC* 3/11a.

no battles had he ever been defeated. Because of this, the court sent him off with great zeal.

Each time that [Ts'ui] Yen-po approached the battlefield, he would always[136] order [T'ien] Seng-ch'ao to perform the "Chuang-shih" songs, which made the armored soldiers eager to fight. Unaccompanied, [Ts'ui] Yen-po would ride on horseback to enter the battle lines, [creating the impression that] there was no one else [on the battleground who dared stand in his way]. His personal bravery exceeded that of everyone in the Three Armies,[137] and his prestige awed all barbarians into subjugation. Within a period of two years, word of his victories came one after another in quick succession.

[Mo-ch'i] Ch'ou-nu recruited skillful archers to shoot [T'ien] Seng-ch'ao. At his death, [Ts'ui] Yen-po was so grieved and saddened that, according to his attendants, Po-ya's 伯牙 lamentation over the loss of Chung Tzu-ch'i 鍾子期[138] could not exceed [Ts'ui Yen-po's].

Later, [Ts'ui] Yen-po was hit and killed in battle[139] by a stray arrow. In consequence, his army of fifty thousand men at once collapsed and dispersed.

To the west of the marketplace were the two wards Yen-ku 延酤里 (Wine-buyers' Ward) and Chih-shang 治觴里 (Wine-servers' Ward), the residents of which were mostly in the business of making wine.

Liu Pai-to 劉白墮,[140] a native of Ho-tung,[141] was a master

[136] Adding *ch'ang* 常, "always," after *IS* 4/7b.

[137] *San-chün* 三軍, "Three Armies." According to the *Rites of Chou*, in determining the military strength of the kingdom and state, the kingdom should have six armies (*liu-ch'ün* 六軍); a large state, three armies; a smaller state, two armies (*erh-chün* 二軍); and the smallest state, one army (*i-chün* 一軍). Each army consisted of 12,500 men, therefore three armies totaled 37,500 men. The term *San-chün* is used loosely here. *Chou-li* 28/2a 夏官序官:凡制軍, 萬有二千五百人爲軍. 王六軍, 大國三軍, 次國二軍, 小國一軍.

[138] Whenever Po-ya played his lute, Chung Tzu-ch'i fully understood where the musician cast his mind—now high mountains, now flowing water. After Chung Tzu-ch'i's death, Po-ya destroyed his *chin*—refused to play again, knowing that there was no longer anyone to understand him fully. See *Lü-shih ch'un-ch'iu* 14/80 孝行覽本味篇.

[139] He died on May 25, A.D. 525, in Ching-ch'uan 涇川. See *WS* 9/21a 肅宗紀.

[140] Also known as Liu To 劉墮, he later became a legendary winemaker. The wine, made of grain, was famous for its purity and translucence. See *SCC* 4/8b 河水注 and *CMYS* 7/18b–19b 笨麴幷酒篇.

winemaker. In the sixth month of midsummer, under the burning heat, he preserved his wine in [open-mouthed] jars that were exposed to the sunlight for ten days. The taste of the wine would remain unchanged, [but], when one drank it, it was aromatic and full-flavored. The drinker would be intoxicated for a full month without waking up. When dignitaries in the capital left for the commandery or for frontier posts, they would take some [jars] along as gifts to remote [areas, sometimes] more than one thousand *li* away. Since the wine came from a great distance, it was known as "Stork-goblet wine" (*Ho-shang chiu* 鶴觴酒), or "Donkey-riding wine" (*Ch'i-lü chiu* 騎驢酒). In the Yung-hsi years (A.D. 532–534) Mao Hung-pin 毛鴻賓,[142] Governor of South Ch'ing-chou 南青州,[143] took the wine to his post. He encountered some bandits en route,[144] who drank the wine and became intoxicated. Every one of them was arrested. The wine was therefore also called "Criminal-capturing wine," (*Ch'in-chien chiu* 擒奸酒). Among the wandering knights[145] there was a saying:

> Fear not a drawn bow or sword,
> Fear only Pai-to's spring wine![146]

To the north of the marketplace were the two wards Tz'u-hsiao

For the same story about Liu Pai-to's strong wine, see Yang and Yang, *The Man Who Sold a Ghost*, p. 132.

[141] Modern An-i 安邑, Shansi.

[142] A native and a leader of Pei-ti 北地 commandery (modern northern Shansi), he and his elder brother Mao Hsia 毛遐 raised an army of local people to maintain order. Mao Hung-pin was later captured by Kao Huan's generals. See *PS* 49/25b–26b 毛遐傳.

[143] The text (4/9b) correctly has the character *nan* 南, "southern," which is missing in *TPKC* 233/1b 酒部擒奸酒. The name was changed to *Nan Ch'ing-chou* 南青州 "southern Ching-chou" in A.D. 498 (*WS* 106B/27b) (modern I-shui *hsien* 沂水縣, Shantung).

[144] The text (4/9b) is *feng-lu* 逢路, but *YHNC* 3/12a gives 路逢盜, 飲之即醉, "He met with bandits en route, who drank the wine and immediately became intoxicated," which the translation follows.

[145] The text (4/10a) is *yu-hsia* 游俠, normally an underground organization or an individual unfriendly to the government. For a general description of *hsia* 俠 in Chinese literature, see James J. Y. Liu, *The Chinese Knight Errant* (Chicago, 1967). It covers such fields as prose, poetry, fiction, and drama, ranging from the period of Warring States (403–222 B.C.) to the Manchu dynasty (A.D. 1644–1911).

[146] This couplet rhymes at the end of each line: *tao* 刀, "knife," and *lao* 醪, "sediment." The latter character here is used loosely for wine.

慈孝里 (Ward of Motherly Love and Filial Devotion) and Feng-chung,[147] the residents of which were sellers of inner and outer coffins and handlers of hearse[148] rentals.

Sun Yen, a professional singer of funeral songs, had taken a wife for three years, during which time she [always] slept with her clothes on. Puzzled, [Sun] Yen waited until she was asleep, and then secretly unloosed her clothing. He discovered that his wife had a tail[149] three Chinese feet long, which resembled that of a wild fox. [Sun] Yen was frightened and put her out. On the point of leaving, the wife took a knife, cut off [Sun] Yen's hair, and then ran away. Chased by her neighbors, she changed into a fox and eluded her pursuers. Later, there were more than one hundred thirty persons in the capital city whose hair was cut off by her. At first [the fox] would change into a woman, who would walk along the street, attractively dressed and wearing elegant makeup.[150] Pleased with her appearance, people would draw near to her, at which point she would cut off their hair.[151] At that time any woman clad in bright colors would be pointed to as the fox-spirit. It happened in the fourth month of the second year of the Hsi-p'ing period (May to June A.D. 517), and lasted until the autumn of the same year.[152]

In addition, there were the other two wards: Fu[153]-ts'ai[154] and Chin-ssu, 金肆里 (Ward of Gold Stores), where rich men lived.

[147] That is, Ward of Homage to the Deceased. See Introduction at note 15.

[148] The text (4/10a) gives *erh* 輀, which, according to Tuan Yü-ts'ai (*Shuo-wen chieh-tzu* 14A/39b), should be written *erh* 輛. The component element on the right side of the character *erh* (而) is descriptive of ornaments hanging from a hearse.

[149] Emending *mao* 毛, "hair," to *wei* 尾, "tail," after *TPKC* 447/3b 狐孫巖.

[150] The text (4/10a) is *i-fu ching-chuang* 衣服靚妝. For *ching-chuang* 靚粧, see *WH* 8/8a–b 司馬相如上林賦：靚粧刻飾, "Wearing elegant makeup and rich ornaments." Li Shan's comm.: 郭璞曰：靚粧，粉白黛黑也, "Elegant makeup refers to powder-white and black color."

[151] *IS* (4/8a) has a slightly different wording: 人見而悅之，近者被截髮, "People were pleased with her [appearance] when she came into sight. The hair of those who approached her would be cut off."

[152] *WS* (112/25b–26a 靈徵志毛蟲之孽) keeps a similar account of the episode, which lasted between the spring and the sixth month of A.D. 517. It is supposed to reflect heaven's disapproval of the undue power of the empress. For the same fox story, see Yang and Yang, *The Man Who Sold a Ghost*, p. 131.

[153] The text (4/10b) gives *chün-ts'ai* 準財, *chün* 準 being a scribal error for *fu* 阜.

[154] That is, Ward of the Wealthy. See Chapter 3 after note 186 under the P'u-t'i Temple.

Within a stretch of ten *li*, residents for the most part were artisans, merchants, and tradesmen. Wealthy families[155] lived in a nearby neighborhood. Storied buildings, set with double doors and open screens,[156] faced each other.[157] Covered passageways, connecting one building to another, were within sight of one another. Slaves and maid-servants wore brocades and embroidered articles of gold and silver, and were fed with the five flavors and rarities.[158] In the Shen-kuei years (A.D. 518–519), as artisans and merchants heedlessly usurped sumptuary privileges, it was ruled that they be prohibited from wearing brocade and embroidery or articles of gold and silver.[159] But the law, although enacted, was by no means enforced.

Inside the Fu-ts'ai Ward was the K'ai-shan Temple 開善寺 (Temple of Guidance to Goodness), formerly the residence of Wei Ying, who was a native of Ching-chao 京兆.[160] [Wei] Ying died prematurely, but his wife, from the Liang clan 梁氏, remarried without first

[155] Literally, *ch'ien chih* 千金, "[those whose property amounted to] one thousand [catties] of gold."

[156] *Ch'i shan* 啟扇, here tentatively translated as "open screens". The exact meaning is unclear.

[157] Adding *tui ch'u* 對出 after *IS* (4/8b) and *CT* (4/11b).

[158] This pair of couplets is yet another good example to show how difficult it is to translate parallel prose into good English. The meanings of the individual words are often repetitious, and, in this particular case, the sentences are in reversed word order. The text (4/10b) reads: 金銀錦繡, 奴婢緹衣; 五味八珍, 僕隸畢口, "Articles of gold and silver, brocade and embroidery, what the slaves and maids wore; five flavors and eight treasures, what male servants and slaves ate." Note that the order of verb and object is in reverse. Furthermore, *nu-pei* 奴婢, *nu-li* 奴隸, and *pei-p'u* 婢僕 may come as compounds in different combinations, but they have only one meaning: servants and male or female slaves.

This is a free translation, including *wu wei* 五味, "five tastes," and *pa chen* 八珍, "eight rarities." For *pa chen* 八珍, see Chapter 3 note 101 under the Pao-te Temple.

[159] The Prince of Kao-yang proposed in a memorial that concubines other than those of the nobility be prohibited from wearing brocade, articles of gold, jade, or pearl, and that violators be punished to the same degree as those disobeying an imperial order. He further suggested that servants not be permitted to wear silk, and that slaves be permitted to wear only cotton. Neither should use hairpins and belts of gold or silk. Violators were liable to be caned with one hundred strokes of a bamboo rod. The empress dowager accepted his advice, but was lax in enforcing this new regulation. See *WS* 21A/24b–25a 高陽王雍傳.

[160] A commandery of Yung-chou, northwest of modern Ch'ang-an, Shensi. See *WS* 106C/1a.

observing the entire mourning period. She took[161] Hsiang Tzu-chi 向子集 of Ho-nei as her new husband, but, after her remarriage, she lived in [Wei] Ying's house as she had before. Learning of his wife's remarriage, [Wei] Ying returned in broad daylight; riding on a horse in the company of several men, he appeared up in the foreground of the courtyard, calling, "A-Liang, have you forgotten me?" Out of fear, [Hsiang] Tzu-chi drew an arrow and shot him, causing him to fall to the ground.[162] Immediately [Wei Ying] changed into a man of peachwood, and the horse he rode changed into one made of thatch. The several followers in his company also changed into men made of reeds.[163] The woman of the Liang clan, terrified, donated the residence for use as a temple.[164]

Hou Ch'ing 侯慶, a native of Nan-yang,[165] had a bronze image of Buddha that was more than one Chinese foot[166] high. He was the owner of an ox that he wanted to sell, in order to use the [acquired] money for gold-leafing or parcel-gilding. Because of an emergency, he used the cash for other purposes. Two years later, [Hou] Ch'ing's wife, a woman of the Ma clan 馬氏, suddenly dreamed of the image, which told her: "You and your husband have owed me a gilding for so long without [my demanding] recompense. Now I am taking your son, [Hou] Ch'ou-to [侯]醜多, as compensation for [your failure to] gild [me]." When the woman of the Ma clan woke up, she was ill at ease. At dawn, [Hou] Ch'ou-to fell ill and died. [Hou] Ch'ing was [then] fifty years old, and he had only this son. The mourning voices moved even the passersby. On the day of [Hou] Ch'ou-to's death, the image itself[167] turned gold; its light shone on

[161] Emending *yüeh* 約, "to invite," to *na* 納, "to take in" after *IS* (4/8b), *TPKC* (371/5a 精怪凶器梁氏) and *FYCL* (43/511).

[162] Emending *ying-hsüan erh tao* 應弦而倒, "to fall in response [to the released] string," to *ying chien erh tao* 應箭而倒, "to fall in response [to the released] arrow," after *IS* (4/8b) and *TPKC* 371/5a.

[163] Possibly they all changed into funerary articles (*ming-ch'i* 明器).

[164] *YYTT* (13/68 冥蹟篇) keeps a record of the same story. It may have been based on the *Ch'ieh-lan chi*.

[165] Modern Nan-yang *hsien* 南陽縣, Honan.

[166] The text (4/11a) gives *chang* 丈, "ten Chinese feet," rather than *ch'ih* 尺 "one Chinese foot." *CS* (4/162) argues that Hou Ch'ing, as an ordinary citizen, could not own any Buddhist image of this size; hence the translation.

[167] Emending 像自然金色 to 像自有金色 (substituting the character *yu* 有 for *jan* 然) after *IS* (4/9a); the original version is an incomplete sentence.

neighboring [houses] in all four directions, and those who lived in the same ward all smelled something fragrant. Young and old, Buddhist devotees and laymen alike, all came to take a look. Yüan Shun 元順,[168] Vice-President on the Left, Department of State Affairs (*Shang-shu tso p'u-yeh*)[169] changed the name of Fu-ts'ai Ward to Ch'i-hsieh Ward 齊諧里 (Ward of Fictitious Tales),[170] since he had heard of strange things that had taken place so frequently in the ward.

The area two *li* east to west and fifteen *li* north to south—bounded in the east by the Yen[171]-ku [Ward], in the west by the Chang Fang Creek 張方溝,[172] in the south by the Lo River, and in the north by the Mang Mountain—was collectively known as the Shou-ch'iu Ward 壽丘里 (Ward of Longevity Hill). Since the residents were members of the royal family,[173] the area was referred to by the general public as the Princes' District (*Wang-tzu fang* 王子坊).

This was the time when peace reigned within the four seas, and the various states in all outlying lands[174] paid regular tribute to China. Court archives[175] had nothing but jubilation to record, while the four seasons followed each other smoothly without the occurrence of

[168] The text (4/11b) reads Yüan Chen 元稹. *CS* (4/162–163) suggests that *Chen* 稹 is an error for *Shen* 慎, which in turn is a mistake for *Shun* 順. Yüan Shun was the son of Yüan Ch'eng, Prince of Jen-ch'eng, a learned member of the imperial family and a ranking official between A.D. 516 and A.D. 528, when he was murdered. The reasoning of *CS* is strengthened by a *YHNC* (3/12a) entry that actually gives Yüan Shun as the man's name. For Yüan Shun, see *WS* 19B/22b–27b and *MCCS* plate 127.

[169] The text (4/11b) gives *Shang-shu yu p'u-yeh* 尚書右僕射. The translation follows *YHNC* (3/12a) which gives *Tso p'u-yeh* 左僕射 instead. The *YHNC* entry agrees with *WS* 19B/26b.

[170] Ch'i-hsieh is the name of an ancient narrator of strange stories. See *Chuang-tzu* 1/3 逍遙遊.

[171] The text (4/11b) reads *t'ui* 退, which is a mistake for *yen* 延.

[172] The creek under the Chang Fang Bridge. See Chapter 4 at note 297 under the Yung-ming Monastery.

[173] *IS* (4/9a–b) reads *huang-tsung so li yeh* 皇宗所立也, "established by members of the royal family," of which *li* 立 is an error. *YHNC* (3/12a) gives *chieh huang-tsung so chü* 皆皇宗所居, "occupied completely by members of the royal family."

[174] Literally, *pa-huang shuai-chih* 八荒率職, "[countries] in eight corners fulfilled their [vassal] obligations." For *pa-huang* 八荒, see Liu Hsiang 劉向, *Shuo-yüan* 說苑 (*SPTK so-pen*) 18/82 辨物篇：八荒之內有四海, 四海之內有九州, 天子處中而制八荒耳, "Within the eight corners are the four seas; within the four seas, nine provinces. The Son of Heaven is located in the center and controls the eight corners."

[175] Literally, *p'iao-nang chi ch'ing* 縹囊紀慶. *P'iao-nang* is blue cloth used as wrappings for books; hence, books, records. For *p'iao-nang*, see *WH* 2a 序：詞人

natural calamities.[176] The masses were well-to-do, [enjoying] good harvests and pleasant customs. Widowers and widows had not heard of dog food or pig fodder [that they might have to eat at times of famine]; the lonely and single ones had not seen horse- or cattle-rugs [that they might have to wear against cold].[177] As a result, [such aristocrats as] imperial clansmen, dukes and marquises, empresses' relatives and princesses, enjoying the riches [yielded by] mountains and seas,[178] and living on the wealth [reaped from] rivers and forests, competed among themselves in building gardens and residences, and showed off against each other. There were imposing gates and spacious rooms, cavernous houses and joined suites, lofty buildings that generated breezes, and storied structures where mist arose. High terraces and scented towers[179] were built in every household, [while] flowering trees and winding ponds were [found] in every garden, [all characterized by] the green of peach and plum trees in summer, and the blue-green cypress and bamboo in winter.

Among all, that of [Yüan] Ch'en 元琛, Prince of Ho-chien 河間王, was the finest, and he was always in competition against [the Prince of] Kao-yang. [Yüan Ch'en] constructed a Wen-pai Hall 文柏堂 (Hall of Grained Cypress) that resembled the Hui-yin Palace 徽音殿 (Palace of Benevolent Voices). There he installed a jade water-well, [complete with] golden pails[180] and multicolored silk[181] hoisting

---

才子, 則名溢於縹囊, "For the literati and the gifted men, their names are overflowing the records."

[176] Literally, *yü chu t'iao ch'en* 玉燭調辰. For *yü-chu* 玉燭, see *Erh-ya* 6/5a 釋天: 四時和謂之玉燭, "When the four seasons follow each other in harmony, it is called *yü-chu*."

[177] Literally, 鰥寡不聞犬豕之食, 煢獨不見牛馬之衣, "Widows and widowers have heard nothing about the fodder of dogs and pigs; orphans and the unmarried have never seen the rugs for cattle and horses." For the reverse of this couplet, see *HS* 24A/16b 食貨志: 故貧民常衣牛馬之衣, 而食犬彘之食, "Therefore the poor people had to wear horse- or cattle-rugs and eat dog or pig fodder."

[178] Literally, *shan shan-hai chih fu* 擅山海之富. For its origin, see *SC* 106/30 吳王濞傳: [吳王]能薄賦斂, 使其衆, 以擅山海利, "[Prince of Wu] was able to reduce taxation, utilize his masses, and reap profit from the mountains and seas."

[179] The text (4/12a) reads *fang shu* 芳樹, "scented trees," but the translation follows *CS* (4/163) which suggests that *fang shu* 芳樹 be emended to *fang hsieh* 芳榭, "scented towers" (*CT* 4/13b also gives 芳榭).

[180] *I-ch'ieh-ching yin-i*, 8/355 瓦瓶, 汲水器也.

[181] Emending to *i wu-se k'uei wei sheng* 以五色繢爲繩, "to make rope of multicolored silk" after *YHNC* 3/12b. (*CT* [4/13b] gives *i wu-se ssu hsü wei sheng* 以五色絲續爲繩, "to connect multicolored silk and make it into a rope.")

rope. The three hundred female entertainers were beauties of national fame. He had a maid by the name of Chao-yün 朝雲 (Morning Clouds), who was skillful at playing the flute and at singing the "T'uan-shan" 團扇歌 ("Song of the Circular Fan")[182] and "Lung-shang" 隴上聲 ("Song of Lung-chou")[183] songs. When [Yüan] Ch'en was Governor of Ch'in-chou 秦州, various branches of the Ch'iang 羌 tribesmen staged a rebellion. After repeated unsuccessful campaigns, [Yüan] Ch'en ordered Chao-yün be disguised as an impoverished old woman, who begged food while playing her flute. Upon hearing [the flute], the Ch'iang all sobbed and repeatedly told each other: "Why should we give up ancestral graveyards and [household] wells and be plundering here in the mountain valleys?" They immediately led one another to surrender. The people of Ch'in[184] had a saying:

> Fast horses and strong lads,[185]
> Are inferior to an old woman playing a flute.

While in Ch'in-chou, [Yüan] Ch'en was for the most part without meritorious achievements. In search of famed horses, he sent envoys to the Western Regions, who reached as far away as the kingdom of Po-ssu.[186] There he acquired a steed [capable of running] one thousand *li* a day. It was named the Chase the Wind Bay (*Chui-feng ch'ih-chi* 追風赤驥). Next best were ten odd horses able to run seven hundred *li* a day. Each of them was given a name, [fed with such equipment as] silver for their troughs [and] gold for their ring-locks.[187] The other princes bowed to his superior wealth.

In conversation with others, [Yüan] Ch'en often said: "Under the

[182] 團扇歌 or 團扇郎歌, a love song created by Hsieh Fang-tzu 謝芳姿, a maid of the sister-in-law of Wang Min 王珉 (A.D. 361–388), who was in love with Wang Min (then president of the Central Secretariat). The song comes in three lines: three, five, five characters for each line, with the last characters in the second and third lines in rhyme. See *YFSC* 45/353 淸商曲辭團扇郎歌.

[183] See notes 124 and 125 of this chapter.

[184] Southwest of modern T'ien-shui 天水, Kansu.

[185] *Chien-erh* 健兒, "agile fighters," and *k'uai-ma* 快馬, "fast-running horses," are complementary. See *YFSC* 25/234 折楊柳歌辭：健兒須快馬，快馬須健兒.

[186] See Chapter 3 at note 173 under the Hsüan-yang Gate.

[187] Literally, [*i*] *chin wei so-huan* [以] 金爲鎖環 "ring-locks made of gold." The text (4/12b) suggests this as a type of ring device to hold the trough in position, but the exact meaning is unclear.

Chin, Shih Ch'ung,[188] though a commoner, was even able [to have] multicolored pheasants' feathers[189] and the softest fox fur skins,[190] [eat] painted eggs[191] and [burn] carved firewood for fuel. How much more should a heaven[-ordained] prince of the Great Wei have? I am not ostentatious and extravagant at all!"

In the rear of his garden was constructed the Ying-feng Hall 迎風館 (Hall to Welcome the Breeze) [decorated with] latticed windows and metal bowls for hanging lamps. There were a jade phoenix holding a bell [in its mouth] and a gold dragon with a ring halfway [in its mouth]. [One would also find] white apricots and red plums, their branches entering the eaves, and female entertainers on the towers picked and ate them from their seats.

[Yüan] Ch'en often gathered members of the royal household [at his mansion], and displayed all his treasures [for them]: more than one hundred gold vessels and silver jars, about the same amount of [gold or silver] bowls, footed containers, plates, and boxes. Among other drinking vessels were several scores of quartz bowls, agate cups,[192] glass bowls, ruby goblets—such marvelous craftsmanship was not to be found in China. All came from the Western Regions.

He further brought out female entertainers and all his famed horses and invited all the various princes on an inspection tour of his storerooms. Embroidered woolens, pearls, jades, gauze [as transparent as] ice,[193] crepe [as light as] mist,[194] filled the interiors.

[188] For Shih Ch'ung 石崇, see Chapter 1 at note 220 under the Chao-i Nunnery and *Chin-shu* 33/25b–32a.

[189] Literally, *chih t'ou* 雉頭, "pheasants' heads"; the colored feathers collected from pheasants' heads were sewn on garments.

[190] Skins of the foreleg area are considered the softest and warmest, and also purest in color.

[191] The text (4/12b) reads *mao* 卯, the fourth of the twelve Terrestrial Branches, but *TPKC* 236/7b 奢侈元琛 and *YHNC* (3/12b) give *luan* 卵, "egg"; hence the translation.

Both "painted eggs" and "carved firewood" are exaggerated statements of luxurious life among wealthy men in olden times. See *Kuan-tzu* (*SPTK so-pen*) 12/72 侈靡篇:雕卵然後瀹之,雕橑然後爨之, and Tsung Lin, *Ching-ch'u sui-shih chi* (*SPPY*) 6a: 古之豪家,食稱畫卵, "In ancient times, extravagant families were known to eat painted eggs."

[192] Emending to *ma-nao pei* 瑪瑙杯, "agate goblets," after *CT* (4/14b).

[193] Literally, *ping-lo* 氷羅, "icy gauze."

[194] Literally, *wu-hu* 霧縠, "misty gauze," of which, according to Tuan Yü-ts'ai (*Shuo-wen chieh-tzu* 13A/7b 糸部), *hu* 縠 is the equivalent of modern *chou-sha* 縐紗, "crepe silk."

Embroidered and patterned silk,[195] heavy or light gauze,[196] fine silk,[197] [garments of] *ko-yüeh* 葛越 grass,[198] coins, and pongee were simply too numerous to be tabulated.

[Yüan] Ch'en suddenly turned to [Yüan] Jung 元融, Prince of Chang-wu 章武王,[199] and said: "I do not regret that I have not seen Shih Ch'ung. Rather I regret that Shih Ch'ung was unable to see me!"

[Yüan] Jung, by nature greedy, violent, and insatiable in his desires, sighed with a sense of self-pity at the sight of [Yüan Ch'en's treasures]. Unexpectedly, he fell ill and slept at home for three days without getting up. [Yüan] Chi 元繼, Prince of Chiang-yang 江陽王,[200] came over to express sympathy for his illness, and said: "Your wealth can compete [with Yüan Ch'en's]. Why should you sigh with envy to this extent?"

[Yüan] Jung said: "I have always thought that [the Prince of] Kao-yang was the one man wealthier than myself. Who would have

[195] Literally, *hsiu-hsieh* 綉纈, "embroidered silk." Ku Yeh-wang 顧野王, *Yü-p'ien* 玉篇 (*SPTK so-pen*) 27/97 糸部：五綵備也, "*Ts'ai* means silk complete with five colors."

[196] Literally, *ch'ou ling* 紬綾, meaning heavy and light gauge of silk fabric, respectively. *Shou-wen chieh-tzu* 13a/8a 糸部：[紬], 大絲繒也, "*Ch'ou* is silk of heavy gauge." Tuan Yü-ts'ai comm.: 大絲, 較常絲爲大也, "Heavy-gauge silk means it is heavier than the average." *Shou-wen chieh-tzu*, 13A/8b 糸部：東齊謂布帛之細者曰綾, "In the eastern part of Ch'i (modern Shantung), light-gauge silk or other fabric is known as *ling*."

[197] That is, *ts'ai* 綵. *HS* 91/7b 貨殖傳：文采千匹, "one thousand bolts of silk." Yen Shih-ku's comm.: 帛之有色者曰采, "*Ts'ai* refers to colored silk."

[198] *Shu-ching* 6/13a 禹貢：島夷卉服. Legge 3, p. 111, "The Tribute of Yu": "The wild people of the islands brought garments of grass." Comm.: 南海島夷草服葛越, "The barbarian islanders wore garments of *ko-yüeh* grass." Sub-comm.: 葛越, 南方布名, 用葛爲之, "*Ko-yüeh* is the name of cloth made of *ko* (a kind of bean stalk)."

Ordinarily Yüeh refers to the name of an ancient state, corresponding to modern Chekiang and Fukien provinces. According to the sub-commentary, it is used here as part of a common noun.

[199] Yüan Jung had been Governor of Ping-chou, Ch'ing-chou, Supervisor of Archives, and Protector of the Army within the Capital (*Chung-hu-chün*). He was a corrupt official. See *WS* 19C/23a–b.

[200] Yüan Chi (d. A.D. 529) had been the Grand Commandant, Chief Palace Attendant, Grand Tutor, and Chief of Ministers under Emperor Su-tsung (regnant A.D. 515–528). He was another well-known corrupt prince of the Wei. See *WS* 16/13a–15a.

anticipated that while I looked ahead, [someone more powerful] would suddenly show up in the rear?"[201]

[Yüan] Chi said with a smile: "You are just like [the self-proclaimed emperor] Yüan Shu 袁術 in Huai-nan 淮南, who did not realize that there was yet [another serious contender] on earth, Liu Pei."[202]

Suddenly [Yüan] Jung leapt up [from his sick bed], set out wine, and had music played.

At that time the country was rich; state coffers and treasuries were inundated.[203] As a result, countless coins and silks were stored exposed in the galleries. When the empress dowager bestowed on various officials bolts of silk, the latter bore away as many as they wanted. The court officials carried away as much as their physical strength permitted.[204] Yüan Jung and Li Ch'ung, the Marquis of Ch'en-liu, were [the only two] who had overloaded themselves with the silk. As a result, they stumbled to the ground and injured their ankles.[205]

[201] *Chan chih tsai ch'ien* 瞻之在前 is a quotation from the *Lun-yü* (9/5a 子罕), which should have two sentences if quoted in full (the next sentence is: *hu yen tsai hou* 忽焉在後). Waley, *The Analects of Confucius*, p. 140: "I (that is, Yen Hui) see it in front; but suddenly it is behind." The dialogue, as it appears in the text (4/13b), stops at the end of the first sentence—a style of conversation known as *hsieh-hou-yü* 歇後語, "stop-short."

[202] A reference to Yüan Shu 袁術 (d. A.D. 199), who, in cooperation with Lü Pu, (a warlord killed in A.D. 198), defeated Liu Pei in a battle and therefore did not consider him a serious contender for power. A few years later, Yüan Shu himself, defeated by Ts'ao Ts'ao, would have liked to seek refuge in his nephew Yüan T'an's 袁譚 stronghold. His passage, however, was blocked by Liu Pei, the same person he had despised before. Frustrated, Yüan Shu fell ill and died in disgrace. See *HHS* 105/5b–9b 袁術傳 and 105/9b–15a 呂布傳.

[203] The affluent state described here is also referred to in *WS* 110/10a 食貨志.

[204] Emending *kuo hsing* 過性, "surpass human nature," to *kuo jen* 過任, "overdid," after *TPKC* 165/2b 廉儉部崔光.

[205] *WS* 13/17b (宣武靈皇后傳) treats Yüan Jung and Li Ch'ung separately. It reads: "[Li] Ch'ung came to injure his back, and [Yüan] Jung, his foot. Contemporaries have a saying [as follows]:

Ch'en-liu and Chang-wu 陳留章武
Injures his back or breaks his thigh. 傷腰折股
The greedy and notorious 貪人敗類
Have brought disgrace to our enlightened rulers!" 穢我明主

Note that the last characters at the end of the first, second, and last lines (*wu*, 武, *ku* 股, and *chu* 主) rhyme.

Ts'ui Kuang,[206] the Chief Palace Attendant, stopped at two bolts. The empress dowager asked, "Why so few?" [Ts'ui Kuang] replied, "Your subject has two hands, and so is only able to take two bolts. I have had enough."

Court celebrities greatly respected his honesty.

After the Ho-yin incident,[207] the Yüans were [almost] completely exterminated. The residences of princes and marquises were for the most part converted into temples. In the lanes within the Shou-ch'iu Ward, Buddhist monasteries [and temples] were in view of each other. Abodes for the pure celibate clustered[208] here and there in the shadow of high-rising stūpas. On the eighth day of the fourth month,[209] many ladies and gentlemen in the capital city would go to the Ho-chien Temple.[210] After viewing the splendid galleries and verandahs, all of them would sigh with admiration, believing that even the immortals' abode in P'eng-lai Island could not be any better. After entering the rear garden, they came into sight of the winding streams and ditches [underneath] the high and rugged steps. Red lotus flowers rose above the surface of the pond; green duckweed floated on the water. Suspended beams linked the pavilions, and tall trees pierced the clouds. They would all express their admiration,[211] imagining that the Rabbit Park of Prince Liang must be inferior.[212]

The Chui-hsien Temple 追先寺 (The Temple in Memory of the

For Li Ch'ung, see Chapter 2 at note 149 under the Cheng-shih Monastery and Chapter 3 at note 204 under the Temple of Prince of Kao-yang. *TC* 149/4a–b has a full account of this story, which seems to have been based on the *Ch'ieh-lan chi*.

[206] For Ts'ui Kuang, see Chapter 2 at note 110 under the Ch'in T'ai shang-chün Monastery and also at note 148 of the same chapter.

[207] For the Ho-yin episode, see Chapter 1 at note 59 under the Yung-ning Monastery.

[208] Literally, *yü ch'i* 鬱起, "rise up in great numbers."

[209] This festival marked the commemoration of the Buddha's birthday, when the Buddhist images in various temples would be put on parade.

[210] Most likely this temple was the former residence of the Prince of Ho-chien, which had been converted into a temple.

[211] That is, "*chi, chi* 嘖嘖," sound of admiration.

[212] For the Rabbit Park, see Chapter 4 at note 11 under the Ch'ung-chüeh Temple.

Deceased Father)[213] was located in the Shou-ch'iu Ward.[214] It was [formerly] the residence of [Yüan] Lüeh 元略,[215] Prince of Tung-p'ing 東平王, Chief Palace Attendant and President, Department of State Affairs.

[Yüan] Lüeh at birth was of outstanding intelligence,[216] and, even as a youth, was extremely mature. He immersed himself in his studies,[217] and was unswearing in his love of the way of basic principles. During the Shen-kuei years (A.D. 518–519), he was the Attending Secretary within the Imperial Yellow Gate. When Yüan Ch'a acted as a dictator and murdered the prime minister,[218] [Yüan] Lüeh secretly plotted with his elder brother, [Yüan] Hsi 元熙, Prince of Chung-shan 中山王 and Governor of Hsiang-chou,[219] to raise a righteous army and eliminate the criminals from around the emperor. But their heroic plans bore no result [as] a rift developed among the schemers. [Yüan] Lüeh's three[220] brothers all fell victim.[221] Yüan Lüeh, the only survivor, [managed] to escape to the east of the [Yangtze] River. Hsiao Yen had long heard of [Yüan] Lüeh's fame. Once he had seen his sagacity and his outstanding literary talents, he held [Yüan Lüeh] in great respect. [Hsiao Yen] asked [Yüan Lüeh],

[213] Emending *Chui-kuang ssu* 追光寺 to *Chui-hsien ssu* 追先寺 after *YHNC* 3/12b.

[214] Adding the four characters *tsai Shou-ch'iu li* 在壽丘里, "in Shou-ch'iu Ward" after *YLTT* 13823/7b.

[215] Fourth son of Yüan Ying, Prince of Chung-shan 中山王. For his biography, see *WS* 19C/15a–16a and *MCCS* plate 139.

[216] A contraction of *k'e-ch'i k'e-i* 克岐克嶷 (*Shih-ching* 17.1/11a [ode 245, verse 4, line 4] 大雅生民). Waley, *Book of Songs*, p. 242: "Well he straddled/Well he reared" is not a precise translation. Karlgren's version is: "then he was able to (straddle =) stride, to stand firmly" (*The Book of Odes*, p. 201).

[217] Literally, *po-hsia chün-shu* 博洽羣書.

[218] Literally, *nüeh-chia tsai-fu* 虐加宰輔, which refers to the execution of Yüan I, Prince of Ch'ing-ho in A.D. 520. For Yüan I, see Chapter 1 at note 198 under the Ching-lo Nunnery, Chapter 4 before note 1 under the Ch'ung-chüeh Temple.

[219] West of modern Lin-chang *hsien* 臨漳縣, Honan. For Yüan Hsi, see *WS* 19C/11b–14b; *MCCS* plate 134.

[220] The text (4/14b) gives *ssu* 四, "four," which is a mistake for *san* 三 "three." See below.

[221] Ten days after Yüan Hsi's uprising, his subordinates turned against him and effected his arrest. Yüan Hsi and his three sons were all subsequently killed. See *WS* 19C/13b (Yüan Hsi's biography) and 14b (Yüan Ching-hsien's biography).

"How many are there in Lo-yang as talented as Your Highness?"

In reply, [Yüan] Lüeh said: "While at the court, I was only appointed to fill a vacancy.[222] As to the vast number of excellent officials serving my nation, they were like drake-ducks and phoenixes[223] whose wings touch [in the flock], or medlar and camphor[224] [so abundant] to make shade. As to those of my caliber, Chao Tzu 趙咨[225] [of the Wu] said it before, by cartloads and bushels—too numerous to be counted."

Hsiao Yen laughed heartily.

He then ennobled [Yüan] Lüeh as the Prince of Chung-shan, with a fief of one thousand households, and honored him with courtesies comparable to those of the emperor's own sons. In addition, [Yüan Lüeh] was appointed Grand Warden of Hsüan-ch'eng 宣城太守,[226] given a musical troupe, and one thousand sword-bearing soldiers. [Yüan] Lüeh's administration was well known for its honesty and strictness. Dignitaries east of the Yangtze were extremely haughty, but whenever they saw [Yüan] Lüeh arriving at the court, they watched his every move[227] with trepidation. Soon afterwards he was promoted to General of the Trustworthy and Mighty (*Hsin-wu chiang-chün*), and concurrently Governor of Heng-chou 衡州.[228]

In the first year of Hsiao-ch'ang (A.D. 525), Emperor Ming, with

[222] Literally, *ch'eng fa she kuan* 承乏攝官, a typical expression of humility meaning that Yüan Lüeh was employed not because of his qualifications but because of an opening. The phrase is a quotation from *Tso-chuan* Ch'eng 2 15/12b: Legge 5, p. 345: "... and to undertake the office [of your charioteer], so supplying your present need." Tu Yü's comm.: 攝承空乏.

[223] Literally, *yüan luan chieh i* 鴛鸞接翼, "wing to wing, the *yüan* and *luan* (of the phoenix family)."

[224] *Ch'i* 杞, "medlar," and *tzu* 梓, "camphor," (*catalpa kaempferis*) are fine woods; hence good timber. *Kuo-yü* 17/124 楚語上:其[楚]大夫皆卿才也, 若杞梓皮革焉, "The lords of the state of Ch'u are as talented as you (that is, Ch'ü Chien 屈建), and [as precious as] medlar, camphor, and hide." Wei Chao's comm.: 杞梓, 良材也, "Medlar and camphor are good timbers."

[225] Chao Tzu of the Wu was sent in A.D. 200 as an envoy to the Wei. In reply to Emperor Wen of the Wei (regnant A.D. 220–226), Chao Tzu said: "[In our country] we have eighty or ninety persons who are unusually wise. As for men of my caliber, there are cartloads-full and bushels-full, impossible to give a clear account." See *Wu-chih* 2/16b–17a 吳主權本紀 commentary.

[226] Modern Hsüan-cheng 宣城, Anhui.

[227] Literally, *mo pu tan ch'i chin-chih* 莫不憚其進止.

[228] Modern Ying-te *hsien* 英德縣, Kwangtung.

the promise that [Yüan] Lüeh be returned, pardoned Chiang Ko 江革,[229] a native of the Wu [region] and one of Hsiao Yen's great generals, but Hsiao Yen said: "We are prepared to lose Chiang Ko, but cannot be without Your Highness." [Yüan] Lüeh replied: "Your subject has suffered catastrophies in his family, and, [in consequence], the bare bones [of the murdered] have not yet been collected [for decent burial]. I beg to return to my own court so as to look after both the living and dead." Then he sobbed bitterly. Hsiao Yen pitied him and sent him home, with a gift of five million [coins], two hundred catties of gold, five hundred catties of silver, along with silk, embroideries, and precious baubles too numerous to mention. In addition, the emperor in person led the various officials to the bank of the [Yangtze] River to send him off. More than one hundred people presented him, as farewell gifts, poems of five characters per line which each of them had composed. In each case, he was treated with all the respectful courtesy due an intimate.[230]

No sooner had [Yüan] Lüeh crossed the Huai River[231] than he was appointed by Emperor Ming [of the Northern Wei] as Chief Palace Attendant, Prince of I-yang[232] 義陽王 (Prince of Righteousness and Enlightenment), with a fiefdom of one thousand households. Upon his arrival at the palace, a rescript [issued in his honor] read [as follows]:

"In the former days, Liu Ts'ang's 劉蒼[233] fondness for good deeds

[229] Chiang Ko was an official of the Ch'i (A.D. 479–502), but later joined the Liang (A.D. 502–557). As a Senior Administrator in the office of the General Quelling the North, he was captured in A.D. 525 when the general's headquarter in P'eng-ch'eng (modern Hsü-chou, Kiangu) fell into the hands of the Northern Wei. Repatriated in the same year, he died in his native Liang ten years later. For his biography, see *Liang-shu* 36/4b–8a.

[230] The text (4/15b) reads *ch'in* 親, "intimate." *Ch'in* is preferable, since it agrees with a statement in the preceding paragraph that the prince was treated "with courtesies comparable to those of the emperor's own sons," but *IS* (4/12a) gives *tz'u* 此, "this," instead.

[231] Then the border line between the Northern Wei and Liang of the Southern Dynasties.

[232] I-yang bordered on the Liang. Modern Hsin-yang *hsien* 信陽縣, Honan.

[233] Liu Ts'ang, the eighth son of Emperor Kuang-wu, was ennobled as Prince of Tung-p'ing (modern Tung-p'ing *hsien*, Shantung) in A.D. 41. When asked by Emperor Ming (regnant A.D. 58–75) what he enjoyed most in his fiefdom, the prince replied: "Doing good deeds is most enjoyable." See *HHS* 72/11a 東平憲王蒼傳.

benefitted [his fiefdom] at Tung-p'ing 東平, and Ts'ao Chih's 曹植[234] literary skill greatly inspired [the people of his fiefdom] Ch'en 陳. Because of this, each of them distinguished himself as a force of solidarity between the feudal lords[235] and their master and brilliantly demonstrated the principle governing their relationships.[236] Chief Palace Attendant [Yüan] Lüeh, Prince of I-yang, by birth comes from [the ranks of] those vassals and has for years rendered meritorious [achievements]. Inwardly he is accommodating and outwardly luminous. His elder and younger brothers were similarly outstanding. Seeing what was right, they forgot their family's [interests]. They sacrificed their lives and died for the nation. Always We will speak of their loyalty and martyrdom. What day could We forget them?

"Although he once served the state of Liang while he was released from his duties[237] [in his home land], he is now returning to his [native] court. Both determined and principled, [his integrity] will last for ever. His nobility will soon be transmitted in [the court] paintings[238] and will shine as bright as the sun and moon.

"Prior to [Yüan] Lüeh's arrival, We have enfeoffed him as [the Prince of] I-yang, so as to match the title with his principles. But his fief is in the borderland, and he is now living on revenues that have come from other fiefs. We have sought for two or three [other fiefs], none of which is completely satisfactory.[239] Indeed, his virtues should be suitably [rewarded] by a fief, in memory of past valor. Let his fief

[234] Ts'ao Chih, enfeoffed as the Prince of Ch'en in A.D. 232. See *Wei-chih* 19/36b.

[235] Literally, *sheng-piao p'an-shih* 聲彪磐石, "distinguished himself for his loyalty to the emperor." *SC* 10/3 孝文本紀:高帝封王子弟地, 犬牙相制, 此所謂磐石之宗也, "Emperor Kao-tsu (regnant 206–195 B.C.) ennobled his sons with fiefs, interlocked like dog's teeth. This is to assure [their loyalty to the emperor and mutual assistance among themselves] as solid as a large stone." Sub-comm.: 言其固如磐石, "Meaning the solidarity is comparable to that of a large stone."

[236] Literally, *i-yü wei-ch'eng* 義鬱維城. *Shih-ching* 17.4/20a (ode 234, verse 7, line 6) 大雅板:宗子維城. Cheng Hsüan's comm.: 宗子謂王之適子. "*Tsung-tzu* (king's relations) means his legitimate heirs."

P'an-shih 磐石, "a great stone," and *wei-ch'eng* 維城, "an alliance of cities," both refer to assistance among feudal lords and their loyalty to the king.

[237] Literally, *shih-tan* 弛擔. *Tso-chuan* Chuang 莊 22 9/22b: 弛於負擔. Tu Yü's comm.: 弛, 去離也, "*Shih* means to be released."

[238] Literally, *ch'uan mei tan ching* 傳美丹青, "to transmit good reputation through red and green (that is, paintings)."

[239] The text (4/16a) reads 寓食他邑, 求之二三, 未爲盡善, the exact meaning of which is not clear. One may surmise that since I-yang bordered on the Liang

be changed to that of Prince of Tung-p'ing, with the same number of households as were previously granted."

Shortly later, he was promoted to President, Department of State Affairs, Palatine Ceremonially Equal to the Three Authorities, Acting Libationer of the Imperial Academy, while retaining his old post as Chief Palace Attendant.

By nature [Yüan] Lüeh was relaxed and had an easy grace. After his return from the south, he became more dignified. Both those in and out of court took his words and conduct as a model. In the first year of the Chien-i period (A.D. 528), he died at Ho-yin.[240] Afterwards, the posthumous rank of Grand Guardian, [Governor of Hsü-chou],[241] and the title Wen-chen 文貞 (Cultured and Principled) were conferred upon him. [Yüan] Ching-shih 元景式,[242] his successor, donated his residence for use as a temple.

The Jung-chüeh Monastery 融覺寺 (Monastery of Harmonious Awakening) established by [Yüan] I, the Wen-hsien 文獻 (The Cultured and Dedicated) Prince of Ch'ing-ho, was located on the south side of the Imperial Drive and outside the Ch'ang-ho Gate. There was a five-storied stūpa, which matched in height the one in the Ch'ung-chüeh Temple.[243] Buddhist halls and monks' rooms filled to overflowing one ward. The bhikṣu T'an-mo-tsui,[244] an expert on Buddhist studies,[245] lectured here on the Mahāparinirvāṇa

---

territory, there was no guarantee of political or economic stability. Hence the translation.

[240] The famous massacre staged at Ho-yin (east of modern Meng-chin, Honan) by Erh-chu Jung, husband of Yüan Lüeh's aunt. Yüan Lüeh died on May 17, A.D. 528 at forty-three *sui*. See *MCCS* plate 139.

[241] See *WS* 19C/16b and *MCCS* plate 139.

[242] That is, Yüan Kuei 元頍 (頍 is the same as 規), styled Ching-shih 景式. See *MCCS* plate 139 (*WS* 19C/16b only mentions his style without giving his *ming*).

[243] The exact meaning of this sentence *yü Ch'ung-chüeh ssu ch'i teng* 與冲覺寺齊等, "equal to the Ch'ung-chüeh *ssu*" is not clear. Originally the Ch'ung-chüeh Temple was also the Prince of Ch'ing-ho's residence. As a very lofty tower was built there, we may surmise that the stūpa in the Jung-chüeh Monastery was comparable in height to the Ch'ung-chüeh Temple tower.

[244] See *Hsü Kao-seng-chuan* 23/624–625 and Chapter 2 at note 49 under the Ch'ung-chen Monastery.

[245] *Ch'an-hsüeh* 禪學, literally, "meditational studies," refers loosely to Buddhist studies and is interchangeable with the terms *I-hsüeh* 義學 (*IS* 4/13a) and *Shih-hsüeh* 釋學 (*YLTT* 13823/8b).

sūtra[246] and the Avataṁsaka sūtra[247] before an audience of one thousand disciples. Having seen this, the Indian monk Bodhiruci[248] held him in great respect and referred to him as a Bodhisattva.

[Bodhi-]ruci was knowledgeable of Buddhist teachings. He was renowned in the Western Lands and called an Arhan (or Arhat) by the barbarians there. Because of his proficiency in the Chinese language and script, he translated some twenty-three[249] works, including the Daśabhūmika sūtra 十地[經論], the Laṅkāvatāra sūtra 楞伽[經], and other śāstras. Even the translations of "golden words" in the Stone Chamber (*Shih-shih* 石室)[250] and of "true transmissions" at the Thatched Hall (*Ts'ao-t'ang* 草堂)[251] could not surpass his.

Whenever [Bodhi-]ruci read T'an-mu-tsui's works on Mahāyāna, he would snap his fingers,[252] make a sign of admiration, and exclaim "How subtle!" He then would render them into his own Indian script and have them transmitted into the Western Regions. Śramaṇa over there often faced eastward to show their respect from a distance. They honored T'an-mu-tsui as the Sage of the East.[253]

[246] Dharmakṣema is the translator of this work (*Ni-p'an* 涅槃) in forty *chüan*.

[247] Buddhabhadra (who arrived in China in A.D. 406) is the translator of this work (*Hua-yen* 華 or 花嚴) in sixty *chüan*. It is known as the Chin 晉, or old, sūtra 舊經 as against the T'ang 唐 or new 新 sūtra translated by Śikṣānanda in about A.D. 700.

[248] For more information about him, see Ch'en, *Buddhism in China*, pp. 182–183, and *Hsü Kao-seng chuan* 1/428–429 唐譯經篇魏南臺永寧寺北天竺菩提流支傳.

[249] According to *Hsü Kao-seng chuan* (1/428–429), he translated some thirty-nine works (totaling one hundred twenty-seven *chüan*) into Chinese, a figure at variance with the *Ch'ieh-lan chi*. For a partial listing of his translation, see *Hsü Kao-seng chuan*, 1/428.

[250] The text (4/16b) comes in a parallel prose couplet that reads:

石室之寫金言,

草堂之傳眞教.

The Shih-shih 石室, "Stone Chamber," is an indirect reference to the "Sūtra of Forty-two Sections" rendered into Chinese by Kāśyapa Mātaṅga after his arrival in Lo-yang in about A.D. 67. It was housed in the Stone Chamber of the Orchid Terrace (Bureau of Archives, see Chapter 3 n. 48 under the Ta-t'ung Temple); hence the allusion.

[251] The Ts'ao-t'ang Monastery was the place where Kumārajīva (A.D. 344–413, var. 409) translated Buddhist works into Chinese after his arrival in Ch'ang-an in A.D. 401. Both "golden words" and "true transmissions" refer to Buddhist scriptures.

[252] *Tan-chih* 彈指, an expression of greetings among the Indians during the period under discussion. See Mather, *A New Account*, p. 86 note 2.

[253] The title "Sage of the East," which implies the recognition of China as a

The Ta-chüeh Monastery 大覺寺 (Monastery of the Great Awakening), located more than one *li* to the west of the Jung-chüeh Monastery, was originally the residence of [Yüan] Huai, Prince of Kuang-p'ing, who donated it for use as a monastery. It overlooked the Mang Mountain to the north, the junction of Rivers Lo [and I (?)][254] to the south, the palaces to the east, and the flag pavilion[255] to the west. The grounds were magnificent[256] and truly scenic. Therefore the monument inscription written by Wen Tzu-sheng[257] reads: "It faces the water and backs on the mountain. On its left is the court, and on its right is the marketplace." It is truly so.

Images of seven Buddhas[258] were placed in the hall, which was formerly [Yüan] Huai's living quarters. [The beautiful view of] woods, ponds, and elevated pavilions matched that of the Ching-ming Monastery.[259] When the spring breezes brushed the trees, the orchids unfolded their purple petals. When the autumn frost descended on the grasses, chrysanthemums yielded their yellow blossoms. Famous monks and distinguished masters would gather here in tranquil contemplation in order to eliminate disturbing illu-

---

center of Buddhism, had been applied earlier to Tao-an 道安 (A.D. 312–385) by Kumārajīva. See *WS* 114/6a 釋老志 and *Kao-seng chuan* 5/354.

[254] The text (4/17a) reads *Lo jui* 洛汭, *jui* 汭 meaning the junction of two rivers. In addition to the Lo River, the other river within sight was the River I.

[255] That is, *Ch'i-t'ing* 旗亭. For its origin, see Chapter 2 at note 16 under the Lung-hua Temple.

[256] Emending *ch'an kao* 禪臯 to *shen kao* 神臯 after *IS* 4/13b. For *shen kao* 神臯, see *WH* 2/2b 張衡西京賦:寔惟地之奥區神臯. "They are indeed the auspicious and sacred areas of the land." Li Shan's comm.: 廣雅曰:臯, 局也, 謂神明之界局也. "*Kao* means an area. It refers to a sacred area."

[257] The title of this essay is *Ta-chüeh ssu pei* 大覺寺碑 "The Memorial of Ta-chüeh Temple." See below. For Wen Tzu-sheng, see Chapter 2 at note 124.

[258] Identification of the Seven Buddhas varies from one source to another. The *Dīrghāgama Sūtra* 長阿含經, as quoted in *FYCL* 139B/140 七佛部, gives the following seven:

Vipaśyin 毗婆尸, the first of the seven Buddhas of antiquity;
Śikhin 尸棄, the second of the seven Buddhas, born in Prabhadvaja;
Viśvabhū 毗舍婆, the third of the seven Buddhas, who converted 130,000 persons on two occasions;
Krakucchanda 拘樓孫, the fourth of the seven ancient Buddhas;
Kānakamuni 俱(拘)那含牟尼, the fifth of the ancient Buddhas;
Kāśyapa 迦葉, the sixth of the seven ancient Buddhas;
Śākyamuni 釋迦, the historical Buddha.

[259] For the Ching-ming Monastery, see Chapter 3.

sions. In the Yung-hsi years (A.D. 532–534), after the ascension to the imperial throne of the Prince of P'ing-yang,[260] a five-storied[261] brick stūpa was built, the masonry of which was marked with incredible dexterity and unrivaled beauty. Wen Tzu-sheng, Drafter of the Central Secretariat, received an imperial order to prepare an inscription.[262]

The Yung-ming Monastery 永明寺 (Monastery of Eternal Brilliance), located to the east of the Ta-chüeh Monastery, was established by Emperor Shih-tsung (regnant A.D. 499–515) during a time when studies of Buddhist scriptures and [worship of] Buddhist images acquired tremendous vogue in Lo-yang. Śramaṇas of foreign countries, staff and sūtras in hand, flocked[263] to this happy land.[264] The monastery was therefore built to accommodate them. Row after row of tall bamboo were in the courtyard, while lofty pine trees brushed the eaves. Exotic flowers and rare plants grew in profusion in the area along the stairways. More than three thousand śramaṇas from one hundred [different] countries [congregated here].

> Monks came to China from as far as Ta-Ch'in,[265] the furthermost country in the western land. It was the western extreme of the universe. Its people lived in the countryside, tilling, weeding,[266] spinning, and weaving. In the city, houses were in close proximity to one another. They imitated the Chinese costumes, carts, and horses.[267]

[260] The Prince of P'ing-yang was the third son of Yüan Huai. He became the emperor in A.D. 532. See Chapter 2 at note 257 under the P'ing-teng Monastery and *WS* 11/10a.

[261] See Chapter 2 after note 257 under the P'ing-teng Monastery.

[262] An incomplete version of this work is available in Ou-yang Hsün's *I-wen lei-chü* (facsimile ed., Taipei, 1960) 77/1b–2a 內典部下寺碑. It does not include the two sentences quoted above at note 257 in the text.

[263] Literally, *hsien lai fu tsou* 咸來輻輳, "All came like spokes [to a hub]."

[264] A reference to *Shih-ching* 5.3/12b (ode 113, verse, line 6) 魏風碩鼠: 適彼樂土. Waley, *Book of Songs*, p. 309: "And go to that happy land."

[265] That is, the Byzantine Empire, also known as Li-hsüan 黎軒, believed to be 39,400 *li* away from P'ing-ch'eng (T'a-t'ung, Shansi), the old capital of the Northern Wei. "Ta-Ch'in" was a name given by countries in Central Asia because of the resemblance of its costumes, carriages, and banner with those of China. See *WS* 102/16b 大秦國.

[266] Adding *keng-yün* 耕耘 after *HCTY* 4/15a.

[267] The text (4/17b) reads *i-fu chü-ma, i-i Chung-kuo* 衣服車馬, 擬儀中國,

To the south was the state of Ko-ying 歌營國,[268] which was very distant from the [Wei] capital. Its customs were different from those of China, and since olden days it had never been in contact with China, not even during the Former and Later Han, nor during the Wei [of the Three Kingdoms]. Only recently did śramaṇa Buddhabhadra[269] come from there. He said of his [journey]:

"Going northward for one month, I arrived at the state of Chü-ya 句雅國.[270] Traveling northward again for eleven days, I reached the state of Tien-sun 典孫國.[271] Traveling northward for another thirty days, I came to the state of Fu-nan 扶南國,[272] which, with a territory of five thousand square *li*, was the largest and most powerful among all barbarian states in the south. It was very populous, producing such valuables as pearls, gold, jade, quartz, and large quantities of betel nuts. Going north from the state of Fu-nan for one month, I arrived at the state of Lin-i

---

"They imitated Chinese costumes, carts, and horses," which bears a striking resemblance to the *WS* (102/16b) account. The latter is: *i-fu chü-ch'i, i-i Chung-kuo* 衣服車旗, 擬儀中國, "They imitated Chinese costumes, carts, and banners."

[268] Also transliterated as Chia-ying 加營, which Fujita Toyohachi identifies as Kulam (Ho Chien-min, tr., *Chung-kuo Nan-hai ku-tai chiao-t'ung ts'ung-k'ao* (Shanghai, 1936), "Yeh-tiao, Ssu-tiao chi Ssu-k'o-tiao k'ao," 葉調斯調及私訶條考, p. 557). Paul Pelliot ("Quelque textes chinois concernant l'Indochine hindouisée," *Études asiatiques* 2 [1925], 243–263), however, believes this state should be located to the south of the Malay Peninsula. Su Chi-ch'ing, on the other hand, asserts that Ko-ying stands for Koyam, an abbreviation for Koyampadi or Koyammuturu, an ancient island state in southern India ("Chia-ying-kou k'ao," *Nan-yang hsüeh-pao* 7:1 [1951], 18–24); see also Sugimoto Naojirō, *Tōnan Ajia-shi kenkyū* 1 (Tokyo, 1968), p. 516.

[269] The text reads P'u-t'i pa-t'o 菩提拔陁, which Édouard Chavannes identifies with Buddhabhadra. See Ch'en, *Buddhism in China*, p. 109 and Feng Ch'eng-chün, tr., *Shih-ti ts'ung-k'ao hsü-pien* (Shanghai, 1933), p. 45.

[270] The text (4/18a) gives *Kou* 勾 for *Chü* 句 through a scribal error. The state is also written as Chiu-chih *kuo* 九稚國 and Chü-chih *kuo* 勾稚國. See *Liang-shu* 54/7a 海南傳扶南國. Paul Pelliot theorizes that *chih* 稚 is an error for *li* 離, and that Chiu-li 九離, on its part, is another transliteration of Chü-li 拘利, a nation mentioned in *T'ung-tien* 188/22b–23a 邊防典南蠻邊斗. See also Feng Ch'eng-chün, *Shih-ti ts'ung-k'ao hsü-pien*, p. 13.

[271] Emending Sun-tien 孫典 to Tien-sun 典孫. The kingdom of Tun-sun 頓遜, identified with Tien-sun 典孫, is mentioned in *Liang-shu* 54/7a 海南傳扶南國. It corresponds to the modern Malay Peninsula.

[272] It corresponds to modern Cambodia.

林邑國,[273] and after leaving the state of Lin-i, I entered Hsiao Yen's kingdom." More than one year after his arrival in Yang-chou,[274] Buddhabhadra followed Fa-jung 法融, a monk of Yang-chou, and came to the capital. Asked by some śramaṇas of the capital[275] about customs in the south, Buddhabhadra replied:

"In ancient times in the state known as Nu-tiao 奴調國,[276] people rode in four-wheeled carriages drawn by horses. The state of Ssu-tiao 斯調國[277] produced fire-proof cloth (*huo-huan-pu* 火烷布), which was made of bark. The bark would not burn even in flames. People in all these states in the south lived in walled cities where precious and beautiful things were abundant. By custom, the people were honest, decent, simple, upright, and righteous. These countries were in communication with the Western Regions,[278] Ta-Ch'in, An-hsi 安息 (Parthia), and Shen-tu 身毒 (India). They set out in three or four different directions,[279] and, by taking boats under favorable winds, reached [their destinations] in no more than one hundred days. As a rule they believe in Buddhism, have love for life and abhor killing."

To the west of the monastery was the I-nien Ward 宜年里 (Deserving Longevity Ward),[280] wherein the two residences of

[273] That is, Champa (modern Vietnam), famous for such products as tortoise shells, cowries, and cotton trees. See *Liang-shu* 54/1b–2a 林邑傳.

[274] That is, Yang-chou 揚州, which during the Liang was a vast territory including what is known today as Kiangsu, Chekiang, and Fukien provinces. See Hung I-sun, *Pu Liang chiang-yü chih* (*Erh-shih-wu-shih pu-pien* ed.) 1/11.

[275] Adding the two characters *ching shih* 京師, "capital," after *IS* 4/14a.

[276] According to Su Chi-ch'ing ("Chih-hu-li ta-chiang yü Chia-na-tiao chou k'ao" 枝扈黎大江與迦那調洲考 as quoted in *CC* p. 236), the correct text should be *Ku nu-tiao kuo* 古奴調國, identified as the state of Kurnadvipa (one of the modern South Sea Islands). Our text (4/18a) *ku yu nu-tiao kuo* 古有奴調國 is erroneous. See also Sugimoto, *Tōnan Ajia-shi kenkyū* 1, pp. 482–83, 493–94.

[277] According to *Nan-chou i-wu chih* 南州異物志 (as quoted in *TPYL* 787/3a 四夷部南蠻斯調國), Ssu-tiao 斯調 was an island state about three thousand *li* to the southeast of Ko-ying. Fujita Toyohachi identifies this nation with Ceylon. See Ho Chien-min, tr., *Chung-kuo Nan-hai ku-tai chiao-t'ung ts'ung-k'ao*, p. 570.

[278] Emending *Hsi kuo* 西國, "Western Kingdoms," to *Hsi-yü* 西域, "Western Regions," after *IS* 4/14b.

[279] The text (4/18b) is *huo san fang ssu fang* 或三方四方, "perhaps three directions, four directions," the exact meaning of which is obscure.

[280] Emending I-niu li 宜牛里 to I-nien li 宜年里 after *YHNC* (3/13a).

[Yüan] Ching-hao 元景皓,[281] Prince of Ch'en-liu 陳留王, and Hu Yüan-chi 胡元吉,[282] Chief Palace Attendant and Duke of An-ting 安定公,[283] were located.

[Yüan] Ching-hao was the son of [Yüan] Tsu 元祚, Prince of Ch'en-liu and Governor of Ho-chou 河州,[284] whose posthumous title was Chuang 莊. By temperament Ching-hao was humble and broadminded. As a youth, he was already known for his tolerance, love for others, and hospitality to the literati.[285] His generosity extended to everyone. He had long been skillful at delivering philosophical discourses on Buddhist teachings.[286] As a result, half of his residence was donated for use as a temple, where monks were housed to chant and texts of several Mahāyāna sūtras were introduced simultaneously. Furthermore, he invited four master monks in the capital—Ch'ao 超, Kuang 光, Hsien 晛, Jung 榮,[287] and Bodhiruci, the Indian authority on Tripiṭaka, and others, to participate in

[281] Yüan Ching-hao, son of Yüan Tsu 元祚, a member of the imperial clan of the Wei, was later killed by Kao Yang 高洋 (later Emperor of Northern Ch'i, regnant A.D. 550–559), in the latter's drive against the royalists of the Wei. See *PCS* 41/10a 元景安傳.

[282] Style of Hu Hsiang 胡祥. Son of Hu Kuo-chen 胡國珍, he had been Minister within the Palace (*Tien-chung shang-shu*), Director of the Central Secretariat (*Chung-shu chien*), and Chief Palace Attendant. For his biography, see *WS* 83B/7b–9a.

[283] Name of a commandery created during Northern Wei. It is located in modern Honan.

[284] The text (4/18b) gives *Ho-nei* 河內, of which *nei* 內 is an obvious mistake for *chou* 州. *Chou* 州, as a province, was under the rule of a governor, whereas *chün* 郡, as a commandery, had a grand warden as its chief executive. See *PS* 15/32a 陳留王虔傳.

[285] Emending *shih* 事 to *shih* 士 after *IS* 4/14b. *Hao-shih* 好士 is a compliment, while *hai-shih* 好事, "to be fond of meddling," is not.

[286] Literally, *Tao chia* 道家 "The school of the Way," which means Buddhism here.

[287] These four monks have not been positively identified, but *WS* (114/14a–24a 釋老志) lists Seng-ch'ao 僧超 and Chih-tan 智誕 (*WS* 114/17a gives 誕 for 晛, the latter being a possible corruption for 誕). Kuang 光 may refer to Hui-kuang 慧光 (*Hsü Kao-seng chuan* 21/606–608 齊鄴下大覺寺釋慧光傳), and Jung 榮 might stand for Tao-jung 道榮. Tao-jung is often referred to in Chapter 5. *Kou-ch'en* (4/18a) suggests Seng-hsien 僧暹, Hui- (a substitute for *Hui* 慧) kuang 惠光, Tao-hsi 道晞, and Fa-jung 法榮, all touched upon in *WS* 114/24b 釋老志.

Tsukamoto Zenryū offers a more detailed discussion of the four monks. See his *Gisho Shaku-Rō-shi no kenkyū*, pp. 226, 256, and 307.

the deliberations. Men gifted in every other field also came to the gatherings.

At the time there was a certain Meng Chung-hui 孟仲暉,[288] the Court Guest, who was a native of Wu-wei 武威[289] and whose father [Meng] Pin [孟]賓 had been the Grand Warden of Chin-ch'eng 金城.[290] [Meng Chung-]hui was intelligent and mastered [Confucian] as well as Buddhist teachings. He had an exhaustive knowledge of the Four Noble Truths.[291] He often came to the temple to discuss [Buddhist teachings] with the śramaṇas, and because of this he was called Master of the Mystery 玄宗先生 by his contemporaries. Subsequently, he had a life-size[292] dry-lacquered statue [of Buddha] made, whose marks and signs were so sumptuous as to be a rarity in the contemporary world. It was placed on the Sumeru Shrine[293] in [Yüan Ching-]hao's anterior hall. In the second year of the Yung-an period (A.D. 529), every night the image would walk around its base, leaving sunken footprints on the ground. Thereupon the dignitaries and commoners, thinking it curious, come here for a view. As a result, countless numbers of them wanted to become Buddhist devotees. In the third year of the Yung-hsi period (A.D. 534), it suddenly disappeared by itself, and nobody ever knew of its whereabouts. In the winter of the same year, the capital was moved to Yeh. In the fifth year of the Wu-ting period (A.D. 547), [Meng Chung-]hui, as the Chief Administrator under the Governor[294] of Lo-chou, made another attempt to locate the image, but there was no trace of it.[295]

[288] No additional information is available for Meng Chung-hui and his father Meng Pin.

[289] Modern Wu-wei, Kansu.

[290] Modern Lan-chou 蘭州, Kansu.

[291] Literally, *Ssu-ti* 四諦, that is, *k'u* 苦, "misery"; *chü* 聚, "accumulation of passion"; *mieh* 滅, "extinction of passion"; and *tao* 道, "the path that leads to the extinction of passion."

[292] *Jen chung* 人中. See also Chapter 2 at note 56 under the Ch'ung-chen Monastery.

[293] The text (4/18a) reads *Hsü-yü-mi pao-tso* 須臾彌寶座, "the holy seat of Sumeru." Hsü-mi 須彌 is the translation of Sumeru, and Hsü-mi pao-tso 須彌寶坐 (*tso* 坐 also written *tso* 座) is a holy throne for Buddha. The character *yü* 臾 is perhaps an interpolation.

[294] The text (4/19b) gives *k'ai fu* 開府, "palatine." The governor to whom this passage refers cannot be identified.

[295] From the next paragraph to the end of this chapter, the description is unrelated

Seven *li* outside the Ch'ang-ho city gate was the Chang-fen Bridge, a stone levee built during the Western Chin[296] to restrain the torrential waters of the Ku River from rushing toward the city wall and damaging a great many people's dwellings. It was intended to divert the rising water into the Lo River; hence the name Chang-fen Bridge 長分橋 (Bridge to Divide the Water at Its Crest). Someone, however, maintained that this was the camping site of General Chang Fang's 張方 army in his expedition against the Prince of Ch'ang-sha 長沙王, as instructed by the Prince of Ho-chien 河間王 of Ch'ang-an.[297] Thus, it was named Chang Fang Bridge. Of the two explanations, one could not be sure which one was correct. Now because of a phonetic error among the populace, it is known as Chang Fu-jen Bridge 張夫人橋 (Mrs. Chang's Bridge).[298] Court officials often came here to send off or to welcome back their colleagues.

To the west of the Chang-fen Bridge was the Ch'ien-chin Dam 千金堰 (Dam Worthy of One Thousand Taels of Gold).[299] It was so named because it yielded a daily profit of one thousand taels of gold by utilizing the water power [to produce flour].

The dam was built under the auspices of Ch'en Hsieh 陳勰,[300]

to the Yung-ming Monastery under discussion. *Ch'ung-k'an* (4/36b) therefore treats all of them as footnotes, which, according to the author, should be moved up to the section dealing with the T'iao-yin and Yüeh-lü Wards (under the Hsi-yang Gate of this chapter).

[296] Literally, *chung ch'ao* 中朝. For a discussion of *chung-ch'ao* 中朝, see Chapter 1 at note 167 under the Yung-ning Monastery and under the Ch'ang-ch'iu Temple of the same chapter.

[297] See *Chin-shu* 59/38b–42b 河間王顒傳 and 60/16a–18b 張方傳.

[298] Phonetically, a contraction of "fu-jen" yields the sound "fen."

[299] The exact locality of the dam is controversial. It is determined either at twenty-five *li* west of Lo-yang (Yang Ch'üan-chi's 楊佺期 *Lo-yang chi* 洛陽記 as quoted in Li Shan's comm. for *WH* 30/14b 沈約三月三日率爾成篇) or fifteen *li* east of Ho-nan *hsien* (*SCC* 16/7a 穀水注 quoting *Ho-nan shih-erh-hsien-ching-pu* 河南十二縣境簿).

[300] Ch'en Hsieh's personal name is written as Hsieh 勰 in the text (4/19b). Ch'en Hsieh was appointed by Emperor Wen of the Chin on the recommendation by Juan Chi, one of the Seven Sages of the Bamboo Grove, who often received gifts of wine from Ch'en Hsieh. In the process of construction, Ch'en Hsieh is said to have found underground six antique bronze, dragon-shaped water receptacles. The dam was also known, then, as the Chiu-lung-yen 九龍堰 "Nine-dragon Dam." See *SCC* 16/7b 穀水注 quoting *Yü-lin* 語林.

formerly Messenger Director of the Waters (*Tu-shui shih-che* 都水使者). [A labor force of] one thousand males was provided annually for its continued maintenance.

The mention of water power in this paragraph is an obvious reference to the many water mills built along the dam for business purposes. See also Chapter 3 at note 13 under the Ching-ming Monastery.

Chapter 5

NORTHERN SUBURBS (*Ch'eng-pei* 城北)

The Ch'an-hsü Temple 禪虛寺 (Temple of Meditation on the Void) was on the western side of the Imperial Drive outside[1] the Ta-hsia Gate. In front of the temple were the Military Parade Grounds (*Yüeh-wu ch'ang* 閱武場), where armored soldiers trained in [mock] battles at year's end or during the slack season for farming. One thousand chariots and ten thousand horses were customarily here [during such exercises].

Ma Seng-hsiang 馬僧相,[2] was a *yü-lin* (plumed forest) guard skillful at wrestling games.[3] He could throw a halberd as high as the top of a tree one hundred Chinese feet above the ground, whereas Chang Chü-ch'ü 張車渠,[4] a *hu-pen* (tiger-rushing) guard, was able to throw a sword ten Chinese feet above the tower.[5] When Emperor [Hsiao-ming] watched the games from the tower, he often ordered these two to engage one another in wrestling.

Under the Western Chin,[6] the Military Exercise Grounds

[1] *CS* (5/179) suggests the inclusion of the character *wai* 外, "outside," which is not in the text.

[2] *YLTT* 13824/1a gives Feng Seng-hsiang 馮僧相 instead.

[3] The text (5/1a) is *ti-chiao* 觝角, but *chiao-ti* 角觝 is more conventional in Chinese literature. For its origin, see *SC* 87/36 李斯傳：[二世]方作觳抵優俳之觀；*HS* 6/27b 武紀：[元封]三年春作角抵戲. The game often involved wrestling, acrobatics, archery, and horse racing.

[4] Adding *ch'ü* 渠 after *YLTT* 13824/1a. A bodyguard (*pei-sheng tso-yu* 備身左右) loyal to Empress Dowager Hu, he and a score of others were killed by Liu T'eng after their abortive uprising in A.D. 520 against the latter. See *PS* 13/20a 宣武靈皇后胡氏傳.

[5] The text (5/1a) is *lou* 樓, which might have been a raised platform as part of the review stand.

[6] The Western Chin is indicated by the term *chung-ch'ao* 中朝. See Chapter 1 at

(*Hsüan-wu ch'ang* 宣武場) were located northwest of the Ta-hsia Gate, but today [this site] is the Kuang-feng Park 光風園 (Park of the Bright and Breezy), where alfalfa[7] grows.

The Ning-hsüan[8] Temple 凝玄寺 (Temple of Harmonious Awakening) established by the eunuch Chia Ts'an 賈璨, Governor of Chi-chou 濟州刺史,[9] was located on the east side of the Imperial Drive one *li* outside the Kuang-mo Gate. It was within the so-called Yung-p'ing Ward 永平里 (Ward of Eternal Peace).

Author's note:[10] This was the same site where the shrine[11] of "the Supreme Emperor-Father of the Han"[12] stood.

In the early years after the capital was moved [to Lo-yang, Chia Ts'an][13] sponsored the creation of this ward and built a house in it. At

---

note 7 under the Yung-ning Monastery, note 167 under Ch'ang-ch'iu Temple of the same chapter, and also Chapter 4 at note 296 under the Yung-ming Monastery.

Actually, the grounds had been in use during the Wei and Western Chin periods. The "Chu-lin ch'i-hsien lun" 竹林七賢論, as quoted in the *SCC* 16/13b 穀水注, makes a mention of Wang Jung 王戎 (A.D. 234–305) then a boy of seven years and later a member of the "Seven Sages of the Bamboo Grove," as among those on the reviewing stand. See also *Shih-shuo hsin-yü* B/25a 雅量篇 (Mather, *A New Account*, p. 181). For Emperor Wu's (regnant A.D. 265–290) review under the Chin, see *Shih-shuo hsin-yü* B/36b 識鑒篇 (ibid., p. 198).

[7] Alfalfa, usually called *huai-feng* 懷風, is also known as *kuang-feng* 光風 for its bright color. A favorite food of horses, it is also suitable for human consumption. See *Hsi-ching tsa-chi* 1/2 and *CMYS* 3/15a.

[8] Emending to Ning-hsüan 凝玄 after *IS* (5/1a) and *YLTT* (13824/1a).

[9] *WS* 94/18b gives *Ts'an* 粲 as Chia's personal name. A eunuch partisan of the Yüan Ch'a and Liu T'eng clique, he was responsible for the initial downfall of Empress Dowager Hu in A.D. 520. Following her restoration to power in A.D. 525, Chia Ch'an was first moved out of the capital, then murdered soon after in Chi-chou. See *WS* 94/18a–b.

[10] This is the only case in which the author used the character *chu* 注, "note," to draw a line between the note and the main text (*Ho-chiao* 5/1a–b), but Ch'en Yin-k'o considers the presence of this character more accidental than intentional ("Tu *Lo-yang ch'ieh-lan chi* shu hou" A/600–605.

[11] The text (5/1b) reads *kuang* 廣, "wide", which, according to *CS* (5/180), might have been a corruption for *miao* 廟 "temple." The abbreviated form of *miao* 廟 is 庿 (or 庙), which has a striking graphic resemblance to *kuang* 廣. The location of this shrine, however, is not given elsewhere.

[12] That is, father of the founder of the Han, Liu Pang, otherwise known as Kao-tsu 高祖.

[13] Adding *Ts'an* 璨 at the suggestion of *CS* 5/181.

the time of his mother's death, he donated the house to be made into a temple.

It occupied an elevated and conspicuous site, overlooking the city walls and palaces. Rooms and corridors were both splendid and beautiful, [surrounded by] forests of bamboo and cypress. Indeed, it was a place where one could practice celibacy and set his heart at rest. Countless princes and ranking officials came to visit here and composed poetry or songs.[14]

In the northwestern section of Lo-yang was the Shang-shang Ward 上商里 (Ward of the Upper Shang),[15] where the Yin refractories,[16] objects of derision, were settled [on the order of the victorious Chou]. Emperor Kao-tsu renamed it Wen-i Ward 聞義里 (Ward of Hearing of the Righteous).

[Against this Yin background], soon after moving the national capital to Lo-yang, court officials residing in the ward were derided one after another,[17] [resulting in] the eventual exodus of them all. The only ones who stayed were the tilers,[18] the producers of earthenware for the capital. Contemporaries made up a song that reads:

[14] The text (5/1b) is *wu-yen* 五言, meaning poems in the style of five characters per line. The term 五言 is, therefore, used here loosely to mean poetry or songs.

[15] The text (5/1b) is Shang kao ching 上高景 (*IS* 5/1b gives Shang-kao li 上高里). According to *HHS* 59/6a, Emperor Kuang-wu gave Pao Yung 鮑永 a residence in the Shang-li 商里 in Lo-yang, a location identified with the Shang-shang Ward in the northeast of the capital city, so named because it was originally a settlement of the Yin (or Shang) people. (Before Emperor P'an-keng 盤庚 [regnant 1525–1506 B.C.] moved the capital to Yin 殷 [west of modern Yen-shih 偃師, Honan]; Yin is also known as Shang.) The *HHS* entry agrees with the *Ch'ieh-lan chi* in both historical background and geographical location of the ward in question. *HHS* 59/6a 鮑永傳:[光武]賜永洛陽商里宅. Comm.: 東觀記曰:賜洛陽上商里宅. 陸機洛陽記曰:上商里在洛陽東北, 本殷頑人所居, 故曰上商里宅也.

[16] For the origin of the term *wan min* 頑民, "refractories," see *Shu-ching* 16/1a 多士序:成周既成, 遷殷頑民. Legge 3, p. 10: "Preface to the Shoo King": "When Ching Chow was completed, the obstinate people of Yin were removed to it." K'ung An-kuo's comm.: 殷大夫士心不則德義之經, 故徙近王都教誨之.

[17] To establish geographical and genealogical relationships between the Lo-yang residents and the Yin people was a favorite satirical practice among intellectuals of the time. See the exchange of such remarks between Ch'eng Yen 成淹 and Wang Su (*WS* 79/3b 成淹傳).

[18] Literally, *tsao wa che* 造瓦者, "those who make tiles"; possibly all makers of earthenware are included.

Compare with Ho Ping-ti's translation, "Lo-yang, A.D. 495–534," p. 88.

In the northwest section of Lo-yang[19] is the Shang-shang Ward,[20]
The scorned refractories of the Yin formerly here resided.[21]
Now the dwellers are makers of earthenware jars,[22]
All others have left, causing shame[23] to those who remain here.

Kuo Wen-yüan 郭文遠, General Cresting the Armies (*Kuan-chün chiang-chün*) was the only [dignitary] who enjoyed[24] living there. His buildings, garden, and woods rivaled those of the feudal lords.[25]

At the time Li Yüan-ch'ien 李元謙[26] of Lung-hsi 隴西[27] took delight in games involving alliteration,[28] and often passed by [Kuo] Wen-yüan's residence. Impressed by the splendor of [Kuo's mansion], he said, "Whose[29] residence[30] is this? Too showy!"[31]
Shìh-shúi tì-ché? Kùo-chīa!

The maidservant Ch'un-feng 春風 (Spring Breeze) stepped out and replied, "Residence of Kuo, General Cresting the Armies."[32]
Kūo Kūan-chūn chīa."

[19] The text (5/1b) reads Lo-yang *ch'eng* 洛陽城 "Lo-yang city," but *IS* 5/1b has only two characters Lo ch'eng 洛城, "Lo [-yang] city." The *IS* version is perhaps better since it limits the line to seven characters to agree with the following three lines. The translation follows *IS*.

[20] Parenthesized phonetics in this and following notes represent those of the Northern Dynasties period. I am grateful to Dr. Ting Pang-hsin for his assistance in providing the phonetics.

Li (ljɛi) 里, which rhymes with *chih* 止, *tzu* 子, and *ch'ih* 耻 in the next three lines.

[21] *Chih* (tśjɛi).

[22] *Tzu* (tsjɛi).

[23] *Ch'ih* (thrjɛi).

[24] Literally, *yu-ch'i ch'i- chung* 遊憩其中, "to live leisurely in it."

[25] Literally *pang chün* 邦君, "rulers of [vassal] kingdoms."

[26] No further information about him is available.

[27] Southeast of modern Lin-t'ao 臨洮, Kansu.

[28] Known as *shuang-sheng* (śɔng-śjɛng) 雙聲 or *t'i-yü* 體語 (*PS* 90/6a–b 藝術徐之才傳), it was a favorite pastime among intellectuals in both Southern and Northern Dynasties.

[29] *Shih-shui* (dźjæi-dźjiɛi) 是誰.

[30] *Ti-che* (diei-drɛk) 第宅.

[31] *Kuo-chia* (kuâ-kæi) 過佳.

[32] *Kuo kuan-chün chia* (Kuak-kuan-kjuen ka) 郭冠軍家.

[Li] Yüan-ch'ien then said: "An ordinary maidservant,[33] [yet] her speech is alliterative!"[34] *Fán-pèi shūang-shēng.*

Ch'un-feng replied, "You rascal.[35] Nonsense!"[36] *Níng-nú màn-mà!*

[Li] Yüan-ch'ien was overwhelmed by the maidservant's talent. As a consequence, the story was passed around in the capital with unanimous applause.

In the Wen-i Ward was Sung Yün's 宋雲[37] residence. [Sung] Yün, a native of Tun-huang 燉煌,[38] went with Hui-sheng 惠生[39] as [Wei] envoys to the Western Regions.[40] In the winter,[41] that is, the eleventh month, of the first year of Shen-kuei period (December A.D. 518 to January A.D. 519),[42] the empress dowager [née Hu] dispatched

[33] *Fan-pei* (bjuam-bjæi) 凡婢.

[34] *Shuang-sheng* (ṣ̂ɔng-śjɛng) 雙聲.

[35] Literally, *ning-nu* (nrɛng-nuo) 儜奴.

Ning is a contraction of *ning-hsing* 寧馨. See Wen T'ing-shih, *Ch'un-ch'ang-tzu chih-yü* (Shanghai?, 1943) 14/32b–33a: 儜即寧馨之合音, 與此字義相對. 又宋以來, 詞曲多稱彼人爲那人, 那字亦寧馨合音, "*Ning* is a contraction of *ning-hsing*; its sound and meaning fit well here. In the *tz'u* and songs written after the Sung [dynasty], *na-jen* is used to mean 'that man'—*na* is also a contraction of *ning-hsing*."

[36] *Man-ma* (man-mâ) 慢罵.

[37] Sung Yün was the chief delegate to go to India in search of Buddhist scriptures. The following pages are based on his account of the pilgrimage.

[38] Created as a commandery in A.D. 526 under the jurisdiction of Kua-chou 瓜州 (modern Tun-huang, Kansu). See *Tung-Chin Nan-pei-ch'ao yü-ti piao*, 3/283.

[39] Hui-sheng accompanied Sung Yün to India. This and the following sentence about Hui-sheng and Sung Yün's trip to the Western Regions are repetitious. *IS* (5/2a) deletes twenty-three characters in the same paragraph and makes it more meaningful.

[40] For a brief account of Sung Yün's travel to Gandhāra and Udyāna, see also Joseph E. Schwartzberg, ed., *A Historical Atlas of South Asia* (Chicago, 1978), p. 183.

[41] The conventional order for keeping a chronological record is (1) year, (2) season, (3) month, and (4) day. In this case, season (winter) comes after month—an unusual order. The *TPYL* quotation (657/2b 釋部經) omits the character "winter" and is therefore more acceptable.

[42] The exact date of their departure and subsequent return to Lo-yang varies greatly from one source to another. The following is a partial listing:

Source	*Date of Departure*	*Date of Return*
WS 102/19b–20a 西域嚈噠傳	between A.D. 516 and A.D. 518	between A.D. 520 and A.D. 525

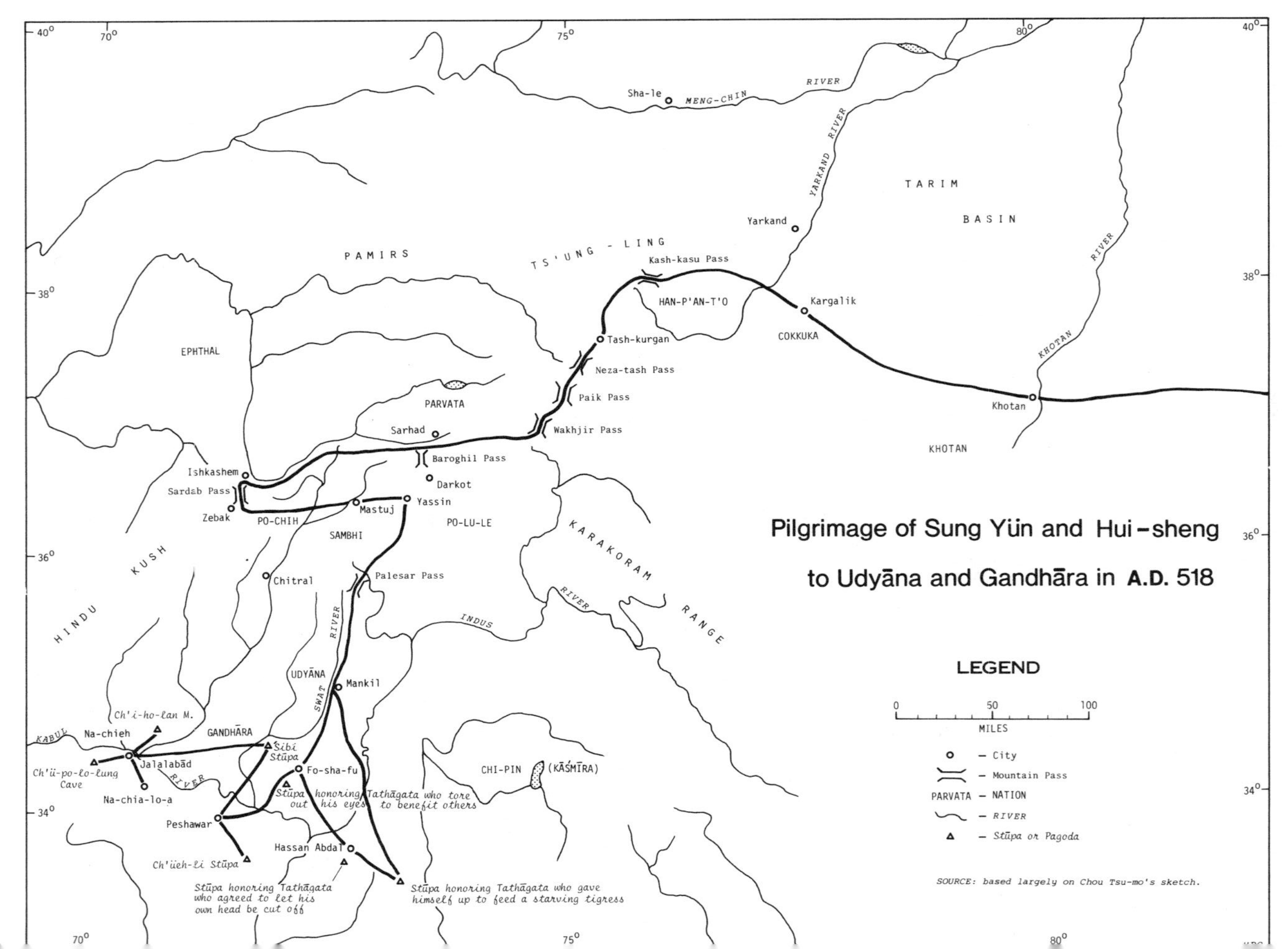

Pilgrimage of Sung Yün and Hui-sheng
to Udyāna and Gandhāra in A.D. 518
LEGEND
0
50
100
MILES
– City
– Mountain Pass
PARVATA – NATION
– RIVER
– Stūpa or Pagoda
SOURCE: based largely on Chou Tsu-mo's sketch.
40°
38°
36°
34°
70°
75°
80°
Sha-le
MENG-CHIN
RIVER
YARKAND RIVER
TARIM
BASIN
Yarkand
PAMIRS
TS'UNG - LING
Kash-kasu Pass
HAN-P'AN-T'O
Kargalik
COKKUKA
Tash-kurgan
Neza-tash Pass
Paik Pass
Wakhjir Pass
KHOTAN RIVER
Khotan
KHOTAN
EPHTHAL
PARVATA
Sarhad
Baroghil Pass
Darkot
Ishkashem
Sardab Pass
Zebak
PO-CHIH
Mastuj
Yassin
PO-LU-LE
SAMBHI
KARAKORAM
RANGE
HINDU
KUSH
Chitral
Palesar Pass
RIVER
INDUS
UDYĀNA
SWAT RIVER
Mankil
Ch'i-ho-lan M.
KABUL
Na-chieh
GANDHĀRA
Sibi Stūpa
Jalalabād
Ch'ü-po-lo-lung Cave
Na-chia-lo-a
RIVER
Fo-sha-fu
Stūpa honoring Tathāgata who tore out his eyes to benefit others
CHI-PIN
(KĀŚMĪRA)
Peshawar
Hassan Abdal
Ch'üeh-li Stūpa
Stūpa honoring Tathāgata who agreed to let his own head be cut off
Stūpa honoring Tathāgata who gave himself up to feed a starving tigress

Hui-sheng of the Ch'ung-ling Temple 崇靈寺 (Temple of Respect for the Efficacious)[43] to go to the Western Regions in search of sūtras. Altogether they acquired one hundred seventy titles, all the best of Mahāyāna classics.

After leaving the capital and traveling westward for forty days, they reached the Ch'ih-ling 赤嶺 (Bare Mountain Range),[44] the western boundary of the state and the location of frontier passes.

The Ch'ih-ling was so named because no vegetation would grow there. On the mountain, birds and mice shared the same caves.

> They belonged to different species but the same zoological family.[45] The male birds and female mice mated together; hence the name "the cave where birds and mice cohabited."

Leaving Ch'ih-ling, and traveling westward for twenty-three

Source	*Date of Departure*	*Date of Return*
PS 97/25a 嚈噠傳	between A.D. 516 and A.D. 518	between A.D. 520 and A.D. 525
WS 114/10a–b 釋老志	A.D. 516	A.D. 522 (winter)
Fo-tsu t'ung-chi 38/355	A.D. 521	A.D. 523
Shih-chia fang-chih B/969	A.D. 518	
Pei-Wei seng Hui-sheng shih Hsi-yü chi (*Taishō* ed.) pp. 866–867	Dec. A.D. 518 or Jan. A.D. 519	A.D. 521

For a French translation of Sung Yün's travels, see Édouard Chavannes, "Voyage de Song Yun dans l'Udyāna et le Gandhāra," *BEFEO* 3 (1903), 279–441. See also Nagasawa Kazutoshi's Japanese translation of the Chinese, entitled *Sōun kōki* in *Tōyō bunko*, vol. 194, first ed. (Tokyo, 1971), pp. 163–216; Uchida Ginpū, "Kōgi Sōun shaku Keisei Seiiki kyūkyōki kōsho josetsu," in *Tsukamoto hakushi shōju kinen Bukkyōshigaku ronsō* (Kyoto, 1961), pp. 113–124.

[43] Emending *Ch'ung-li* 崇立 to *Ch'ung-ling* 崇靈 after *TPYL* 657/2b.

[44] A city by that name close to the river Pu-k'o-yin-ko-erh 布喀音噶爾 (Boukhaingol) bordering on China and the T'u-yü-hun. It lies in modern Ch'ing-hai 青海, (Tsinghai or Kokonor). *Hsin T'ang-shu* (I-wen facsimile ed.) 40/3b–14a 地理志 (under Shan-chou 鄯州) lists a number of cities between Shan-chou 鄯州 and Ch'ih-ling 赤嶺, at an interval of sixty or one hundred *li*. *CC* (5/260) suggests that the *Hsin T'ang-shu* account may have been based on Sung Yün's recorded itinerary.

[45] The story about cohabitation of birds and mice is recorded in many ancient texts, including *Erh-ya* 10/9a 釋鳥 and *HS* 28B/3b–5a 地理志隴西郡, and such accounts seem to have been common in Kansu and Chinese Turkestan. See *I-wen lei-chü* 92/3b quoting *Sha-chou chi* 沙州記 and Hsü Sung, *Hsi-yü shui-tao chi* (Facsimile ed., Taipei, 1966) 5/2a 賽喇木淖爾所受水. The size and color of such birds and mice vary from one source to another, but they belong to "different species of the same family." It is likely that the birds made no nests but lived in the caves of the mice instead.

days, they crossed the Liu-sha 流沙 (Shifting sands)[46] area, and arrived at the kingdom of T'u-yü-hun.[47] While they were en route, it was very cold, windy, and snowy. Blowing sand and flying pebbles filled their eyes. The city of T'u-yü-hun and its vicinity were the only places warmer than elsewhere. The kingdom had a writing system, and costumes[48] similar to those of the Wei. But their customs and political system were of the barbarian type.

Traveling westward for three thousand five hundred *li* from T'u-yü-hun, they arrived at the city of Shan-shan,[49] which had been an independent city-state until the deposal of its king by the T'u-yü-hun. The present king in[50] the city was the second son of the T'u-yü-hun, known as the General Tranquilizing the West (*Ning-hsi chiang-chün*), who had at his command three thousand tribesmen to guard against the Western Barbarians (Hsi-hu 西胡).

Traveling westward from Shan-shan for one thousand six hundred forty *li*, they arrived at the city of Tso-mo,[51] which had a population of about one hundred families. This land was deficient in rainfall, so the people grew wheat by inundating their fields with water. They did not know how to use oxen for cultivation, but they tilled their fields with plows and plowshares.[52] The portraits of Buddha and

[46] Liu-sha, also known as Sha-chou 沙洲, refers to the desert stretching from west of modern An-hsi 安西, Kansu, to T'u-lu-fan (Turfan) 吐魯番, Sinkiang 新疆.

[47] For T'u-yü-hun (in modern Kokonor), see Wada Hironori, "Toyokukon to Nambokuryōchō to no kankei ni tsuite," *Shigaku* 25:2 (1951), 80–103.

[48] Emending *k'uang t'ung Wei* 況同魏 to *i-fu t'ung Wei* 衣服同魏 after *Ch'ung-k'an* 5/39a.

[49] Shan-shan, otherwise known as Lou-lan 樓蘭 during the Western Han, was located to the east of Lopnor. Lou-lan is sometimes translated as Lao-lan 牢蘭 (*Shih-shih Hsi-yü chi* 釋氏西域記, as quoted in *SCC* 2/7a–b). For an exhaustive study of Lou-lan, see Nagasawa Kazutoshi, *Rōran-ōkoku*, in Regulus Library vol. 64 (Tokyo, 1976).

[50] Between *chin ching* 今城, "now the city," and *shih* 是, 'is," *IS* (5/2b) and *CT* (5/3a) have two additional characters *nei chu*, 內主, "within ruler." Hence, the translation.

[51] Tso-mo 左末, which Thomas Watters (*On Yuan Chwang's Travels in India, 629–645 A.D.*, 2 vols., London, 1904–1905, II, 343–344) identifies as modern Charchan, is also transliterated in Chinese as Ch'ieh-mo 且末 (*Pei-Wei seng Hui-sheng shih Hsi-yü chi*, p. 866 and *WS* 102/4a 西域傳), Chü-mo 沮末 (*Ta-T'ang Hsi-yü chi* 12/140), or 沮沫 (*Shih-chia fang-chih* A/951 遺跡篇第四).

[52] The text (5/2a) gives *pu-chih yung niu, lei-ssu erh t'ien* 不知用牛, 耒耜而田 which my translation follows. After the character *t'ien* is a blank, followed by two more characters *Chung-kuo* 中國, making the meaning unclear.

Bodhisattva [exhibited here] did not have an Indian appearance, and when they asked the local elders why, they were told that the portraits had been made at the time[53] of Lü Kuang's [Kuchean] Expedition.[54]

Traveling westward from the city of Tso-mo for one thousand two hundred seventy-five *li*, they reached Mo-ch'eng.[55] The fields and flowers near the city were like those of Lo-yang. The only thing unusual here was that the earthen houses were flat-roofed.[56]

Traveling westward from Mo-ch'eng for twenty-two *li*, they arrived at the city of Han-mo 捍麼.[57] Fifteen *li* to the south of the city was a large monastery that housed some three hundred monks and a gold statue of Buddha. The statue, sixteen Chinese feet high, with imposing appearance and aureole, always faced the east and was never willing to be turned to the west. The elders said: "Orginally, this statue came through the air from the south. The king of Khotan took it home after paying personal homage."

En route, [when the king was at rest], during the night, it suddenly disappeared. [The king] sent someone to search for it, and returned it to the original place. There the king built a stūpa, for which four hundred households were assigned to take care of sprinkling water and sweeping the grounds.[58] If a person suffered pain, and if he put a piece of metal foil on the corresponding spot of the statue, he would, before he knew it, be relieved of the pain.

Men of later times built several thousand Buddhist statues[59] and

[53] Adding *shih* 時, "time," after *Pei-Wei seng Hui-sheng shih Hsi-yü chi*, p. 866.

[54] The expedition took place between A.D. 383 and 385. See Richard B. Mather, tr., *Biography of Lü Kuang* (Berkeley and Los Angeles, 1959), pp. 31–37.

[55] Identified by Ting Ch'ien, *Sung Yün ch'iu-ching-chi ti-li k'ao-cheng*, in *Che-chiang t'u-shu-kuan ts'ung-shu* (Hangchow, 1915) as Mo-kuo 末國. Also see *Liang-shu* 54/34a. It was also the site of Ching-chüeh *kuo* 精絕國 of the Han.

[56] The text (5/3a) is *p'ing-t'ou* 平頭, "flat-headed," the exact meaning of which is not clear, and which is here tentatively translated as "flat-roofed."

[57] *TPYL* (657/4b 釋部[像]) quotes the *Ch'ieh-lan chi* and gives Han-mo 捍麼 (west of modern Yü-tien), which is identified as Han-mi 扞彌, and P'i-mo 媲摩 in the *Ta-T'ang Hsi-yü chi* 12/139–140. See also Sir Mark Aurel Stein, *Ancient Khotan: Detailed Report of Archaeological Explorations in Chinese Turkestan* (Oxford, 1907), I, pp. 455–460.

[58] The assignment of certain numbers of households to render manual services for temples is a Northern Wei institution initiated by T'an-yao 曇曜. See Ch'en, *Buddhism in China*, p. 154 ff.

[59] Literally, "statues sixteen Chinese feet tall"—the symbolic height of Buddha.

stūpas in the neighborhood. Colored canopies and banners hung over them in the tens of thousands—of these more than half originated from the Wei. The *li* 隸 (clerical) script written on the banners was for the most part dated the nineteenth year of T'ai-ho (A.D. 495), the second year of Ching-ming (A.D. 501), and the second year of Yen-ch'ang (A.D. 513).[60] There was only one banner, where an examination of the reign and year showed it to date from the time of Yao-Ch'in.[61]

Traveling westward from the city of Han-mo for eight hundred seventy-eight *li*, they arrived at the kingdom of Yü-tien 于闐 (Khotan).[62] The king wore [on his head] a gold crown shaped like a cock's comb.[63] In the back was suspended a piece of raw silk two Chinese feet in length and five Chinese inches in width for decoration. Among his insignia were a drum, a horn, a metal gong, a set of bow and arrows, two halberds, and five lances. On his left and right he had fewer than one hundred armed attendants.[64] By custom, women wore trousers and waist bands, and galloped on horseback in the same way as the men. They cremated the deceased, and they then collected the bones and where they interred them they built a stūpa. The mourners would cut short their hair and slash[65] their faces in

[60] The importance of these three dates is not clear.

[61] Identified by Chavannes ("Voyage de Song Yun," p. 393 n. 6) as the banner of Fa-hsien 法顯, the first important pilgrim who left China in A.D. 399 for India in search of Buddhist sūtras. See Ch'en, *Buddhism in China*, pp. 89–93.

The text (5/3b) gives Yao-Ch'in 姚秦, but *IS* (5/3b) gives Yao Hsing 姚興 (regnant A.D. 394–416). The translation follows *IS*.

[62] See Chi Pin, tr., "Yü-tien kuo k'ao" ("Utenkokukō") by Hori Kentoku, *Yü-kung* 4 (September 1935), 67–82.

[63] For the *chin-tse* 金幘, "golden crown," see *Liang-shu* 54/33b 于闐國傳.

[64] Literally, *tso yu tai tao* 左右帶刀. "the attendants on both the left and right carried knives."

[65] To slash the face as an expression of sorrow was a Hsiung-nu custom followed by the people of other countries in the Western Regions. See *HHS* 49/12a 耿秉傳: 匈奴聞秉卒, 擧國號哭, 或至梨面流血, "When the Hsiung-nu heard about [Keng] Ping's death, everyone in the country cried out. Some even slashed their faces to cause bleeding." Comm.: 梨即剺字, 古通用也. 剺, 割也, "*Li* 梨 is the same as *li* 剺; they were interchangeable in ancient times. *Li* 剺 means to slash." *Hsin T'ang-shu* 122/27b 郭元振傳: 召爲太僕卿, 將行, 安西酋長有剺面哭送者, "[Kuo Yüan-chen] was summoned [by the court] to be the supervisor [of the Court] of Imperial Stud. By the time of his departure, some chieftains of the An-hsi [area] slashed their face, cried out, and sent him off."

order to express their sorrow. When their [shortened] hair grew back to four Chinese inches long, they stopped mourning. The king was the only one exempt from cremation after death. Instead, [his corpse] would be placed in a coffin, which was interred in the distant countryside. A shrine would be built for sacrifices and he would be commemorated[66] from time to time.

Previously,[67] the king of Yü-tien had not believed in Buddhism. A barbarian[68] merchant brought a monk named P'i-lu-chan 毗盧旃 (Vairocana)[69] to the south of the city and had him wait beneath an apricot tree. He then went to see the king and asked for forgiveness, saying, "Now, without authorization, I have taken in an alien monk, who is now in the south of the city beneath an apricot tree." Upon hearing this, the king was enraged.[70] He immediately set out to see P'i-lu-chan. P'i-lu-chan then spoke to the king: "Tathāgata[71] sent me to come here, and he ordered Your Highness to construct a stūpa[72] with a top shaped like an overturned plate as a way to assure the everlasting prosperity of your reign." The king said: "If you would show me the Buddha, I would then comply with your request." P'i-lu-chan rang a bell and told Buddha [about this], and Buddha instantly ordered Lo-hou-lo 羅睺羅 (Rāhula)[73] to change into the shape of a Buddha, showing his real appearance in the sky. The king, placing his knees, elbows, and head on the ground [to express his utmost respect], immediately had a shrine built underneath the apricot tree and had a portrait of Rāhula painted. Rāhula then suddenly disappeared. The king of Yü-tien again had a hall built to

[66] Chavannes ("Voyage de Song Yun," p. 396 n. 2) suggests *ssu* 思, "think," as a mistake for *ssu* 祀, "sacrifice." But *i shih ssu chih* 以時思之, "at times think of him," is a direct quotation from *Hsiao-ching* 9/3a 喪親章, so Chavannes's suggestion is irrelevant.

[67] Adding *hsi* 昔, "in the past," after *CS* 5/189.

[68] Adding *hu* 胡, "barbarian," after *TPYL* 968/2b 果部杏.

[69] Also known as Mahāvairocana, he is considered by some as the Tathāgata who reveals the far-reaching treasure of his eye, that is, the sun.

[70] Emending *hu nu* 忽怒, "suddenly angry," to *fen-nu* 忿怒, "angry," after *TPYL* 968/2b 果部杏.

[71] *Ju-lai* 如來, that is, Tathāgata. For *Ju-lai* 如來, see *Fan-i ming-i chi* 1/3 十大弟子篇.

[72] Emending *ch'ü* 軀, "body," to *so* 所, "place," after *CS* 5/190.

[73] For Lo-hou-lo 羅睺羅 (Rāhula), one of the ten chief disciples of Śākyamuni, the master of the esoteric.

house the portrait [and display it]. Now the reflection of the plate-shaped [stūpa top] often appeared outside of the house, and all of those who saw it would devotedly worship it. Inside of the house was Pi-chih-fo's 僻支佛 (Pratyeka Buddha) shoe,[74] which has remained intact to this day. It was not made of leather, nor of silk, but of some unknown material.

Author's note: The domain of Yü-tien was only a little more than three thousand *li* from east to west.

On the twenty-ninth day of the seventh month, in the second year of the Shen-kuei period (September 8, A.D. 519), they entered the state of Chu-chü-po 朱駒波 (Cokkuka).[75] Here the people were mountain dwellers who grew the five grains in vast quantities. They ate noodles and other wheat products[76] and refrained from butchery. The [only] meat consumed was taken from animals that had died naturally. The customs and spoken language were similar to those of Yü-tien, while the written language was like that of Brahmins [in India]. Within five days one could travel across the state.

Early in the eighth month (early September), they entered Han-p'an-t'o 漢盤陀 (modern Tashkurghan).[77] Traveling westward for

[74] *SCC* (2/5a–b 河水注) refers to the same object as made of stone, but *YYTT* (10/57) agrees with the *Ch'ieh-lan chi* account.

For P'i-chih *fo* 辟支佛 (Pratyeka Buddha, one who is diligent and zealous in seeking wisdom, loves loneliness and seclusion), see *Fan-i ming-i chi* 1/10 三乘通言篇.

[75] Also transliterated as Chu-chü-po 朱俱波 (*WS* 102/10a 于闐疏勒傳), Chu-chü-p'an 朱俱槃 (*Hsin T'ang-shu* 221A/22b 疏勒傳), Che-chü-chia 遮拘迦 (*SPC* 12/103), and K'an-chü-chia 斫句迦 (*Ta-T'ang Hsi-yü chi* 12/135).

Identified by P. C. Bagchi (*CS* 5/191) as Cokkuka between the Yarkand and Tisnaf Rivers.

[76] Emending *mien mai* 麵麥, "wheat noodles," to *mai fu* 麥麩, "wheat and bran," after *IS* 5/4a.

[77] Also transliterated and written as K'o-p'an-t'o 渴槃陁 (*WS* 102/20a 渴槃陁傳), 渴盤陁 (*Liang-shu* 54/34a 渴盤陁), Ho-p'an-t'o 喝盤陁, Han-t'o 漢陀, K'o-fan-t'an 渴飯檀, or K'o-lo-t'o 渴羅陀 (*Hsin T'ang-shu* 121A/22b 疏勒傳) and Chieh (?)-p'an-t'o 朅盤陀 (*Ta-T'ang Hsi-yü-chi* 12/133). It lay in what is known today as Tashkurghan and in the Sarikol area. See Mizutani Shinjo, ed., *Dai-Tō Seiiki ki* (*in Chūgoku koten bungaku taikei*, Tokyo, 1971), p. 384 n. 1. See also Chang Hsing-lang, *Chung-hsi chiao-t'ung shih-liao hui-pien*, 6 vols. (Peiping, 1930), 6, 313; and Feng Ch'eng-chün, tr., *Hsi T'u-chüeh shih-liao* (a translation of *Documents sur les T'ou-Kiue occidentaux* by Édouard Chavannes, St. Petersburg, 1903; Shanghai, 1934), pp. 93–94.

For K'o-p'an-t'o and other neighboring countries that Sung Yün visited, see

six days, they ascended the Ts'ung-ling Range.[78] Traveling westward again for three days, they arrived at the city of Po-yü 鉢盂.[79] Traveling three more days they reached the Pu-k'o-i Mountain 不可依山 ("Unreliable" Mountain), where it was very cold. The mountain was snow-clad in winter and summer alike.

In the mountain was a pond wherein an evil dragon lived. A group of three hundred[80] merchants once stopped on the bank of the pond and stayed there, when the dragon, in a fit of anger, inundated[81] [the land around the pond] and drowned the merchants. Upon hearing of this, the king of [Han-]p'an-t'o abdicated in favor of his son, and went to the state of Wu-ch'ang[82] to study the spells of Brahmins. Within four years he had learned all the arts. Upon his return, he resumed his position as king, and went to the pond to exorcise the dragon. The dragon changed itself into a man, and repented before the king. The king then moved it to the Ts'ung-ling Range, which was more than two thousand *li* from this pond. The present king was the thirteenth-generation descendant [of the monarch under discussion].

Westward from this point, the mountain path was steep and sloping. [There were] banks one thousand *li* long, and a precipice rising eighty thousand Chinese feet above the ground. Here indeed were great obstacles [to be faced by] travelers. By comparison, the T'ai-hang[83] and Meng-men 孟門[84] ranges were really not im-

---

Matsuda Hisao, *Kodai rekishichirigaku-teki kenkyū* (revised ed., Tokyo, 1974), "Gisho Seiikiden no gimmi" 魏書西域傳の吟味.

[78] That is, the Pamirs.

[79] *IS* (5/4a) gives Po-meng 鉢猛. No identification is available.

[80] *San-pai* 三百, "three hundred," is added after a quotation of the *Ch'ieh-lan chi* in *TPKC* 418/6a 龍類宋雲, but the *TPYL* (930/3a 鱗介部龍) quotation of the same source reads *wu-pai* 五百, "five hundred."

[81] Emending *chou* 呪, "curse," which agrees with *IS* (5/4a) and *CT* (5/6a), to *fan* 汎, "overflowing," that is, to drown them by inundation, after the *TPYL* and *TPKC* quotations referred to in note 80.

[82] *IS* (4/4a) reads Wu-ch'ang 烏萇, which is the state of Udyāna. For Wu-ch'ang 烏萇, see below at note 113.

[83] For the T'ai-hang, see Chapter 2 at note 247 under the P'ing-teng Monastery and note 128 in Chapter 3.

[84] The Meng-men range is located to the east of the T'ai-hang near Hui-hsien 輝縣, Honan. Both T'ai-hang and Meng-men are referred to in the *SC* (65/15 吳起傳) as strategic points.

passable, and the Yao Pass 崤關[85] and Lung-pan 隴坂[86] were simply flatlands. After setting out from the Ts'ung-ling Range, [they found] the altitude increasing with every step, and it took four days before they were able to reach the summit. Once there it looked like low land,[87] but actually it was already halfway to heaven.

Here at the top of the mountain was the country of Han-p'an-t'o.

From the west of Ts'ung-ling Range, all waterways flowed westward into the West Sea (Hsi-hai 西海).[88] The local people considered themselves to be living halfway between heaven and earth. They grew crops by flooding their fields with water [from a dam]. When they heard that in China [farmers] waited for rainfall for farming, they laughed: "How can Heaven's time be counted on?" To the east of the city was the Meng-chin River 孟津河,[89] which flowed northwest toward Sha-le 沙勒.[90]

In the high steep parts of the Ts'ung-ling Range there was no vegetation. It was the eighth month (September) [when they were there], and it was already cold. The north wind forced the wild geese [to fly southward], and snow scudded over one thousand *li*.

In the middle of the ninth month (late October), they entered the state of Po-ho 鉢和 (Parvata, in modern Wakhan) which was located in a deep valley of high mountains where hazardous paths were the rule. The city where the king resided was sheltered by the mountains. For the people's clothing and ornaments, there was nothing but felt. The ground was very cold, so people lived in caves. Wind and snow were both violent and biting, so human beings and animals relied on

[85] Same as Yao-shan 崤山, which is the east end of the Han-ku Pass 函谷關, Shensi.

[86] Northwest of Lung-hsien 隴縣, Shensi, a strategic point in the western section of the Han-chung 漢中 area.

[87] The text (5/5b) is *i yüeh chung hsia* 依約中下, the exact meaning of which is unclear.

[88] Adding three characters *ju Hsi-hai* 入西海, "into the West Sea," after *IS* 5/4b and *CT* 5/6b. The phrase is perhaps derived from *HS* 96A/17a 西域傳:于闐之西, 水皆西流, 注西海, "West of Yu-tien, all waterways flow westward into the West Sea."

[89] Identified as the Fu-hsi-to River 負徙多河 (the Sita), by Chang Hsing-lang, *Chung-hsi chiao-t'ung* 6 古代中國與印度之交通, p. 213 n. 15; and Li Kuang-t'ing, *Han Hsi-yü t'u-k'ao* (1870 ed.) 1/13a, in a note quoting the *T'ang-shu*.

[90] Same as Shu-le 疏勒, modern K'o-shih ko-erh 喀什噶爾 (Kachgar). See Feng Ch'eng-chün, *Hsi T'u-chüeh* p. 92 and Chang Hsing-lang, *Chung-hsi chiao-t'ung* 6, 313 n. 16.

each other [for survival]. In the borderland to the south of this state was a large snowy mountain, where the snow melted in the morning but froze again in the evening. It looked like a jade cliff.[91]

In the early part of the tenth month (mid-November), they reached the state of Yen-ta 嚈噠 (Russian Turkestan, Ephthal or Hephthalitai),[92] a rich land where endless mountains and rivers came into view. There were no walled cities for residences; [the area] was kept in good order by a patrolling army. The people lived in felt [tents], moving from one place to another in pursuit of water and pasture lands: they moved to cooler areas in summer and warm regions in winter. The natives were simple rustic folk,[93] unversed in writing, the rites, or moral precepts. They did not know how *yin* and *yang*[94] alternate. [They did not know about] a common and a leap year, an intercalary month, or a month of thirty or twenty-nine days.[95] But they used twelve months to make up a year.

The state received tribute from a number of countries: from Tieh-lo 牒羅[96] in the south to as far as Ch'ih-le 勅懃[97] in the north, from Yü-tien in the east to Po-ssu 波斯[98] in the west. Altogether [delegates from] more than forty countries came to pay tribute and offer congratulations [on appropriate occasions].[99]

The king lived in a large felt tent that was forty paces (*pu*) square and lined with [hanging] carpets on all sides. He wore a garment of

[91] A comparable account of this state is also available in *WS* (102/20a) 鉢和國. It reads in part: 其土尤寒, 人畜同居, 穴地而處, 又有大雪山, 望若銀峯, "It was particularly cold. People and animals lived together in caves. There was a great snowy mountain, which resembled a silver cliff."

[92] Emending Ho-ta 嗽噠 to Yen-ta 嚈噠 after *WS* (102/19a 嚈噠傳 *IS* 5/5a reads 㖤噠). The people of Yen-ta were a branch of the Ta-yüeh-chih, the Indo-Scythians who resided in Central Asia.

[93] Literally, *hsiang-t'u pu-shih wen-tzu* 鄉土不識文字. Here *hsiang-t'u* 鄉土 is translated freely.

[94] For *yin* and *yang*, see Chapter 2 note 175.

[95] The text (5/6a) is *yüeh wu ta-hsiao* 月無大小, "[They knew not] the difference between a plus and a common month." It perhaps refers to the lunar system.

[96] Identified as modern Tirhut by Chang Hsing-lang, *Chung-hsi chiao-t'ung* 6, 313 n. 20.

[97] That is, modern Tölöo or Teulès. See Feng Ch'eng-chün, *Hsi T'u-chüeh* p. 157 n. 3.

[98] That is, Persia, modern Iran.

[99] Literally, *ch'ao-ho* 朝賀, "To pay tribute at court and offer congratulations [as occasions demanded]."

brocade and sat in a golden chair supported by four phoenixes as legs. When he received envoys from the Great Wei, he bowed twice and knelt down to receive the rescript. At audiences, one man would call out, then step forward, in response to the shouting of an announcer. At a later call, they would withdraw when the latter shouted again. This is the only way that audiences were held. Music was never present at the scene.

The queen of Yen-ta also wore a brocade garment, the train of which, three Chinese feet long, was lifted by an attendant. She also wore a cornered[100] [turban] eight Chinese feet in length and three Chinese feet on the diagonal.[101] It was adorned with pearls[102] in rose and five other colors on top. When the queen went out, she was seated in a golden, bejeweled sedan, carried on the back of a "six-tusked" white elephant.[103] Wives of ranking officials would accompany her under umbrellas. On their heads, each seemed to wear a cornered turban[104] that was round and trailing. [Such head pieces] presented the appearance of a gem-decorated canopy of precious materials.

There were differences, it was observed, between the noblemen and commoners. Of all the four barbarians,[105] they were by far

[100] Literally, *i-chiao* 一角, "a cornered or horned [turban]." These three sentences are misplaced under "three Chinese feet long." The translation follows the sentence order as suggested in *CS* 5/196 and *CC* 5/288.

[101] The text (5/6b) gives *ch'i* or *chi* 奇, which has the same meaning as *hsieh* 衺 (old script for modern 斜, meaning "diagonal"). See *CC* 5/295, note 7.

[102] Adding the character *chu* 珠, "pearls," after *CS* 5/196–197.

[103] The text (5/7a) reads *ju tso chin-ch'uang, i liu-ya pai-hsiang ssu shih-tzu wei ch'uang* 入坐金牀, 以六牙白象四獅子爲牀. According to *CS* (5/197), *shih-tzu ch'uang* 師子牀 (sinihāsana) is a bejeweled sedan chair placed on the back of an elephant. The text uses the character *ch'uang* 牀 twice in as many sentences and thus sounds repetitious.

For the "six-tusked white elephant," see Chapter 1 at note 169 under the Ch'ang-ch'iu Temple.

[104] The text (5/7a) gives *yu chiao* 有角, "to have a cornered [turban]." According to *WS* (102/19a), it was customary among the Yen-ta women to knot the corners of their turbans to indicate how many hushands they had. Hsüan-tsang 玄奘 (*Ta-T'ang Hsi-yü chi* 12/131 呬摩呾羅國) claimed that this custom originated among the Turks.

[105] The text (5/7a) is *ssu-i* 四夷, "four barbarians," normally meaning the four barbarians bordering on China's east, west, north, and south. Here the term seems to refer to the state of Yen-ta as more powerful than the four others in the same area: the Tieh-lo, Ch'ih-le, Po-ssu and Yü-tien.

the strongest and largest. They did not worship Buddha but for the most part believed in non-native gods instead.[106] They slaughtered animals, ate the meat, and used the "seven treasures"[107] [to adorn] their utensils. There were many valuables and rarities among the tribute offered to them by various other states.

The state of Yen-ta was more than twenty thousand *li* away from the capital city (that is, Lo-yang).

Early in the eleventh month (early to mid-December), they arrived at the state of Po-chih 波知 (modern Zebak).[108] A very small territory, they tranversed it in seven days. The people were mountain dwellers and maintained a meager livelihood. Their customs were violent and discourteous; they showed no respect for the king, and when the king traveled he had few escorts.

This state had a river that was very shallow in former years. Later the current was cut off by a mountain slide, splitting the stream into two ponds.[109] Poisonous dragons occupied them. Many were the calamities and misfortunes. [The dragons] delighted in rainstorms in summer and deep piles of snow in winter. Travelers passing by often met with difficulties on account of this. The snow produced white rays that dazzled men, forcing them to close their eyes. Consequently they could not see a thing. They could have a safe passage only if they offered sacrifices to the Dragon-king.[110]

In the middle of the eleventh month (mid- to late December), they entered the state of She-mi 賒彌國 (Sambhi), which was located at a short remove from the Ts'ung-ling Range. The land was barren, and the people by and large poor and distressed. The path was steep and dangerous, barely passable for a single person or a horse. A straight

[106] Possibly Zoroastrianism.

[107] The definition of the seven treasures varies from one source to another. Generally, the terms refer to such valuables as gold, silver, lapis lazuli, crystal, agate (or coral), rubies, and amber. See Chiang-liang-yeh-she, tr., *Fo-shuo Kuan-wu-liang-shou fo ching* (*Taishō* ed.), p. 342.

[108] The text (5/7a) gives Po-ssu 波斯, *ssu* 斯 being an error for *chih* 知. See Fujita Toyohachi, *Hui-ch'ao wang Wu-t'ien-chu chuan chien-shih* (Peiping, 1931), pp. 83b–84a.

[109] *WS* (102/20b 波知國) gives three, rather than two, ponds, occupied by the dragon, its wife, and its son.

[110] The text (5/7b) is 祭祀龍王, 然後平復. The term *p'ing-fu* 平復, "restoration to normalcy," seems to refer to the lost vision. The translation is based on *WS* 102/20b, which reads: 行人經之, 設祭乃得過; 不祭, 多遇風雨.

road connected the state of Po-lu-le 鉢盧勒 (Bolora)[111] and the state of Wu-ch'ang, where an iron-chain bridge served as a suspended passageway. Beneath was bottomless space; on the sides, there was nothing to hold on to, and in an instant, one might fall eighty thousand Chinese feet [to one's death]. As a result, travelers refused to go by this route when they heard about it.[112]

In the early twelfth month (January to February A.D. 520), they entered the state of Wu-ch'ang,[113] which bordered on the Ts'ung-ling Range to the north and India to the south. The climate was mild. The territory covered several thousand square *li*. Products were as abundant as in Lin-tzu[114] of the Holy Continent 神州 (China), and the beautiful fields[115] were equal to the best land of Hsien-yang 咸陽.[116] [It was] the site where Pi-lo 轉羅 (Viśvanatara) gave up his children,[117] and the place where Mahāsattva offered his own blood to feed [a hungry tigress].[118] Although former traditions had faded, local customs were still observed. The industrious king, a vegetarian

[111] Same as Po-lu-lo 鉢露羅 (Bolora) in the *Ta-T'ang Hsi-yü chi* 3/31. Also see *WS* 102/20b under She-mi *kuo* 賒彌國, and *Hsin T'ang-shu* 221B/8b under Hsiao Po-lü 小勃律.

[112] Literally, 是以行者望風謝路耳, "As a result, travelers would gaze at the wind and decline to take [this] route." *WS* 102/20b (She-mi *kuo*) states explicitly that Sung Yün was unable to reach this state because of the hazards involved.

[113] Also written as Wu-ch'ang 烏萇 (*WS* 102/20b), Wu-ch'ang 烏長 (*Kao-seng Fa-hsien chuan*, p. 858 and *SCC* 1/5b 河水注), Wu-ch'a 烏荼 (*K'ai-yüan shih-chiao lu* 6/543 and *Fan-i ming-i chi* 3/1098), and Wu-chang-na 烏仗那 (*Ta-T'ang Hsi-yü chi*) 3/28.

For a detailed study of Wu-ch'ang (on the bank of modern Swat or Svat River), see Mizutani, *Dai-Tō Seiiki ki*, pp. 99–100 nn. 1 to 7; and A. Cunningham, *The Ancient Geography of India*, I, *The Buddhist Period* (London, 1871), pp. 69–70.

[114] Lin-tzu was a major metropolis in the ancient state of Ch'i. See Chapter 2 note 134.

[115] A reference to *Shih-ching* 16.2/16a (ode 237, verse 3, line 1) 大雅緜：周原膴膴. Waley, *Book of Songs*, p. 248: "The plain of Chou was very fertile."

[116] The capital city of the ancient state of Ch'in near modern Sian, Shensi.

[117] Pi-lo is also known as Hsü-ta-na 須大拏 (Sudāna) who, against the will of his wife, gave up a son and a daughter to serve as slaves of a Brahmin. Buddha was a reincarnation of this prince. See Sheng-chien, tr., *T'ai-tzu Hsü-ta-na ching* (*Taishō* ed.), p. 422; and *Ta-T'ang Hsi-yü chi* 2/25 under Chien-t'o-lo *kuo* 健馱羅國.

[118] A reference to Mahāsattva, the youngest son of King Mahāratha, who fed a tigress and its newly born cubs with his own blood. Mahāsattva was an incarnation of the future Tathāgata. See Fa-sheng, tr., *P'u-sa t'ou-sheng ssu-o-hu ch'i-t'a yin-yüan ching* (*Taishō* ed.), pp. 426–427.

of long standing, worshiped Buddha from morning to night, beating drums and blowing conch-trumpets. *P'i-p'a*, harps, pan-pipes, and *hsiao* 簫 flutes—he had them all. He attended to state affairs only after midday. If [a criminal] deserved the death penalty, he would not be subject to instant execution. Instead, he would be transferred to a deserted mountain area where he was free to drink and eat,[119] but nature was allowed to determine his fate. [A person] suspected of a crime would be asked to take some medicine that would prove whether he was innocent or guilty.[120] If found to be guilty, he would be summarily dealt with according to the seriousness [of the crime he had committed]. The land was fertile and large in population, including all types of grains and five varieties of fruits.[121] At night one could hear the tolling bells here and everywhere in the domain.[122] The land abounded in rare flowers, which bloomed in succession in all seasons.[123] Buddhist monks as well as laymen plucked the flowers and offered them to the Buddha.

When the king received Sung Yün, the latter said, "I came here as an envoy of the Great Wei."[124] The king then bowed, placing [one] hand on his own head[125] and receiving the rescript [brought by Sung Yün] with the other. Learning that the Empress Dowager [Hu] upheld Buddhist teachings, the king instantly faced eastward, held his palms together, and paid the greatest respect from this remote [land]. He sent a man who understood the Wei language[126] to ask Sung

[119] Literally, *jen ch'i yin cho* 任其飲啄, "Let him drink and peck."

[120] The text (5/8a) is *ch'ing cho tse yen* 清濁則驗, "Innocent (clear) or guilty (dirty) is verified."

[121] The text (5/8a) is *pai-ku* 百穀, "hundred crops," and *wu-kuo* 五果, "five fruits." According to the *Fan-i ming-i chi* (3/88 五果篇), the "five fruits" refer to (1) stone fruits (such as dates and apricots), (2) soft-skinned fruits (such as pears), (3) shell fruits (such as coconuts and walnuts), (4) cone-fruits *kuei-kuo* 檜果 (such as pine seeds), and (5) five-cornered fruits *wu-chiao kuo* 五角果 (such as beans).

[122] Literally, 夜聞鐘聲, 遍滿世界, "At night one could hear bells [reverberating] everywhere in the world."

[123] Literally, *tung hsia hsiang chieh* 冬夏相接, "Winter followed summer in the production of such flowers."

[124] Emending 國王見宋雲云:大魏使來 to 國王見大魏使宋雲來 after *IS* 516a.

[125] A custom prevailing in this area to show the utmost respect. *Mu-t'ien-tzu chuan* 穆天子傳 (*SPTK so-pen*) 2/6: 吾乃膜拜而受. Kuo P'u's 郭璞 (A.D. 276–324) comm.: 今之胡人禮佛, 擧手加頭, 稱南膜拜者, 即此類也.

[126] The nineteen characters between "learning" (Chinese *wen* 聞) and "Wei languages" (Chinese *Wei-yü* 魏語) are not found in *IS* 5/6a.

Yün, "Are you not the one who has come from the place where the sun rises?"[127]

In reply Sung Yün said, "In the east, my country borders on a vast expanse of sea, where the sun rises. What you have said is indeed ture."

The king again asked, "Does that country produce sages?"

Sung Yün told him all about the virtues of the Duke of Chou, Confucius, Chuang[-tzu], and Lao[-tzu], then about the Silver Watchtower and Golden Hall of the P'eng-lai Mountains[128] where immortals and sages lived. He also talked about the divination skill of Kuan Lu 管輅,[129] medical technique of Hua T'o 華陀,[130] and the magical power of Tso Tz'u 左慈[131]—he told him about each such thing item by item.

The king then said, "If what you said is true, then your country is a Buddha Land. After death I would like to be reincarnated in that country."

Thereafter Sung Yün and Hui-sheng went out of the city to look for the sites where Tathāgata had preached. On the east of the river was a place where Buddha dried his garments. Previously, when Tathāgata came to Wu-ch'ang to convert [the populace],[132] the dragon-king was so infuriated as to cause a violent rainstorm drenching the inside and outside of Buddha's saṅghāṭī (*seng-chia-li* 僧迦梨).[133] When the rain stopped, the Buddha was at the foot of a

[127] This sentence ends with the particle *yeh* 也, which is an equivalent of *yeh* 耶, the latter signifying a question. See Wang Yin-chih, *Ching-chuan shih-tz'u* (Peking, 1956; a facsimile of 1868 ed.) 24/98–100.

[128] One of the three fabulous islands in the eastern sea where immortals lived. The other two islands were Fang-chang 方丈 and Ying-chou 瀛州. See *HS* 25A/12b 郊祀志; also see Chapter 1 at note 287 under the Ching-lin Monastery.

[129] Kuan Lu (A.D. 208–256) was a famous diviner of Wei during the Three Kingdoms period. See *Wei-chih* 29/19a–43b.

[130] A famous physician of Wei during the Three Kingdoms period, who was killed on the order of Ts'ao Ts'ao (A.D. 155–220). See *HHS* 112B/5b–8a.

[131] A well-known magician of the Later Han (A.D. 25–220) and a contemporary of Ts'ao Ts'ao (A.D. 155–220). See *HHS* 112B/12b–13b.

[132] For more information about Tathāgata's attempt at converting the populace, see *Ta-T'ang Hsi-yü chi* 3/28, *Fo-shuo p'u-sa pen-hsing ching* B/116; Chia-pa-t'o-lo, tr., *Shan-chien lü-p'i-p'o-sha* (*Taishō* ed.) 2/685; and An Fa-ch'in, tr., *A-yü-wang chuan* (*Taishō* ed.) 4/116 摩田提因緣.

[133] Also transliterated as *seng-chia-ti* (saṃghāṭi) 僧伽胝 (*CC* 5/310), a patch-garment of a monk reaching from shoulders to the knee and fastened around the waist. See Takakusu Junjirō, tr., *Nankai kiki naihō den* (Kyoto, 1913), p. 54.

boulder facing east and drying his kāṣāya (*chia-sha*).[134] After the passage of so many years, the marks were as sharp as new. Not only were the seams clearly visible, but also all the fine details were as if new. If one should go there for a quick look, he might not be able to get a clear view, but if he should scrape the spot, the patterns would become all the more vivid.[135] There were stūpas at the sites where the Buddha had sat and where he dried his garments.

To the west of the river was a pond in which a dragon-king lived. On the shore of the pond was a monastery that housed more than fifty monks. Whenever the dragon-king worked his charms, the king would offer prayers and throw gold, jade, and other valuables into the pond. And, when the latter [articles] were washed ashore, he would order the monks to collect them. The monks of the monastery relied on[136] the dragon for a living. Contemporaries called the place the Dragon-king Monastery.

Eighty *li* to the north of the capital city were the footprints where Tathāgata had stepped on a stone, over which a stūpa was subsequently built to shelter it. The spot looked like a piece of muddy ground on which someone had stamped. It had no fixed boundaries—sometimes it was long; at other times, short. Now a monastery was built there, housing seventy or more monks.

Twenty paces to the south of the stūpa were a spring and a rock. Buddha, whose nature was pure, once chewed a willow branch.[137] After it was stuck in the ground, it grew. By this time it has grown into a huge tree, called by the Indians *p'o-lou* 婆樓.[138]

To the north of the city was the T'o-lo Monastery 陀羅寺, which had the largest number of Buddhist relics. The stūpa was high and large, and the monks' cells were crowded off to the side. It had six thousand[139] golden statues arranged in a circle. The king's annual assemblies[140] all were held here, and every one of the monks of the

[134] For *chia sha* 袈裟, see *Fan-i ming-i chi* 7/212–213.

[135] For more information about this stone, see *Ta-T'ang Hsi-yü chi* 3/28.

[136] The text (5/9a) reads *tai* 待, "awaits," but *TPYL* 930/3a 鱗介部龍 is *shih* 恃, "to rely upon." The translation follows the latter.

[137] Also known as *ch'ih-mu* 齒木, the willow branch that was used by Indians to cleanse the teeth. See Takakusu, *Nankai kiki naihō den*, p. 55.

[138] Identity unknown.

[139] *IS* (5/7b) reads *liu shih* 六十, "sixty."

[140] This perhaps refers to the quinquennial assembly touched upon in the *Ta-T'ang Hsi-yü chi* 1/5 under Ch'ü-chih *kuo* 屈支國.

nation came, gathering like clouds. Seeing the monks' strict observance of rigorous discipline, and watching such models of morality, Sung Yün and Hui-sheng held them in special respect. As a consequence, [the visiting monks] bought and emancipated two slaves—one male and one female—to provide such services as water-sprinkling and ground-sweeping for the monastery.

Traveling through the mountains southeastward from the capital city for eight days, they arrived[141] at the place where Tathāgata, in his ascetism, gave himself up to feed[142] a starving tigress. The high mountains presented a majestic appearance, and perilous cliffs soared into the clouds. Auspicious trees and sacred fungi grew on top [of the cliffs] in clumps. The forest and fountains were beautiful, and colors of the flowers dazzled one's eyes. Sung Yün and Hui-sheng contributed some of their traveling money to build a stūpa at the summit, including a stone monument with an inscription in the *li* (clerical) style to record the achievements of the Wei. On the mountain there was a Shou-ku Monastery 收骨寺 (Monastery of Collected Bones), which housed more than three hundred monks.

More than one hundred *li* to the south of the capital city was the place where Tathāgata, while in the state of Mo-hsiu 摩休,[143] cut off his skin to be used as paper,[144] and broke off a bone to be used as a pen. The spot was sheltered by a stūpa built by Aśoka. The structure was one hundred Chinese feet high. At the place where [Tathāgata] broke off a bone, the marrow flowed onto a stone and was visible there. Upon examination, [one found its] viscosity and color as rich and glossy as if it were fresh.

Five hundred *li* to the southwest of the capital city was the

[141] Adding the character *chih* 至, "arrive," after *CS* 5/203.

[142] Adding the character *ssu* 飼 (or *i* 飴) according to the title of a famous sūtra devoted to this subject. The title is *P'u-sa t'ou-sheng ssu-o-hu ch'i-t'a yin-yüan ching* (p. 424), as noted earlier. It deals with the youngest son of Mahāratha, Prince Mahāsattva, who let out his blood to feed a tigress and its newly born cubs, which were unable to find food for themselves. See *P'u-sa t'ou-sheng ssu-o-hu ch'i-t'a yin-yüan ching* p. 426; Shao-te and Hui-hsun, trs., *P'u-sa pen-sheng man lun* (*Taishō* ed.) 1/332–333 投身飼虎緣起第一; *Hsien-yü ching* 賢愚經 1/352 摩訶薩埵以身施虎品第二; and K'ang Seng-hui, *Liu-tu chi-ching* (*Taishō* ed.) 1/2 布施度無極章第一.

[143] Mo-hsiu is perhaps identifiable with Mo-yü 摩愉 (Masura) as recorded in *Ta-T'ang Hsi-yü chi* 3/29. See *CC* 5/314.

[144] For the sake of recording the holy law (*chieh* 偈, gāthā), the Buddha as Brahmā-Sahaṁpati (the father of all living things) cut off a piece of his own skin to be used as paper. See *Fo-shuo p'u-sa pen-hsing ching* C/119.

Mountain Shan-ch'ih 善持山,[145] whose sweet springs and delicious fruits are referred to in the sūtras. It was warm and mild in the valley, where grasses and trees were green [even] in winter. This was the first month of spring,[146] and warm breezes had already begun to blow. Birds chirped in spring trees; butterflies danced in clusters of flowers. Far away in an isolated land, and seeing such beautiful scenes, Sung Yün felt homesick from the bottom of his heart. As a result, he succumbed once again to an old illness that forced him to lie in bed for more than one month. He recovered only as the result of a Brahmin's incantation.

In the southeastern section of the summit was Prince [Sudāna's] stone chamber. It consisted of one door, which led to two rooms. Ten paces in front of the prince's chamber was a large square stone on which the prince was said to sit often. Aśoka built a stūpa on the site to commemorate this event.

One *li* south of the stūpa was the thatched cottage of the prince.

One *li* from the stūpa and fifty paces to the northeast of the mountain was the spot where the prince's two children ran around the tree refusing to be taken away, and were whipped by the Brahmin until their blood flowed, staining the earth. The tree was still there.[147] The place where they bled was now changed into a spring.

Three *li* to the west of the chamber was the site where the lion, which was the incarnation of Śakra (T'ien-ti shih-chia 天帝釋迦),[148] crouched to prevent Madrī (Man-ch'ü 嫚胠) [from reaching her

[145] Same as T'an-t'e-shan 檀特山 (*WS* 102/21a 烏萇國) and Tan-to-lo-chia-shan 彈多落迦山 (Dantaloka). See *Ta-T'ang Hsi-yü chi* 2/25 under Chien-t'o-lo *kuo* 健馱羅國.

[146] Literally, *t'ai-ts'u yü-ch'en* 太簇御辰, "[when] the third semi-tone in a standard ancient pitch pipe is in season," that is, the third month or early spring. For *t'ai-ts'u* 太簇, see *Li-chi* 14/9a–b 月令孟春之月.

[147] According to the *T'ai-tzu Hsü-ta-na ching* (p.422), Prince Sudāna was forced out of his home for twelve years. There he met with and studied under the saint A-chou-t'o 阿周陀 (also known as Acyuta, see note 150 below), staying in a thatched cottage built by himself. A Brahmin requested that both his children—a son and a daughter—be given away as slaves. Although the prince complied with the request, the children and his wife Princess Madri refused to leave him. As a result, both children were beaten to the point of bleeding by the demanding Brahmin. Meanwhile, Śakra transformed himself into a lion to prevent Princess Madri's further interference.

[148] According to Indian mythology, Śakra is one of the ancient gods who fights the demons with his thunderbolt. Buddhism adopted him as its defender, though he is considered inferior to a Buddha or any who have attained bodhi.

children].[149] Marks of the hair, tail, and claws [of the lion] were all distinctly visible on the rock. The cave of A-chou-t'o (Acyuta)[150] and the place where Shan-tzu 閃子[151] waited upon his blind parents were both commemorated by the erection of a stūpa.

In the mountain there were seats of the five hundred Arhans of olden days. They were arranged north to south in two rows, with the seats facing one another [so that] the seats were opposite one another in the same numerical sequence, exactly facing the ones in the correct order. There was a large monastery that housed two hundred monks.

At a point to its north where the prince drank from the spring was another monastery. Several donkeys customarily carried provisions to the mountain top. Without drivers, the donkeys would come back and forth all by themselves. They left for the monastery at 3 to 5 A.M. and returned at noontime,[152] often in time for the monks' lunch. This, then, [was due to] Śiva (Shih-p'o-hsien 濕婆僊), the stūpa-guardian.

In the monastery there had been a śramaṇa 沙門 (novice) who, while smearing himself with ashes,[153] became so absorbed that he reached the stage of complete rest. When seized by the karmadāna (*wei-na* 維那)[154] he was found, surprisingly enough, to have passed away.[155] As a result, Śiva smeared ashes in his place. At the site, the king built a shrine for Śiva, along with a gilt image of his likeness.

Across the summit was the P'o-chien Monastery 婆姧寺 built by

[149] See note 147.

[150] Transliteration is as given by Chavannes, "Voyage de Song Yun," p. 414.

[151] The text (5/10b–11a) reads *men-tzu* 門子, *men* 門 being a mistake for *shan* 閃 (same as 睒, see *CS* 5/207). Chavannes ("Voyage de Song Yun," p. 414) mistranslated 門子 as "the disciples." According to Sheng-chien, tr., *Fo-shuo shan-tzu ching* (*Taishō* ed.), pp. 438–440, at the age of ten Shan-tzu lived with and waited upon his blind parents in the mountain. One day he was critically wounded by the king, who shot him by mistake while hunting. Learning of the boy's utmost devotion to his parents, Śakra appeared and saved his life.

[152] The same story about the donkeys is available in *WS* 102/21a 烏萇國. See also *Yu-yang tsa-tsu hsü-chi* (*SPTK so-pen*) 8/159.

[153] Emending *ch'u-hui* 除灰, "remove ashes," to *t'u-hui* 塗灰, "smear with ashes," after *CS* 5/209. Pāṁśupatas, followers of Śiva, smeared themselves with ashes as a way of spiritual discipline.

[154] Superintendents of works in a monastery.

[155] Literally, *p'i lien ku li* 皮連骨離, "the skin was attached but the bones had gone."

Yeh-ch'a 夜叉 (Yakṣa).[156] It had eighty monks. According to them, Arhans and Yakṣas often came here to worship, sprinkle water, sweep the grounds, and fetch fuel. They would not permit the ordinary monks to stay within the monastery. When the monk Tao-jung 道榮[157] of the Great Wei reached here, he came to worship and then left—he dared not stay.

In the middle of the fourth month in the first year of the Cheng-kuang period (mid-May A.D. 520), they entered the state of Ch'ien-t'o-lo (Gandhāra, in the north of modern Punjab), where the land was similar to that of Wu-ch'ang. Originally known as the state of Yeh-po-lo 業波羅國 (Gopāla), it was conquered by [the ruler of] Yen-ta who installed Ch'ih-ch'in 勅懃[158] as the king. Now two generations of this family had reigned. The present king[159] was violent, cruel, and frequently carried out killings. He did not believe in Buddhism but indulged himself in worshiping ghosts and spirits. All the inhabitants were Brahmins who respected Buddhist teaching and enjoyed reading sūtras. It was deeply against their will to suddenly have [this man as] such a king. Relying on his military power, [the king] had been fighting for more territory against Chi-pin 罽賓 (Kāśmīra, modern Kashmir)[160] for three years. The king attacked his enemy [with a force of] seven hundred combat elephants, each

[156] Yeh-ch'a are demons in the earth, in the air, or in the lower heavens. They are malignant, and devourers of human flesh. See *Fan-i ming-i chi* 2/44 八部篇.

[157] No additional information about Tao-yao 道藥 is available, but Chavannes ("Voyage de Song Yun," p. 383 n. 4) believes him to be the same Tao-jung referred to elsewhere in the *Ch'ieh-lan chi*.

[158] *PS* (97/26b) reads *Ch'ih-te* (identified as Tegin by Chavannes, "Voyage de Song Yun," p. 416). For a study of Tegin as a title of the Turkish nobility, see Mori Masao, *Kodai Toruko minzokushi kenkyū*, vol. 1, 3rd ed. Tokyo, 1976), pp. 299 ff., and p. 380 n. 1.

For Gandhāra, see Alfred Foucher, "Notes sur la ǵeographie ancienne du Gandhāra," *BEFEO* 1 (1901), 322–369.

[159] Chavannes, ("Voyage de Song Yun," p. 417 n. 6) gives the king's name as Mihira Kula (regnant A.D. 515–550). See also Foucher, "Notes," pp. 348 ff., and Mark Stein, *Kalhana Rajatarangini* (Delhi, 1961), pp. 43–48.

[160] According to *WS* 102/17b, Gandhāra stretched eight hundred *li* from east to west and three hundred *li* from south to north. On all four sides it was protected by mountain ranges. This natural strategic situation is perhaps the main reason that encouraged the king to undertake a protracted war.

For Chi-pin, see Shiratori Kurakichi, "Keisenkoku kō," in *Seiikishi kenkyū* (Tokyo, 1941), pp. 377–462.

carrying ten men armed with swords and clubs.[161] Swords to strike against the enemy were attached to the trunk of each elephant. The king, as a rule, stayed at the frontier all day long without returning [to his residence]. His army grew weary and his people overburdened. [As a result,] the masses sighed with resentment.

Sung Yün presented the imperial rescript to the king at the latter's military camp. The king, defiant and discourteous, received the rescript while sitting. Realizing that distant barbarians were difficult to control, Sung Yün yielded to his arrogance and did not reprimand him. The king then sent an interpreter to speak to Sung Yün, saying, "You have come across many states and traveled on many hazardous roads. Do you feel tired and weary?"

Sung Yün replied: "Our Emperor is deeply interested in Mahāyāna [and ordered me] to search for sūtras from afar. Hazardous as the journey has been, I dare not make mention of weariness. You, oh great king, take personal charge of the Three Armies and come to this borderland from a great distance. Is Your Majesty not tired with the sudden changes of the climate from cold to hot?"

The king replied: "As I am unable to conquer this small country, hearing your question makes me ashamed of myself."

At first Sung Yün thought that the king, as a barbarian, was beyond reproof by the standard of Chinese protocol. He therefore let the king receive the rescript while sitting. Now after some dialogue, he found the king to have human feelings after all. As a consequence, he reprimanded [the king], saying: "Mountains differ in height: some are high but others are low. Rivers vary in size: some are big but others are small. Among men who live in the world, there are also high or low [positions]. The kings of Yen-ta and Wu-ch'ang both bowed to the rescript and then received it. How can Your Majesty alone [be exempted] from bowing?"

In reply the king said, "If I see the Wei ruler in person,[162] I will of course bow to him. But [now] I am [only] receiving his letter; I am [therefore] reading it while sitting. This is by no means surprising. When a man receives a letter from his parents, he will still read it while sitting. Since [the ruler of the] Great Wei is just like a parent of

[161] That is, *ch'a* 楂, "driftwood."

[162] Adding *ch'in* 親 after *IS* 5/9b.

mine, I shall likewise read his rescript while sitting. I do not see any impropriety here."

[Sung] Yün had no way to prevail upon him. Subsequently the king sent [Sung] Yün to a monastery and gave him a very meager allowance.

At that time the state of Pa-t'i 跋提[163] gave two lion cubs to the king of Ch'ien-t'o-lo. When [Sung] Yün and the others viewed them, they remarked on their fierce natures. None of the pictures in China captured their likeness.

Thence they traveled westward for five days before reaching the place where Tathāgata [agreed to] be beheaded in compliance with someone's request.[164] There too were a stūpa and a monastery that housed more than twenty monks.

Traveling westward again for three days,[165] they reached the Great Hsin-t'ou River 辛頭大河 (the Indus). On its western bank was the site where Tathāgata transformed himself into a giant *mo-ho* 摩竭 (makara) fish, which, leaping out of the river for twelve years, had offered its meat to help [the needy and sick]. A stūpa was built there to commemorate this episode, and marks of fish scales were still visible on the rock.[166]

Traveling again for three days,[167] they reached the city of Fo-sha-

[163] The text (5/12b) reads Pa-pa-t'i *kuo* 跋跋提國, but *IS* (5/10a) gives only Pa-t'i *kuo* 跋提國, which perhaps refers to Pa-ti-yen 拔底延 (Baktria, modern Balkh), the capital city of Yen-ta. See Chavannes, "Voyage de Song Yun," p. 418 n. 5.

[164] The site is identified as modern Shah Dheri ("Voyage de Song Yun," p. 418 n. 8; and Cunningham, *Ancient Geography*, p. 115).

At the request of an old Brahmin, Tathāgata agreed to let himself be beheaded. The head was bound to a tree, but the Brahmin, who wanted to cut off Tathāgata's head by himself, was only able to hit a branch of the tree. See Chih-ch'ien, tr., *P'u-sa pen-yüan ching* (*Taishō* ed.) B/64 月光王品第五.

[165] The text (5/13a) reads *san yüeh* 三月, "three months," but should be *san jih* 三日, "three days," in view of the short distance involved. *IS* (5/10b) reads 三日.

[166] Name for a legendary fish in Indian mythology, sometimes identified as a whale. See Hsin-hsing, *Fan fan yü* (*Taishō* ed.) 7/1032 魚名第三十九：摩伽羅魚王, 亦云摩竭, 譯曰鯨魚.

As a sea monster, Tathāgata had for twelve years offered bits of his blubber or flesh to cure those suffering from skin disease. *Fo-shuo p'u-sa pen-hsing ching*, B/119.

[167] Emending *shih-san* 十三, "thirteen," to *san* 三, "three," after *IS* (5/10a). This city was on the west bank of the Indus River, which Sung Yün had just visited. It should not take thirteen days to travel between these two points. Hence the translation follows *IS*.

fu 佛沙伏,[168] where the land was fertile. The city walls were stately and erect; the population large and flourishing; its woods and springs were lush and numerous. The land was also rich in precious articles, and the customs were refined and good. In and out of the city, there were [quite a few][169] ancient temples, where famous monks and their virtuous followers were known for their noble and rarefied conduct. One *li* to the north of the city was the Pai-hsiang (White Elephant) Palace, where all Buddhist relics consisted of stone. They were imposing, beautiful, and numerous. Each statue was completely plated in gold, producing a dazzling effect on the viewers. In front of the monastery was a tree to which the white elephants were tied; hence, the name of the monastery.[170] Its flowers and leaves were like those of date trees, but its fruit would not ripen until late winter. The local elders said "When this tree ceases to exist, Buddhism will also be extinguished." Inside the monastery was a picture depicting the bestowal of a son and a daughter to a Brahmin by the prince and his wife.[171] Every Hu-barbarian 胡人 sobbed bitterly upon seeing it.

Traveling westward for another day, they reached the place where Tathāgata tore out his eyes to benefit others.[172] There was also a stūpa and a monastery. On the rock of the latter were the imprints of Chia-yeh *fo* 迦葉佛 (Káśyapa Buddha).[173]

Traveling westward for another day, they rode in a boat across a

[168] Identified as the city Pa-lu-sha 跋虜沙 (Paluṣa) by Chavannes ("Voyage de Song Yun," p. 419 n. 5). It is referred to in the *Ta-T'ang Hsi-yü chi* 2/25.

[169] The text (5/13a) reads *fan yu ku ssu* 凡有古寺, which is not a complete sentence. The phrase "quite a few" in the translation is added to make the sentence complete.

[170] The prince was driven out of the home by his father when he gave away the latter's favorite white elephant. Hence, the name of the monastery. See *T'ai-tzu Hsü-ta-na ching*, p. 419.

[171] While living in the T'an-t'e Mountain, the same prince gave away his own son and daughter to a Brahmin who wanted to keep them as slaves. See *T'ai-tzu Hsü-ta-na ching* (p.422) cited above and note 147 of this chapter.

[172] In his previous life, Tathāgata as a prince agreed to have both his eyes torn out as the ingredient of a drug to benefit the ailing masses. The two eyes, however, were returned to him intact on the order of Śakra. See *Fo-shuo p'u-sa pen-hsing ching* C/120; and Chu Fa-hu, tr., *Mi-le p'u-sa so-wen pen-yüan ching* (*Taishō* ed.), p. 188.

[173] Chia-yeh *fo* was a Buddha of Brahmin origin, believed to have a height of one hundred sixty feet. See Seng-yu, *Shih-chia p'u* (*Taishō* ed.) 1/9.

deep waterway,[174] which was more than three hundred paces wide.

Traveling southwestward for sixty *li*, they reached the city of Ch'ien-t'o-lo.[175] Seven *li* to the southeast of the city was the Ch'üeh-li 雀離 stūpa.[176]

According to the *Account of Tao-jung*, [the stūpa] was located four *li* east from the city.

Now [one must] trace the origin of this stūpa. When Tathāgata was in this world, he and his disciples wandered around converting people in this land. He pointed to the east of the city, saying, "Two hundred[177] years after my nirvāna, a king by the name of Chia-ni-se-chia 迦尼色佳[178] (Kaniṣka) will build a stūpa in this place." Two hundred years after the Buddha's nirvāna, a king named Chia-ni-se-chia indeed came out to visit the eastern part of the city, where he saw four boys building a stūpa by piling up cow-dung to the height of about three Chinese feet. Instantly the boys disappeared before the king.[179]

According to the *Account of Tao-jung*, the boys chanted *chieh* 偈 (gāthā)[180] to the king from high in the air.

Perplexed by the boys' [actions], the king immediately built a stūpa to shelter the one built by the boys, but the latter gradually heightened itself, surpassing the king's stūpa in height and rising

[174] According to Chavannes ("Voyage de Song Yun," p. 420 n. 4), the waterway was located at a point where the Svat and Kabul met.

[175] This city, the capital of Ch'ien-t'o-lo (Gandhāra), is also known as Fu-lou-sha 弗樓沙 (*Kao-seng Fa-hsien chuan*, p. 858) and Pu-lu-sha 布路沙 (*Ta-T'ang Hsi-yü chi* 2/22 under the Chien-t'o-lo *kuo*). It corresponds to modern Peshawar (*CS* 5/214).

[176] *PS* (97/26b Ch'ien-t'o *kuo* 乾陁國) places the stūpa at seven *li* to the southeast of the city. It was seven hundred Chinese feet high, with a circumference of three hundred paces (*pu*, or one thousand eight hundred Chinese feet). The meaning of this renowned stūpa and its exact spelling remain controversial.

[177] Emending *san-pai* 三百, three hundred," to *erh-pai* 二百, "two hundred," after *FYCL* 51/615.

[178] The king (regnant A.D. 120) was of Yüeh-chih 月支 origin. His ancestors resided in Bactria around 140 B.C. His name is also transliterated as Chia-ni-se-chia 迦膩色迦 (*Ta-T'ang Hsi-yü chi* 2/22 ff.).

The king sponsored the construction of many stūpas, among which the present one, the Sheng-t'a 聖塔 (Holy Stūpa; *Ta-T'ang Hsi-yü chi* 2/22 ff.) and the Ch'üeh-li are best known.

[179] For more information about this episode, see *Kao-seng Fa-hsien chuan*, p. 858.

[180] *Chieh* 偈 (gāthā), a metrical hymn or chant that often appears in sūtras, is usually four, five, or seven characters to the line.

above it. It did not stop growing in height until it had risen four hundred Chinese feet above the ground. The king, in addition, broadened the foundation of his stūpa to more than three hundred paces.

> According to the *Account of Tao-jung*, [the foundation] was more than one hundred ninety paces.

From then on, the structural wood[en pillars installed on the foundation of the king's stūpa] began to match [the one of cow-dung].

> The *Account of Tao-jung* reads: "The pillars, [each] at least thirty Chinese feet high, were all built on foundation platforms of patterned stone[181] supported by joists to which corbel brackets were attached. Altogether it was thirteen stories [high]."

On the top of the stūpa was an iron post three hundred Chinese feet high, to which golden plates in thirteen tiers were attached. The total height was seven hundred Chinese feet above the ground.

> The *Account of Tao-jung* reads: "The iron post was eighty-eight Chinese feet high and eighty spans (*wei* 圍) in girth. Golden plates pile up in fifteen tiers. Altogether it rose six hundred thirty-two Chinese feet above the ground."[182]

After the construction was completed, the dung-stūpa remained there three hundred paces[183] to the south of the large one. At the time a Brahmin, suspecting that the stūpa was not made of [cow-]dung, tried to find out with his hand. Consequently, a hole was created. Even though the stūpa had survived many, many years, the dung had still not decayed. When incense paste was used to seal the hole, the hole could not be filled up. Now the [cow-dung stūpa] was sheltered under a T'ien-kung 天宮 (Heavenly Palace).[184]

Since the Ch'ueh-li Stūpa constructed itself, the stūpa had three times caught fire (*t'ien-huo* 天火, heavenly fire), but it was completely restored each time, as the king had it repaired. [This was because] the

[181] The text (5/14a) gives 悉用文木爲陛階, "all used grained wood as foundation platform" as against 悉用文石爲陛堦, "all used grained stone as foundation platform" in *IS* 5/11a. The translation follows *IS*.

[182] The size, height, and actual features of this stūpa are a subject of debate among scholars. But it seems certain that the wooden stūpa had thirteen stories, topped by an iron mast and supported by a five-storied foundation with a circumference of between 1,800 and 2,400 Chinese feet.

[183] Emending *san pu* 三步, "three paces" (three *pu*), to *san pai pu* 三百步, "three hundred *pu*," after *FYCL* 51/615.

[184] T'ien-kung (devapura) is the abode of gods. The term is used here figuratively.

elders said, "Buddhism would be extinguished if the stūpa should be swept by 'heavenly fire' a seventh[185] time."

> The *Account of Tao-jung* states: In repairing the stūpa, the king found no one able to raise the iron post up after the completion of the woodwork. The king then built four high towers, one for each corner, where he placed much gold, silver, and other precious things. With his wife and princes all on top [of the tower],[186] the king burned incense and scattered flowers. With utmost reverence they prayed[187] [for Buddha's assistance]. Thereupon, in one stroke, [the iron post] was hoisted up by winding a rope in a pulley. Therefore the Hu-barbarians all said, "The assistance came from the four heavenly kings (devarāja).[188] Otherwise, [this post] could never have been lifted by human efforts."

All Buddhist relics[189] within the stūpa were made of gold and jade, and their effects changed so continually as to defy description.[190] At dawn when the morning sun began to rise, the golden bells radiated brilliantly; when a soft breeze gently arose, the precious bells sounded in harmony. Among all stūpas in the Western Regions, this one was by far the best.

At the time when the stūpa was just completed, it was covered with a net sewn with rare[191] pearls. Several years later, the king thought to himself, "This pearl net is worth ten thousand measures of gold. After my death, I fear someone may steal it. Furthermore, I am afraid that if the stūpa is in disrepair, no one will fix it."

He then had the net removed and placed in a bronze cauldron,

[185] Emending *so* 所, "by" used in the passive voice, to *ch'i* 七, "seven," after *FYCL* 51/614 and *Ta-T'ang Hsi-yü chi* 3/23.

[186] Adding *lou* 樓, "towers," after *IS* 5/11b.

[187] Emending *ching* 精, "essence," to *ch'ing* 請, "beg," at the suggestion of Chavannes ("Voyage de Song Yun," p. 425 n. 4). The full phrase is *chih hsin ching shen* 至心精神, which could also mean "to exercise greatest sincerity and animate spiritual power."

[188] They are the four guardians of the world: Dhṛtarāṣṭra in the east, Virūḍhaka in the south, Virūpakṣa in the west, and Vaiśravaṇa in the north.

[189] Emending *wu shih* 物事, "things," to *fo shih* 佛事 after *FYCL* 51/615 and *IS* 5/11b. *Fo shih* 佛事 as a term appears quite often in the *Ch'ieh-lan chi*.

[190] The text is *ch'ien-pien wan-hua, nan-te erh ch'eng* 千變萬化, 難得而稱, "One thousand changes and ten thousand transformations it is hard to praise."

[191] *IS* 5/11b reads *chen* 珍, "rare," but the text (5/15a) and *TPYL* 658/4a 釋部塔 both give *chen* 眞, "real." The two graphs are perhaps interchangeable.

which was interred at a point one hundred paces to the northwest of the stūpa. Above was planted a tree known as *p'u-t'i* 菩提 (bodhi), whose branches stretched out in all directions and whose thick foliage blocked out the sky. Underneath the tree in each of the four directions were statues of seated Buddha,[192] each fifteen Chinese feet high. Four dragons guarded the pearls; if someone entertained the idea of thievery, he would immediately[193] meet with disaster. The king engraved an epitaph on a stone, commanding that if in the future the stūpa should be in disrepair, he would trouble worthies of later periods to sell the pearls [buried underneath] and use the money to fix it.

Fifty paces to the south of the Ch'üeh-li Stūpa was a perfectly round stone stūpa, which rose to a height of twenty Chinese feet. It had such magic powers as to presage good or bad luck for men.[194] Of those who touched it, if it was one who would have good fortune, golden bells sounded in response. If it was one who would have ill fortune, the bells failed to sound, even when shaken. Now, since Hui-sheng was in a distant country, he was afraid of an inauspicious return [trip], so he bowed to the holy stūpa and begged for some evidence. He then touched it with his finger, and heard the bells ring in response. After receiving this indication, he felt at ease. Later, he indeed had a happy return [trip].

At first, when Hui-sheng left the capital, the empress dowager [née Hu] ordered him to take one thousand multicolored banners, each one hundred Chinese feet long. [He also received] five hundred incense bags made of brocade, in addition to [another] two thousand banners given him by princes and ministers. While en route from Yü-tien to Ch'ien-t'o-lo, he gave all the Buddhist materials away [to the monasteries he visited]. In this way he used them up, except for one hundred-foot banner that the empress dowager had given him, and that he was prepared to offer to the stūpa of King Shih-p'i 尸毗 (Śibi).[195] Sung Yün, [on his part], gave two slaves—one male and one female—to serve for life the Ch'üeh-li Stūpa, sweeping the

[192] See also *Ta-T'ang Hsi-yü chi* 2/22 under Chien-t'o-lo *kuo*.

[193] Emending *tze* 則, "then," to *chi* 即, "immediately," after *IS* 5/12a and *TPYL* 658/4a 釋部塔.

[194] Literally, *shih jen* 世人, "men of the world."

[195] Śibi is also transliterated as Shih-p'i-chia 尸毗迦 (Śivika) (*Ta-T'ang Hsi-yü chi* 3/29 under Wu-chang-na *kuo*). He was the ruler of the city of T'i-p'o-t'i 提婆提 (Devapati), India.

ground and sprinkling water. Hui-sheng, too, by saving from his travel allowance, was able to select a skilled artisan to copy in bronze [the following pictures]: one Ch'üeh-li Stūpa, and four other stūpa depicting the transformation of Śākya[muni].[196]

Thereafter they traveled westward for seven days, and, after having crossed a large river, they reached the place where Tathāgata, as King Śibi, saved the life of a dove. A stūpa and a monastery were built [to commemorate this event]. Long ago the granary of King Śibi was burned, scorching the stored rice. The rice was still in existence at that time. Anyone who took one grain would be free of malaria forever.[197] The people of this land were permitted the medicine[198] only when they needed it.

> The *Account of Tao-jung* reads: "After arriving in the state of Na-chia-lo-a 那迦羅阿[199] (Nagarahāra, in modern Jalalabad, Afganistan) [we found] a piece of Buddha's bone from the top of his skull, square [outside] and round [inside,][200] four inches long

---

King Śibi was the transformation of Tathāgata in his previous life. Both the dove and hawk were transformations of Śakra and Viśvakarman, who plotted jointly to test Tathāgata's determination. The dove (the transformation of Viśvakarman), being pursued by the hawk (the transformation of Śakra), sought shelter under the armpit of King Śibi. The hawk asked the king for the release of the dove, saying that otherwise it (the hawk) would be starved to death. The king then cut off his own flesh with a sharp knife to feed the hawk. See *P'u-sa pen-sheng man lun* A/333 to 334 尸毗王救鴿命緣起第二; *Fo-shuo p'u-sa pen-hsing ching* C/119; Chiu-mo-lo-shih (Kumārajīva), *Ta-chih-tu lun* 35/314 釋報應品第二, *Hsien-yü ching* 1/351 梵天請法六事品第一 and *Liu-tu chi ching* 1/1 布施度無五章第一.

196 This refers to the four most famous stūpas in northern India, each of which was built at the site where Tathāgata performed noble deeds. The sites were: (1) where Tathāgata tore out his eyes, (2) where he offered himself to feed a starved tiger, (3) where he cut off his own hand to benefit others, and (4) where he cut off his own flesh to save the life of a dove.

197 There is also a reference to the medicinal effect of scorched rice in the *YYTT* 10/57 物異篇.

198 The text (5/16b) is *hsü chin-jih ch'ü-chih* 須禁日取之, "It should be taken on forbidden days," but *IS* (5/12b) reads *hsü yao-jih ch'ü-chih* 須藥日取之, "It should be taken when the medicine is needed." The translation follows the latter since the meaning of "forbidden days" is unclear. *TPYL* 839/10b 百穀杭 reads *hsü i-wei yao* 須以爲藥, "It would be taken as medicine." See also Iriya Yoshitaka, *Rakuyō garan ki*, p. 112 n. 78.

199 The following quotations from *Tao-jung's Account* are unrelated to Sung Yün's travel. Even the wording does not reflect any editing by the author.

200 The text (5/16b) reads *fang yüan* 方圓, "square and round," the exact meaning of which remains unclear. My interpretation follows Chinese tradition, which considers round inside and square outside as ideal.

and beige in color. At the lower end of the bone was a hole [big enough] to insert a finger; lining the inside were [tiny pockets] as numerous[201] as the cells of an inverted hornet's nest. The Ch'i-ho-lan Monastery 耆賀濫寺[202] we visited had in its possession a thirteen-patch kaṣāya of the Buddha. Measured with a ruler, some [of the patches] were long; others short. There was also a pewter staff of Buddha's. Seventeen Chinese feet long and gold-plated, it was deposited in a water pail that was also gold-plated. Its weight varied from time to time: when it was heavy, one hundred men could not lift it, but when it was light, two persons could handle it.

"In the city of Na-chieh 那竭 there were Buddha's teeth and hair, which were placed in a jeweled box and worshiped [by the people] day and night.[203] Arriving at the Ch'ü-po-lo-lung Cave 瞿波羅龍窟,[204] we saw the shadow of the Buddha. The cave had an opening toward the west. When we viewed the shadow at a distance of fifty paces,[205] the many radiant marks were clearly [revealed]. But when we took a closer look, they were indistinct and invisible. If one touched it by hand, he could only feel the stone wall. But, as he slowly stepped back they would begin to appear.

[201] Emending *shan-jan* 閃然, "flashingly," to *ch'u-jan* 閦然, "numerously," at the suggestion of *CS* 5/221.

[202] Ch'i-ho-lan is the Chinese transliteration of khakkhara, the staff held by Buddhist monks when begging for food. According to the *Kuo-seng Fa-hsien chuan* (pp. 858–859), the Buddha's robes and his staff were kept separately, but the *Ta-T'ang Hsi-yü chi* (2/21 under Lan-po *kuo* 濫波國) asserts that they were placed together in the same room.

[203] The depository of Buddha's hair and teeth in this city (capital of Nagarahāra) is also referred to in the *Kao-seng Fa-hsien chuan* (pp. 858–859), but when it came to Hsüan-tsang's time, the teeth were already lost. See *Ta-T'ang Hsi-yü chi* 2/21 under Hsiao Su-tu *ch'eng* 小窣堵城.

[204] The text (5/16b) reads Ch'ü-lo-lo-lu 瞿羅羅鹿, which makes little sense. *CS* (5/223) suggests that one of two *lo* 羅 characters should be deleted, and the last character *lu* 鹿 is a mistake for *k'u* 窟. *CC* (5/347, n. 12), on the other hand, suggests that the name of the place be read Ch'ü-po-lo-lung 瞿波羅龍, and the text should be rephrased to read 瞿波羅龍見佛影窟, 戶向西開, 卻行五十步. The translation follows the latter version. In any event, the text contains significant interpolations that defy reasonable interpretation.

[205] On the basis of *Ta-T'ang Ta-tz'u-en-ssu San-tsang-fa-shih chuan* by Hui-li (*Taisho* ed., 2/229 from A-ch'i-ni *kuo* 阿耆尼國 to Chieh-jo-chü-she *kuo* 羯若鞠闍國), *CC* (5/223) suggests that the text be changed from *shih-wu pu* 十五步, "15 paces," to *wu-shih pu* 五十步, "fifty paces."

Their appearance was so unique that few other places in the world have anything like it.

"In front of the cave was a square rock on which were Buddha's [foot] prints. One hundred paces to the southwest of the cave was the site where Buddha had washed his garment.[206] One *li* to the north of the cave was the Mu-lien Cave 目連窟 (Mandgalyāyana).[207] To the south of the [Ch'ü-po-lo-lung] Cave was a hill, at the foot of which was a large stūpa that rose to a height of one hundred Chinese feet. It was built with the great[208] Buddha's own hands. The elders said that if the stūpa should [one day] sink into the ground, Buddhism would perish. Altogether the Buddha built seven stūpas. To the south of the large one[209] was an inscription reportedly written by Tathāgata. The inscription appeared in the barbarian characters (Sanskrit) and is still clearly legible today."

Hui-sheng stayed for two years in Wu-ch'ang. It would be difficult to record in detail the minor variations in the customs of the Western barbarians, which by and large were similar. It was not until the second month of the second year of the Cheng-kuang period[210] that he returned to the national capital.[211]

[Yang] Hsüan-chih's note: *Hui-sheng's Traveling Account* 惠生行紀 did not give us details. Now I have also quoted from the

[206] For more information about the Buddha's footprints and the place where he washed his garment, see *Ta-T'ang Hsi-yü chi* 2/21 under Chieh-lo-ho *kuo* 揭羅曷國.

[207] Mu-lien was one of Buddha's disciples; also known as Mu-chien-lien 目犍連. See *Fan-i ming-i chi* 1/15 十大弟子篇.

[208] Emending *liu* 六, "six," to *ta* 大, "big," after *IS* 5/13a and *CT* 5/19a. *CS* (5/224) suggests that *liu* 六 is a mistake for *ch'i* 七, "seven" (*Ch'i-fo* 七佛, "seven Buddhas," are referred to in Chapter 4 under the Ta-chüeh Monastery), but in light of the text immediately following, his suggestion does not seem acceptable. The translation follows *CC* (5/341) in changing *liu* 六 to *ta* 大.

[209] See note 208 above.

[210] Emending Cheng-yüan 正元 to Cheng-kuang 正光.

The text (5/17a) should read *san-nien* 三年 rather than *erh-nien* 二年.

According to Hui-sheng's travel account, he left Lo-yang in the eleventh month of the first year of the Shen-kuei period (December A.D. 518 to January 519), and arrived in Wu-ch'ang in the early twelfth month of the same year (January to February A.D. 520), where he stayed for two years after his visit to Ch'ien-t'o-lo in the middle of the fourth month (mid-May) in A.D. 520. Taking into consideration the time he spent on the return trip, he would not have been able to reach Lo-yang before the third year of Cheng-kuang (A.D. 522).

[211] Literally, *T'ien-ch'üeh* 天闕, "the Heavenly Palace."

Account of Tao-jung and the *Private Records of Sung Yün*[212] to make up its deficiencies.

The capital city was twenty *li*[213] from the east to the west and fifteen *li* from the south to the north. It had a total of one hundred ninety thousand and more households. Excluding monasteries, shrines, palaces, and such government buildings as *fu* 府 (ministries) and *ts'ao* 曹 (bureaus), [the city was divided into] wards, [each being] the equivalent of three hundred square paces. It also had four gates. For each gate, there were two *li-cheng* 里正 (ward superintendents), under whom were four *li* 吏 (assistants) and eight *men-shih* 門士 (wardens). There were altogether two hundred twenty wards and one thousand three hundred sixty-seven temples and monasteries. After the moving of the capital to the city of Yeh in the first year of the T'ien-p'ing period (A.D. 534), four hundred twenty-one temples and monasteries still remained in Lo-yang. This number did not include temples and monasteries outside of the city. A detailed listing of such temples and monasteries is given herewith: On the Pei-mang Mountain, the Feng-wang[214] and the Ch'i Hsien-wu Wang 齊獻武王寺[215] monasteries; in the Shih-ch'üeh 石闕 (Stone

[212] *Hui-sheng's Travel Diary Account* (*Hui-sheng hsing chuan* 慧(惠)生行傳) is registered in *Sui-shu* (33/24a 經籍志; in one *chüan*), and *Sung Yün's Account* is recorded in *Chiu T'ang-shu* (I-wen facsimile ed., 46/46b 經籍志; in one *chüan* under the title of *Sung Yün Wei-kuo i hsi shih-i kuo shih* 宋雲魏國以西十一國事) and *Hsin T'ang-shu* (58/32a 藝文志, under the same title). *The Account of Tao-jung* is referred to in Tao-hsüan's *Shih-chia fang-chih* (*Taishō* ed.; B/969 遊履篇; Tao-yao 道藥 (not Tao-jung 道榮) is given as the author's name). These three major works, covering an important chapter in China's relations with the west, are no longer extant. The *Lo-yang ch'ieh-lan chi*, however, preserves some fragments of them in the form of quotations.

[213] Lao Kan, "Pei-Wei," p. 300, suggests that the *li* here refers to wards, the subdivision of a city, rather than a measure of length. But his interpretation does not agree with the city planning as described in *Ti-wang shih-chi* 帝王世紀 and *Chin Yüan-k'ang tao-ti chi* 晉元康道地記 (both are quoted in *HHS* 19/6a 郡國志 comm.). Instead, both *CS* (5/227–228) and *CC* (5/351; Appendix 3, pp. 382 ff.) assert that Yang Hsüan-chih's record includes both the inside and outside of the city of Lo-yang, thus depicting Lo-yang as a rectangular-shaped city (longer east to west than south to north).

[214] That is, Feng Hsi's Monastery.

[215] That is, Kao Huan's Monastery.

ig. 6. The central statue of Buddha (height of head: 4m; statue, 17.14m) and guardians in the Feng-hsien 'emple, Lung-men, Lo-yang

Tower)[216] section—the eastern suburb of the capital—the Yüan Ling-chün 元領軍寺 (Temple of Yüan, General Directing the Army)[217] and Liu Ch'ang-ch'iu[218] 劉長秋寺 (Temple of Liu, the Prolonger of the Autumn) temples;[219] in the Sung Mountains, the Hsien-chü 閒居寺 (Temple of Leisurely Resting),[220] Hsi-ch'an 栖禪寺 (Temple of Living in a State of Meditation), Sung-yang 嵩陽寺 (Temple on the South of the Sung Mountains),[221] and Tao-ch'ang 道場寺 (Temple of Enlightenment)[222] temples; on top of the Sung Mountains, the Chung-ting 中頂寺 (Temple of the Mid-Summit) temple, and, on the eastern slope, the Sheng-tao 升道寺 (Temple of Achieving Enlightenment) temple; in the southern suburb of the city near the Kuan-k'ou 關口 (I-ch'üeh 伊闕, a cliff overlooking the I River), the Shih-k'u 石窟寺 (Temple of the Stone Cave) and Ling-yen 靈巖寺 (Temple of the Auspicious Cliff)[223] temples; [and finally] in the western suburbs of the capital close to the Ch'an 瀍 and Chien 澗 rivers,[224] the Pai-ma and Chao-lo 照樂寺 (Temple to Shine on Happiness) temples.

[216] Emending *shih-kuan* 石關 to *shih-ch'üeh* 石闕 after *IS* 5/13b.

[217] That is, Yüan ch'a's Temple.

[218] That is, Liu T'eng's Temple.

[219] Adding the character *ssu* 寺, "temple," after *CT* 5/20a.

[220] Emending *ch'üeh* 闕 to *hsien* 閒 after *CT* 5/20a. The monastery was built under the reign of Emperor Hsüan-wu (regnant A.D. 499–515). See *WS* 90/3a 馮亮傳 (the text gives 閑居, 閑 being interchangeable with 閒). During the Sui, it was renamed Sung-yo Monastery 嵩嶽寺 (the Sacred Sung Mountain). See Li Yung, *Li Pei-hai chi* (*Ssu-k'u ch'üan-shu chen-pen*, 5/4b–5a)

[221] Referred to in Pi Yüan's *Chung-chou chin-shih chi*, Wang san-i chai ed., 1/14a–b). It was built in May to June A.D. 536.

[222] See *WS* 90/3a cited in note 220 above.

[223] Other monasteries built in I-ch'üeh 伊闕 during the Wei but not mentioned here are: Ch'ien-yüan 乾元 (The First), Kuang-hua 廣化 (To Broaden the Rule), Ch'ung-hsün 崇訓 (To Respect the Instructions), Pao-ying 寶應 (Precious Response), Chia-shan 嘉善 (To Uphold Decency), T'ien-chu 天竺 (The Hindus), Feng-hsien 奉先 (To Worship the Ancestors), and Hsiang-shan 香山 (The Fragrant Mountain). See Wei Hsiang and Lu Chi-lu, *Lo-yang hsien-chih* (1813 ed.) 22/14a 伽藍記.

[224] For the Ch'an and Chien Rivers, see *SCC* 15/26b–28a.

Glossary

chang	ten feet
chen	a military post
ch'en	the equivalent of two hours; a twenty-four hour cycle of day and night is divided into twelve *ch'en*
ch'ih	one Chinese foot = 0.241 metre or 0.788 foot during the Chin
chin	a ford
chin-p'an	golden plates suspended from the corners of a Buddhist stūpa; also an Indian shrine erected at the top of a Buddhist stūpa
chün	a commandery
fang	a district within a city
hsien	a district under a commandery
hsün	the equivalent of seven or eight Chinese feet
hu	a household, normally of five members
li	roughly one-third of an English mile; a ward in a city
ming	given name
pu	a pace (1/300 *li* during the Han)
san-yüan	the "three firsts": the first day of the first month of the new year
shih	a measure of capacity equivalent to ten *tou*
ssu	a temple, monastery, or nunnery
sui	year of age by Chinese reckoning: one is considered two years old following the first new year's day after birth
t'a	a stūpa or pagoda; a storied Buddhist tower
tan	a picul or 100 catties
tou	a liquid measure about 2.45 liters
wan	the equivalent of ten thousand
wei	the equivalent of five Chinese inches

Official Titles

An-tung chiang-chün 安東將軍	General Pacifying the East
Ch'ang-ch'iu (ling) ch'ing 長秋(令)卿	Grand Prolonger of Autumn
Chao-hsüan ts'ao 昭玄曹	Office of Revealed Mysteries or Office of Religious Affairs
Chen-hsi ta-chiang-chün 鎮西大將軍	Generalissimo Governing the West
Chen-pei chiang-chün 鎮北將軍	General Governing the North
Cheng-hsi chiang-chün 征西將軍	General of the Western Expedition
Chi-shih 給事	Supervising Secretary
Chi-shih-chung 給事中	Court Secretary
Chi-shih chung ta-fu 給事中大夫	Ministrant and Palace Grandee
Chi-shih huang-men shih-lang 給事黃門侍郎	Ministrant of the Imperial Yellow Gate
Chi-t'ien 籍田	Office of the Sacred Fields
Ch'i-ping shang-shu 七兵尚書	Minister of Seven Forces
Chia-chieh 假節	Commissioner Holding Imperial Credentials
Chiang-tso ta-chiang 將作大匠	Court Architect
Chiang-tso ts'ao 將作曹	Office of Court Architect
Chien-fu ts'ao 監福曹	Office to Oversee Merits
Chien-i ta-fu 諫議大夫	Grandee Remonstrant
Ch'ien chiang-chün 前將軍	General in the Front
Chih-shu shih-yü-shih 治書侍御史	Associate Censor in charge of Drafting
Chiu-chi fu 九級府	"Nine-story" Office
chu-shu 主書	clerk (court)
Chu-kuo 柱國	Pillar of the State
Chu-tso lang 著作郎	Archivist
Chü-ch'i chiang-chün 車騎將軍	General of Chariots and Horsemen

Chung-hu-chün 中護軍	Protector of the Army within the Capital
Chung-lang chiang 中郎將	Commandant
Chung-po-shih 中博士	Erudite
Chung-san ta-fu 中散大夫	Palace Attendant
Chung-shu chien 中書監	Director of the Central Secretariat
Chung-shu po-shih 中書博士	Erudite of the Central Secretariat
Chung-shu she-jen 中書舍人	Drafter of the Central Secretariat
Chung-shu sheng 中書省	Central Secretariat
Chung-shu shih-lang 中書侍郎	Squire-attendant of the Central Secretariat
Chung ta-fu 中大夫	Palace Grandee
Chung-wai chu chün-shih ta-chiang-chün 中外諸軍事大將軍	Generalissimo in Charge of Internal and External Military Affairs
Chung-yeh-che 中謁者	Palace Internuncio
Feng ch'ao-ch'ing 奉朝請	Court Guest
Fu-chün-fu ssu-ma 撫軍府司馬	Sergeant-at-Arms in the Office of Commanding General in the Army
Fu-kuo ta-chiang-chün 輔國大將軍	Generalissimo Aiding the State
Fu-ma tu-wei 駙馬都尉	Commandant of Attending Cavalry
Hsia-sheng 下省	Bureau in Waiting
Hsiang-kuo 相國	Prime Minister
Hsin-wu chiang-chün 信武將軍	General of the Trustworty and Mighty
Hu-chün fu 護軍府	Office of the Protector of the Army
Hu-pen chung-lang-chiang 虎賁中郎將	Commandant of Tiger-rushing Squires
Huang-men shih-lang 黃門侍郎	Attending Secretary within the Imperial Yellow Gate
I-t'ung san-ssu 儀同三司	Palatine Ceremonially Equal to the Three Authorities
Kou-tun 勾盾	Office of Imperial Palace Parks

Kuan-chün chiang-chün 冠軍將軍	General Cresting the Armies
Kuang-lu ch'ing 光祿卿	Superintendent of the Imperial Household
Kuang-lu ta-fu 光祿大夫	Imperial Household Grandee
K'uang-yeh chiang-chün 曠掖(野)將軍	General of the Wilderness
Kuo-tzu chi-chiu 國子祭酒	Libationer of the Imperial Academy
Kuo-tzu hsüeh-t'ang 國子學堂	Academy for the Sons of the Noblemen
Kuo-tzu po-shih 國子博士	Erudite of the Imperial Academy
Lang 郎	Grandee
Lang-chung-ling 郎中令	Prefect of the Palace Squires
Li-cheng 里正	Ward superintendent
Li-pu shang-shu 吏部尚書	Secretary General of the Ministry of Civil Office
ling 令	prefect
Ling-chün chiang-chün 領軍將軍	General Directing the Army
Ling-chün tso-yu 領軍左右	Commander of Left and Right Palace Guards
Ling Kuo-tzu chi-chiu 領國子祭酒	Acting Libationer of the Imperial Academy
Ling Shang-shu ling 領尚書令	Acting Chief of Ministers
Ling-shih 令史	Foreman Clerk
Ling Ssu-t'u 領司徒	Acting Minister of Public Instruction
Lu Shang-shu shih 錄尚書事	Chief of Ministers
Lü-hsüeh po-shih 律學博士	Erudite of the Law
Lung-hsiang chiang-chün 龍驤將軍	Dragon-soaring General
Men-hsia lu-shih 門下錄事	Clerk of the Palace Gate
Men-hsia (sheng) 門下(省)	Bureau in Waiting for the Emperor's Service
men-shih 門士	wardens
Mi-shu-ch'eng 祕書丞	Assistant Archivist
Mi-shu chien 祕書監	Supervisor of Archives
Ming-t'ang tui 明堂隊	Regiment of the Hall of Illumination
Ning-hsi chiang-chün 寧西將軍	General Tranquilizing the West

Pei chiang-chün 裨將軍	Adjunct General
pei-sheng tso-yu 備身左右	bodyguard
Piao-ch'i chiang-chün 驃騎將軍	General of the Whirling Cavalry
Piao-ch'i ta-chiang-chün 驃騎大將軍	Generalissimo of the Whirling Cavalry
Piao-yung chiang-chün 飈勇將軍	General of Whirlwindlike Bravery
P'ien chiang-chün 偏將軍	General on the Flanks
P'ing-hsi-fu chang-shih 平西府長史	Senior Administrator in the Office of the General Quelling the West
P'ing-pei chiang-chün 平北將軍	General Quelling the North
Po-shih 博士	Erudite
Pu-hsia tu-tu 部下都督	Subordinate Inspector
Pu-ping chiao-wei 步兵校尉	Commandant of Infantry
San-ch'i ch'ang-shih 散騎常侍	Cavalier Attendant-in-Ordinary
San-kung ling-shih 三公令史	Foreman Clerk Assigned to the Three Lords
Shang-shu 尚書	Minister of State Affairs
Shang-shu lang 尚書郎	Secretary in the Department of State Affairs
Shang-shu ling 尚書令	President of the Department of State Affairs
Shang-shu p'u-yeh 尚書僕射	Vice President, Department of State Affairs
Shang-shu sheng 尚書省	Department of State Affairs
Shang-shu tso-ch'eng 尚書左丞	Secretary on the Left, Department of State Affairs
Shang-shu tso p'u-yeh 尚書左僕射	Vice President on the Left, Department of State Affairs
Shang-shu yu-ch'eng 尚書右丞	Secretary on the Right, Department of State Affairs
Shang-shu yu p'u-yeh 尚書右僕射	Vice President on the Right, Department of State Affairs
She-jen 舍人	Drafter
Sheng-huang shu 乘黃署	Bureau of Imperial Carriages
Sheng-huang ts'ao 乘黃曹	Bureau of Imperial Carriages

Shih-ch'ih-chieh 使持節	Commissioner Holding Imperial Credentials
Shih-chung 侍中	Chief Palace Attendant
Shih-yü-shih 侍御史	Attendant Censor
Ssu-chih 司直	Director of Uprightness
Ssu-k'ung 司空	Grand Minister of Public Works
Ssu-ma 司馬	Marshal
Ssu-men po-shih 四門博士	Erudite of the Four Gates
Ssu-nung (ch'ing) 司農(卿)	Minister of Agriculture
Ssu-pu-ts'ao 祠部曹	Office of Sacrifices
Ssu-t'u fu 司徒府	Office of the Minister of Public Instruction
Ssu-t'u kung 司徒公	Grand Minister of Public Works
(Ta) ch'eng-hsiang (大)丞相	Prime Minister
Ta-chiang-chün 大將軍	Generalissimo
Ta-hung-lu 大鴻臚	Great Usher in Charge of State Guests
Ta-ssu-ma 大司馬	Grand Marshal
Ta-ssu-nung (ch'ing) 大司農(卿)	Grand Minister of Agriculture
T'ai-ch'ang ssu 太常寺	Ministry of Grand Ceremonies
T'ai-fu 太傅	Grand Tutor
T'ai-hsüeh po-shih 太學博士	Erudite of the Imperial Academy
T'ai-pao 太保	Grand Guardian
T'ai-p'u ssu 太僕寺	Court of the Imperial Stud
T'ai-p'u-ssu ch'ing 太僕寺卿	Supervisor of the Court of Imperial Stud
T'ai-shih 太師	Grand Preceptor
T'ai-shih ssu-ma 太師司馬	Sergeant-at-Arms in the Office of Grand Preceptor
T'ai-shou 太守	Grand Warden
T'ai-tsai 太宰	Grand Steward
T'ai-ts'ang 太倉	Imperial Granary
T'ai-tzu she-jen 太子舍人	Chamberlain of the Crown Prince

T'ai-wei fu 太尉府	Office of the Grand Commandant
T'ai-wei (kung) 太尉(公)	Grand Commandant
Tao-kuan 導官	Grain Sorters
T'e-chin 特進	Specially Advanced
Ti-i ling-min ch'iu-chang 第一領民酋長	Chieftain of the First Rank in Charge of the People
Tien-chung shang-shu 殿中尙書	Minister within the Palace
Tien-nung 典農	Office of Agriculture
Tien-yü ts'ao 典虞曹	Office of Imperial Parks and Ponds
T'ien-chu ta-chiang-chün 天柱大將軍	Pillar of Heaven and Generalissimo
T'ing-wei ch'ing 廷尉卿	Commandant of Justice
Tso-wei fu 左衞府	Office of the Imperial Guards on the Left
Tsung-cheng 宗正	Superintendent of the Imperial Clan
Tsung-cheng ssu 宗正寺	Office of the Imperial Clan
Tu-chih shang-shu 度支尙書	Minister of Finance
Tu-kuan shang-shu 都官尙書	Minister of Public Works
Tu-shui 都水	Office of Waters
Tu-shui shih-che 都水使者	Messenger Director of the Waters
Tu-tu chung-wai chu chün-shih 都督中外諸軍事	Inspector General of Internal and External Military Affairs
Tu-tu shih-chou chu chün-shih 都督十州諸軍事	Inspector General of Military Operations in Ten Provinces
Tz'u-pu ts'ao 祠部曹	Office of Religion, Department of State Affairs
tz'u-shih 刺史	governor
wan-lang 挽郎	pallbearer
Wei chiang-chün 衞將軍	General of the Guards
Wei-wei ch'ing 衞尉卿	Commandant of the Palace Guards
Wu-k'u shu 武庫署	Office of the Prefect in Charge of Military Provisions
Wu-ping shang-shu 五兵尙書	Minister of Five Forces

yin 尹	Metropolitan Prefect
Ying-shih ts'ao 鷹師曹	Office of Hawks' Trainers
Yu chung-lang chiang 右中郎將	Right Commandant of Palace Squires
Yu kuang-lu ta-fu 右光祿大夫	Palace Grandee on the Right
Yu p'u-yeh 右僕射	Vice President on the Right, Department of State Affairs
Yu-wei fu 右衞府	Office of the Imperial Guards on the Right
yü-lin 羽林	plumed forest (guards)
Yü-lin chien 羽林監	Commander of the Plumed Forest Guards
Yü-shih chung-wei 御史中尉	Chief Censor
Yü-shih t'ai 御史臺	Tribunal of Censors
Yüan-wai san-ch'i shih-lang 員外散騎侍郎	Cavalier Attendant

Chronological Chart

Western Calendar	*Name of Emperor*	*Name and Year of Regnal Period*		IMPORTANT EVENTS
493	Hsiao-wen (Kao-tsu)	T'ai-ho	17	T'o-pa rulers decided to move national capital to Lo-yang
495	,,	,,	19	National capital moved to Lo-yang
496	,,	,,	20	
497	,,	,,	21	
498	,,	,,	22	
499	,,	,,	23	
500	Hsüan-wu (Shih-tsung)	Ching-ming	1	
501	,,	,,	2	
502	,,	,,	3	The Ching-ming Monastery was constructed
503	,,	,,	4	
504	,,	,,	5	
		Cheng-shih	1	A new legal system was codified
505	,,	,,	2	
506	,,	,,	3	The Cheng-shih Temple was constructed
507	,,	,,	4	
508	,,	,,	5	
		Yung-p'ing	1	
509	,,	,,	2	
510	,,	,,	3	
511	,,	,,	4	
512	,,	,,	5	
		Yen-ch'ang	1	
513	,,	,,	2	
514	,,	,,	3	
515	,,	,,	4	Empress Dowager Hu assumed supreme power

Western Calendar	*Name of Emperor*	*Name and Year of Regnal Period*		IMPORTANT EVENTS
516	Hsiao-ming (Su-tsung)	Hsi-p'ing	1	The Yung-ning Monastery was constructed; Yüan Ch'a assumed power
517	,,	,,	2	The construction of the Yung-ming stūpa was completed
518	,,	,,	3	Sung Yün and Hui-sheng started a pilgrimage to India
		Shen-kuei	1	
519	,,	,,	2	
520	,,	,,	3	
		Cheng-kuang	1	Yüan Ch'a assumed supreme power, placed the Empress Dowager Hu under house arrest, and murdered Yüan I
521	,,	,,	2	
522	,,	,,	3	Sung Yün and Hui-sheng arrived in Lo-yang from India
523	,,	,,	4	
524	,,	,,	5	
525	,,	,,	6	Empress Dowager Hu was restored to supreme power
		Hsiao-ch'ang	1	
526	,,	,,	2	Yüan Ch'a was executed
527	,,	,,	3	
528	Prince of Lin-t'ao	Wu-t'ai	1	Erh-chu Jung rebelled and captured Lo-yang; empress dowager was murdered
	Prince of Ch'ang-lo	Chien-i	1	
	Hsiao-chuang (Ching-tsung, same as Prince of Ch'ang-lo)	Yung-an	1	
529	Hsiao-chuang	,,	2	Yüan Hao captured Lo-yang but was soon defeated and killed
530	,,	,,	3	Erh-chu Jung was slain by the emperor. Erh-chu Chao captured Lo-yang and committed regicide
	Prince of Ch'ang-kuang	Chien-ming	1	
531	Chieh-min	,,	2	
	(Emperor Ch'ien-fei)	P'u-t'ai	1	
532	,,	,,	2	
	Hsiao-wu (Emperor Ch'u)	Yung-hsi	1	Emperor Ch'ien-fei was dethroned and murdered

Western Calendar	*Name of Emperor*	*Name and Year of Regnal Period*		IMPORTANT EVENTS
533	Hsiao-wu	,,	2	
534	Hsiao-ching	,,	3	The Yung-ming
		T'ien-p'ing	1	Monastery was burned down
535	Hsiao-ching (Eastern Wei)	,,	2	Northern Wei was split into Eastern and Western Wei
547	,,	Wu-ting	5	Yang Hsüan-chih revisited Lo-yang and wrote the *Ch'ieh-lan chi*
550	,,		8	The Eastern Wei was conquered by the Western Wei

Abbreviations

Frequently Cited Editions of the *Lo-yang ch'ieh-lan chi*

CC Fan Hsiang-yung 范祥雍, *Lo-yang ch'ieh-lan chi chiao-chu* 洛陽伽藍記校注
CS Chou Tsu-mo 周祖謨, *Lo-yang ch'ieh-lan chi chiao-shih* 洛陽伽藍記校釋
CT *Chin-tai mi-shu* 津逮祕書, ed.
Chi-cheng Wu Jo-chun 吳若準, *Lo-yang ch'ieh-lan chi chi-cheng* 洛陽伽藍記集證
Ch'ung-k'an Hsü Kao-juan 徐高阮, *Ch'ung-k'an Lo-yang ch'ieh-lan chi* 重刊洛陽伽藍記
HCTY *Hsüeh-chin t'ao-yüan* 學津討原, ed.
Ho-chiao Chang Tsung-hsiang 張宗祥, *Lo-yang ch'ieh-lan chi ho-chiao* 洛陽伽藍記合校
Iriya Iriya Yoshitaka 入矢義高, *Rakuyō garan ki* 洛陽伽藍記
IS *Ku-chin i-shih* 古今逸史, ed.
Ju-yin-t'ang Ju-yin-t'ang 如隱堂, ed.
Kou-ch'en T'ang Yen 唐晏, *Lo-yang ch'ieh-lan chi kou-ch'en* 洛陽伽藍記鉤沉

General References

BEFEO *Bulletin de l'École Française d'Extrême Orient*
BMFEA *Bulletin of the Museums of Far Eastern Antiquities*
Chin-shu *Chin-shu chiao-chu*
Chou-shu *Chi-chung Chou-shu*
CHWW *Ch'üan Hou-Wei wen*
CMYS *Ch'i-min yao-shu*
CYYCY *(Kuo-li) Chung-yang Yen-chiu-yüan Li-shih yü-yen Yen-chiu-so chi-k'an* (國立)中央研究院歷史語言

研究所集刊 Canton, Peiping and Shanghai, 1928–48; Taipei, 1950–

FYCL	*Fa-yüan chu-lin*
HHS	*Hou-Han-shu chi-chieh*
HJAS	*Harvard Journal of Asiatic Studies*
HS	*Han-shu pu-chu*
IS	*Ku-chin i-shih*
JAOS	*Journal of the American Oriental Society*
Lao-tzu	*Lao-tzu tao-te-ching*
Legge 3	Legge, James, tr. *The Chinese Classics*, 3, *The Shoo King or The Book of Historical Documents*. Reprint, Hong Kong, 1960.
Legge 5	Legge, James, tr. *The Chinese Classics*, 5, *The Ch'un Ts'ew with the Tso Chuen*, Reprint, Hong Kong, 1960.
MCCS	*Han-Wei Nan-pei-ch'ao mu-chih chi-shih*
NCS	*Nan-Ch'i shu*
PC	"*Lo-yang ch'ieh-lan chi* ti chi-t'iao pu-chu"
PCS	*Pei-Ch'i shu*
PS	*Pei-shih*
SC	*Shih-chi hui-chu k'ao-cheng*
SCC	*Shui-ching chu*
SPC	*Li-tai san-pao chi*
SPPY	*Ssu-pu pei-yao*, Shanghai, Chung-hua Book Co., 1927–1935
SPTK	*Ssu-pu ts'ung-k'an*, Shanghai, Commercial Press, 1929–1936
SSCCS	*Shih-san-ching chu-shu*
Taishō	*Taishō shinshū daizōkyō*, Tokyo, 1922–1933
TC	*Tzu-chih t'ung-chien*
TPKC	*T'ai-p'ing kuang-chi*
TPYL	*T'ai-p'ing yü-lan*
trad.	traditional
Tso-chuan	*Ch'un-ch'iu Tso-chuan chu-su*
WH	*Wen-hsüan*
WS	*Wei-shu*
YFSC	*Yüeh-fu shih-chi*
YHNC	*Yüan Ho-nan chih*
YLTT	*Yung-lo ta-tien*
YYTT	*Yu-yang tsa-tsu*

Bibliography

Modern works are listed by author, whereas works of the nineteenth century and earlier are listed by title.

A-yü-wang chuan 阿育王傳. Translated by An Fa-ch'in 安法欽. 7 *chüan*. *Taishō*.

Bielenstein, Hans. *Bureaucracies of Han Times*. Cambridge, 1980.

———. "Lo-yang in Later Han Times." *BMFEA* (Stockholm) 48 (1976), 1–142.

———. "The Restoration of the Han Dynasty, with Prolegomena on the Historiography of the Hou Han Shu," 1–3. *BMFEA* 26 (1954), 1–209; 31 (1959), 1–287; 39 (1967), 1–198.

Bodde, Derk. *Festivals in Classical China: New Year and Other Annual Observances during the Han Dynasty* (206 B.C.–A.D. 220). Princeton, 1975.

Chan, Wing-tsit 陳榮捷, tr. *The Way of Lao Tzu*. New York, 1963.

Chan-kuo-ts'e 戰國策. With commentary by Pao Piao 鮑彪 and Wu Shih-tao 吳師道. 10 *chüan*. *SPTK so-pen*.

Chang Hsing-lang 張星烺. *Chung-hsi chiao-t'ung shih-liao hui-pien* 中西交通史料滙編. 6 vols. Peiping, 1930.

Chang Kuo-kan 張國淦. *Li-tai shih-ching k'ao* 歷代石經考. Peiping, 1930.

Chang Ping-lin 章炳麟. "Hsin-ch'u san-t'i shih-ching k'ao" 新出三體石經考. 1 *chüan*. In *Chang-shih i-shu hsü-pien* 章氏遺書續編, vol. 3. Edited by Ch'ien Hsüan-t'ung 錢玄同 et al. Peiping, 1933.

Chang Tsung-hsiang 張宗祥, ed. *Chiao-cheng San-fu huang-t'u* 校正三輔皇圖. Shanghai, 1958.

———. *Lo-yang ch'ieh-lan chi ho-chiao* 洛陽伽藍記合校. Shanghai, 1930.

Chao-lun 肇論. Translated by Seng-chao 僧肇. *Taishō*.

Chao-te hsien-sheng Chün-chai tu-shu chih 昭德先生郡齋讀書志. By Chao Kung-wu 晁公武. 5 *chüan* (each divided into 2 sections), plus 2 *chüan* of supplements. *SPTK*.

Chao Wan-li 趙萬里. *Han-Wei Nan-pei-ch'ao mu-chih chi-shih* 漢魏南北朝墓志集釋. 10 + 1 *chüan*, with 612 plates. Peking, 1956.

Chavannes, Édouard. *Documents sur les T'ou-kiue occidentaux*. St. Petersburg, 1903.

———. "Voyage de Song Yun dans l'Udyāna et le Gandhāra." *BEFEO* 3 (1903), 279–441.

Chen Chi-yun. See under Ch'en Ch'i-yün.

Chen-i-t'ang ts'ung-shu 眞意堂叢書. By Wu Tzu-chung 吳自忠. Comp., Huang-ch'uan 璜川. 1811.

Ch'en Ch'i-yün 陳啓雲. *Hsün Yüeh (A.D. 148–209); The Life and Reflections of an Early Medieval Confucian*. Cambridge, 1975.

Ch'en Chung-fan 陳鍾凡. *Han-Wei Liu-ch'ao san-wen hsüan* 漢魏六朝散文選. Shanghai, 1956.

Ch'en, Kenneth K. S. 陳觀勝 *Buddhism in China: a Historical Survey*. Princeton, 1964.

Ch'en Yin-k'o 陳寅恪. *Ch'en Yin-k'o hsien-sheng ch'üan-chi* 陳寅恪先生全集. 2 vols. Taipei, 1977.

Ch'en Yüan 陳垣. *Erh-shih-shih shuo-jun piao* 二十史朔閏表. I-wen facsimile ed., Taipei, 1977.

Ch'eng Shu-te 程樹德. *Chiu-ch'ao lü k'ao* 九朝律考. 2 vols. Facsimile ed., Taipei, 1965.

Chi-chung Chou-shu 汲冢周書. With commentary by K'ung Chao 孔晁. 10 *chüan*. *SPTK so-pen*.

Chi Pin 紀彬, tr. "Yü-tien kuo k'ao" 于闐國考 ("Utenkokukō" by Hori Kentoku 堀謙德). *Yü-kung* 禹貢 4 (September 1935), 67–82.

Chi-yün 集韻. Edited by Ting Tu 丁度 et al. 10 *chüan*. *SPPY*.

Ch'i-min yao-shu 齊民要術. By Chia Ssu-hsieh 賈思勰 (fl. ca. A.D. 520). 10 *chüan*. I-wen facsimile ed., Taipei, 1959(?).

Chiao-shih pi-cheng cheng-chi 焦氏筆乘正集. 6 *chüan*. *Hsü-chi* 續集 8 *chüan*. By Chiao Hung 焦竑 (1541–1620). In *Kuo-hsüeh chi-pen ts'ung-shu* 國學基本叢書. Taipei, 1968.

Chin-shih ts'ui-pien 金石萃編. By Wang Ch'ang 王昶 (1725–1806). Ching-hsün-t'ang 經訓堂 ed. 160 *chüan*. 1805.

Chin-shu chiao-chu 晉書斠注. Annotations and commentary by Liu Ch'eng-kan 劉承幹 et al. (*Chin-shu* by Fan Hsüan-ling 房玄齡 576–648, 130 *chüan* + 3 *chüan* of Yin-i 音義 by Ho Ch'ao 何超 with preface of 747). I-wen facsimile ed., 1927. Taipei, 1957(?).

Chin-tai mi-shu 津逮祕書. Compiled and published by Mao Chin

毛晉 (1599–1659). I-wen facsimile ed., Taipei, 1964.

Ching-chuan shih-tz'u 經傳釋詞. By Wang Yin-chih 王引之 (1766–1834). 10 *chüan*. Facsimile of 1868 ed., Peking, 1956.

Ching-ch'u sui-shih chi 荊楚歲時記. By Tsung Lin 宗懍 (ca. A.D. 483–503 – ca. 561–566). *SPPY*.

Ching-te ch'uan-teng lu 景德傳燈錄. By Tao-yüan 道原. 30 *chüan*. *SPTK*. (Ching-te is the name of a year period [1004–1007]).

Chiu T'ang-shu 舊唐書. By Liu Hsü 劉煦 (887–846) et al. 200 *chüan*. I-wen facsimile ed., Taipei, 1956.

Chou-i 周易. See *I-ching*.

Chou-li 周禮. With commentary by Cheng Hsüan 鄭玄 (A.D. 132–200) and sub-commentary by Chia Kung-yen 賈公彥 (fl. 627–656). 42 *chüan*. I-wen facsimile *SSCCS* ed., Taipei, 1955.

Chou Tsu-mo 周祖謨. *Lo-yang ch'ieh-lan chi chiao-shih* 洛陽伽藍記校釋. 5 *chüan*. Peking, 1963.

Chou Yen-nien 周延年. *Lo-yang ch'ieh-lan-chi chu* 洛陽伽藍記注. 5 *chüan*. Wu-hsing 吳興 (?), 1937.

Chou Yi-liang. See under Zhou Yi-liang.

Chow Tse-tsung 周策縱, ed. *Wen Lin* 文林, *Studies in the Chinese Humanities*. Madison, Wisc., 1968.

Ch'u-tz'u 楚辭. Commentary by Wang I 王逸 (d. A.D. 158) and Hung Hsing-tsu 洪興祖 (1090–1155). 17 *chüan*. *SPTK so-pen*.

Ch'üan Han wen 全漢文. Compiled by Yen K'o-chün 嚴可均 (1762–1843). 63 *chüan*. In *Ch'üan shang-ku San-tai Ch'in-Han San-kuo Liu-ch'ao wen* 全上古三代秦漢三國六朝文. I-wen facsimile ed., Taipei, 1961.

Ch'üan Hou-Wei wen 全後魏文. 60 *chüan*. I-wen facsimile ed., Taipei, 1961.

Ch'üan Liang wen 全梁文. 74 *chüan*. I-wen facsimile ed., Taipei, 1961.

Chuang-tzu 莊子. By Chuang Chou 莊周 (ca. 369 – ca. 286 B.C.). With commentary by Kuo Hsiang 郭象 (d. A.D. 312). 33 *chüan*. *SPTK so-pen*.

Chugoku koten bungaku taikei 中國古典文學大系. Tokyo, 1974.

Ch'un-ch'ang-tzu chih-yü 純常子枝語. By Wen T'ing-shih 文廷式 (1856–1904). 40 *chüan*. In *Wen T'ing-shih ch'üan-chi* 文廷式全集. Shanghai(?), 1943.

Ch'un-ch'iu Ku-liang-chuan chi-chieh 春秋穀梁傳集解. With commentary by Fan Ning 范寧 (A.D. 339–401). 20 *chüan*. I-wen facsimile *SSCCS* ed., Taipei, 1955.

Ch'un-ch'iu Kung-yang-chuan 春秋公羊傳. With commentary by Ho Hsiu 何休 (129–182). 28 *chüan*. I-wen facsimile *SSCCS* ed., Taipei, 1955.

Ch'un-ch'iu Tso-chuan chu-shu 春秋左傳注疏. With commentary by Tu Yü 杜預 (A.D. 222–284) et al. 60 *chüan*. I-wen facsimile *SSCCS* ed., Taipei, 1955.

Chung-chou chin-shih chi 中州金石記. By Pi Yüan 畢沅 (1730–1797). 5 *chüan*. Wang-san-i chai 望三益齋, Chiao-ch'uan 蛟川, 1882(?).

Chung-kuo K'o-hsüeh-yüan K'ao-ku-yen-chiu-so Lo-yang kung-tso-tui 中國科學院考古研究所洛陽工作隊. "Han-Wei Lo-yang-ch'eng ch'u-pu k'an-ch'a" 漢魏洛陽城初步勘查. *K'ao-ku* 考古 4 (1973), 198–208.

———. "Han-Wei Lo-yang-ch'eng nan-chiao ti Ling-t'ai i-chih" 漢魏洛陽城南郊的靈台遺址. *K'ao-ku* 1 (1978), 54–57, with 3 illustrations (one in color) following p. 72.

de Crespigny, Rafe. "The Harem of Emperor Huan: A Study of Court Politics in Later Han." In *Papers in Far Eastern History* 12. Canberra, 1975, 1–42.

———. *Official Titles of the Former Han Dynasty as Translated and Transcribed by H. H. Dubs*. Canberra, 1967.

Crump, James I. Jr., tr. *Intrigues: Studies of the Chan-kuo Ts'e*. Ann Arbor, 1964.

Cunningham, Alexander. *The Ancient Geography of India*. I, *The Buddhist Period*. London, 1871.

Dien, Albert E. "The *Yüan-hun Chih* (Accounts Of Ghosts with Grievances): A Sixth Century Collection of Stories." *Wen-lin* 文林 (Madison, Wisc., 1968), 211–228.

Dubs, Homer H., tr. *The History of the Former Han Dynasty by Pan Ku*. 3 vols. Baltimore, 1938–1955.

Eberhard, Wolfram. *A History of China*. Berkeley and Los Angeles, 1971.

Ebrey, Patricia Buckley. *The Aristocratic Families of Early Imperial China*. Cambridge, 1978.

Encyclopaedia Britannica. Chicago, 1971.

Erh-shih-wu-shih pu-pien 二十五史補編. 6 vols. Shanghai, 1935–1937.

Erh-ya 爾雅. With commentary by Kuo P'u 郭璞 (A.D. 276–324). 3 *chüan*. I-wen facsimile *SSCCS* ed. Taipei, 1955.

Erh-ya i-shu 爾雅義疏. By Hao I-hsing 郝懿行 (1757–1825). 19 *chüan*. *SPPY*.

Études asiatiques. Publiée à l'occasion du vingt-cinquième anniversaire de l'École française d'Extrême-Orient par see membres et ses collaborateurs. 2 vols. Paris, 1925.

Fa-men ming-i chi 法門名義集. By Li Shih-cheng 李師政. *Taishō*.

Fa-yen 法言. By Yang Hsiung 揚雄 (53 B.C.–A.D. 18). 13 + *yin-i* 音義. 1 *chüan*. *SPPY*.

Fa-yüan chu-lin 法苑珠林. By Tao-shih 道世. 120 *chüan*. *SPTK so-pen*.

Fan fan-yü 翻梵語. By Hsin-hsing 信行. 10 *chüan*. *Taishō*.

Fan Hsiang-yung 范祥雍. *Lo-yang ch'ieh-lan chi chiao-chu* 洛陽伽藍記校注. 5 *chüan*. Shanghai, 1958.

Fan-i ming-i chi 翻譯名義集. By Fa-yün 法雲. 7 *chüan*. *SPTK so-pen*.

Fang-kuang ta Chuang-yen ching 方廣大莊嚴經. Translated by Ti-p'o-k'o-lo 地婆訶羅. 12 *chüan*. *Taishō*.

Fang-yen shu-cheng 方言疏證. *Fang-yen* by Yang Hsiung, *shu-cheng* by Tai Chen 戴震 (1723–1777). 13 *chüan*. *SSPY*.

Feng Ch'eng-chün 馮承鈞, tr. *Hsi T'u-chüeh shih-liao* 西突厥史料 Shanghai, 1934; facsimile ed., Taipei, 1962.

———. *Hsi-yü Nan-hai shih-ti k'ao-cheng i-ts'ung*, 6th Series 西域南海史地考證譯叢第六編. Facsimile ed., Taipei, 1962.

———. *Shih-ti ts'ung-k'ao hsü-pien* 史地叢考續編. Shanghai, 1933.

Fo-shuo Kuan-wu-liang-shou fo ching 佛說觀無量壽佛經. Translated by Chiang-liang-yeh-she 畺良耶舍. *Taishō*.

Fo-shuo p'u-sa pen-hsing ching 佛說菩薩本行經. 3 *chüan*. *Taishō*.

Fo-shuo shan-tzu ching 佛說睒子經. Translated by Sheng-chien 聖堅. 1 *chüan*. *Taishō*.

Fo-shuo shih-erh yu ching 佛說十二遊經. Translated by Chia-liu-t'o-ch'ieh 迦留陀伽. *Taishō*.

Fo-shuo t'ai-tzu jui-ying pen-ch'i ching 佛說太子瑞應本起經. Translated by Chih-ch'ien 支謙. 2 *chüan*. *Taishō*.

Fo-tsu t'ung-chi 佛祖統紀. By Chih-ch'ing 志磐. 54 *chüan*. *Taishō*.

Foucher, Alfred. "Notes sur la géographie ancienne du Gandhāra." *BEFEO* 1 (1901), 322–369.

Franke, Otto. *Geschichte des chinesischen Reiches*. 5 vols. Berlin and Leipzig, 1930–1952.

Frankel, Hans H. "Fifteen Poems by Ts'ao Chih: An Attempt at a New Approach," *JAOS* 84 (January–March 1964), 1–14.

Fujita Toyohachi 藤田豐八. *Hui-ch'ao wang Wu-t'ien-chu chuan*

chien-shih (Kai-chō ō Gotenjiku den senshaku) 慧超往五天竺傳箋釋. Peiping, 1931.

Funaki, Katsuma 船木勝馬. "Hokugi no Seiiki kōtsū ni kansuru shomondai." I 北魏の西域交通に関する諸問題 in *Fukuoka Nishi Nihon shigaku* 福岡西日本史学 4 (1950), 46–69; II in *Hakusan shigaku* 白山史学 (Tōyō Daigaku Hakusan Shigakkai 東洋大学白山史学会), 2 (1956), 1–10.

de Groot, J.J.M. *Universismus, die Grundlage der Religion und Ethik, des Staatswesens und der Wissenschaften Chinas*. Berlin, 1918.

van Gulik, Robert H. *Hsi K'ang and His Political Essay on the Lute*. Tokyo, 1968.

Hai-nei shih-chou chi 海內十洲記. By Tung-fang Shuo 東方朔 (ca. 161–ca. 87 B.C.). *IS* edited by Wu Kuan 吳琯 (1571 *chin-shih*). Facsmile ed., Shanghai, 1937.

Han Hsi-yü t'u-k'ao 漢西域圖考. By Li Kuang-t'ing 李光廷 (1812–1880). 7 + 1 *chüan*. N.p., 1870.

Han-shu pu-chu 漢書補注. *Han-shu* by Pan Ku 班固 (A.D. 32–92), with commentary by Yen Shih-ku 顏師古 (A.D. 581–645). *Pu-chu* with supplementary commentary by Wang Hsien-ch'ien 王先謙. 100 *chüan*, I-wen facsimile ed., Taipei, 1955.

Han-Wei Nan-pei-ch'ao mu-chih chi-shih. See Chao Wan-li.

Han-Wei shih-ching k'ao 漢魏石經考. By Liu Ch'uan-ying 劉傳瑩. T'un-ch'eng 沌城, 1886.

Han-Wei ts'ung-shu 漢魏叢書. Edited by Wang Mo 王謨. I-wen facsimile ed., Taipei, 1967.

Hashimoto Masukichi 橋本増吉. "Reidaikō" 霊台考. *Shigaku* 史学 13:4 (1934), 1–23.

Hatanaka Jōen 畑中浄円. "*Rakuyō garan ki* no sho hanpon to sono keitō" 洛陽伽藍記の諸版本とその系統. *Ōtani gakuhō* 大谷学報 30:4 (June 1951), 39–55.

Hatani Ryōtai 羽渓了諦. *Seiiki no Bukkyō* 西域の佛教. Kyoto, 1914.

Hattori Katsuhiko 服部克彥. *Hokugi Rakuyō no shakai to bunka* 北魏洛陽の社会と文化 and *Zoku* 續. 2 vols. Kyoto, 1965 and 1968.

Hawkes, David. *Ch'u Tz'u, the Songs of the South*. London, 1959.

Ho Chien-min 何健民, tr. *Chung-kuo Nan-hai ku-tai chiao-t'ung ts'ung-k'ao* 中國南海古代交通叢考. Shanghai, 1936.

Ho Peng-yoke 何丙郁. *The Astronomical Chapters of the Chin-shu*. Paris, 1966.

Ho Ping-ti 何炳棣. "Pei-Wei Lo-yang ch'eng-kuo kuei-hua" 北魏洛陽城郭規劃. *CYYCY, Symposium in Honor of Dr. Li Chi on*

His Seventieth Birthday 1, 1965, 1–27.

———. "Lo-yang, A.D. 495–534; A Study of Physical and Socio-Economic Planning of a Metropolitan Area." *HJAS* 26 (1966), 52–101.

Holzman, Donald. *La vie et la pensée de Hi K'ang (223–262 A.P.J.C.)*. Leiden, 1957.

Hori Kentoku 堀謙德. *Kaisetsu Seiiki ki* 解說西域記. Tokyo, 1912.

Hou-Han shu chi-chieh 後漢書集解. *Hou-Han shu* by Fan Yeh 范曄 (A.D. 398–445), with commentary by Li Hsien 李賢 (A.D. 651–684) and Ssu-ma Piao 司馬彪 (fl. ca. A.D. 270). *Chi-chieh* (collected annotations) by Wang Hsien-ch'ien. 10 + 80 + 30 *chüan*. I-wen facsimile ed., Taipei, 1955.

Hsi-ching tsa-chi 西京雜記. By Liu Hsin 劉歆 (ca. 46 B.C.–A.D. 23). 6 *chuan*. *SPTK so-pen*.

Hsi-yü shui-tao chi 西域水道記. By Hsü Sung 徐松 (1781–1848). 5 *chüan*. Facsimile ed., Taipei, 1966.

Hsiao, Kung-ch'üan 蕭公權. *A History of Chinese Political Thought*. Translated by F. W. Mote. Vol. 1. Princeton, 1979.

Hsien-yü ching 賢愚經. Translated by Hui-chüeh 慧覺 et al. 13 *chüan*. *Taishō*.

Hsin T'ang-shu 新唐書. By Ou-yang Hsiu 歐陽修 (1007–1072), Sung Ch'i 宋祁 (998–1061), et al. 225 *chüan*. I-wen facsimile ed., Taipei, 1956.

Hsiu-hsing pen-ch'i ching 修行本起經. Translated by Chu Ta-li kung-k'ang-meng-hsiang 竺大力共康孟詳. 2 *chüan*. *Taishō*.

Hsü Hsiao-mu chi chien-chu 徐孝穆集箋注. *Hsü-hsiao-mu chi* by Hsü Ling 徐陵 (A.D. 507–583). *Chien-chu* (annotations and commentary) by Wu Chao-i 吳兆宜. 6 + 1 *chüan*. *SPPY*.

Hsü Kao-juan 徐高阮. *Ch'ung-k'an Lo-yang ch'ieh-lan chi* 重刊洛陽伽藍記. 2 vols. Taipei, 1960.

Hsü Kao-seng chuan 續高僧傳. By Tao-hsüan 道宣. 30 *chüan*. *Taishō*.

Hsü Ku-wen yüan 續古文苑. Compiled by Sun Hsing-yen 孫星衍 (1753–1818). 20 *chüan*. Yeh-ch'eng shan-kuan 冶城山館 ed., 1812.

Hsü Shih-ying 許世瑛. "*Shih-shuo hsin-yü* chung ti-i-shen ch'eng-tai-tz'u yen-chiu" 世說新語中第一身稱代詞研究. *Tan-chiang hsüeh-pao* 淡江學報 2 (1963), 19–21.

Hsüeh-chin t'ao-yüan 學津討原. Compiled and published by Chang Hai-p'eng 張海鵬 (1755–1816).

Huai-nan-tzu 淮南子. By Liu An 劉安 (d. 122 B.C.). With commentary by Hsü Shen 許愼 (fl. A.D. 100) and Kao Yu 高誘 (fl. A.D. 205–212). 21 *chüan*. *SPTK so-pen*.

Hucker, Charles O. "Governmental Organization of the Ming Dynasty." *HJAS* 21 (1958), 1–66.

Hughes, E. R. *Two Chinese Poets*. Princeton, 1960.

Hung-ming chi 弘明集. By Seng-yu 僧佑 (d. early 6th cent.). 14 *chüan*. *Taishō*.

Hurvitz, Leon. *Wei Shou on Buddhism and Taoism*. Kyoto, 1956.

I-ch'ieh-ching yin-i 一切經音義. By Hui-lin 慧琳. 100 *chüan*. *Taishō*.

I-ching 易經. With commentary by Wang Pi 王弼 (A.D. 226–249), Han K'ang-po 韓康伯 (fl. A.D. 371), Lu Te-ming 陸德明 (d. ca. A.D. 627), and Hsing Shou 邢璹 (fl. A.D. 737). 10 *chüan*. I-wen facsimile *SSCCS* ed., Taipei, 1955.

I-wen lei-chü 藝文類聚. Compiled by Ou-yang Hsün 歐陽珣 (A.D. 557–641) et al. 100 *chüan*. Facsimile ed., Taipei, 1960.

Iriya Yoshitaka 入矢義高, ed. *Rakuyō garan ki* 洛陽伽藍記. In *Chūgoku koten bungaku taikei* 中國古典文學大系. Tokyo, 1974.

Jao Tsong-yi 饒宗頤 and Paul Demiéville, eds. *Airs de Touen-Houang (Touen-houang k'iu). Textes à chanter des huitième-dixième siècles*. Paris, 1971.

Jih-chih-lu chi-shih 日知錄集釋. *Jih-chih-lu* by Ku Yen-wu 顧炎武 (1613–1682); *chi-shih* (collected commentaries) by Huang Ju-ch'eng 黃汝成 (1799-1837). 32 *chüan*. *SPPY*.

Ju-yin-t'ang 如隱堂. Publisher of the *Lo-yang ch'ieh-lan chi*, possibly by Lu Ts'ai 陸采 (1497–1537). I-wen facsimile ed., Taipei, n.d.

K'ai-yüan shih-chiao lu 開元釋教錄. By Chih-sheng 智昇 (fl. A.D. 730). 20 *chüan*. *Taishō*.

Kan-chu chi 紺珠集. By Chu Sheng-fei 朱勝非. 13 *chüan*. A.D. 1137 hand copy housed at Harvard-Yenching Library, Cambridge.

Kanda Kiichirō 神田喜一郎. "Rakuyō garanki jo sakki" 洛陽伽藍記序劄記. *Tōyōshi kenkyū* 東洋史硏究 9 (July 1947), 71–94.

Kao-seng chuan 高僧傳. By Hui-chiao 慧皎. 14 *chüan*. *Taishō*.

Kao-seng Fa-hsien chuan 高僧法顯傳. By Fa-hsien. 1 *chüan*. *Taishō*.

Karlgren, Bernhard. *The Book of Odes*. Stockholm, 1950.

Kracke, Edward A., Jr. *Civil Service In Early Sung China 960–1067*. Cambridge, 1953.

Ku-chin chu 古今注. By Ts'ui Pao 崔豹. 3 *chüan*. Facsimile *IS* ed. Shanghai, 1937.

Ku-chin i-shih 古今逸史. Edited by Wu Kuan 吳琯 (1571 *chin-shih*). Facsimile ed., Shanghai, 1937.

Kuan-tzu 管子. With commentary by Fang Hsüan-ling 房玄齡, pseudonym Yin Chih-chang 尹知章 (fl. A.D. 705). 24 *chüan*. *SPTK so-pen*.

Kuang Hung-ming chi 廣弘明集. By Tao-hsüan 道宣. 30 *chüan*. *Taishō*.

Kuang-ya shu-cheng 廣雅疏證 *Kuang-ya* by Chang I 張揖 (fl A.D. 227–232). *Shu-cheng* (annotations and commentary) by Wang Nien-sun 王念孫 (1742–1832). 10 *chüan*. *SPPY*.

Kuang-yün 廣韻. Revised by Ch'en P'eng-nien 陳彭年 (fl. A.D. 986). 5 *chüan*. *SPPY*.

Kuo Pao-chün 郭寶鈞. "Lo-yang ku-ch'eng k'an-ch'a chien-pao" 洛陽古城勘察簡報. *K'ao-ku t'ung-hsün* 考古通訊 1 (1955), 9–21.

Kuo-yü 國語. With commentary by Wei Chao 韋昭 (A.D. 204–274). 21 *chüan*. *SPTK so-pen*.

Lao Kan 勞榦. "Lun *Hsi-ching tsa-chi* chih tso-che chi ch'i ch'eng-shu shih-tai" 論西京雜記之作者及其成書時代. *CYYCY* 33 (1962), 19–34.

———. "Pei-Wei Lo-yang ch'eng-t'u ti fu-yüan" 北魏洛陽城圖的復原. *CYYCY* 20A (1948), 299–312.

Lao-tzu Tao-te ching 老子道德經. By Lao-tzu 老子 (ca. 300 B.C.). With commentary by Ho-shang kung 河上公 (pseudonym). 2 *chüan*. *SPTK so-pen*.

Lau, D. C., tr. *Mencius*. Baltimore, 1970.

Legge, James, tr. *The Chinese Classics*. 5, *The Ch'un Ts'ew with the Tso Chuen*. Reprint, Hong Kong, 1960.

———. *The Chinese Classics*. 3, *The Shoo King or The Book of Historical Documents*. Reprint, Hong Kong, 1960.

Li-chi 禮記. With commentary by Cheng Hsüan and Lu Te-ming, and sub-commentary by K'ung Ying-ta 孔穎達 (A.D. 574–648). I-wen facsimile *SSCCS* ed., Taipei, 1955.

Li Pei hai chi 李北海集. By Li Yung 李邕. 6 *chüan*. *Ssu-k'u ch'üan-shu chen-pen* 四庫全書珍本 Series 4, vol. 212. Shanghai, 1934–1935.

Li-shuo-pien 蠡勺編. By Ling Yang-tsao 凌揚藻. 40 *chüan*. *Ling-nan i-shu* 嶺南遺書 ed., Canton, 1863.

Li-tai san-pao chi 歷代三寶記. By Fei Ch'ang-fang 費長房. 15 *chüan*. *Taishō*.

Liang-shu 梁書. By Yao Ch'a 姚察 (A.D. 533–606) and Yao Ssu-lien 姚思廉 (d. A.D. 637). 56 *chüan*. I-wen facsimile ed., Taipei, 1956.

Lieh-hsien chuan 列仙傳. By Liu Hsiang 劉向 (79–8 B.C.). 2 *chüan*. Facsimile *IS* ed., Shanghai, 1937.

Lieh-tzu 列子. Attributed to Lieh Yü-k'ou 列禦寇. 8 *chüan*. *SPPY*.

Liu, James J. Y. *The Chinese Knight Errant*. Chicago, 1967.

Liu Ju-ling 劉汝霖. "Liu-ch'ao ch'ieh-lan chi hsü-mu" 六朝伽藍記敍目. *Shih-fan ta-hsüeh yüeh-k'an* 師範大學月刊 13 (1934), 40–58.

Liu-tu chi ching 六度集經. Translated by K'ang Seng-hui 康僧會. 8 *chüan*. *Taishō*.

Liu Wen-hsien 劉文獻. *Han shih-ching I-li ts'an-shih chi-cheng* 漢石經儀禮殘石集證. Taipei, 1969.

Lo Ken-tse 羅根澤. "*Lo-yang ch'ieh-lan chi* shih-lun" 洛陽伽藍記試論. *Wen-hsüeh i-ch'an* 文學遺產 298, *Kuang-ming jih-pao* 光明日報 (January 31, 1960).

Lo-yang ch'ieh-lan chi 洛陽伽藍記. Facsimile *Hsüeh-chin t'ao-yüan* ed., Shanghai, 1922.

Lo-yang ch'ieh-lan chi chi-cheng 洛陽伽藍記集證. By Wu Jo-chun 吳若準. 5 + 1 *chüan*. *SPPY*.

Lo-yang hsien-chih 洛陽縣志 (of Chia-ch'ing 嘉慶 period, 1796–1820). By Wei Hsiang 魏襄 and Lu Chi-lu 陸繼輅. 60 *chüan*. Lo-yang, 1813.

Lo-yang Po-wu-kuan 洛陽博物館. "Lo-yang Pei-Wei Yüan Shao mu" 洛陽北魏元邵墓. *K'ao-ku* 4 (1973), 218–224, 243.

Loewe, Michael. *Ways to Paradise*. London, 1979.

Lü-chün-t'ing 綠君亭, ed. *Lo-yang ch'ieh-lan chi* 洛陽伽藍記. Compiled by Mao Chin 毛晉. 1599–1659. I-wen facsimile ed., Taipei, n.d.

Lü-shih ch'un-ch'iu 呂氏春秋. By Lü Pu-wei 呂不韋 (ca. 240 B.C.). With commentary by Kao Yu 高誘 (fl. A.D. 205–212). 26 *chüan*. *SPTK so-pen*.

Lun-yü 論語. With commentary by Ho Yen 何晏 (d. A.D. 249) and subcommentary by Hsing Ping 邢昺 (A.D. 930–1010). 20 *chüan*. I-wen facsimile *SSCCS* ed., Taipei, 1955.

Mao-shih ts'ao-mu niao-shou ch'ung-yü shu 毛詩草木鳥獸蟲魚疏. By Lu Chi 陸璣. 2 *chüan*. *Ts'ung-shu chi-ch'eng* 叢書集成 facsimile ed., with preface by Ting Yen 丁晏 (1794–1875) dated 1855. Shanghai, 1935–1937.

Mather, Richard B., tr. *Biography of Lü Kuang*. Berkeley and Los Angeles, 1959.

———, tr. *A New Account of Tales of the World*. Minneapolis, 1976.

Matsuda Hisao 松田寿男. *Kodai rekishichirigaku-teki kenkyū* 古代歴史地理学的研究. Revised ed. Tokyo, 1974.

Meng-tzu 孟子. With commentary by Chao Ch'i 趙岐 (A.D. 109–201). 14 *chüan*, each divided into 2 parts. I-wen facsimile *SSCCS* ed., Taipei, 1955.

Mi-le p'u-sa so-wen pen-yüan ching 彌勒菩薩所問本願經. Translated by Chu Fa-hu 竺法護. *Taishō*.

Mizuno Seiichi 水野清一. "Rakuyō Eineiji kai" 洛陽永寧寺解. *Kōkogaku ronsō* 考古學論叢 10 (January 1939), 111–128.

Mizutani Shinjo 水谷真成, ed. *Dai-Tō Seiiki ki* 大唐西域記. In *Chūgoku koten bungaku taikei*. Tokyo, 1971.

Mori Masao 護雅夫. *Kodai Toruko minzokushi kenkyū* 古代トルコ民族史研究. Vol. 1, 3rd ed., Tokyo, 1976.

Mori Shikazō 森鹿三. "Hokugi Rakuyōjō no kibo ni tsuite" 北魏洛陽城の規模について. *Tōyōshi kenkyū* 東洋史研究 11:4 (1952), 36.

———. "Itsu-shū-sho Sakurakukai to Hokugi Dai-Rakuyōjō" 逸周書作雒解と北魏大洛陽城 *Tōyōshi kenkyū* 11:4 (1952) 22–35.

———. "Rō Kan shi no Hokugi Rakuyōjōzu-teki fukugen o hyōsu" 労榦氏の北魏洛陽城図的復原を評す. In *Tōyōgaku kenkyū* 東洋学研究 Tokyo, 1970, pp. 229–243.

Mu-t'ien-tzu chuan 穆天子傳. With commentary by Kuo P'u 郭璞 (A.D. 276–324) 6 *chüan*. *SPTK so-pen*.

Nagasawa Kazutoshi 長澤和俊. *Rōran-ōkoku* 楼蘭王国 in Regulus Library vol. 64. Tokyo, 1976.

———. *Sōun kōki* 宋雲行紀 in *Tōyō bunko* 東洋文庫 vol. 194. Tokyo, 1971.

Nan-Ch'i shu 南齊書. By Hsiao Tzu-hsien 蕭子顯 (A.D. 439–537). 59 *chüan*. I-wen facsimile ed., Taipei, 1956.

Nan-ch'uang chi-t'an 南窗紀談. By an unknown author. *Hsüeh-hai lei-pien* 學海類編 ed., Reprint, Shanghai, 1920.

Nan-fang ts'ao-mu chuang 南方草木狀. By Hsi Han 嵇含 (ca. A.D. 304). 3 *chüan*, 40 illustrations. Facsimile ed., Shanghai, 1955.

Nan-hua chen-ching 南華眞經. See *Chuang-tzu*.

Nan-shih 南史. By Li Yen-shou 李延壽 (ca. A.D. 629). 80 *chüan*. I-wen facsimile ed., Taipei, 1956.

Nan-ts'un cho-keng lu 南村輟耕錄. By T'ao Tsung-i 陶宗儀. 30 *chüan*. Yü-lan ts'ao-t'ang 玉蘭草堂 (Ming) ed. N.p., n.d.

Nan-yang hsüeh-pao 南洋學報. Singapore, after 1940.

Needham, Joseph. *Science and Civilisation in China*. Vols. 1–5. Cambridge, 1954–1974.

Nien-erh-shih ta-chi 廿二史劄記. By Chao I 趙翼 (1727–1814). 36 *chüan*. *SPPY*.

Nishijima Sadao 西嶋定生. "Tenkai no kanata" 碾磑の彼方. In his *Chūgoku keizaishi kenkyū* 中国経済史研究. Tokyo, 1966.

Ōchō Enichi 横超慧日. *Hokugi Bukkyō no kenkyū* 北魏仏教の研究. Kyoto, 1970.

Pai Chien 白堅. *Wei shih-ching ts'an-shih chi* 魏石經殘石集. Shanghai (?), 1930.

Pai-hu-t'ung te lun. See *Po-hu-t'ung te lun*.

Pao-p'u-tzu 抱朴子. By Ko Hung 葛洪 (fl. A.D. 317–350). 70 *chüan*. *SPTK so-pen*.

Pei-Ch'i shu 北齊書. By Li Te-lin 李德林 (A.D. 530–590) and Li Pai-yao 李百藥 (A.D. 565–648). 50 *chüan*. I-wen facsimile ed., Taipei, 1956.

Pei-shih 北史. By Li Yen-shou 李延壽 (fl. ca. A.D. 629). 100 *chüan*. I-wen facsimile ed., Taipei, 1956.

Pei-Wei seng Hui-sheng shih Hsi-yü chi 北魏僧惠生使西域記. *Taishō*.

Pelliot, Paul. "Quelque textes chinois concernant l'Indochine hindouisée." *Études asiatiques* 2 (1925), 243–263.

Po-hu-t'ung te lun 白虎通德論. By Pan Ku 班固 (A.D. 32–92). 10 *chüan*. *SPTK so-pen*.

Po-wu chih 博物志. By Chang Hua 張華 (A.D. 230–300). Edited by Wu Kuan 吳琯 (1571 *chih-shih*). 10 *chüan*. *IS*. Facsimile ed., Shanghai, 1937.

Pu Liang chiang-yü chih 補梁疆域志. By Hung I-sun 洪齮孫 (1773–1816). 4 *chüan*. *Erh-shih-wu-shih pu-pien* ed., Shanghai, 1935–1937.

P'u-sa pen-sheng man lun 菩薩本生鬘論. Translated by Shao-te 紹德 and Hui-hsün 慧詢. 16 *chüan*. *Taishō*.

P'u-sa pen-yüan ching 菩薩本緣經. Translated by Chih-ch'ien 支謙. 3 *chüan*. *Taishō*.

P'u-sa t'ou-sheng ssu-o-hu ch'i-t'a yin-yüan ching 菩薩投身飼餓虎起塔因緣經. Translated by Fa-sheng 法盛. 1 *chüan*. *Taishō*.

des Rotours, Robert. *Traité des fonctionnaires et de l'armée, tr. de la*

Nouvelle histoire des T'ang. 2 vols. Leiden, 1948.

———. *Le Traité des examens, traduit de la Nouvelle histoire des T'ang*. Paris, 1932.

San-kuo chih chi-chieh 三國志集解. *San-kuo chih* (*Wei-chih* 魏志, 30 *chüan*; *Shu-chih* 蜀志, 15 *chüan*; and *Wu-chih* 吳志, 20 *chüan*) by Ch'en Shou 陳壽 (A.D. 233–297). Commentary by P'ei Sung-chih 裴松之 (A.D. 372–451); *chi-chieh* (collected annotations) by Lu Pi 盧弼 (preface of 1936). Peking, 1957.

Schwartzberg, Joseph E. *A Historical Atlas of South Asia*. Chicago, 1978.

Shan-chien lü-p'i-p'o-sha 善見律毗婆沙. Translated by Chia-pa-t'o-lo 伽跋陀羅. 18 *chüan*. *Taishō*.

Shan-hai ching 山海經. With commentary by Kuo P'u 郭璞. 18 *chüan*. *SPTK so-pen*.

Shang-shu 尚書. See *Shu-ching*.

Shang-shu ta-chuan 尚書大傳. Ascribed to Fu Sheng 伏生 (fl. ca. 206 B.C.). Commentary by Cheng Hsüan. Collation by Ch'en Shou-ch'i 陳壽祺 (1771–1834). 5 + 1 *chüan*. *SPTK so-pen*.

Shih-chi hui-chu k'ao-cheng 史記會注考證. *Shih-chi* by Ssu-ma T'an 司馬談 (d. 112 B.C.) and Ssu-ma Ch'ien 司馬遷 (ca. 145–ca. 86 B.C.). Commentary by P'ei Yin 裴駰 (fl. A.D. 465–475) (Ssu-ma Chen 司馬貞 first half of 8th cent.), and Chang Shou-chieh 張守節 (A.D. 737). *K'ao-cheng* (verifications) by Takigawa Kametarō 瀧川亀太郎. 130 *chüan*. I-wen facsimile ed., Taipei, 1957 (?).

Shih-chia fang-chih 釋迦方志. By Tao-hsuan 道宣. 2 *chüan*. *Taishō*.

Shih-chia p'u 釋迦譜. By Seng-yu 僧祐. 5 *chüan*. *Taishō*.

Shih-ching 詩經. Commentary by Mao Heng 毛亨 (early 2nd cent. B.C.) and Cheng Hsüan; sub-commentary by Lu Te-ming and K'ung Ying-ta. I-wen facsimile *SSCCS* ed., Taipei, 1955.

Shih-liu-kuo ch'un-ch'iu chi-pu 十六國春秋輯補. By T'ang Ch'iu 湯球. 100 *chüan*. Kuang-ya shu-chü 廣雅書局, ed. Canton, 1895.

Shih-men tzu-ching lu 釋門自鏡錄. By Huai-hsin 懷信. 2 *chüan*. *Taishō*.

Shih-ming 釋名. By Liu Hsi 劉熙 (fl. ca. A.D. 196). 8 *chüan*. *SPTK so-pen*.

Shih-shih yao-lan 釋氏要覽. By Tao-ch'eng 道誠. 3 *chüan*. *Taishō*.

Shih-shuo hsin-yü 世說新語. By Liu I-ch'ing 劉義慶 (A.D. 403–444).

Commentary by Liu Chün 劉峻 (A.D 462–521). 3 *chüan*. I-wen facsimile ed., Taipei, 1964.

Shih-t'ung 史通. By Liu Chih-chi 劉知幾 (A.D. 661–721). 20 *chüan*. *SPTK*.

Shih-t'ung t'ung-shih 史通通釋. *T'ung-shih* by P'u Ch'i-lung 浦起龍 (b. 1679; 1730 *chin-shih*). 20 *chüan*. *SPPY*.

Shiratori Kurakichi 白鳥庫吉. "Keisenkoku kō" 罽賓國考. In *Seiikishi kenkyū* 西域史研究. Tokyo, 1941.

Shu-chih. See *San-kuo-chih chi-chieh*.

Shu-ching 書經. Commentary by K'ung An-kuo 孔安國 (pseudonym); sub-commentary by Lu Te-ming and K'ung Ying-ta. I-wen facsimile *SSCCS* ed., Taipei, 1955.

Shu-i chi 述異記. By Jen Fang 任昉 (A.D. 460–508). 2 *chüan*. *Han-Wei ts'ung-shu* 漢魏叢書 ed. Compiled by Wang Mo 王謨. Late 18th cent. I-wen facsimile ed., Taipei, 1967.

Shui-ching chu 水經注. *Shui-ching* by Sang Ch'in 桑欽; *chu* (commentary) by Li Tao-yüan 酈道元 (d. A.D. 527). 40 *chüan*. I-wen facsimile ed., Taipei, 1959(?).

Shuo-wen chieh-tzu Tuan chu 說文解字段注. *Shuo-wen chieh-tzu* by Hsü Shen 許慎. *Chu* (commentary) by Tuan Yü-ts'ai 段玉裁 (1738–1815). 30 + 2 *chüan*. *SPPY*.

Shuo-yüan 說苑. By Liu Hsiang 劉向. 20 *chüan*. *SPTK so-pen*.

Sickman, Laurence, and Alexander Soper. *The Art and Architecture of China*. London, 1956; new ed., 1968.

Ssu-k'u ch'üan-shu tsung-mu t'i-yao 四庫全書總目提要. 200 *chüan*. I-wen facsimile ed., Taipei, n.d.

Ssu-pu pei-yao 四部備要. Shanghai, 1927–1935.

Ssu-pu ts'ung-k'an 四部叢刊. Shanghai, 1929–1936.

Ssu-shih-chai chi 思適齋集. By Ku Kuang-ch'i 顧廣圻 (1776–1835). 18 *chüan*. Shanghai, 1849.

Stein, Sir Mark Aurel. *Ancient Khotan: Detailed Report of Archaeological Explorations in Chinese Turkestan*. 2 vols. Oxford, 1907.

———. *Kalhana Rajatarangini*. Delhi, 1961.

Straughair, Anna. *Chang Hua: A Statesman-poet of the Western Chin Dynasty*. Canberra, 1973.

Su Chi-ch'ing 蘇繼廎. "Chia-ying-kuo k'ao" 加營國考. *Nan-yang hsüeh pao* 南洋學報 7:1 (1951), 18–24.

Sugimoto Naojirō 杉本直治郎. *Tōnan Ajia-shi kenkyū* I 東南アジア史研究. Revised ed., Tokyo, 1968.

Sui-shu 隋書. By Wei Cheng 魏徵 (A.D. 580–643). 85 *chüan*, I-wen facsimile ed., Taipei, 1956.

Sui-shu ching-chi-chih k'ao-cheng 隋書經籍志考證. By Chang Tsung-yüan 章宗源 (1752?–1800). *Erh-shih-wu shih pu-pien* 二十五史補編 ed., Shanghai, 1935–1937.

Sui-shu ching-chi-chih k'ao-cheng. By Yao Chen-tsung 姚振宗. 52 *chüan*. *Erh-shih-wu-shih pu-pien* ed., Shanghai, 1935–1937.

Sun Hai-po 孫海波. *Wei san-tzu shih-ching chi-lu* 魏三字石經集錄. I-wen facsimile ed., Taipei, 1975.

Sung-shu 宋書. By Shen Yüen 沈約 (A.D. 441–513). 100 *chüan*. I-wen facsimile ed., Taipei, 1956.

Ta chih-tu lun 大智度論. Translated by Chiu-mo-lo-shih 鳩摩羅什 (Kumārajīva). 100 *chüan*. *Taishō*.

Ta-pan nieh-p'an ching 大般涅槃經. Translated by Fa-hsien 法顯 3 *chüan*. *Taishō*.

Ta-T'ang Hsi-yü chi 大唐西域記. By Hsüan-tsang 玄奘 (ca. A.D. 596–664). *SPTK so-pen*.

Ta-T'ang nei-tien lu 大唐內典錄. By Tao-hsüan 道宣. 10 *chüan*. *Taishō*.

Ta-T'ang Ta-tz'u-en-ssu San-tsang-fa-shih chuan 大唐大慈恩寺三藏法師傳. By Hui-li 慧立 and Yen-ts'ung 彥悰. 10 *chüan*. *Taishō*.

Tai-tzu Hsü-ta-na ching 太子須大拏經. Translated by Sheng-chien 聖堅. *Taishō*.

T'ai-p'ing huan-yü chi 太平寰宇記. By Yüeh Shih 樂史. 200 *chüan*. Wen-hai 文海 facsimile [1803] ed., Taipei, 1963.

T'ai-p'ing kuang-chi 太平廣記. By Li Fang 李昉 (A.D. 925–996) et al. 500 *chüan*. Soochow, 1806.

T'ai-p'ing yü-lan 太平御覽. By Li Fang et al. Facsimile ed., Peking, 1959.

Taishō shinshū daizōkyō 大正新修大藏經. Tokyo, 1922–1933.

Takakusu Junjirō 高楠順次郎, tr. *Nankai kiki naihō den* 南海寄歸內法傳 Kyoto, 1913.

T'ang Ch'ang-ju 唐長孺. *Wei-Chin Nan-pei-ch'ao shih lun-ts'ung hsü-pien* 魏晉南北朝史論叢續編. Peking, 1959.

T'ang Yen 唐晏. *Lo-yang ch'ieh-lan chi kou-ch'en* 洛陽伽藍記鉤沉. Shanghai, 1915.

T'ang Yung-t'ung 湯用彤. *Han-Wei Liang-Chin Nan-pei-ch'ao fo-chiao shih* 漢魏兩晉南北朝佛教史. 2 vols. Facsimile of 1938 ed., Taipei, 1965.

Teng Ssu-yü 鄧嗣禹, tr. *Family Instructions for the Yen Clan, Yen-shih chia-hsün*. Leiden, 1968.

T'ien Su-lan 田素蘭. "*Lo-yang ch'ieh-lan chi* chiao-chu" 洛陽伽藍記校注. In *Kuo-wen yen-chiu-so chi-k'an* 國文研究所集刊 16 (Kuo-li Shih-fan ta-hsüeh 國立師範大學). Taipei, 1972, 1–164.

Ting Ch'ien 丁謙 (1843–1919). *Sung Yün ch'iu-ching-chi ti-li k'ao-cheng* 宋雲求經記地理考證. *Che-chiang t'u-shu-kuan ts'ung-shu* 浙江圖書館叢書. 2nd Series. Hangchow, 1915.

Ting Fu-pao 丁福保 (1874–1952). *Ch'üan Pei-Wei shih* 全北魏詩. In *Ch'uan-Han San-kuo Chin Nan-pei-ch'ao shih* 全漢三國晉南北朝詩. I-wen facsimile ed., Taipei, 1957.

Tjan Tjoe Som, tr. *Po Hu T'ung, the Comprehensive Discussions in the White Tiger Hall*. 2 vols. Leiden, 1949, 1952.

Ts'e-fu yüan-kuei 册府元龜. By Wang Ch'in-jo 王欽若 (A.D. 962–1025.). 1,000 *chüan*. Facsimile ed., Hong Kong, 1960.

Tsukamoto Zenryū 塚本善隆. *Gisho Shaku-Rō-shi no kenkyū* 魏書釋老志の研究. Kyoto, 1961.

Tung-Chin Nan-pei-ch'ao yü-ti piao 東晉南北朝輿地表. By Hsü Wen-fan 徐文范. Preface written by author in 1803. *Erh-shih-wu-shih pu-pien* ed., Shanghai, 1935–1937.

T'ung-tien 通典. By Tu Yu 杜佑 (A.D. 735–812). 200 *chüan*. I-wen facsimile ed., Taipei, 1959.

Tzu-chih t'ung-chien 資治通鑑. By Ssu-ma Kuang 司馬光 (1019–1086). With commentary by Hu San-hsing 胡三省 (1230–1302). 294 *chüan*. I-wen facsimile ed., Taipei, 1955.

Tzu-chih t'ung-chien k'ao-i 資治通鑑考異. By Ssu-ma Kuang. 30 *chüan*. *SPTK so-pen*.

Uchida Ginpū 内田吟風. "Kōgi Sōun shaku Keisei Seiiki kyūkyōki kōsho josetsu" 後魏宋雲釋惠生西域求經記考證序説. In *Tsukamoto hakushi shōju kinen Bukkyōshigaku ronsō* 塚本博士頌壽紀念佛教史学論叢. Kyoto, 1961, pp. 113–124.

Wada Hironori 和田博德. "Toyokukon to Nambokuryōchō to no kankei ni tsuite" 吐谷渾と南北兩朝との関係について. *Shigaku* 史学 25:2 (1951), 80–103.

Waley, Arthur, tr. *The Analects of Confucius*, London, 1938.

———. tr. *The Book of Songs*. New York, 1960.

———. tr. *170 Chinese Poems*. London, 1918.

Wang Kuo-wei 王國維 (1877–1927). "Wei shih-ching k'ao" 魏石經考. In *Kuan-t'ang chi-lin* 觀堂集林: I-wen facsimile ed.,

Taipei, 1956.

Wang Yi-t'ung 王伊同. "The Political and Intellectual World in the Poetry of Juan Chi." *Renditions* 7 (Hong Kong, 1977), 48–61.

———. "Slaves and Other Comparable Social Groups during the Northern Dynasties." *HJAS* 16 (1953), 293–364.

———. "Wu-hu t'ung-k'ao" 五胡通考 In *Chung-kuo-wen-hua yen-chiu-so hui-k'an* 中國文化研究所彙刊 3 (Chengtu, 1943), 57–79.

Wang Yü-ch'üan 王毓銓. "An Outline of the Central Government of the Former Han Dynasty." *HJAS* 12 (1949), 134–187.

Watson, Burton. tr. *Chinese Rhyme-prose, Poems in the Fu Form from the Han and Six Dynasties Periods*. New York, 1971.

———. tr. *The Complete Works of Chuang-tzu*. New York, 1968.

———. tr. *Records of the Grand Historian of China*. 2 vols. New York, 1961.

Watters, Thomas. *On Yuan Chwang's Travels in India, 629–645 A.D.* 2 vols. London, 1904–1905.

Wei-chih. See *San-kuo-chih chi-chieh*.

"Wei san-t'i shih-ching i-tzu k'ao" 魏三體石經遺字考. By Sun Hsing-yen. 1 *chüan*. In *P'ing-chin-kuan ts'ung-shu* 平津舘叢書, vol. 6. Lan-ling 蘭陵, 1806.

Wei-shu 魏書. By Wei Shou 魏收 (A.D. 506–572). 114 *chüan*. I-wen facsimile ed., Taipei, 1956.

Wen-hsüan 文選. By Hsiao T'ung 蕭統 (A.D. 501–531). With commentary by Li Shan 李善 (A.D. 658), Lü Yen-chi 呂延濟, Liu Liang 劉良, Chang Hsien 張銑, Li Chou-lan 李周翰, Lü Hsiang 呂向. 60 *chüan*. I-wen facsimile ed., Taipei, 1956(?).

Weng T'ung-wen 翁同文. "*Lo-yang ch'ieh-lan-chi* pu-pien" 洛陽伽藍記補辨. In I-wen facsimile *Chin-tai mi-shu* ed. of the *Lo-yang ch'ieh-lan chi*. Taipei, n.d.

White, William C. *Tomb Tile Pictures of Ancient China*. Toronto, 1939.

———. *Tombs of Old Loyang*. Shanghai, 1934.

Wilbur, Martin C. *Slavery in China during the Former Han Dynasty, 206 B.C.–A.D.* 25. Revised ed. New York, 1967.

Wilhelm, Richard, tr. *The I Ching or Book of Changes*. 2 vols. New York, 1950.

Wu T'ing-hsieh 吳廷燮. *Yüan-Wei fang-chen nien -piao* 元魏方鎮年表. *2 chüan*. *Erh-shih-wu-shih pu-pien* ed., Shanghai, 1935–1937.

Wu Wei-hsiao 吳維孝. *Hsin-ch'u Han-Wei shih-ching k'ao* 新出漢魏石經考. Shanghai, 1927.

Yang, Hsien-yi 楊憲益, and Gladys Yang, trs. *The Man Who Sold a Ghost*. Hong Kong, 1958: new ed., 1974.

Yang Lien-sheng 楊聯陞. "Hostages in Chinese History." In his *Studies in Chinese Institutional History*. Cambridge, Mass., 1961, pp. 43–57.

———. "Notes on the Economic History of the Chin Dynasty." Ibid., pp. 119–197.

———. "Schedules of Work and Rest in Imperial China." Ibid., pp. 18–42.

Yao Wei-yüan 姚薇元. *Pei-ch'ao Hu-hsing k'ao* 北朝胡姓考. Peking, 1962.

Yen-shih chia-hsün 顏氏家訓. By Yen Chih-t'ui 顏之推 (A.D. 531–591). With commentary by Chao Hsi-ming 趙曦明 (d. 1787 at age 83), Lu Wen-ch'ao 盧文弨 (1717–1796), and Ch'en Ta-hsin 錢大昕 (1728–1804). 7 *chüan*. *SPPY*.

Yen Wen-ju 閻文儒. "Lo-yang Han Wei Sui T'ang ch'eng-chih k'an-ch'a chi" 洛陽漢魏隋唐城址勘查記. *K'ao-ku hsüeh-pao* 考古學報 7 (1955), 117–136.

Ying-tsao fa-shih 營造法式. By Li Chieh 李誡. 4 *chüan*. Facsimile ed., Shanghai, 1954.

Yu-p'o-i-to-she-chia ching 優陂夷墮舍迦經. Translator unknown. *Taishō*.

Yu-yang tsa-tsu 酉陽雜俎. By Tuan Ch'eng-shih 段成式 (fl. A.D. 860). 20 *chüan*. *Hsü-chi* 續集. 10 *chüan*. *SPTK so-pen*.

Yü Chia-hsi 余嘉錫. *Ssu-k'u t'i-yao pien-cheng* 四庫提要辨證. 24 *chüan*. I-wen facsimile ed., Taipei, n.d.

Yü-kung 禹貢. *Journal of Historical Geography*. Peiping, 1934–1937.

Yü-p'ien 玉篇. By Ku Yeh-wang 顧野王 (A.D. 519–581). 30 + 1 *chüan*. *SPTK so-pen*.

Yü Tzu-shan chi chu 庾子山集注. *Yü Tzu-shan chi* by Yü Hsin 庾信 (A.D. 513–581); *chu* (commentary) by Ni Fan 倪璠 (1705 *chu-jen*). 16 *chüan*. *SPPY*.

Yüan Ho-nan chih 元河南志. 3 *chüan*. in Miao Ch'üan-sun's 繆荃孫 (1844–1919) *Ou-hsiang ling-shih* 藕香零拾 ed., Shanghai (?), 1908.

Yüeh-fu shih-chi 樂府詩集. By Kuo Mao-ch'ien 郭茂倩 (fl. 1084). 100 *chüan*. *SPTK so-pen*.

Yün-yü yang-ch'iu 韻語陽秋. By Ko Li-fang 葛立方. 20 *chüan*. I-wen facsimile of 1770 *Li-tai shih hua* 歷代詩話 ed., Taipei, 1956.

Yung-lo ta-tien 永樂大典. Edited by Hsieh Chin 解縉 (1369–1415). Facsimile ed., Taipei, n.d.

Zhou Yi-liang 周一良. "Ling-min ch'iu-chang yü liu-chou tu-tu" 領民酋長與六州都督. In *Wei-Chin Nan-pei-ch'ao shih lun-ts'ung* 魏晉南北朝史論叢. Peking, 1963.

———. "*Lo-yang ch'ieh-lan chi* ti chi-t'iao pu-chu" 洛陽伽藍記的幾條補注. In *Wen-hsien* 文獻 3 (1980). 111–115.

———. "Pei-ch'ao ti min-tsu wen-ti yü min-tsu cheng-ts'e" 北朝的民族問題與民族政策. In *Wei-Chin Nan-pei-ch'ao shih lun-ts'ung* 魏晉南北朝史論叢. Peking, 1963.

Index

Library of Congress Cataloging in Publication Data

Yang, Hsüan-chih, d. 555?
A record of Buddhist monasteries in Lo-yang.

(Princeton library of Asian translations)
1. Temples, Buddhist – China – Lo-yang shih Region – Early works to 1800.
2. Monasteries, Buddhist – China – Lo-yang shih Region – Early works to 1800.
3. Lo-yang shih Region (China) – Description and travel –
Early works to 1800. I. Wang, Yi-t'ung, 1914– . II. Title. III. Series.
BQ6345.L65Y3613 1983 951'.01 83-42586
ISBN 0-691-05403-7